# TALKING NEW ORLEANS MUSIC

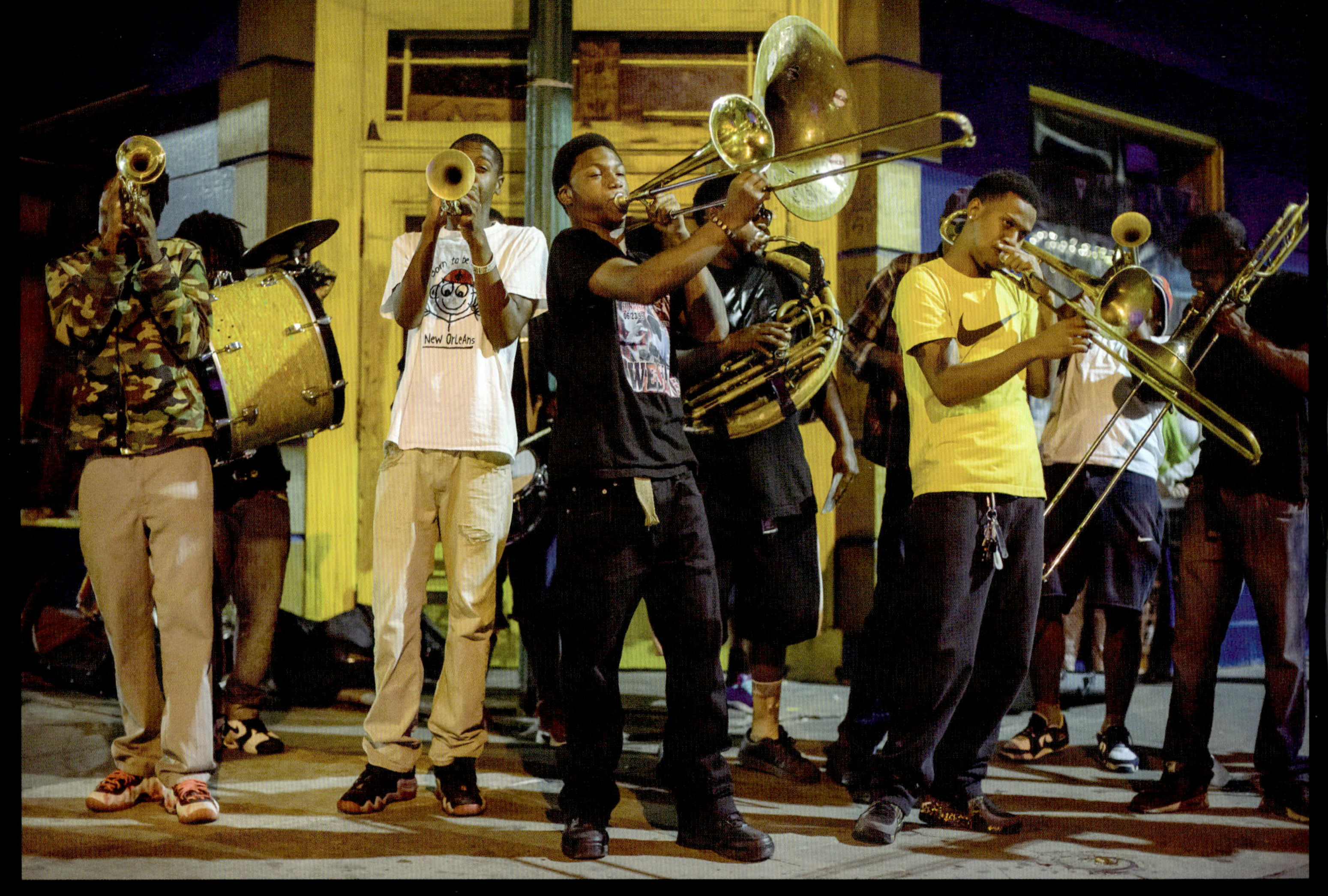



♣ Young Fellaz Brass Band
busking on Frenchmen Street

# TALKING NEW ORLEANS MUSIC

## Crescent City Musicians Talk about Their Lives, Their Music, and Their City

BURT FEINTUCH ✦ Photographs by GARY SAMSON

University Press of Mississippi / Jackson

www.upress.state.ms.us

Designed by Todd Lape

The University Press of Mississippi is a member
of the Association of American University Presses.

Copyright © 2015 by University Press of Mississippi
All rights reserved
Manufactured in Malaysia

First printing 2015

∞

Library of Congress Cataloging-in-Publication Data

Talking New Orleans music : Crescent City musicians talk about
their lives, their music, and their city / [interviews by] Burt Feintuch
; photographs by Gary Samson.
pages cm
Includes index.
ISBN 978-1-4968-0362-7 (cloth : alk. paper) — ISBN 978-1-4968-
0363-4 (ebook) 1. Musicians—Louisiana—New Orleans—Interviews. 2. Musicians—Louisiana—New Orleans—Biography. I.
Feintuch, Burt, 1949– interviewer II. Samson, Gary, photographer.
ML394.T34 2015
780.9763'35—dc23                                   2015005224

British Library Cataloging-in-Publication Data available

# CONTENTS

# TALKING NEW ORLEANS MUSIC

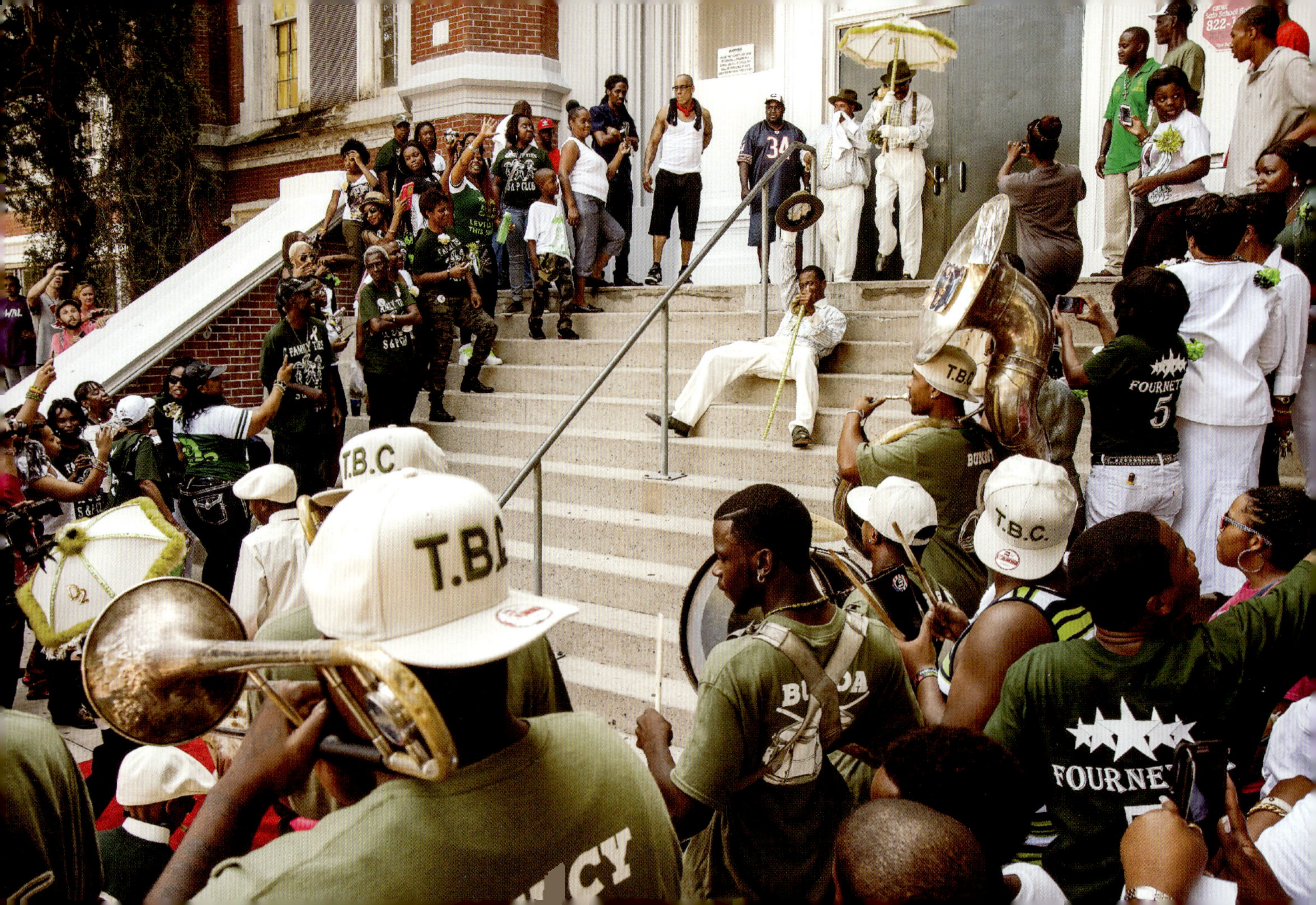

# INTRODUCTION

. . . music to me is just in me. It's in my soul. It's in my heart. It's in my feet. It's in every fiber of my being. It's in my fingertips. It's in my hair. It's in my spirit. I feel it.
—**CHARMAINE NEVILLE**

Being from New Orleans, you're exposed to the culture. You come up in the culture, with the second-line parades, the Mardi Gras, all that. You're exposed to that ever since you were a little kid. Your parents bring you to Mardi Gras in your costume, and you see the Mardi Gras Indians, the brass bands, the jazz funerals, and it becomes part of you.
—**DEACON JOHN MOORE**

I grew up knowing my heritage.
—**BRUCE DAIGREPONT**

One more thing I guess I would say about New Orleans. The funk has not gone away.
—**SCOTT BILLINGTON**

The late New Orleans R&B singer Ernie K-Doe, not someone known for understatement, is often quoted as saying "I'm not sure, but I'm almost certain that all music came from New Orleans." K-Doe's biggest hit, "Mother-in-Law," was written and produced by New Orleans's brilliant Allen Toussaint. Toussaint also played piano on that record. They cut it at Cosimo Matassa's studio on Governor Nicholls Street, on the edge of the French Quarter. About 250 records originating from that studio charted nationally, nearly all involving musicians from New Orleans.

The musicians who played on many of those records pretty much set the beat for decades of American popular music. Deacon John Moore, an interviewee in this book, played guitar on many of those records, including "Mother-in-Law."

Released on New Orleans–based Minit Records, Ernie K-Doe's "Mother-in-Law" was number 1 in 1961 on both *Billboard*'s Hot 100 and R&B charts. In the 1990s, K-Doe began referring to himself as "The Emperor of the Universe" and took to wearing a cape and crown. He had started costuming much

✣ "Coming out the door" at the start of a social aid and pleasure club parade

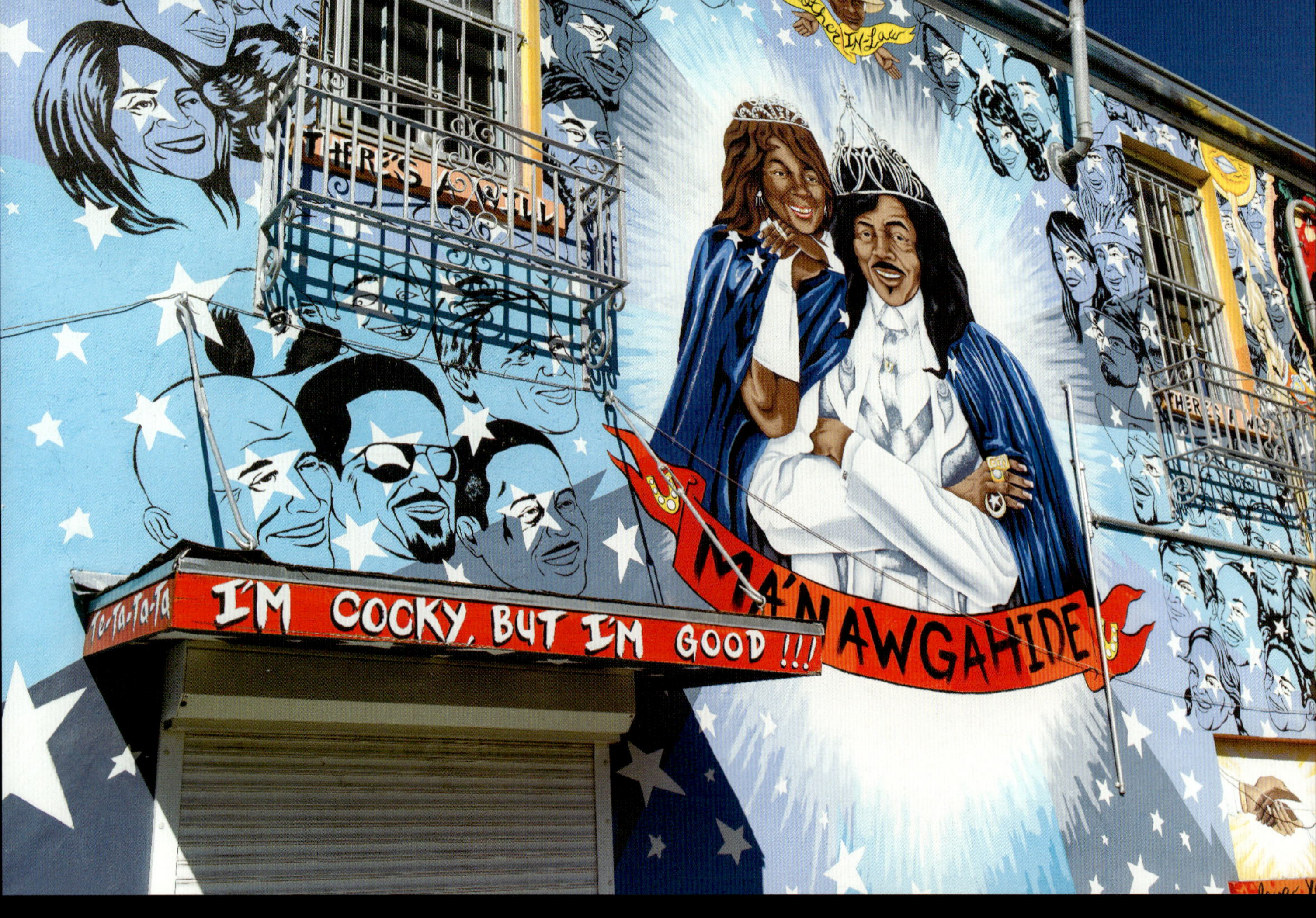

The Mother-in-Law Lounge

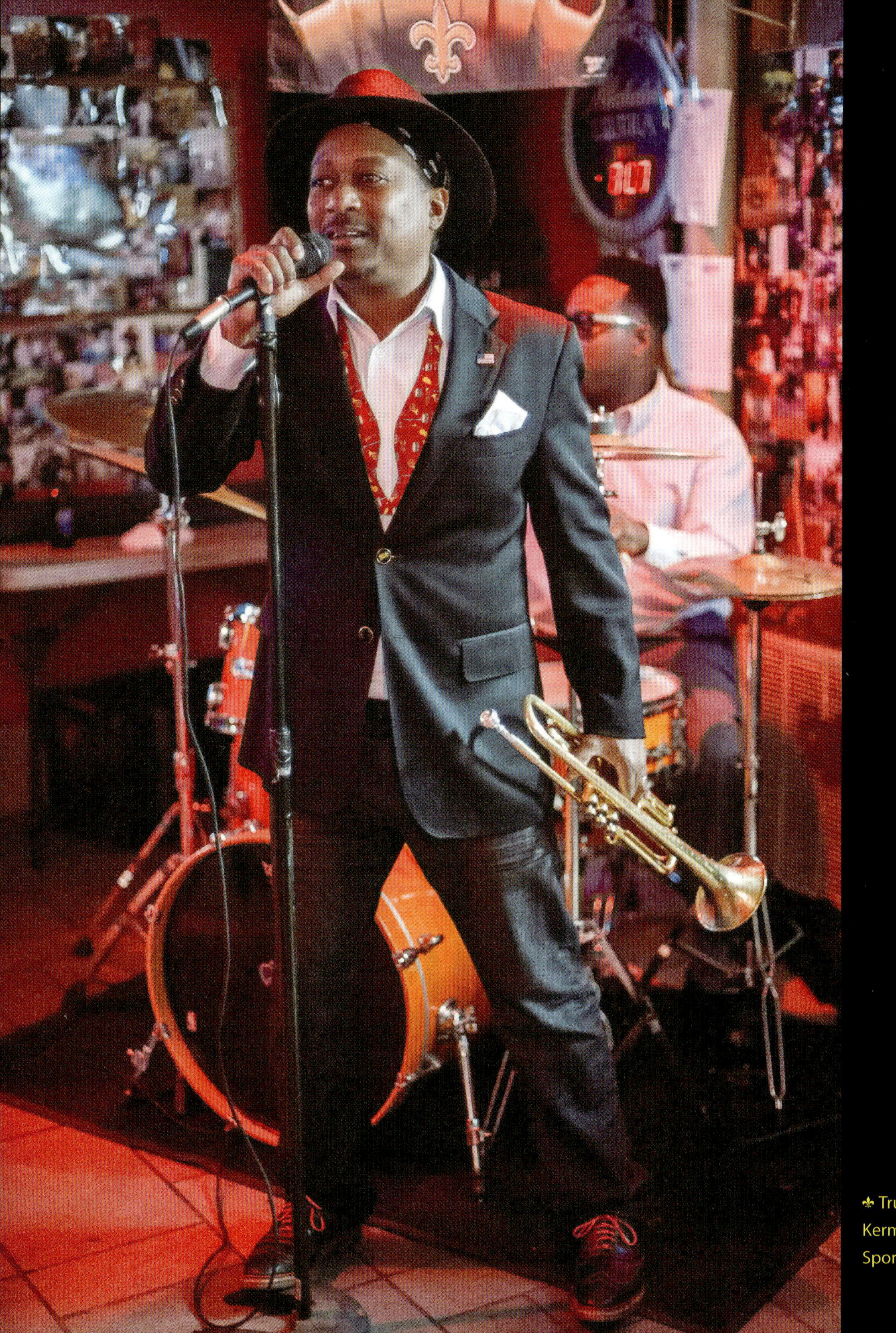



♣ Trumpeter and vocalist
Kermit Ruffins at Bullet's
Sports Bar, Seventh Ward

earlier, though. In his youth, he masked as a Mardi Gras Indian, and he must have been familiar with the unique body of music that's part of that tradition.

In 1994 K-Doe opened the Ernie K-Doe Mother-in-Law Lounge, on the edge of the Treme, one of New Orleans's many musically rich neighborhoods. He died in 2001. At the wake, his cousin, Walter "Wolfman" Washington, whose mother had been one of the two women who raised the Emperor, and with whom he had sung gospel music in his youth, performed. So did the Soul Queen of New Orleans—Irma Thomas—and many others. At the funeral, Sherman Washington, then the leader of the Zion Harmonizers, one of New Orleans's venerable gospel quartets, performed. Deacon John Moore and Allen Toussaint did, too. Walter Washington, Irma Thomas, the aforementioned Deacon John, and the current leader of the Zion Harmonizers, Brazella Briscoe, are all interviewed in this book.

A traditional jazz funeral procession, with an estimated five thousand people, featuring several brass bands and a second line, took K-Doe to St. Louis Cemetery #2, where he was interred near the tombs of many other New Orleans musicians, including jazz musicians Paul Barbarin, Danny Barker, and Louisa "Blu Lu" Barker and R&B musician Earl King. K-Doe's wife, Antoinette, operated the Mother-in-Law Lounge after her husband's death; she was often photographed with a lifelike statue or mannequin of K-Doe, which she had commissioned. She also helped revive the baby-doll tradition, dating to 1912, and rooted in parade and costuming traditions originated by black prostitutes in New Orleans. Charmaine Neville, interviewed herein, is a latter-day K-Doe baby doll.

Antoinette is now buried next to Ernie. The Lounge closed in 2010. On the Martin Luther King Jr. holiday in 2014, exuberant trumpeter and vocalist Kermit Ruffins reopened the Mother-in-Law Lounge. The opening-night party included a large figure of Louis Armstrong—to whom Ruffins is sometimes likened—rocking to the music of trombonist Glen David Andrews and R&B vocals by James Winfield, a.k.a. the Sleeping Giant.

Here's the point: While all the world's music surely didn't come from the Crescent City, there is something about New Orleans where art, culture, and everyday life are all of a piece, all tangled up. One musician leads to another; traditions overlap, intertwine, nourish each other; everyone seems to know everyone else. It is an extraordinarily creative and productive musical hotspot. We can, and should, learn from this place.

Most of what's distinctive about music in New Orleans starts on the street. You find it in families and neighborhoods, in social aid and pleasure clubs, in churches, on local radio, in a web of clubs and other venues, at weddings, parties, funerals, worship services, dances, parades, more parties, and even more parades. It is fundamentally part of the New Orleans vernacular—a local language of music, part of the common culture of everyday life, a language of varied—but interrelated—dialects. And it is tightly woven into the fabric of what is good and successful in a city that has more than its share of difficulty rooted in racism, poverty, violence, corruption, and environmental challenges. Tug on a thread and that leads, seemingly without end, to other musicians, genres, and venues. From the days of early jazz and brass band music through a time when R&B and the city were nearly synonymous, through contemporary brass band music, sissy bounce, and the many other musical forms flourishing today, New Orleans music has been on a roll. Or perhaps I should say that it's been on a stroll, given how much it has to do with the city's streets. No matter how you characterize it, the music just seems to keep on happening.

The music has a way about it that's remarkable—it keeps changing, but it also stays the same. For my father's generation, New Orleans meant Louis Armstrong, King Oliver, Jelly Roll Morton, and the many other pioneers of what today is called traditional jazz. For another generation it means those pioneering rhythm and blues recordings that came mostly from Cosimo's studio, featuring Ernie K-Doe, Fats Domino, Huey "Piano" Smith, James "Sugar Boy" Crawford, Lee Dorsey, Frankie Ford, the Dixie Cups, and a host of others. Some musicians from that era are very much on the scene these days, Irma Thomas, Deacon John, Mac Rebennack—Dr. John, that is—and Art and Aaron Neville among them. For some it's the foundational figures who emerged from that R&B era, stayed more local, and left an indelible musical impression. Henry Roeland Byrd, a.k.a. Professor Longhair, a.k.a. Fess, and James Booker are primary examples, piano professors whose names come up whenever the city's music is the subject.

For still others it's the new wave of music growing from the older local traditions that remain very much part of the city's soundscape today. We can use the Dirty Dozen Brass Band as an example. They were among the first to take older brass band traditions dating to the nineteenth century and bring in funk and bop. Now, many bands, from Rebirth to the Soul Rebels to the all-women Original Pinettes Brass Band (two of whom are interviewed in this book), have created a contemporary brass band tradition. Another example: the Neville Brothers, rooted in New Orleans R&B, especially in the person of Art Neville. They forged a cosmopolitan sound that soaked up influences from around the New World African diaspora but remained indisputably rooted on Valence Street and in the Calliope housing projects.

These days, for many it's the numerous musicians who themselves resist classification—vocalists John Boutté and Charmaine Neville among them (both interviewed in this book)—who are leading attractions in the Crescent City. Or it's bounce, blending hip hop and New Orleans rhythms, sometimes, as in the case of sissy bounce, also blurring gender boundaries (my main regret in this project is my lack of success in interviewing a sissy bounce performer)—see Matt Miller and Stephen Thomas's film on the subject, *Ya Heard Me*. In whatever era and in whatever person you locate the music of New Orleans, the more you listen to one form, the more you can hear it all, with all its roots and flowers. And as the interview here with Dr. Michael White, the noted traditional jazz musician and bandleader, demonstrates, each of those forms is alive and well in New Orleans, with one foot in the tradition and an eye to the future.

If you look at New Orleans culture, it's branches of the same tree. We're doing the same things for the same reasons. It's just that they come out different ways, which is beautiful. I mean, it's hard to believe that an urban area in America, even today, can have unique traditions like we have. Social parades, jazz funerals, brass bands, Mardi Gras Indians still have meaning and vitality in the community, although that meaning may have changed and outside influences have altered the course or direction of some of them somewhat. But they still are very important parts of New Orleans culture today. It's incredible.
—**Dr. Michael White**

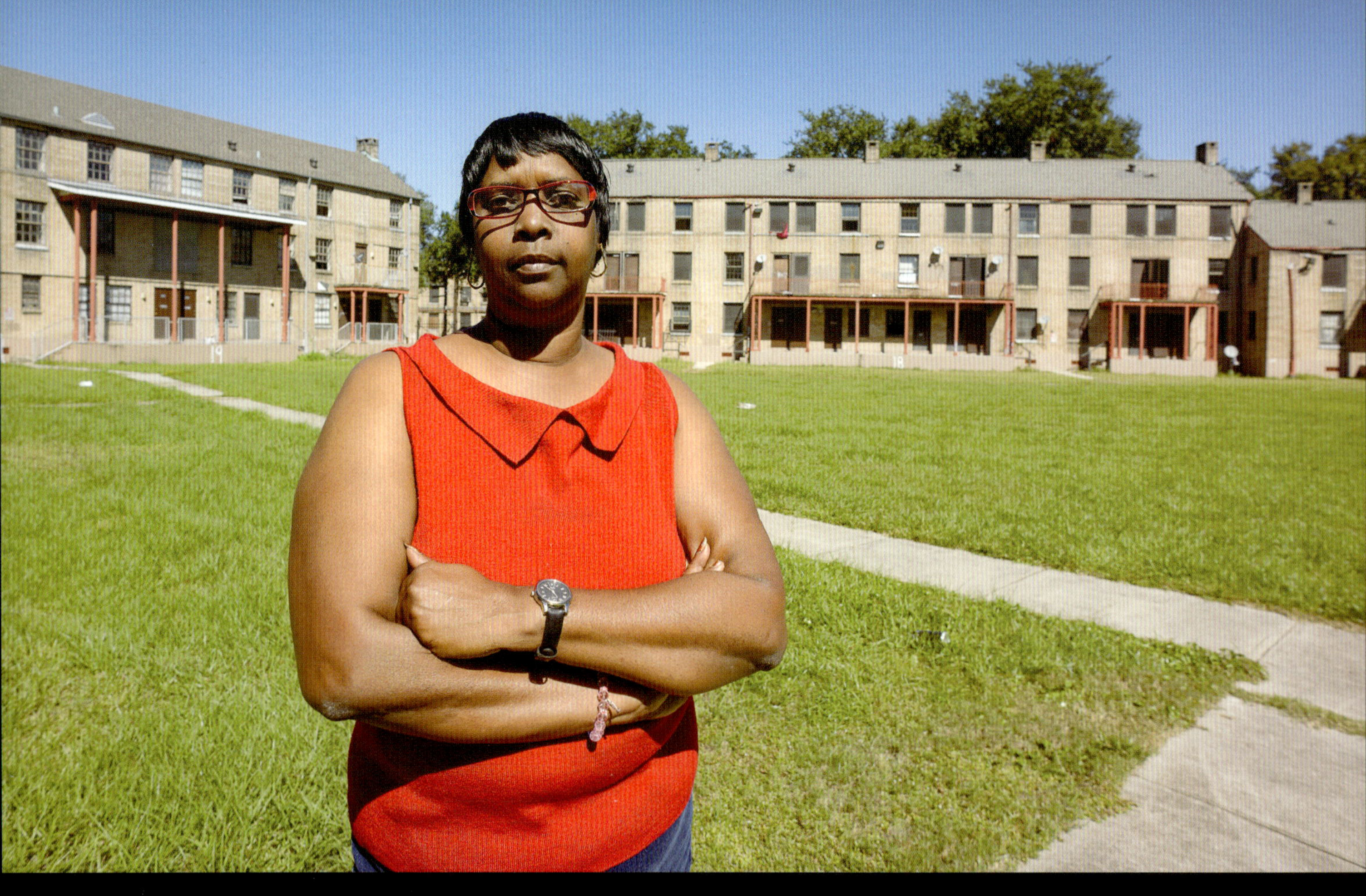

♣ Janet M. Allen, TOPS Coordina-
tor at the former Calliope Projects,

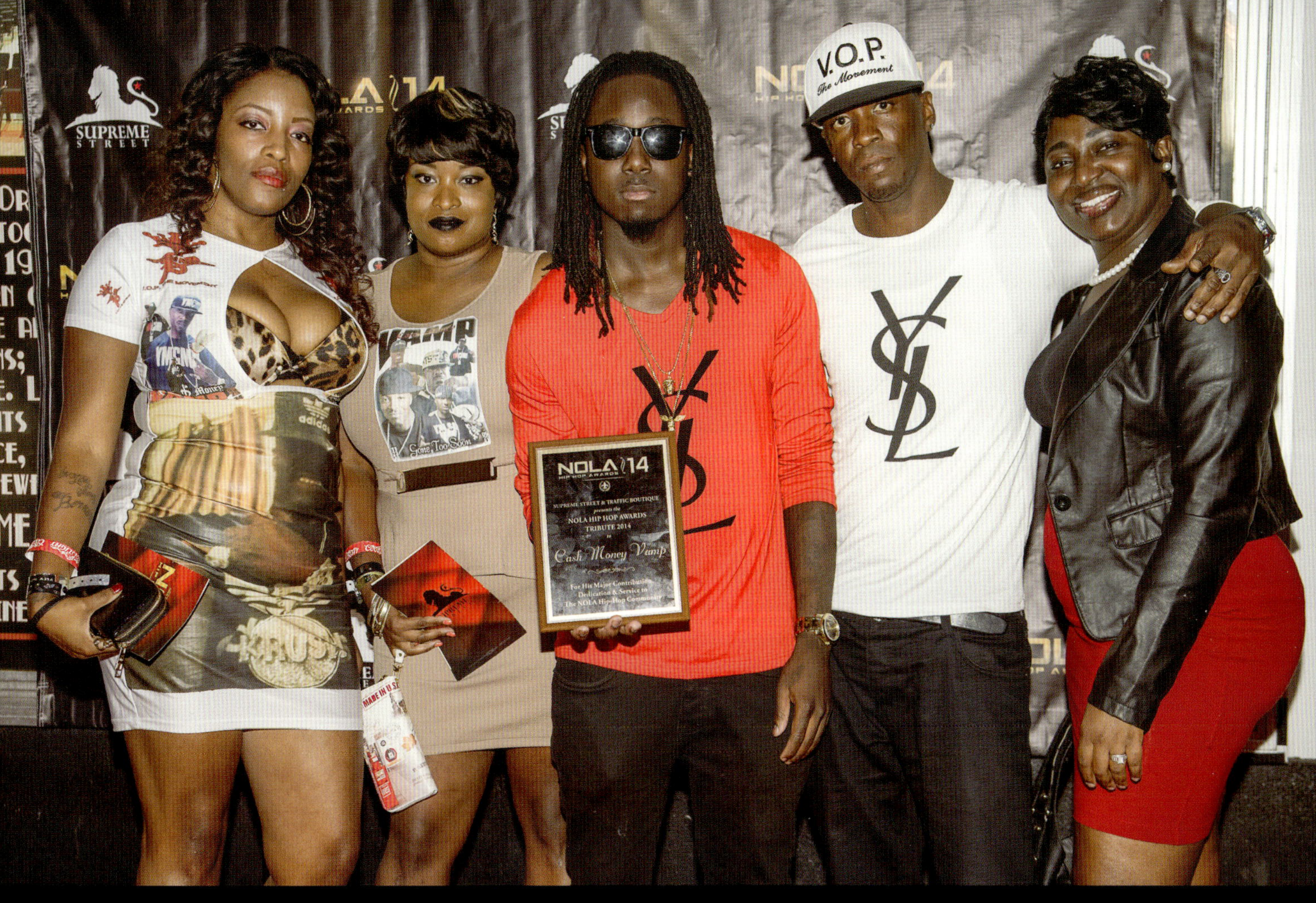


✤ At the 2014 NOLA Hip Hop

Walter "Wolfman" Washington's scream started it off for me. Sometime in the 1980s, I bought an anthology of modern New Orleans music on the Rounder label, and Walter's track sent me looking for his solo recordings. Scott Billington, interviewed herein, produced those recordings. That scream—or is it a cry, a howl?—still grabs me hard, and it led me into what seems to be a never-ending stream of sound from this distinctive, and distinctively American, place. New Orleans screams. It honks. It blats. It wails. It purrs. It messes with time. It messes with pitch. It messes with your feet. It messes with your head. It messes with those parts in between.

New Orleans really does mess with you. The city requires that you give up some of what you thought you knew. Uptown isn't up. Some of Uptown is, in fact, below Central City. On the other hand, sea level may well be above you. The West Bank is mostly south. Whether it's your Indian gang, your family, your krewe, your social aid and pleasure club, your neighborhood, or your church, social association matters more than usual. African American spiritualist churches consider the Native American figure, Black Hawk, a powerful guide. Little People's Place was a bar. You bury your dead above ground. Dixieland is white people's music. And the streets are a stage for what may be the world's best musical theater.

Then there's the food. Like the music, it percolates upward from its humid vernacular roots. Like the music, it's a product of culture with a lower-case *c*. Further, like the music, it achieves its distinctiveness as a result of cultures coming together. The word *gumbo* is generally described as having African roots. Thicken your gumbo with okra, and you're still within the realm of African origins. Use dried and ground sassafras leaves—filé—and you've added the influence of Native Americans. Create a roux—flour browned in fat—and you are likely acting in accordance with French cuisine, although some claim that the New Orleans roux is darker than anything you'll find in French cooking. I can tell you from firsthand experience that Bruce Daigrepont, the excellent Cajun musician in New Orleans and one of this book's interviewees, who traces his ancestry to France, makes a mean gumbo. So does L'il Dizzy's Café, the creole/soul food restaurant in the Treme. If creolization refers to the creative emergence of new forms and identities as a result of cultural groups interacting—sometimes voluntarily, sometimes the result of colonization, slavery, and other imbalances of power—New Orleans must be the capital of creolized cultures in the United States. The food and the music argue that case.

One of the great things about New Orleans culture is that we like to take and transform reality into a new reality, our own independent reality. We do that, of course, with food. We do it with language. We do it, of course, with music. The second-line parade is one of the prime examples of this New Orleans tendency to blend things together that would not normally go together and make something new, interesting, exciting and unique and beautiful out of it.
—**Dr. Michael White**

Back to that scream. Although I had been to New Orleans a number of times before I heard Walter "Wolfman" Washington on that fateful album, it took some time to return. When I did, my partner, folklorist Jeannie Thomas, and I went to d.b.a., a club on Frenchmen Street, to hear Walter and his band, the Roadmasters. Somehow, in that late night of passionate funk and soul, my instincts as a cultural

✦ At Li'L Dizzy's Café, Treme

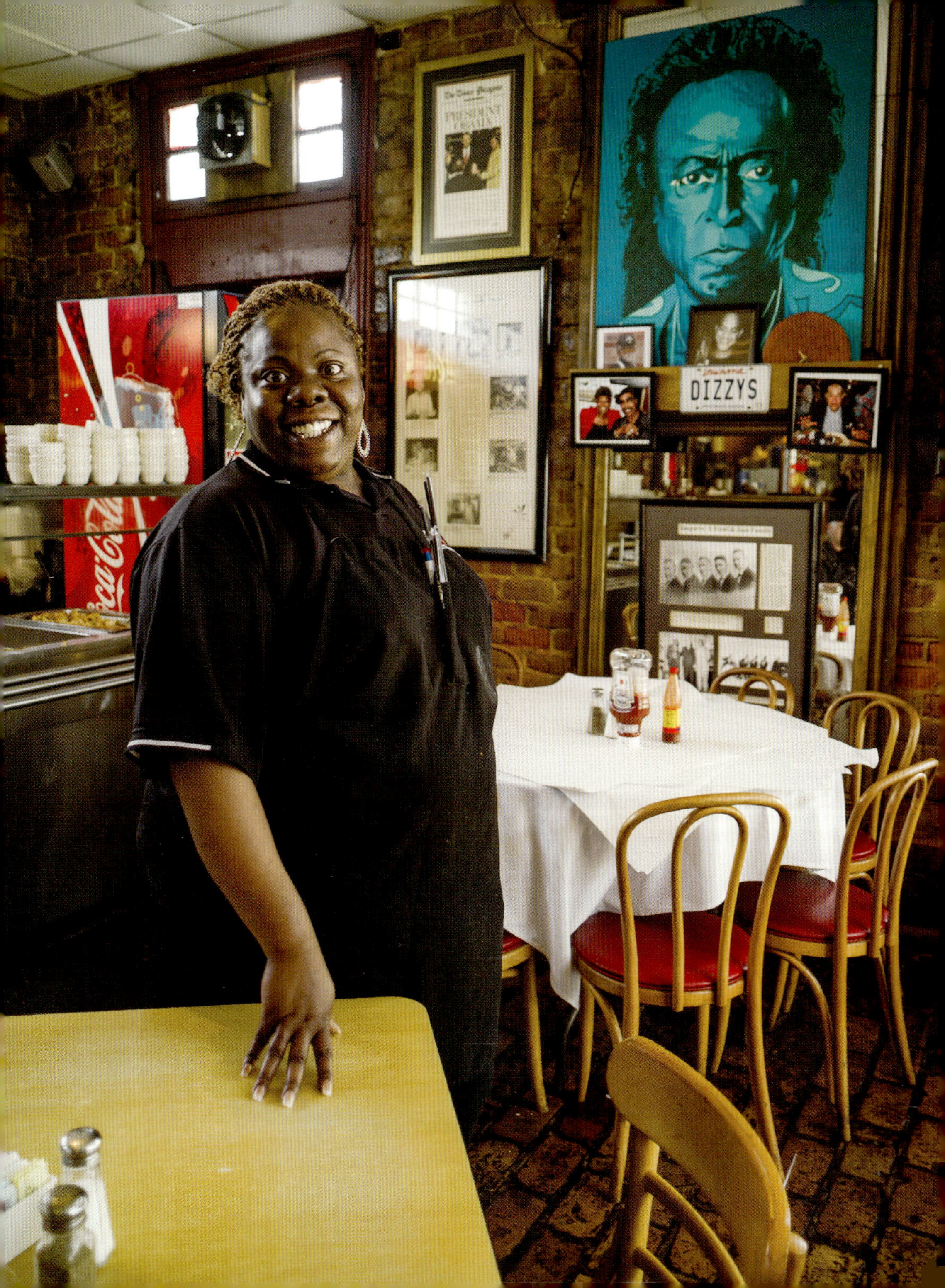

Louisiana
DIZZYS

documentarian and musician kicked in. I wanted to talk to the musicians, to gain some sort of understanding of their lives—the lives that produced their remarkable music. That's the germination of this book. I talked to my friend and collaborator, photographer Gary Samson, about the idea—to do a set of interviews with New Orleans musicians and to illustrate the book richly with photographs. Gary said he was in. The University Press of Mississippi was interested enough to give us an advance contract. Then began the pleasure, and occasional frustration, that made that idea into this book. At the beginning, I had the good fortune of interviewing both Dr. Michael White and Bruce Daigrepont, each of whom was enormously helpful. Subsequent visits to New Orleans, some with Gary, some with Jeannie, some with Gary and Jeannie, all with late nights and very good conversation, yielded the interviews and photographs between these covers. And I eventually caught up with Walter "Wolfman" Washington.

Why these eleven interviewees? Early on, I decided to concentrate on musicians—vocalists and instrumentalists—who in New Orleans would be described as culture bearers. The term implies a heritage of music, learned in the community, rooted in the vernacular, deeply connected to place. While New Orleans's pulsing nightlife has its share of alternative bands, the city's music schools teach their share of Western classical musicians, and recently arrived ethnic groups dance to music produced by members of those communities, you won't find those musicians represented in this book. That's not a comment on their merit or musicality; it has to do with my focus on musicians who represent what is a distinctly New Orleans vernacular in their music. WWOZ, the Crescent City's excellent community radio station devoted to local music, uses the term

*Guardian of the Groove* similarly to the expression *culture bearer*. From the station's website:

> Whether they're musicians, business owners or community leaders, Guardians of the Groove play a significant role in preserving and enhancing the culture of New Orleans. They share a dedication to their craft and a belief in the importance of cultural expression. . . . Guardians combine a respect for those who came before them with hard and essential work to pass the tradition and culture on to its future champions.

*Culture bearers, guardians of the groove.* After the city was very nearly drowned in 2005 by the catastrophic failure of the levees—the worst civil engineering disaster in American history—those terms became loaded, politicized. Poor African Americans, who have been the source of so much of the city's creative brilliance, bore the brunt of that calamity, and as the city struggled to rebuild, culture became an issue. Police harassment of Mardi Gras Indians and second-line parades, not unknown before the flood, seemed to accelerate at a time when devastated communities were doing their best to assert their existence and to claim a right to a future. As the post-Katrina city gentrified, with more affluent residents arriving from elsewhere, complaints of noise in the streets and attempts to regulate street music and parades by city ordinances became more common. In response, organizations such as the New Orleans Social Aid and Pleasure Club Task Force, the New Orleans Musicians Relief Fund, and the Tipitina's Foundation began, or increased, advocacy work on behalf of musicians and their cultural communities, honoring those culture bearers. Some efforts focus on young people, providing band

✦ Trombonist Thomas Grant, Bamboula's, Frenchmen Street

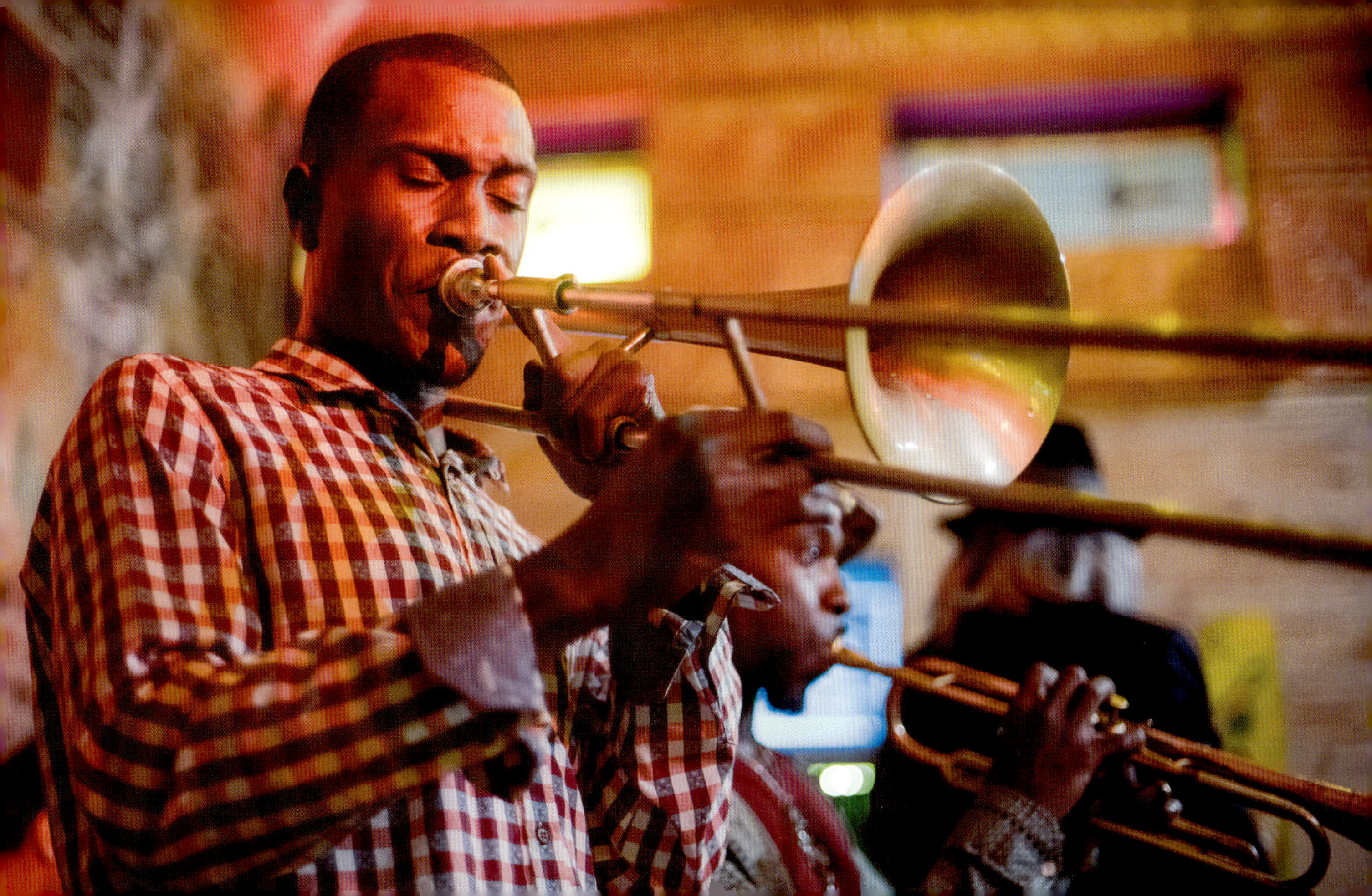

instruments or educational programs to ensure that there will be more guardians of the groove.

> I think that the great tragedy, though, is that so many working poor people were not able to return. And these were often the African American people that were the heart of everything that everybody loves about New Orleans—the jazz, the brass bands, the food, gospel music, the second lines. That's the tragedy to me, that people that owned modest homes went to Atlanta or Houston, wherever they had family. They got new jobs; they put their kids in school. They're paying rent on an apartment in their new place of residence. In the meantime, the bank wanted them to keep paying the mortgage on their wrecked home in New Orleans. And now there are these new regulations calling for the elevation of houses, particularly in the lower Ninth Ward. And there's just no way. The economic barriers are too imposing for people to be able to afford to come back. There's also the kind of ironic thing about New Orleans culture—that it was often those poorest people in which the culture ran most deeply.
> **—Scott Billington**

Ironies do abound. For instance, a city that uses music to draw tourists—many of whom arrive at an airport named for a celebrated local musician—also tries to regulate music, and the root traditions that underlie much of that music, in ways that some say threaten the existence of those musical forms. Tourism has changed the complexion of the audiences, as well. The economics of the local music business don't always reward musicians, especially in those music clubs that take advantage of how many players there are vis-à-vis the limited number of venues. Or consider this: much of the city's musical vitality has to do with second-line parades, which, among other things, are a major source of financial support for brass bands. They're sponsored by social aid and pleasure clubs, benevolent organizations organized in black neighborhoods to provide insurance, burial benefits, and social connections. As the city attempts to regulate those parades, one of its deepest wellsprings of cultural vitality is threatened. A recent research project in New Orleans ranked social aid and pleasure clubs highest of all the organizations and groups in the city when it comes to civic engagement. So, the music seems to be everywhere, but beneath the vitality on the surface, there's fragility.

Concerns about cultural preservation and sustainability are very much part of public discourse in New Orleans, and those conversations can be very heated. Against that backdrop, culture bearers are the guardians of the groove, and that is why this book focuses as it does. The one outlier—my interview with Rounder Records producer Scott Billington—complements the focus on culture bearers. Scott has made records of many of the city's culture bearers, bringing the music to a broad public. He, too, is a guardian of the groove.

These interviews took place in various settings. Some were in interviewees' homes. A couple developed when I caught up with a musician on the road, setting up in a borrowed room. One was in a loud bar on Esplanade. Another took place outside a café further up Esplanade. In two cases, the interviewees came to us, where we were staying in the city. Gary, who is especially interested in environmental portraiture, was sometimes able to make portraits after an interview in a musician's home. In other cases, we were able to document musicians in performance. In some instances, interviewees had another location in mind, and we met them there. John Boutté, who had recently been named New Orleans vocalist of the year, rode his bike to meet us in Armstrong Park.

I approached each interview with a sound recorder and a few notes to fall back on if the conversation didn't flow. I knew I wanted to hear about the interviewees' lives, with an emphasis on those things that shaped them as musicians. I knew that I wanted to hear their thoughts about why New Orleans is such a creative hotspot. And, with the aftermath of the 2005 disaster always nearby, I knew that I wanted to hear about their experiences in and after Katrina. It turns out that by and large I didn't have to ask many questions. People were gracious, engaged, and thoughtful. Even when we got to difficult subjects—racism, violence, horrific experiences after the levees broke—where feelings were intense enough that some people cried, that grace and engagement prevailed. I may not have had to ask many questions, but that's not to say that I was unprepared. I had read and listened as widely and deeply as I could. For me, a highlight of all of this was when Irma Thomas told me that it was clear I had done my homework.

Then I transcribed each of the interviews, researching every unfamiliar name or reference, which turned out to be invaluable, if time- and labor-intensive. Raw interview transcripts are the stuff of research, but because they attempt to reproduce verbatim everything that was said—and because in conversation people don't follow the rules of formal or written English—they can be awkward or uninviting for readers. Consequently, I have edited those transcripts for public presentation, giving priority to preserving each person's distinctive voice. I really want you to hear those voices as you read this book. That means that in some cases I've removed digressions and false starts, reorganized for continuity, and—very

rarely—inserted a word or two for continuity. I've also inserted subheadings to help guide the reader. And in introductory essays that precede each interview, I've tried to provide the reader with sufficient context for reading what follows. Photographers process images with programs such as Photoshop, doing their best to bring out the best qualities of a picture. In a sense, I've Photoshopped these interviews with that same goal. To repeat: I really want you to hear the voices as you read.

What do those voices say? Of course, eleven people don't speak in one voice. And I want to resist making easy generalizations. I prefer to encourage readers to think about what they see here.

There are some things, however, that I want to point out. For instance, there's a great deal of family love and support here—many of the interviewees talk about their family's support for their music as being right at the foundation of their art. Some go farther, as does Deacon John, who told me: "Music talent, in my opinion, is largely a genetic thing. People are just born into music. . . . If you look around New Orleans, you see most of the musicians come from musical families."

Recent research suggests that he's right. Although the subject is controversial, it increasingly seems that musical ability has something to do with genetic factors in multigenerational families (see, for example, this Finnish research: http://www.ncbi.nlm.nih.gov/pubmed?Db=pubmed&Cmd=ShowDetailView&TermToSearch=23460800). Many of the interviewees in this book talk about their families, both as conduits for talent and as having established a supportive environment for developing those talents. Loving—and musical—mothers and fathers are important.

The interviewees also speak about neighborhood. Many talked early in their interviews about

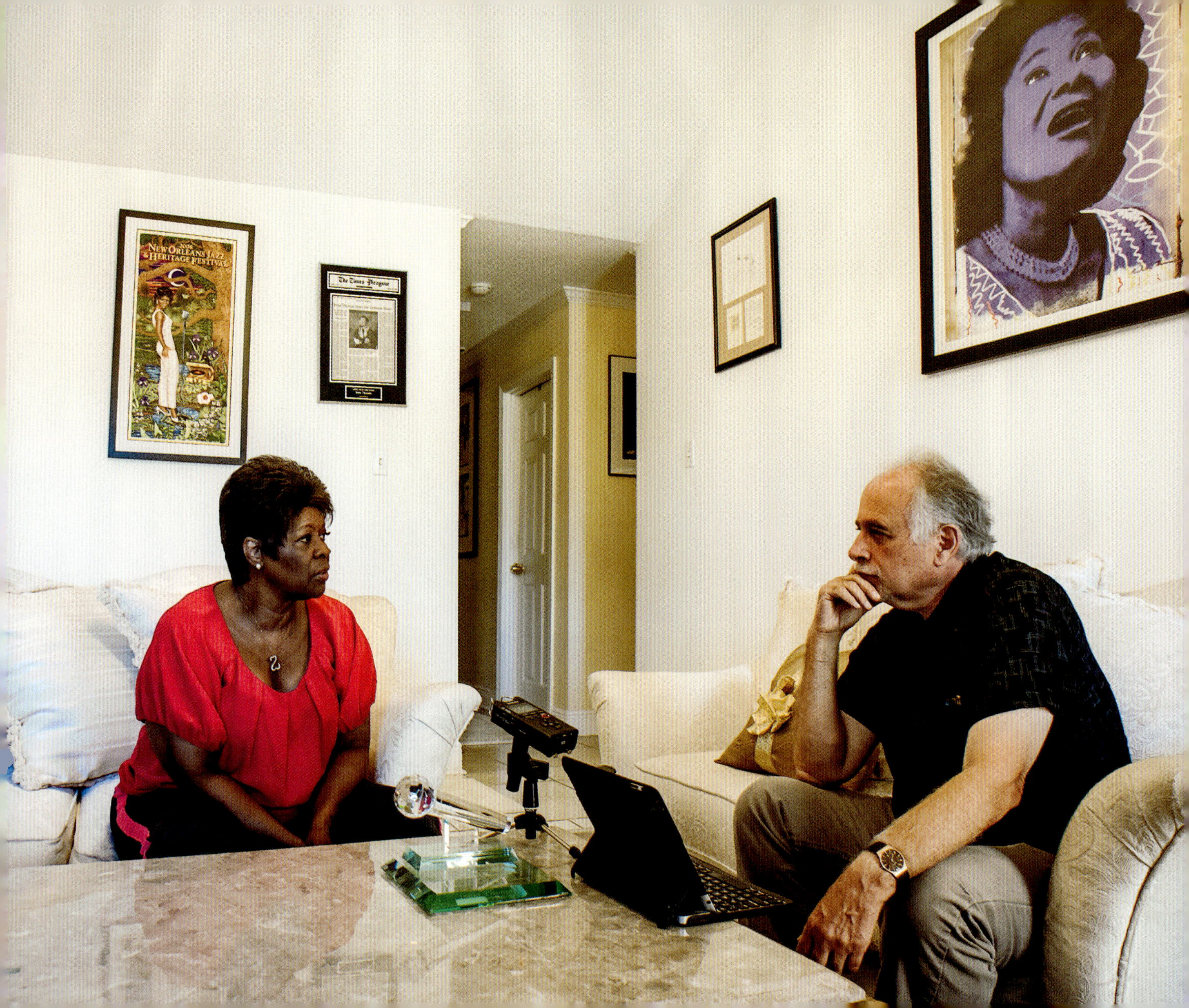

where they come from in the city and about living in an environment rich in music. John Boutté's "Treme Song" puts some of that into musical form. But whether it's people talking about harmonizing on street corners or watching Mardi Gras Indians in the lower Ninth, many of the musicians here grew up in a place where music was part of the public realm. You'd hear it from your front porch, on your way home from school, during Carnival. It is part of the soundscape of daily life.

> Growing up in the Lower Ninth was fabulous. I mean everybody was a musician.
> —**Charmaine Neville**

Pay attention, too, to the role of local institutions. Whether it's the schools with their marching bands, or nightclubs such as the late, lamented Dew Drop Inn—one of the South's leading music venues during segregation—or the church, New Orleans has managed to support an infrastructure that allowed people to learn their musical craft and provided venues for performing it. Clubs in New Orleans, by the way, have no mandated closing time. Although this is less the case these days, musicians could be playing sets long after clubs in other cities had closed for the night. Note how many interviewees talk about the role of the church, too. The importance of local record labels and of Cosimo Matassa's recording studio can't be overstated, particularly during one of the several periods that might be described as golden eras of New Orleans music. Matassa died in September 2014, just as this book was going to press.

Another key local institution is WWOZ, the remarkable community radio station so devoted to the city and its music. Festivals, especially Jazz Fest, have helped increase the music's economic base. An estimated 435,000 people attended the 2014 festival; imagine the economic implications of that, along with the less measurable way in which it helps drive a remarkable world of music. And note how often Jazz Fest comes up in these interviews. Underneath it all, too—in the cultural bedrock—are those less formal institutions that bring people together, among them the all-important social aid and pleasure clubs and the Indian gangs.

Jazz Fest's official name is the New Orleans Jazz and Heritage Festival. That word *heritage* comes up a number of times. Bruce Daigrepont speaks of growing up very aware of his, and of the role of a festival in setting the direction for his life in music. At an even more foundational level, a number of interviewees talk about the importance of heritage. Although they probably wouldn't use this term, they portray New Orleans as culturally conservative, reluctant to give up what matters, slow to join the cultural and commercial mainstream of American life.

> And down here in New Orleans, we're still very close to our heritage. Sometimes it's like you can't see the forest for the trees, because you're living with it. Then you have to want to know where it's coming from, and research it. It's not always given to you.
> —**John Boutté**

It's not all good news, though. From segregation and racism to the indignities of playing for the tip jar, from the lingering effects of what some call *the federal flood* to the fact of frightening violence and desolation on those same streets from which the music comes, many of the musicians here tell stories of overcoming, or living with, terribly destructive challenges.

Finally, throughout, there's home. When the levees broke, the result was incalculable damage and

✦ Irma Thomas being interviewed by Burt Feintuch at her home in New Orleans East

disruption in the lives of many of the people in this book. In some cases, it took years to be able to come back. But they did come back, even when many others were unwilling or unable to return. Whenever I asked about that, the answers were essentially that New Orleans's distinctiveness is too much to give up. I would add that New Orleans is the basis of the musical success of many of the interviewees, providing an economic base—fragile as it often is—that is lacking in the lives of many of the people who didn't return. But it is home, and in accounts from many of the people who couldn't come back, you hear a longing for that distinctive place. It took Irma Thomas and her husband, Emile Jackson, quite some time to rebuild and return. But, as she says,

> People used to ask us, "Why are you moving back?" Why not? It's home. You know. I mean, that storm didn't do us anything; it was the after-effects of what happened that did the damage.
>
> It's home. It's where I grew up. It's where I got my roots. This is the place where I'm comfortable.

I'm envious of the people whose voices are here. Each is living life on his or her terms, at least to some extent. Each is following an enduring passion. Each is in a physical place and spiritual location that they love. Each came of age in a community that recognized their interest and passions and nurtured them. As best I can tell, no one is rich in the conventional sense, but many would say that they're blessed.

There's also pain here, from poverty, racism, and violence. There is hard work, although people don't speak much about it. There is single-mindedness. There is, as I've mentioned, not a lot of money. There is a great deal of family love. There's a fair amount of reckless abandon.

Only nuns from New Orleans will get up and second-line.

**—Charmaine Neville**

In reality, life in the Big Easy isn't all that easy for most of its citizens. Could that be one reason why the music is so important, so vital? *Art Saves Lives* reads a sign we saw in the city. A recent CBS television documentary, *The Whole Gritty City*, makes the same point, showing how Crescent City high school marching bands literally do save lives, providing alternative pathways for young people. In a world where so much music is placeless and faceless, shaped by machines, distributed online and heard in isolation, and only of the moment, the persistent musical richness of New Orleans provides another model. I believe that the rest of us can learn important things from the people who make the music; I hope you will think about that as you read what they have to say.

**—BURT FEINTUCH**
Portsmouth, New Hampshire
August 2014

# DR. MICHAEL WHITE

Clarinetist, composer, music and culture historian
Leader, Dr. Michael White and the Original Liberty Jazz Band

[ Interviewed March 2, 2010, in Durham, New Hampshire ]

In his day job, Dr. Michael White is a professor at Xavier University in New Orleans, where he holds the Rosa and Charles Keller Jr. Endowed Chair in the Arts and Humanities. Twenty-four hours a day, though, he's a dean of traditional jazz, both in New Orleans and in the rest of the world. A clarinetist, bandleader, and composer, he is, in his gentle but firm way, on a mission, representing a traditional art form deeply rooted in New Orleans culture and history. New Orleans traditional jazz is his calling, his vocation. In recognition of his pivotal role in that tradition, the National Endowment for the Arts awarded him a National Heritage Fellowship in 2008.

What is now called traditional jazz was once simply *jass* or *jazz*. It is the root of all the forms of jazz—swing, bop, free, and beyond—that came later. Its precise origins can't be pinpointed, but it has elements of ragtime, nineteenth-century classical and "society" music, blues, and other musical forms and styles that were part of the of the polyphony of New Orleans's musical neighborhoods. Bruce Raeburn, from the Hogan Jazz Archive at Tulane University, points out that in the era in which jazz was born, the city had a large appetite for music, thanks to what he describes as an "endless succession of private and public social rituals" that required

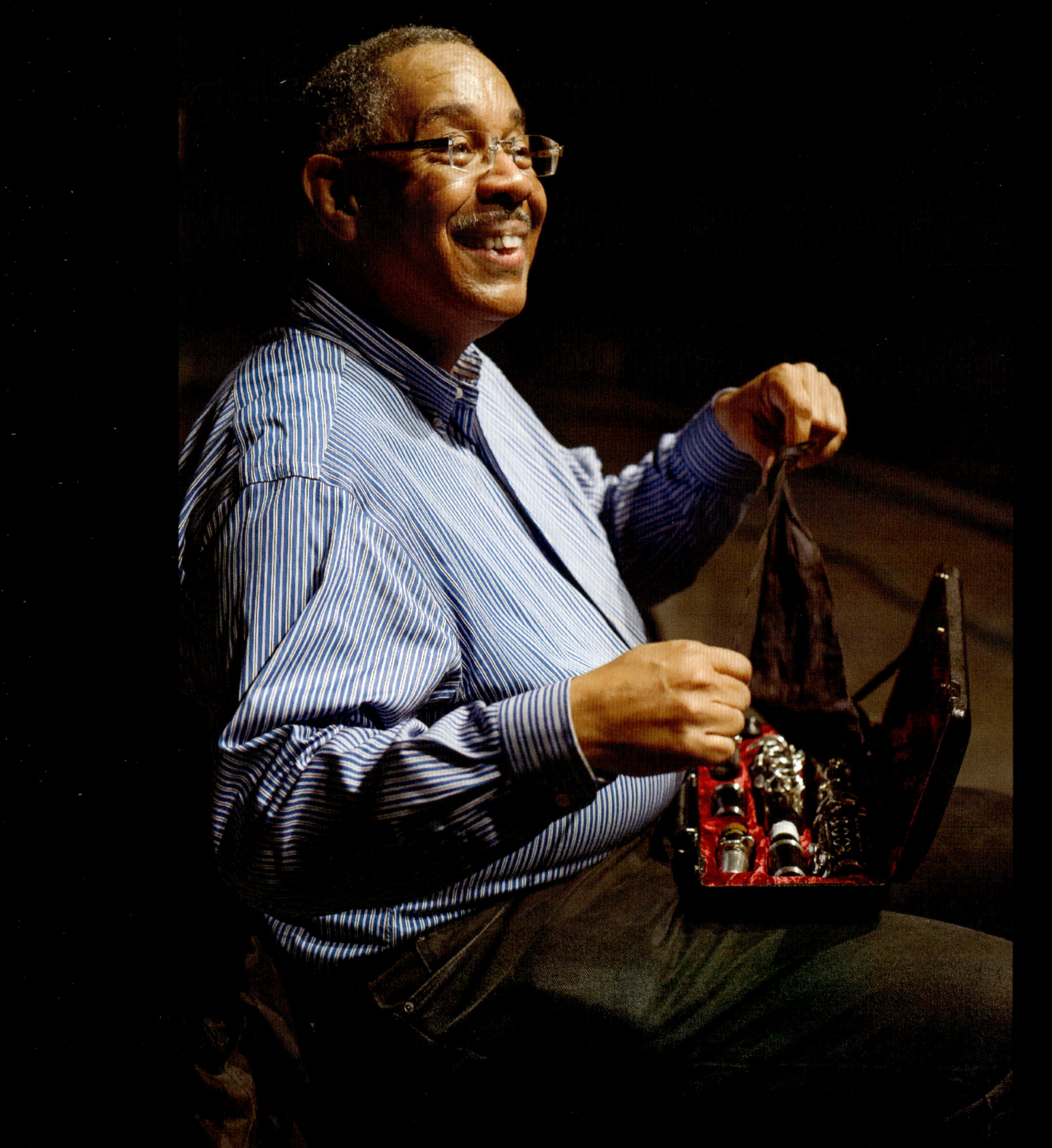

music. Debutante balls, picnics, processions, brothels, Carnival, and many other kinds of events and settings were energized by music. At the same time, sexualized forms of dance were emerging. (See Raeburn's very helpful, concise essay: http://www.knowla.org/entry/546/.) All of this required hot music, and the early New Orleans jazz ensembles provided it. Influential players and composers—King Oliver, Buddy Bolden, Jelly Roll Morton, Kid Ory, Sidney Bechet, and, of course, Louis Armstrong—headlined the music. But the music was in the air, and it was all around.

Typically, a traditional jazz ensemble is fronted by three instruments—cornet or trumpet, clarinet, and trombone. A rhythm section—drums, bass or tuba, guitar or banjo, piano—keeps the pulse going while the front-line musicians improvise, together and as soloists, over, under, and around a melody. New Orleans jazz codified a new kind of freedom in African American culture, and it became a sensation. Historians sometimes say its heyday ended in the 1930s, but it has always been played in New Orleans and it has fierce devotees worldwide. It's a living, breathing music, not something for the archive. And even with the proliferation of white Dixieland ensembles, some of which seem to be parodies of the form, it's an African American music.

Michael White came up in a way that mirrors the experience of many musicians in New Orleans. Music in the streets, around the neighborhood, and in the extended family has been the soundtrack of his life. His family lived in the Ninth Ward when he was young, and he grew up playing with Fats Domino's children. The family moved uptown to Carrollton, where Mahalia Jackson came from. Music was all around—he remembers Mardi Gras, second-line parades, brass bands, Zulu (the early African American social aid and pleasure club) parades, and other music in the commons. Seeing the (still) legendary St. Augustine Marching Band, a high school band easily a hundred strong, parade down the street left an indelible impression. He went to St. Augustine, an institution with a remarkable record of educating African American young men during segregation. The marching band produced a similarly accomplished set of alumni, including Michael White and trumpeter and composer Terence Blanchard. This was the beginning of how, as he says, Michael "drifted into jazz."

Stints with influential senior musicians—Doc Paulin and Danny Barker gave him experience in brass bands dedicated to the tradition and to instilling discipline and an appreciation of history in younger players. Barker's Fairview Baptist Church Marching Band has an extraordinary roster of alumni, including Wynton Marsalis, Herlin Riley, Kirk Joseph, Branford Marsalis, Gregg Stafford, Leroy Jones, and Michael White. Of playing in Doc Paulin's group, Michael says,

> It was a great thing for me, because I got to know the meaning of jazz. I got to see jazz in its natural environment, if you will: in the community where people dance to it. And what I eventually came to see is that the music was an expression of these people's lives, spirits, aspirations, hopes, desires. It was the embodiment of the New Orleans persona in sound. When I started to see jazz that way, then that really changed my life.

That, to me, is the heart of Michael White's music. As he says in this interview, his music comes from a distinctively New Orleans cultural foundation, where music stands for freedom, for democracy, for joy. It's all of a piece, "branches of the same tree," as he says. The music of Mardi Gras Indians, of brass bands, of the church, of traditional jazz musicians comes from the same roots, and they do many of the same things. His concern is that these key elements of culture not be watered down and that they be appreciated, understood, and perhaps most of all, valued for what they are. He really is a man on a mission.

He's also a wonderful player and bandleader. With the Original Liberty Jazz Band, he has made many records; much of his recent output is on the Basin Street Records label, a company entirely dedicated to New Orleans music.

✦ Dr. Michael White preparing for a workshop, Durham, New Hampshire

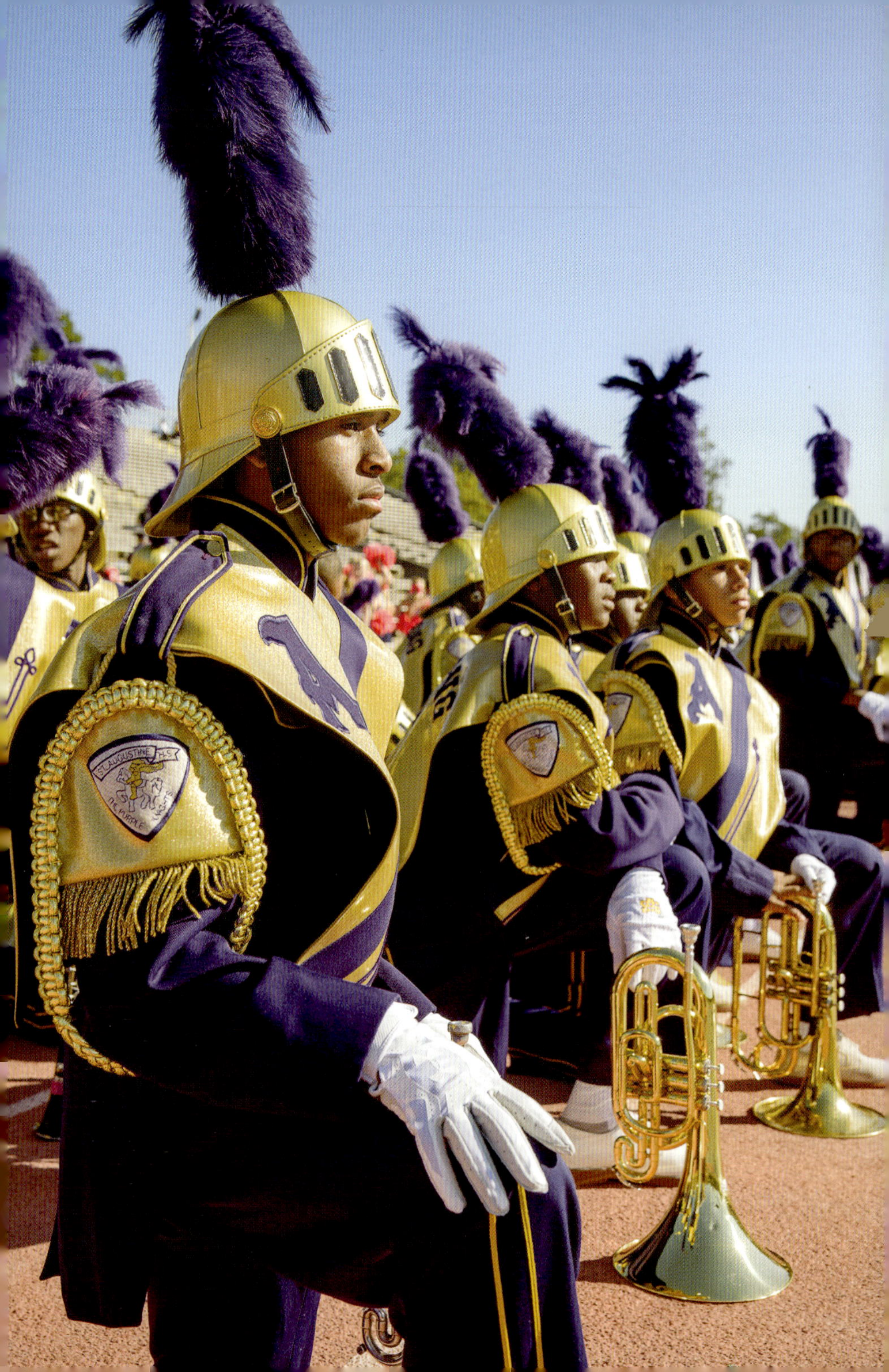

The band itself is made up of musicians who share his devotion to traditional jazz. On stage, they dress in dark suits, a reflection of a shared belief that the music should be represented with dignity. It is striking that a music as joyful and free as the jazz he plays also has that dignity. In a sense, that's his argument about New Orleans itself.

## An Early Consciousness of Music

I was born in New Orleans, November 29, 1954, and my first few years I lived in the Ninth Ward section, in Lizardi Street. Music was all around in some form or another. I actually happened to live around the corner from Fats Domino. I went to school at Saint David Elementary Catholic School with some of his kids.

So there was always a consciousness of music. I remember my mother had some Fats Domino records that she played all the time. I can just see those little Imperial 45s now. There was always a sense that Fats Domino was this famous musician. I remember his kids saying one time—you know kids brag about their parents—"My daddy, he has so much money he has to keep it in the safe at home." Everybody's like, "Wow." I remember that.

But I didn't really get into music until I moved, at the age of eight, up into the Carrollton section of New Orleans. At that time there were still a lot of segregation issues. I went to school in Uptown New Orleans, to Holy Ghost Elementary School, and I didn't really get into music until I was in eighth grade, when I went to Saint Joan of Arc. In eighth grade I started playing clarinet. My aunt used to play around the house, and she played classical music. She had had a music scholarship in college, and two or three times a year she would pull out the clarinet and these ancient, crumbling, music books that she had. I remember the pages were almost brick colored—that's how old they were. She would play some of those classical tunes that she had played at school. I liked the sound of the instrument.

Music is everywhere when you're in New Orleans, and at that same time I remember going to Mardi Gras Parades, seeing Mardi Gras Indians and brass bands. I didn't know what they were at the time. The thing that impressed me the most was going to a Zulu club parade. This was long before the Zulu club was regulated to a certain route and all of that. They would go anywhere—and you had to find them.

I remember going to a Zulu parade on Jackson Avenue in New Orleans with my mother. I was about nine years old. All of a sudden I heard this thunder coming up the street. It scared me to death. There was this roar, and everybody was saying, "That's Saint Aug, that's Saint Aug!" That was the Saint Augustine High School Marching 100 Band, and when they finally came within view I could see these guys that looked like giants. They were dressed like knights. They had on purple and gold uniforms with shiny gold helmets with spikes pointing up, and they were in a perfect line. They had these white buckskin shoes. They looked like one person with all that movement. They moved with precision—high steps. This was the loudest sound that you ever wanted to hear. And they looked like an army, like a legion of soldiers that were so powerful. I remember my mother saying, "You like that?" "Yeah." "You want to play with that band?" "Yeah." So since an early age I wanted to do that.

So, when I got into high school, I went to Saint Augustine, and I started taking music lessons with the band director, Edwin Hampton. I took private lessons with him for three-and-a-half years and played in the band. The first year, I was a color guard. The second two years, I played in the marching band,

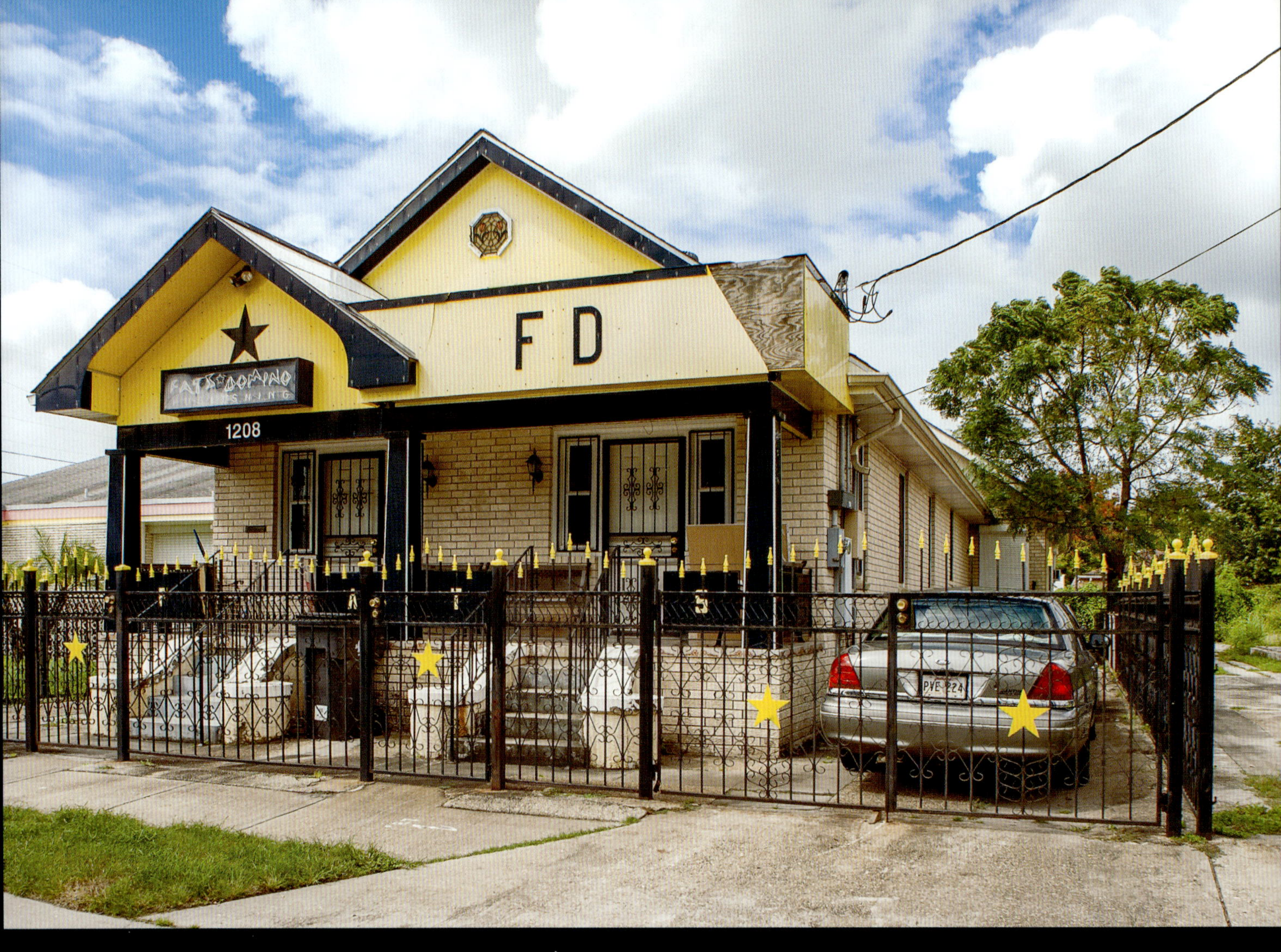

✦ Fats Domino's house,

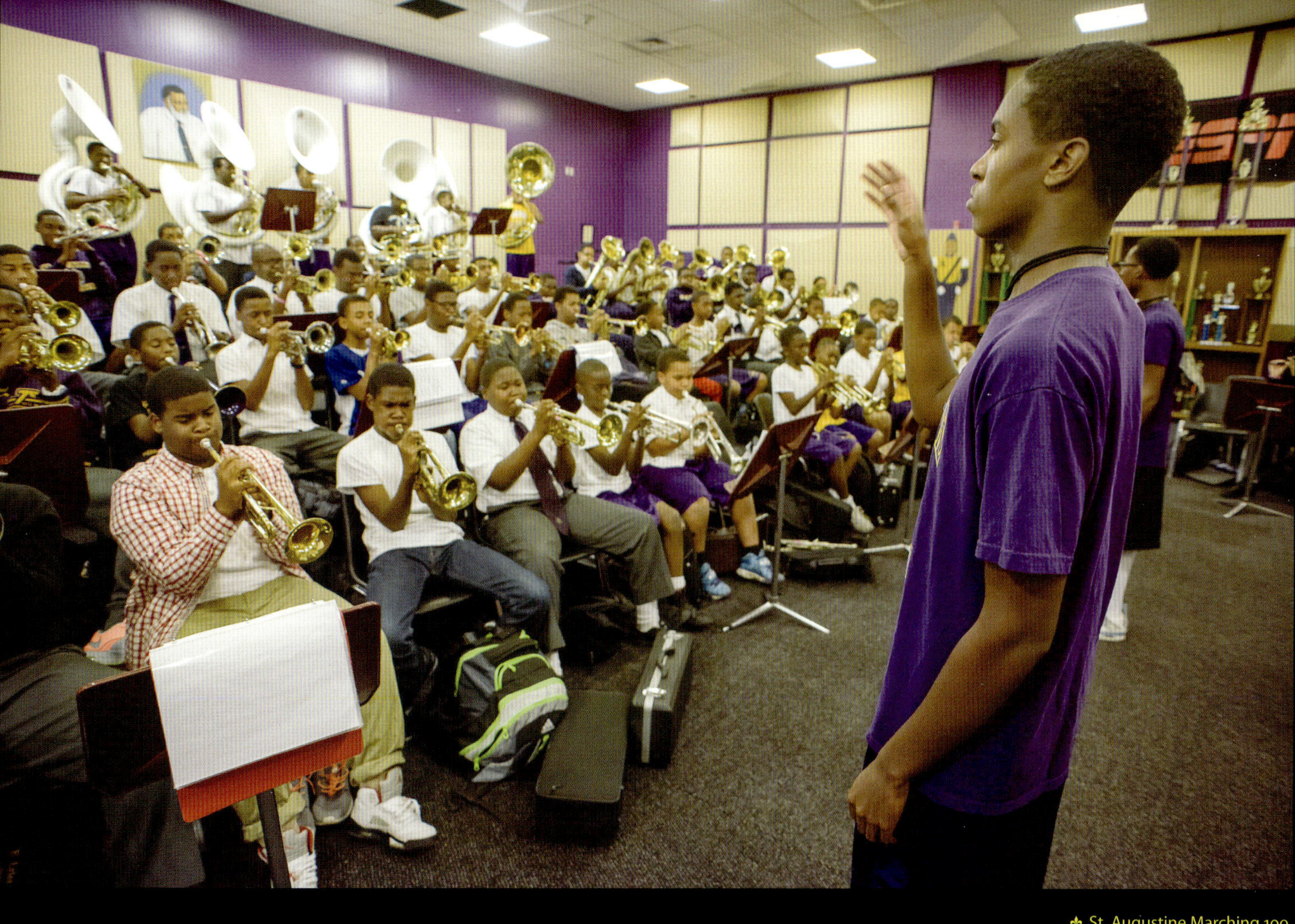



St. Augustine Marching 100
rehearsal, school band room

and three of those years I was in the concert band. That was my beginning in music. But in terms of jazz, like a lot of people, I almost missed the boat. I almost missed the boat because at that time there was not a lot of consciousness of jazz where I was living, and it was difficult to really get to it and know that it existed and what it was. So, I almost missed the boat.

When I finished high school I didn't want to major in music. At that time I didn't like classical music, although I love it now. I didn't want to become a music teacher, and I didn't see any other outlet for me. So I majored in Spanish and went all the way through college and graduate school—got a master's and a doctorate in Spanish. But I had been practicing music all along, playing along with songs on the radio, playing scales, and playing out of the book and stuff like that.

### Drifting into Jazz: Doc Paulin, Fairview Baptist, Danny Barker, Young Tuxedo Brass Band

Then I sort of drifted into jazz. I started going to Jazz Fest. I would see these older musicians, and I was like, "Wow. This music is great." Then when I was a junior in college at Xavier I saw one of the members of the band, Big Al Carson, who is a singer today on Bourbon Street in the French Quarter. He was a tuba player back then. He played in a brass band, and he used to tell me about it, and he said "Man, yeah, I've been playing these parades on weekends and making a little money and having a good time." I was like, "Wow, I would love to do that." I really didn't know anything about it, but I said, "Would you tell the guys if they ever need somebody . . . ?"

By that time I had heard a couple records and knew the basis of a couple of songs—"The Bourbon Street Parade," "The Saints," "Just a Closer Walk"—some of those songs. And a few weeks later I met the bandleader at Jazz Fest. He was this old musician. I introduced myself. It was Ernest "Doc" Paulin. I said, "I'm that guy that Big Al told you about." He said, "Oh yeah, you young people. Y'all ain't no good. If I call you for a job are you going to show up?" I said, "Yeah." "You going to be on time?" "Yeah." "You going to dress right?" "Yeah." "No, I know, y'all aren't no good. Young people."

To my great surprise a couple of weeks later he called me, and that was the beginning. I played with him, went to his house, had a military-type inspection, which he did for all of his jobs. This was the only band that I ever played in where you don't go to the job; you go to the bandleader's house. So you go to his house, and there you are. Then he brought us over, and we played at a Baptist Church parade in Marrero. I remember that very well.

That was the beginning of what was sort of a four-year apprenticeship playing with older, more experienced musicians—learning songs, learning style. I played in a lot of social club parades in the community and jazz funerals. That was the training ground that so many other jazz musicians had in the early days, but I didn't know that at the time. It was a great thing for me, because I got to know the meaning of jazz. I got to see jazz in its natural environment, if you will: in the community where people dance to it. And what I eventually came to see is that the music was an expression of these people's lives, spirits, aspirations, hopes, desires. It was the embodiment of the New Orleans persona in sound. When I started to see jazz that way, then that really changed my life.

Other people have said that I played as a young guy with the Fairview Brass Band, but, really, it's yes and no. If you see pictures of the old Fairview Brass

Band you'll see a little guy on the clarinet that 90 percent of everybody would think is me. Quite a few people swear up and down it's me. He does look like I used to look when I was a young kid. But it's definitely not me. It's a young guy named Gene Mims. I joined the Fairview Baptist Church Band when I was twenty-one years old. I was at Xavier. I had already played in Doc Paulin's brass band, and it just so happened I met Danny Barker, who was teaching African American music at Xavier, the same class I teach now. We talked, and he told me about the Fairview Band, and I joined the band and played with them for a couple of years.

That was the second generation of the Fairview Baptist Church band. We used to play in the French Quarter for tips, and we used to have some other jobs—occasional parades, things like that. So, yeah, I was in the Fairview, but in the second generation and, like I said, I was an old kid. I was twenty-one years old, when some of the other guys were anywhere from around ten to fifteen. It was unusual for the brass band to be associated with the church, because no other brass band was, as far as I know. But that association for the kids in the band was minimal. We practiced at the church once a week, and that was it. Other than that we didn't have direct contact with the church or go to services or functions there.

I joined the musicians union in 1979 and then I joined the Young Tuxedo Brass Band. What happened was that by that time I was in grad school at Tulane, and a couple of guys that I knew were in the band—in the Young Tuxedo. They used to come up and play jobs at Tulane University every spring. One time when they played I sat in with them. The bandleader heard, and he liked me, and then I started playing occasional jobs with them—parades and things. So, I played with the Tuxedo band for a number of years. Nowadays they don't do a lot of work, but when they get together I still play with them some.

### Family, Creativity, and Music

I grew up Catholic. I didn't hear a lot of Baptist hymns and sanctified music and all that until later. If you come up in New Orleans, you know Mahalia Jackson came from there, and, of course, everybody had Mahalia Jackson records somewhere. So you'd hear that, but I wasn't really around gospel music until later. In fact, I remember that first church parade I ever played. We played hymns in an uptempo jazz style in the brass band. It was a church anniversary parade, so before the parade started they had services in the church. We were in the back of the church, and I got to hear people singing there. Later on, I heard a lot of gospel music in Baptist and sanctified churches because with some of the older musicians I knew, we would go to wakes and funerals. You would hear incredible singing—choirs and individual soloists and musicians.

Were my parents musical? In a word, no. But, artistic, yes. My grandmother was very creative. She actually invented a way of making spun sugar candy roses that became well known—enough to get her a feature article in the *New Yorker* in 1949 and a full spread layout feature in *Ebony* in 1952. That one-person operation that she had paid for my mother, my aunt, and my uncle to go to college, and partly for my uncle to go through medical school. It was an important thing, and I think that gift was passed down.

By the same token, on my mother's father's side of the family there was music and there was musical

talent. I didn't find out about this until later. But a lot of my connection to the music, I just have to say, is spiritual, and a lot of those things kind of jump out at you with time. I found out that we're related to a musical family that goes back to the first generation of jazz musicians. In the family were musicians like Papa John Joseph, who was a bass player, and his brother, Willie Joseph, who was a clarinetist. They both were in the first generation of jazz musicians.

Papa John actually ran a barber shop that was a half block from Buddy Bolden's house. Buddy Bolden's house is still standing. I passed by there last week, but the barber shop is now torn down. That "shaving parlor" used to be a congregating place for musicians. Even Buddy Bolden used to hang out there. They would book jobs from the barber shop. During times when business was slow they would rehearse there.

Papa John Joseph was reportedly the first saxophonist in all of jazz. He bought a C-melody saxophone and played with one of the brass bands early on. He played a little clarinet too, mandolin, guitar, but he was mainly a bass player. During the New Orleans revival period he recorded with Kid Thomas and George Lewis, and he made the historic 1963 three-month tour of Japan with George Lewis that helped to spark a New Orleans jazz revolution over there that's still going on today. Papa John Joseph died as the oldest living jazz musician. He was born in the late 1870s. He died—he was really eighty-nine but everybody said ninety—while playing at Preservation Hall. He had played a solo on "When the Saints Go Marching In" and then he dropped dead right after that.

His brother, Willie Joseph, recorded in 1927 with Louis Dumaine. Very few New Orleans bands actually recorded in New Orleans, but Louis Dumaine was one of them. There was a cousin of the family, Earl Fouche—well, my mother is a Fouche. He was also related to the Josephs, and he played alto saxophone and clarinet with Sam Morgan's Jazz Band. He recorded on those classic eight songs that Sam Morgan recorded in 1927 in New Orleans.

So there were musicians in the family that go back. There were others. In later years I found out about other musicians in other genres, and it's almost shocking to believe that musical heritage could really literally be in the blood without you directly knowing about it, but I guess it is. I found that I'm related to a trumpet player and composer named Renald Richard. In the 1940s he played trumpet, and he was playing with Ray Charles.

Because New Orleans had a special sound, a lot of the early rhythm and blues people went down to New Orleans. So we find people like Little Richard or Ray Charles either really getting their start or jump-starting their career in New Orleans, using New Orleans bands and musicians and recording there. So, Ray Charles came down to New Orleans. One of the early touring bands that he formed had New Orleans musicians—Renald Richard was a trumpet player. And one night Renald brought a song to Ray Charles, saying, "I wrote this song up for you." Ray Charles listened to it, he liked it, he recorded it, and it was one of his early hits, "I Got a Woman."

Renald Richard comes to New Orleans, doing Jazz Fests, every year. We always get together and have lunch, and we talk about his life on the road, we talk about Ray Charles, we talk about the song. I think Kanye West, the rapper, put one line of the song in his "Gold Digger" rap song and that Renald got a lot of royalties for that. He wrote other songs for Ray Charles as well, and all of that's documented.

Then I have another cousin in the family who I'm pretty sure you've heard many times. I didn't find

out about him until later, but he's still living, still performing, and I run into him. He lives in California, but I've seen him more in Europe than in the States—the tenor saxophonist Plas Johnson. You might not know the name, but you know the music. You've heard him before, because he was a featured soloist with Henry Mancini. He is the guy who plays the melody and the solos in the recording of "The Pink Panther." And "Peter Gunn" and a lot of other stuff. You've heard him. So, that's Plas Johnson. He's also in the family.

I also have several cousins from that same side of the family that are playing music today. Renald's son, Thaddeus Richard, plays piano, but he also played alto saxophone, and for a while he was with Paul McCartney in Wings. We have people in the family that have done a lot.

So I come from a musical family that I didn't know about. That's good in a way, because it shows that kind of ability and musical tendencies and talents do seem to be passed down in the genes. But the thing that I'm most, I guess you could say, proud of and connected to is the traditional jazz music— we have people that were around and participated with the very earliest jazz musicians. I mean, Papa John Joseph played with people like King Oliver and Kid Ory. They were involved with those guys. That's quite a legacy—to discover all those all of a sudden. That lets you understand why you feel the way you feel about music. It's not just something with you, but it's something that's been passed on for generations in your family.

The strange thing about it is that I discovered a lot of coincidences once I started to find out about family members, once I was in the business. I lived on the same street that was a corner street where the barber shop was. The cousin, Willie Joseph, is buried in a cemetery on that street, and the cemetery was a half a block from my house. Papa John himself used to live on that street and several other important musicians. So that street was kind of important: Liberty Street. It really was interesting to find out about all of that musical activity in the family later. Like I said, it did help make sense of, a lot more sense, of my own life and feelings. But it was good to find my own way into it and then discover all these people. Wow. And then to discover that at some point all of the early relatives, all of them, played clarinet. That was unusual.

Willie Joseph recorded on clarinet. Sometimes I listen to his style, and it's like we have similar influences. It's almost frightening. There really were a lot of coincidences. You know—streets, people we played with, places we played. It's really, really interesting. So, you think that there's something else going on there beyond just genes and the blood and coincidence.

**Authenticity**

I was in college, really, when I discovered my interest in traditional jazz. You see, there's this thing in New Orleans. There's this commercialized version of jazz known as Dixieland, and the powers-that-be would make you think that that's authentic New Orleans jazz. Then all of a sudden you discover that ain't it. That is a commercial imitation. That is like fast food compared to a chef. That's like soup compared to gumbo.

Then you find out that there's a music that has a real meaning, a special individual sound, and it's about something. It's about people's lives; it's not about money and commercialism. It involves all

kinds of passions and emotions. Yes, it's dance music, and it's for a good time, but it's like the story of people's lives is in this music. It's expressed by the music, and it's an outgrowth of the music, and the music is an outgrowth of it. So it's something very special, and that discovery transformed my life. First, for me, it was in the parades.

It's a coincidence that for years I was in Doc Paulin's jazz band. That was like school—a different kind of school. You know, I'm in college and grad school during the week, and then on the weekends I was in this other kind of school learning about music, learning about jazz, learning about social clubs and Mardi Gras Indians and all of these things. Not through study at that point but firsthand, being out there.

And then I had another sort of schooling. After I left Doc Paulin's band and joined the musician's union, then I got to know, and actually play with, more than three dozen musicians born between the late 1890s and 1910. I got to see several people on the same instrument, and I learned so much about individuality and personal expression and how to convert individual feelings and passions into your own sound and your own expression. A lot of those older musicians became my friends, musical colleagues, bandmates, roadmates, and that was a great learning experience for me.

That's not something you could get in any school. All of those different musical personalities were just incredible. Every one of them taught me lessons one way or the other. Certainly not formally, for the most part—just observing and listening to their own individual versions.

It's like a living version of a philosophy on life that breeds individualism and collectivism at the same time, and also promotes nonconformity in a conformist structure. It's freedom within confines. In other words, an acting out of democracy—democratic ideas and principles and in such a way that it offered the philosophy of possibility—considering different possibilities and blends that were new, different, exciting, personal, meaningful. So, that was a whole lot of training, in a sense not just about music but about life. I didn't realize this at the time, of course. This is only years later when those dots started to connect.

A lot of people that grew up in New Orleans—my age, and even older—missed the authentic, traditional New Orleans jazz experience. You could be right in New Orleans and never see it. It's sort of like people think about Nashville country music, and you go to Nashville and you don't see country music everywhere like you think. But there's some commercial tourist thing, and that's far removed from Nashville reality in a lot of cases.

That's kind of like what it was. It was like traditional New Orleans jazz had different branches. Some of it was considered tourist music, and most of what you heard on television and saw in the papers was Dixieland. That's a more commercial music, and it wasn't coming from the black community. So it didn't sound like anything that I related to, really. It was like this is sort of a comic, corny music.

And then you discover real New Orleans jazz, and you're like "Wow, wow, what is this?" I'm moved spiritually. My whole life is changed for days at a time. I'm shaking on the inside. I feel beauty. I see a whole another side of life. What kind of music is this? You see that, and it is hard to get to sometimes. Because authentic New Orleans jazz, when I was coming up, was not in schools. It was not on the radio. For the most part, it was not promoted by the businesses and powers-that-be. More commercial forms were.

## Social Aid and Pleasure Clubs

It was almost an unknown, or hidden, thing. There was a half-hour jazz club radio show on Sundays, if you could find the radio station—an AM station—and I used to listen to that show. I would say maybe half to two-thirds of the music they played was in the authentic vein. I went to Jazz Fest. I saw some of the older, authentic players there. But where the music was accessible, ironically, what I would consider the biggest traditional jazz events, were social club parades. There are many clubs in New Orleans in the black community, called social aid and pleasure clubs, and along with those were benevolent societies. Those were self-help groups that started, really gained momentum, after the Civil War, during Reconstruction. When jazz came along, the music sort of paralleled the goals and objectives of these clubs. So they became the biggest sponsors of jazz music—at dances, at picnics, at other functions, and eventually in their annual parades and their jazz funerals for dues-paying members. Funerals were called *funerals with music*. Today they're known as jazz funerals.

Those social clubs were very, very important. There were dozens of these social clubs all over New Orleans. They continue that tradition of parades—annual parades, holiday parades—and they are in the community. Nowadays they get a little publicity but back, even in the mid-'70s, when I started in 1975—you did not know they were going on. They are like the complete opposite of Mardi Gras parades. Everyone knows about Mardi Gras, but these are very different. There are no floats, no masks, no throws, no balloons or beads or anything like that—very, very different kind of parade.

They have three important parts to the social club parade. First is the club, which can come in several divisions, which can be divided by age and gender. The club is usually dressed in bold, sometimes clashing, colors. But the colors don't clash because everybody's wearing them—which is another take on that whole concept of possibility and change, transformation, inclusion, collectivism. But anyway, there's a social club. Then another important part to the social club parade was the brass band. There would be two, three, four uniformed brass bands. In the early days of jazz they had special band uniforms that looked like circus band uniforms, more or less. In more modern times, at least the '20s or '30s, people would wear black and white—black pants, white shirt, black tie—a black suit, basically, with a white band cap. The brass bands, of course, played traditional New Orleans jazz, leisurely up-tempo style, for dancing. They would play songs like blues songs, hymns, marches, folk songs, but all in the traditional New Orleans jazz style.

And then the third important component was the dozens, hundreds, up to thousands, of anonymous faces that would appear from nowhere when the music starts. Those are the people that follow the parade. They're called *second liners*. So with these kinds of parades, it's not like Mardi Gras or Macys or something you look at, say, "Oh that's nice," and then you go home. No, you become a part of the parade. The parade goes along and collects people—dozens and dozens more every time you look up—and they follow along cheering, and then they dance like the club members do.

It's dancing that we know of as the second line, which is a free-form dance based on West African tradition. In fact, much of those parades are related to traditional West African processions—even down to the ornaments. Most people think, "Oh, that's a New Orleans thing." But things like use of a

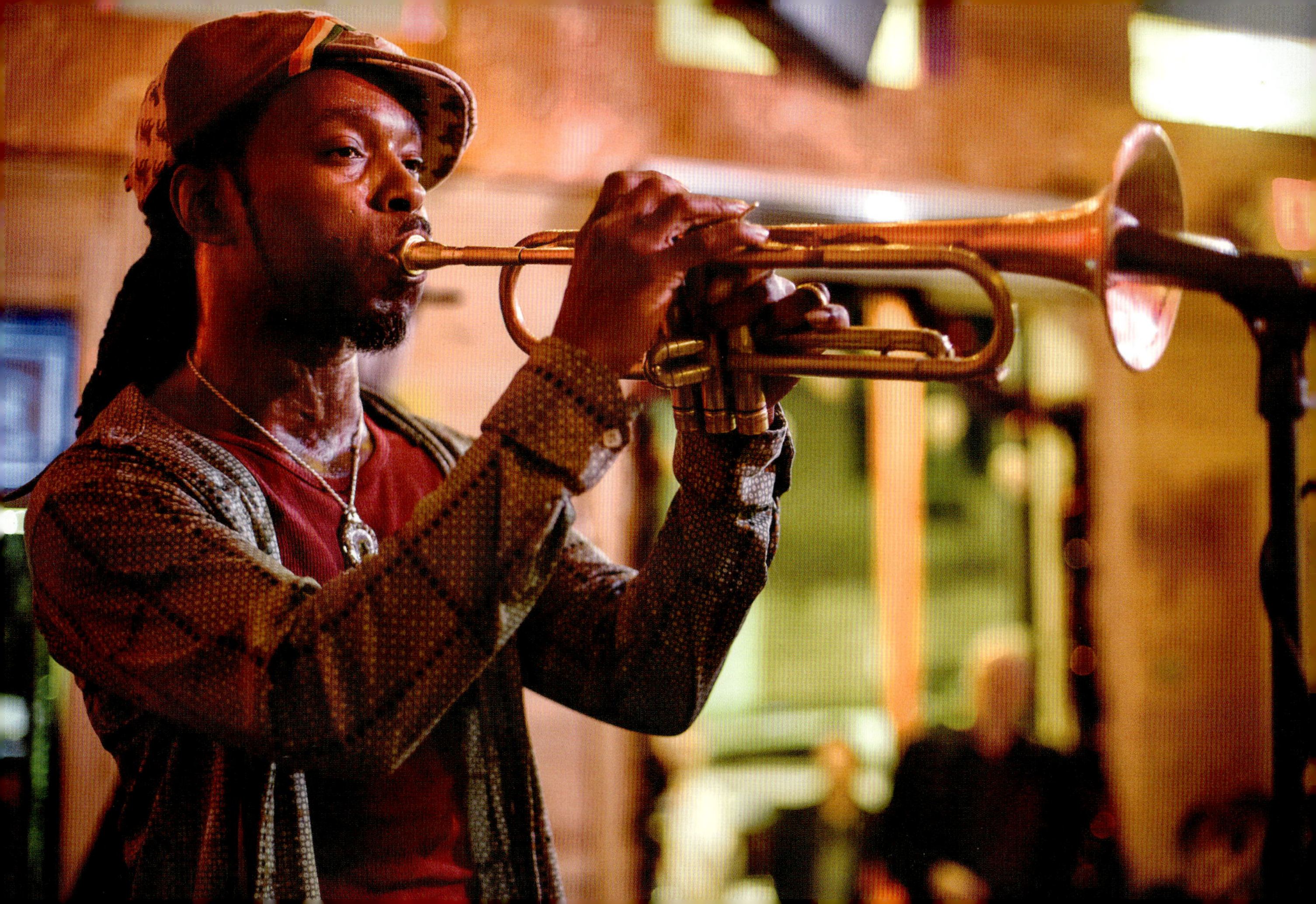

handkerchief and the umbrella—of course in West Africa the umbrella is a symbol of social status or royalty and the more elaborate the colors or the larger the umbrella the more status or height the person has. In New Orleans there are umbrellas and handkerchiefs and this free-form, creative dance. But it still has a certain look and feel to it, and it parallels the music, and the music parallels the dance, and, in fact, they creatively feed off of each other.

So, that's a social club parade in New Orleans. They usually go down big streets in various New Orleans neighborhoods. It's usually only one club that parades at a time. Everybody's on foot, and it's a tremendous thing. Sometimes the people in the club will spend tremendous amounts of money on their outfits. Certain colors, suits—bold colors, as I mentioned—certain kinds of shoes or boots. They have accessories, like hats and fans and baskets, umbrellas, handkerchiefs, that they use to dance with. It's quite a thing to see. Some of the clubs try to outdress each other. Who's going to have the best outfits this week? As opposed to next week.

So you might see things that really are striking and catch the eye. I mean, you might see a club that has lime green as theme. They might have six different shades of lime green, and they might not look like they would blend together. But because everybody is wearing them, they will blend together. Lime green shoes, lime green socks, lime green belt, lime green shirt, jacket, another color of lime green hat, lime green basket, and all of that. That presents some interesting things to think about in terms of redefining what works and what doesn't work—redefining concepts of beauty, of culture, of what's acceptable, what's not acceptable. It's sort of like dissonance in music, but visual dissonance. I'm sure there's a term for that. Things that normally would not fit together,

would be thought to clash: just because so many people are wearing them and the attitude with which they wear them, they don't clash. They become beautiful and majestic and bold and powerful. That was the purpose of all those parades—a sense of unity, a sense of strength in hard times. And it was a way of transforming.

One of the great things about New Orleans culture is that we like to take and transform reality into a new reality, our own independent reality. We do that, of course, with food. We do it with language. We do it, of course, with music. The second-line parade is one of the prime examples of this New Orleans tendency to blend things together that would not normally go together and make something new, interesting, exciting and unique and beautiful out of it.


**Mardi Gras Indians**

The Mardi Gras Indians are another branch of the same tree. I mean, the Indian parade is all about, on one hand, fun and good times, but it's also about a psychological method of transformation from whatever your social conditions are. Most of the Indians—like the second line social club members—come from the poor segments of society. But on the days of the parades, or when the Indians are practicing or the Indians are parading or the Indians are sewing, they've transformed their lives from poverty and second-class citizenship to something of beauty, of majesty, of power, of respect. They've transcended the confines of normal society and earthly restrictions, and they've become something completely different. That's psychological; it's visual; it's physical; and it's displayed before the entire community, so everybody sees that.

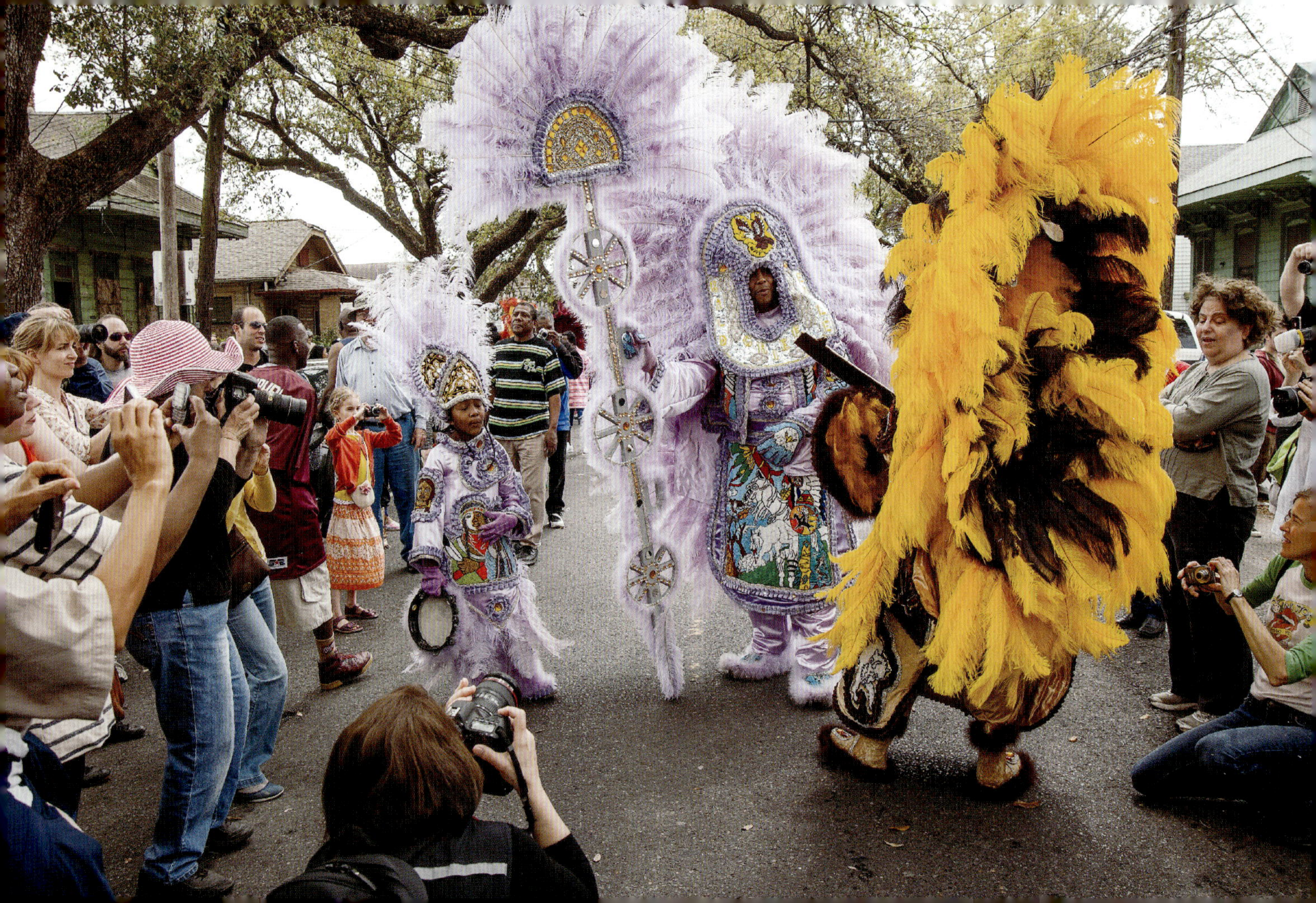

You might be a janitor in everyday life but on second line Sunday you're something special. People are looking at you; people are respecting you and the way you dance and the attitude you have; you're royalty. You know, you're not an Indian on Super Sunday or Mardi Gras day or Saint Joseph's Day—you're an Indian all year long. The mask is what you have to do to maintain that Indian status. Your day job, or whatever, doesn't matter. So, you transform that concept of reality.

Even though originally Mardi Gras Indians made their own music, at times they've had brass bands play. I've played Super Sunday with brass bands before. It was a great thing.

Donald Harrison Jr. is a real Mardi Gras Indian and a jazz musician. His father was a chief. And his sister is a queen. His whole family is involved in that. At Xavier I sponsor concerts and programs every semester on some aspect of New Orleans culture, as the Keller Endowed Chair in the Humanities. We just did a program featuring the music and talking about the life and contributions of Sidney Bechet. Donald played soprano sax with my band, and it was a great program. But even then, he would come to rehearsals with material and sketches of his Indian costume, and he was working on it then. You know that thing that they say about how the Indians start working the day after Mardi Gras on the suit for the next Mardi Gras? Well, a lot of them do work year round; I mean that's part of their tradition. And I realize that it's not about just the idea, "Oh, men like to sew." What it's about is that the mindset of the Indian—proud, majestic, free, bold, rebellious, powerful—stays with you year round. You're making this suit that represents your heart, your spirit, your soul, and it's with you every day, wherever you go. It stays with you year round.

What becomes a mask and what becomes a reality? Reality is what's with you every day. This is how you feel inside no matter what society sees when it looks at you, or your economic status, or education level or whatever. This is how you define yourself. This is what you are. And you reinforce those concepts by sewing every day, by meeting, by practicing throughout the year. I mean, imagine a Mardi Gras Indian practice. It's not like a jazz band. They're not learning new songs and a whole new way of playing every time. No—it's a way of reaffirming the connection and the bond, reaffirming that status and that transformation—that type of unity and that type of freedom that comes along with that Indian persona.

## Branches of the Same Tree

I've been studying this stuff for a long, long time and thinking about it. Over the last few years the dots started to connect, and I started not only to have a much, much deeper appreciation for everything, but to understand how it all blends together—not only in New Orleans but in the cultural world and where it all comes from. So it's great to see that and have those traditions. I realize, for instance, the Indians don't look like traditional jazz bands. Their parades don't look like social club parades or jazz funerals. But they're all connected—it's all coming from the same tree. It's done for different reasons.

If you look at New Orleans culture, it's branches of the same tree. We're doing the same things for the same reasons. It's just that they come out different ways, which is beautiful. I mean, it's hard to believe that an urban area in America, even today, can have unique traditions like we have. Social parades, jazz funerals, brass bands, Mardi Gras Indians still have meaning and vitality in the community, although that meaning may have changed and outside influences have altered the course or direction of some of them somewhat. But they still are very important parts of New Orleans culture today. It's incredible.

Sometimes over the last few years I've been accused of being *re*-something. *Re*-create, *re*-do, *retro*, *re*-this, *re*-that, *re*-, *re*-nothing. You have to understand when I came along into music, the only music that they had in the black community—in the jazz funerals and social aid and pleasure club parades—was authentic, traditional New Orleans jazz. That was not re-creating. That was what was ongoing and living. And when people played the music they were playing the music creatively—it was what was pertinent to community and community life at the time. When I got involved in that, I mean, we were playing whatever we created.

Then, when I got involved with the older musicians, I had started reading about jazz history, started listening to recordings, and certainly, in terms of clarinet, coming under the influence of people like Johnny Dodds, George Lewis, Sidney Bechet, Edmond Hall, and dozens of others who recorded. But the truth is that I wasn't trying to recreate anything. I was playing with the musicians who were playing the music that they always played—I was just developing along with them. It was not a recovery attitude or, "Let me go back and find this old music that's gone." The music wasn't gone. It was alive all over New Orleans. It wasn't publicly known as such and wasn't promoted as such, but it was authentic traditional New Orleans music. Jazz was in the black community in the brass bands, sometimes in social aid and pleasure clubs, sometimes in dances and events for old folks homes and things like that.

Traditional, authentic, traditional New Orleans jazz was a functional music then. In the community it was a functional music, too, in parts of rich, Uptown New Orleans. In a lot of homes in the Garden District and along Saint Charles they would have parties, and they would have traditional jazz bands. When I started playing with the older musicians, a lot of the guys that played at Preservation Hall and whatever, some of them were also were still playing other kinds of jobs, not only in the hall. So, New Orleans jazz was still a functional music when I came along, and I was playing in it. The whole idea of trying to *re*-create and *re*-whatever didn't even enter the picture.

Now, later on, I have to admit that I did become so fascinated by the music that I really got into the music of the 1920s that nobody was playing, because it's tough as hell—Jelly Roll Morton and King Oliver music with their approach and arrangements and key changes and introductions and breaks and different parts and different kinds of harmonies and all of that. I got into that. But to me that was just an extension of what I was already doing. It wasn't a sense of trying to go back and recreate a music of the past. You know, a lot of the guys that I played with, the older musicians, had played with Jelly Roll Morton and King Oliver and Louis Armstrong and Sidney Bechet. And some of them recorded with them. So those people were still very much alive to me and in the minds of those musicians that played with them.

I mean, you know, it's one thing to talk about—let's say Sidney Bechet—but to sit next to Danny Barker and have him playing the same rhythms behind you that he played on the great Sidney Bechet records: it's not like you're recreating anything. This man is playing what he plays. So now you're developing yourself, and you're playing. It wasn't like I was trying to recreate Sidney Bechet. I was trying to define myself within that tradition.

## Authenticity and Democracy, Freedom and Majesty

How do I think I'm seen in New Orleans and beyond? Oh, that's funny. That's really funny. I don't think in America, in general, there's an awareness of traditional New Orleans jazz, authentic New Orleans Jazz. There are Dixieland bands all over America. There are Dixieland festivals all over America. There's more than one every week somewhere in America, and they're usually for people who are Dixieland fans, as such. There's not a general awareness, even among them, that there's an authentic New Orleans jazz that sounds very, very different from Dixieland. Because in New Orleans there's a lot of Dixieland. That's what they promote, and people think, "Oh that's it." No, that's not it. That's not it.

It's really interesting. When I started coming up in New Orleans, a lot of the musicians who were my age, but especially older than me, when they saw that I was getting into the more authentic style—Johnny Dodds and George Lewis and all this—a lot of people laughed at me. Some of them thought I was nuts. One guy told me one time, I'll never forget it—he thought I was retarded or something because I didn't have any bebop in my playing. That's what he said. But later he said, "But then I found out you had education, and now I see where you're coming from."

I got encouragement—and discouragement—from different people. A lot of people were willing to let traditional music die. They didn't see any value in it. They thought it wasn't hip. It was old man's music.

Some people thought it was Uncle Tom music, and what it was all about was being submissive and one step removed from being a slave or a minstrel. So a lot of people missed the boat. They didn't see what the music was really about, the whole idea that the music was a representation of democracy, of freedom, once again, like the Indians and everything else—of transformation, of majesty, of power—all of those things in the music. A lot of people didn't see that. It wasn't hip. A lot of jazz musicians were playing modern jazz, bebop, Coltrane-influenced and later, and even if they played traditional music they weren't really playing traditional style. They played traditional songs, what I used to call "under protest." You know, "I will play it if I have to make money, but I'm going to play it my way." *My way* meant playing as modern jazz as possible.

In my mind, New Orleans jazz is not a song or a repertoire. It's a style or approach that can be applied to many songs. I played a job at the Snug Harbor a couple weeks ago with my band, and I did a kind of risky thing. I pulled this song out on them because I feel kinship now, more than ever, to Haiti and I found out that one of the most popular Haitian folk songs, "Ayiti Cheri," has the same structure as a lot of songs we play. So I pulled out this song, and I said, "Fellas, just follow me." You know, at the beginning I'll play the melody, Caribbean rhythm. The next thing you know we're playing it, Caribbean-style—and then we turn it into New Orleans jazz. It came out nice, very nice. So New Orleans jazz is an approach to playing, not a set of songs. Like other forms, New Orleans jazz is a language. There's a lot of freedom in it, but it has a certain direction that it goes in. If you're not going down that stylistic direction, if what you play sounds like Dizzy Gillespie or something, it's not traditional New Orleans jazz, plain and simple.

On clarinet, I was really the only one—and one of the very few on any instrument—who was that serious about the authentic New Orleans jazz sound and into the older musicians. So, in my day I only hung out with the older guys. I was one of the few younger musicians playing at Preservation Hall. I played there for twenty-four years, and I played with all of the older musicians. I was frequently the only one in the band not in their seventies. I was in my twenties, and I was playing with guys seventy, seventy-five. People would laugh at me. But the older musicians loved it, because they thought it was great that one of their own was interested in their music. Otherwise it was somebody from England or Central Europe, Japan or somewhere. They helped me, and they encouraged me, and it was great to have that because I saw the value in the music; I saw the things that it had to offer. I saw the greatness of the music. So, for the most part I ignored younger musicians. When I say *younger musicians* I mean the rhythm and blues generation and on down. And they ignored me.

But then, with time, a lot of them had to play traditional music, one way or the other, for economic purposes. With time it changed quite a lot. I mean, one of my great surprise encouragements came from Ellis Marsalis early on. When he first heard me, he just looked at me, and he stood up and he shook his head. Ellis can be very intimidating in his own way. He just looked at me, and he shook his head, and I was like, "What's the matter?" You know, I was waiting for some kind of insult or put-down; I was waiting for him to say something like, "You know you're archaic; you should be dead" or something like that. But he said, "You're amazing to me." And I was like, "Oh lord, here it comes." He said, "You know, twenty years ago you could not have existed." And I was thinking, "Oh lord, here it goes," and he said, "But

it's a great thing you're doing," he said, "Keep doing what you're doing." I was surprised by that, and that encouraged me. Of course the older musicians were great encouragement. But, coming from Ellis Marsalis, a respected modernist and all that—that was a meaningful thing for me at the time.

## Can You Say Something New in an Old Tradition?

Nowadays I think I'm viewed for the most part as a traditional musician. And I discovered later on that I could write a few songs. I think I've helped to do something that was always a question plaguing me—how to maintain tradition and yet to be innovative; how to contribute to tradition. I think if you look at the two main periods of New Orleans jazz, in terms of records anyway, the classic period and then the revival period, there's really no next step. So what do you do in the next step? How do you maintain the greatness of traditional New Orleans jazz, yet say something new and different? That's a tough one. You don't want to sound like a poor imitation of Coltrane. You have this rich tradition here. You have this spirit here. You have these concepts of tone and rhythm—exploit those.

So the question is, how do you say something new with an old tradition? Well, when I first formed my bands, I used older musicians; I didn't pay attention to guys my age, or ten, twenty, thirty years older. I used the older musicians—forty, fifty, sixty years older. My first Original Liberty Jazz Band was Chester Zardis, born in 1900, on bass. It was Sadie Goodson, born in 1900, on piano; Danny Barker, born in 1909, on banjo. It was Louis Nelson on trombone, born in 1902. I had a couple of younger guys, but that was it.

✷ Trumpeter and vocalist Gregg Stafford with Dr. Michael White and the Original Liberty Jazz Band, workshop, Durham, New Hampshire

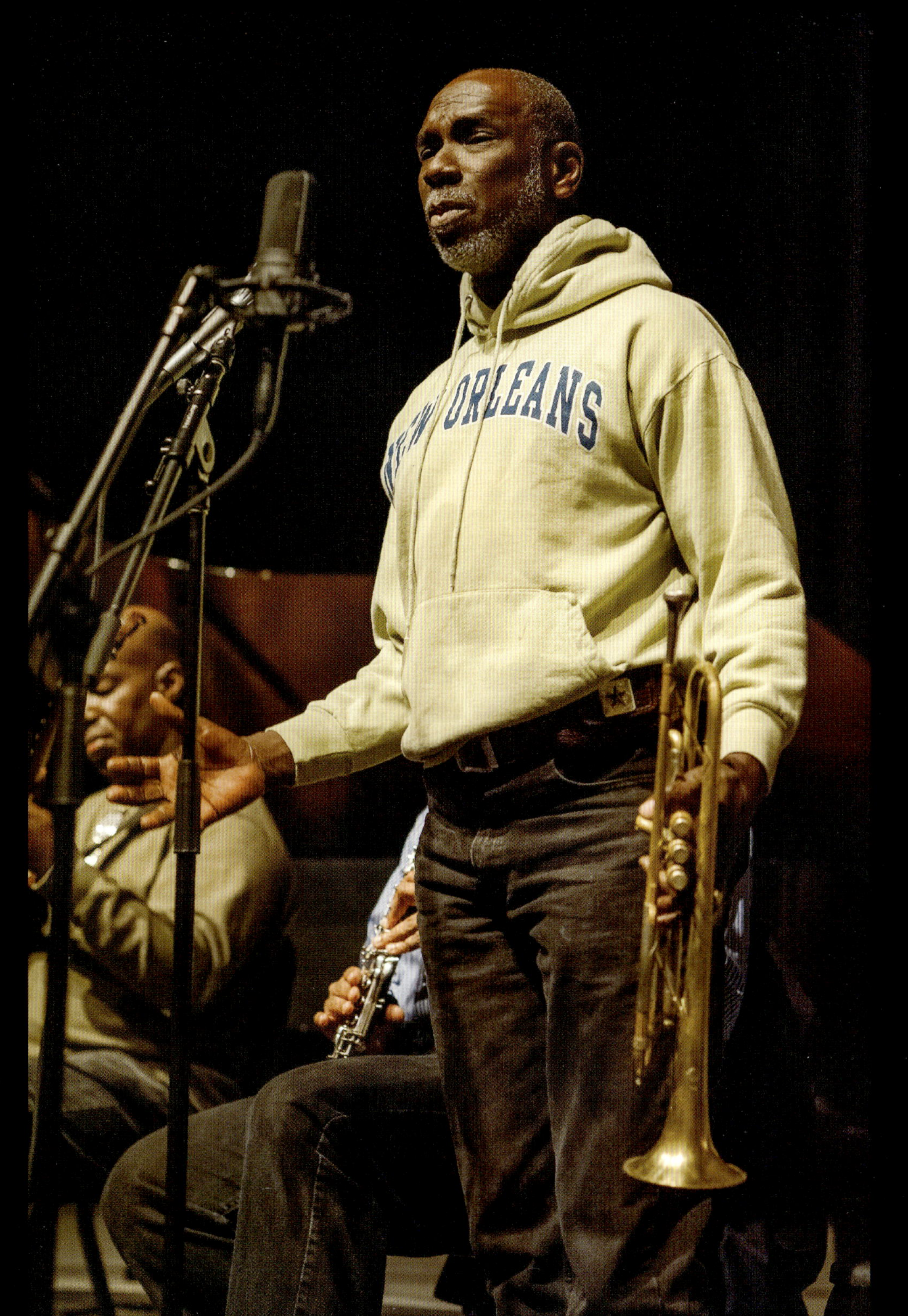

Nowadays I think it's really kind of interesting—I think a lot of people realize now the value of tradition. I've done what I can though lectures and playing the music—that this is a great music, a powerful music, a spiritual music, and one of the world's special musics. I think that I've done enough things to gain respect in some good circles with that. Of course, you always have people who think anything older than yesterday needs to be destroyed. And some people try to accuse you of being a retro something or that you're anti-anything modern, but the thing is every time I play I try to create original phrases, and I use my own contemporary life's experiences when I'm playing—things that come to me now.

So, when we play it's contemporary to us. It's coming from our life experiences. But we're using the principles of the older tradition. What I've also done is I started writing songs—seriously for the first time in 2004, and then, after Katrina, really seriously. And I discovered what I think is a new way of playing New Orleans jazz, which is to use your own personal experiences, the principles of the music, and blend sometimes with other ethnic folk music.

For example, on my latest CD, *Blue Crescent,* I have some songs that mix New Orleans jazz with Caribbean music, North African music, French music. But it's traditional music, and I write traditional forms, like hymns and spirituals. I have a dirge, "Katrina." Some of it is a little bit on the revival side, but none of it really sounds just like the George Lewis stuff or the '20s stuff. It has its own character. You have diehard jazz fans that think you should play the same songs, and they want to hear somebody sound like George Lewis or something. You hear that a lot in Europe. But I realize that you have to do not exactly what they did—you have to do like they did, which

means I'm just using the things they used. I'm using personal experience, environment.

## Personal Creativity and the Tradition

Musically, I'm liable to use any influences in my music. Some people think I'm a diehard traditionalist and all that. And I believe in traditional music, but I have, since Katrina, experimented, played African music, Cuban music, in different bands, not my own, and even completely free avant-garde jazz. I listen to pop music; I listen to rap; I listen to rhythm and blues; I listen to all kinds of modern jazz. And elements of those things come into my music.

There's no reason to copy somebody's playing or try to recreate the sound they had, because it's going to be different. Johnny Dodds, George Lewis—their lives were based on their experiences. I have an iPhone that I can't figure out yet—give me another two or three years, I'll have it mastered. I have a computer; I've had experiences different from what their experiences were. I went through the civil rights movement, Vietnam, political assassinations.

I've had many different kinds of experiences. Those experiences—good, bad, ugly—those emotions should be in music. They should come out in the music. They're not in King Oliver's music; they're not in Bunk Johnson's music because that's not their experiences. So mine do come out. I mean I listen to Coltrane, I listen to Albert Ayler, I listen to all kinds of things. I've been able to convert experiences and musical influences into the language of New Orleans jazz. I'm not copying anyone's music, but I've taken rap songs, I've taken 50 Cent's songs, and played them on traditional jobs, because they had a similar structure that would lend itself to that kind of style. I'll pull it out, tell the band a couple of words, and we're playing it. There are other things that come from pop music that I've used sometimes, not consciously, but they're there. I mean, you have a rich well of life experiences and sources, so why not use them in the music?

It's been interesting to me: First of all, I've gotten to the stage and the age where I don't care what people think, one way or the other. I get a lot of awards and accolades. When I go back to New Orleans this Saturday I'm going to be named the Louisiana State Humanist of the Year by the Louisiana State Endowment for the Humanities. I was just named in the *OffBeat* magazine, clarinetist of the year. I've gotten to the stage where I don't care about that stuff. That doesn't define me. It's nice, I guess, but it really doesn't mean a heck of a lot to me. I'm fortunate to have this tradition, and I have to keep realistic parameters on myself.

For me, if we can play before an audience—not jazz fans, not necessarily people who come there to expect something—and move them, give them something that they can relate to and feel, then that's the greatest compliment of all to me. That's the greatest award, when you have somebody that will say, "Oh, I didn't know what to expect." Some people will say, "I thought this was going to be Dixieland, but it's not, it's something else," or, "I never heard jazz before but I love this." A guy came to us last night and said, "I don't cry much, but you all made me cry twice last night." I know that what we're feeling and expressing relates to people today. I'm not thinking about trying to recreate anything. I'm trying to think about expressing genuine, universal human passion and emotion in the musical language of New Orleans. So, when we can do that I feel good.

Right now, if I pull out my CD player, I have Sade's latest CD in there, *Soldier of Love.* Haven't heard it yet, but, might be something in there. Consciously or subconsciously. I might be on the job playing "Way Down Yonder in New Orleans," and a little melodic phrase from that might come out. And I'm like, wow. Sometimes I'm like, where did that come from? What is that? And sometimes I figure it out. Sometimes I don't. But, I think that's what Armstrong did. That's what Coltrane did. You know—their musical experiences. My objective is to use the principles of the music that, when I came up as a musician, was around me.

This is sort of like what Duke Ellington said— Ellington said he was trying to put in music the lives of his people. When we play, I still see certain second-liners, certain musicians and people that I knew, certain expressions, certain parts of New Orleans. They're in the back of our—not just mine, but the other guys in the band too—in the back of our heads. We talk about this all the time: somebody's sense of humor, some kind of way of playing. You try to convert what that means to musical sound and expression. So, to me it's never been a dead music. I've never thought, "Let me try to recreate this thing that came from these people where I came from." No.

What's going to happen after guys like me, after we pass? Understand, I deal with this question every day of my life. It's a tough call. The commercial powers that be, educational powers that be, musical powers that be, political powers that be, don't really know or care about authentic New Orleans jazz. Plain and simple. It's a cult music all around the world. People will kill you about it. Argue about it. They write. They play the music. They visit clubs. They promote record companies. They do all kinds of things. Make pilgrimages to New Orleans. But in New Orleans, there's very little consciousness of authentic. Even with some of the success I've had, people think it's me. They don't realize that what I'm doing is an extension of a tradition and an approach. They just think I have something different, something special. It's not me. It's not the guys in my band. Well, individually, we have something. But it's coming from somewhere. And that's a whole rich tradition that for the most part is being covered over and dying out.

## Young People and the Importance of New Orleans' Music

Since Katrina I think a lot of people have realized the importance of New Orleans music. And I've assisted. I've helped some of the younger brass bands—in particular the Hot 8—try to get into learning about traditional brass band style and values. We have an ongoing relationship. I talked to Benny Pete, the leader of the band, a couple of days ago, and, in fact, I'm going to do a program at Xavier in April, called "The Culture of Second Line." I'll be having them and my own band play. We're going to have a panel of people, and I'll talk a little bit about the different meanings of second line. We'll have some people there to demonstrate second-line dancing—the philosophy behind it, the music behind it, what it means to New Orleans people and culture.

I realize as time goes on that it's almost like a foreign language to younger people. That's because it's such a confusing concept when you put this umbrella term, *New Orleans music*, out there. The lines are very blurred between what is New Orleans music and what isn't. Is it New Orleans rhythm and blues? Is it funk? Is it traditional jazz? Is it Dixieland? Is it modern brass band? With time, partly because of the constant infusion of commercialism in traditions, from the Indians and brass bands and social clubs and all that—those lines have become kind of erased and blurred. So now that umbrella term, *New Orleans music*, can mean a whole lot of things to a whole lot of people.

A young person coming up today can't do what I did—play with someone who was born four or five years before Louis Armstrong. Kid Thomas Valentine, sitting down, playing the trumpet with this unique style that sounds like he's talking and fussing at the same time. But there's a beauty of it; he can make his horn sound like a baby crying and sit down and talk about what it was like playing dances in the old days. Or Chester Zardis telling you what it was like playing on an advertising wagon, where they chained the wheels together on the wagons, and two bands were competing. Or what it was like to play in the old dance halls. Or somebody telling me what Sidney Bechet really sounded like. Or what it was like to go out in Chicago to the Lincoln Gardens and listen to King Oliver's band every night as a young inspired kid, and then finally being able to join that band. And what it was like to record with Johnny Dodds, or Armstrong. Or what was Jelly Roll Morton really talking about that's not in Lomax's book and not on the Library of Congress records? That made all that alive for me. And then, like I say, it was the traditional music out on the streets; older musicians you would never know or hear anything about. They lived for those parades. That's what they did. You don't have that any more.

A lot of the younger musicians in New Orleans don't know what authentic traditional music is. They've never heard it, and it's foreign to them when they do hear it. They can't relate to it. They don't realize that that's where they come from. So it's hard for them to get to that. Nowadays brass band music in general is simpler—they have complex heads, but when it gets down to improvisation, a lot of the music is not as involved as some of the traditional songs in terms of the harmonic structure. So, it's hard for them to learn how to play those old songs. It's hard for them to learn the concepts involved in New Orleans jazz.

I help people out individually. Usually, no money's involved, no publicity. It's just somebody that I talk to or calls me. It's "Meet me at Xavier" at a certain time. A session might last a couple hours. We listen to recordings of whatever instrument they play. I talk to them about listening to all the different people. If you want to define the style that your instrument is, what the role of your instrument is, listen to maybe half a dozen or ten people who played the instrument on a recording. Listen to these guys playing the same song. What is alike, and what's different? That will tell you what the role of the instrument is. Then we talk about it. And we sit down and actually play some things, and work on content. We talk about the history.

It's tough, because there's not encouragement for that. Unfortunately, we're in an age today where the level of development is not encouraged to be what it was before. When I joined the brass band, you served an informal apprenticeship. Old men would look at you and say, "Oh, you're not doing this right. You need to work on this or that." I remember Doc Paulin telling me, "You're too light on that clarinet. Too light." "What, do I need suntan or . . . ?" No, what he was saying, and I figured it out and started working on it, was that he needed a broader, louder, more powerful sound to cut through all those brass instruments. So I talked to older musicians, I practiced, and I developed because of him.

But nowadays, you have younger guys, same age as I was, who don't necessarily have the level of musical training that kids used to have. We used to have really good high school bands—teachers and really good bands. Those were feeding grounds for all the New Orleans musicians. Everything is different nowadays. The level of a lot of things is a lot lower. It's hard for kids to come along. For a lot of people I was a hope. "Oh wow, everybody wants to see us dead, and there are no young black musicians playing authentic style." Then, all of a sudden, here I come. So, I'm hoping. Every time I see a little kid—you know, four or five years old—and we're playing, and he has a starry look in his eyes, I'm thinking, "Is he going to be one of the ones to keep this up when he gets older?"

I remember a George Lewis recording, *George Lewis Plays Hymns*. At the end of the recording, they interviewed him, and he said, "I'm thinking after we go, there's not going to be anybody to continue this music." He died before I started playing, but maybe, just maybe, people will hear us, and they'll realize that there is something going on, something special. I've had some successes in getting other people involved in playing traditional music—Wynton Marsalis and many others, on different levels. But to have that really taken as a serious creative thing that relates to both your life and the art of the music, that's tough. That's tough.

But there's a tremendous amount of talent in New Orleans. Music is part of community life. You see it some now, and before Katrina it was a very common thing to see kids—I would see this every week—coming from school, walking down the street or standing at a bus stop, playing a trombone or a trumpet, or a couple of kids together, beating on a drum or something. There's an awareness of music, and a lot of kids—not a lot, but some kids—got into the habit of going out to the French Quarter and playing for tips, doing things like that. Forming little brass bands. There was a lot of encouragement, and I think there should be, to encourage younger people to play. But unfortunately, some of the people in power positions—agents, promoters—exploit the kids. And unfortunately, some well-meaning tourists, sometimes they'll say stuff like, "Oh, you're great. Louis Armstrong," and all this stuff. A lot of the kids sort of get kind of pushed out there before they develop. A lot of times some festival will take kids or younger bands from New Orleans just because they're from New Orleans and they have spirit. And also because they're not experienced, and they can get them cheap.

You find young bands that tour in Europe and make records and get attention, get write-ups, articles in newspapers, pictures in the paper. And they think they've made it. It's like, "If what we're doing works, why change it?" That keeps them from growing and developing; it kind of messes things up really. You don't have that apprentice kind of process like when I came along, that really helps people to grow and continue. So there's no real encouragement; they see no reason to learn authentic traditional music. They don't realize that some kid from Japan, maybe the same age, can play authentic traditional music from New Orleans that they know nothing about. It doesn't hit them like that. I mean, of course the guy in Japan is playing for different reasons from the guy in New Orleans.

So it's very difficult to convince people to play traditional New Orleans music. There are not a lot of good traditional bands in New Orleans. There are bands, but as far as authentic music and really good bands and creative bands, there aren't many. It's hard for young people to get excited about that music. But with that said, I've had people younger than me come along—like some of the guys I brought up here—Herman Lebeaux, Kerry Lewis. Herman's in his thirties; Kerry's in his forties. You know, they come along. And sometimes younger ones come along. But it's difficult.

For a lot of people, I think it's sort of like going down a path. I can give you a lot of analogies. But it's like—if you're trying to get from point A to point B, do you want to go down a road that's been cut out already, get there quick and easy, simple; or do you want to cut your own path through the bushes to get there, the harder way, the long way, the more difficult way? You know, you have to eat, and you're in a hurry. Do you go to McDonalds, or do you go to a restaurant with a chef, and it's going to take a while to get your food? A lot of people take the quick and easy route. It's a lot easier than playing collective improvisation, because you can't practice that. That's hard to do—to realize that you're going to go out there and exactly what you're going to play is not pre-planned: the melody, the chord structure, and all of that. It depends on what the trumpet player is doing. It depends on the feel of the rhythm section. It comes when it comes—where the spaces are. That's harder to do than simple one-change, funk-type solos.

Yes, it's difficult. If I were a young musician coming up today, it would be very hard for me to find out that there was this authentic New Orleans jazz and what it is, exactly. It would be very hard to find out, even in New Orleans. When you talk about black kids coming along, there is this culture of modern brass bands, with its own standards and values, and those are very different from the more traditional music. Even though they come from the same musical wellspring, it's a very, very different thing. You find a lot of guys that play in the modern brass bands. They've worked out certain kind of riffs and a few songs here and there. But they can't just come and play with another group, or play even some of the simple, common traditional songs. And everybody thinks, "Oh, you're from New Orleans . . ." No, it just doesn't go like that.

So it's tough. I try to talk to young people that might seem interested. I show them the values. I talk about history. I talk about tradition. I talk about what the music has to offer in terms of being an individual and a collective world. I talk about the fact that if you're a musician and you want to play funk and pop music and rap and all, that's great. But you're competing in a very, very large framework, and it's hard to excel and to distinguish yourself and have a life and a career. Most people end up not doing so well. And I say that you look at other styles of music and you can find value but not necessarily millions and millions of dollars and major mass publicity. But you can certainly find a way of expressing yourself that has meaning and value beyond the big money or whatever. It's hard for people, because to get to it nowadays you have to study. And who wants to study? You have to listen to records. You have to buy records, spend money. You have to spend time. You need to read about the lives of these musicians, spend time talking to people who've been there and know. Who wants to spend time doing that? You have to educate yourself. You have to motivate yourself and educate yourself. I see a lot of people doing it in Japan, in Canada, Scandinavia. But in New Orleans, in America—forget it.

But I don't know. You never really know. It's hard to predict what's going to happen. Even though it doesn't look good, I don't predict the end of traditional music. People have been trying to do that since the '30s. They said, "When Kid Thomas dies, it's all over. When Percy Humphrey dies, it's all over. When this one dies . . ." Yet it's still here. Like I said, from my perspective it doesn't look good, but you never know who you influence out there. You never know who's listening. It could be some kid you never see, who might be thirteen years old, fifteen, eighteen, listening. And, you know, in the next few years he might be out there. There might be several of them. I think there are a lot of things that could motivate people. Money, which, of course, is not the best motivator. Pride. Culture. Ancestry. Sense of tradition. Sense of individuality. Trying to do something really different, something that has meaning. Expression of culture. There are a lot of possible motivators out there.


**After the Storm**

I think in a general sense New Orleans musicians are struggling to come back after Katrina. In New Orleans there are a variety of musical styles today. People are grappling for position, so to speak. You still have traditional jazz people, brass bands, Dixieland people, your modern jazz guys, your college-age modern jazz guys, your R&B people, your folk music people, and all kinds of blends and mixtures, and all of that's going on. All of these guys are trying to get back into music.

On a personal level, after Katrina I have a greater sense of urgency and greater sense of grief than I've ever had before. Tragedy. Loss. I think those things have become part of my music, to give me a little more passion in my playing. Experiences post-Katrina have certainly fueled new compositions. But Katrina, in a sense, washed away, if you will, a lot of the security I had in life. So, I think, musically it washed away some of the limitations I had, conceptually, and it opened me up, not to go out seeking other styles but to be receptive when they came. And they came.

Since Katrina I've done so many things that I've never done before, never even thought about. My musical tastes have always been wide—I've always listened to all styles of music, and I like all styles of music—but I never played a lot of things like I'm playing now. I mean I've done everything from—I recorded with a Cuban group, played some jobs with them out of New York, Juan Carlos Formell. You've heard of Juan Formell from Los Van Van in Cuba? His son—great guitarist and singer. He has a sort of post–Buena Vista kind of Cuban folk and jazz music. It's great. I've played some with him and recorded.

I'm playing now in New Orleans with an African group, with guys from West Africa, with a balafon, with a djembe drum, dundun, mixed with various New Orleans musicians—Jason Marsalis on vibraphone, Bruce Sunpie Barnes on accordion, myself on clarinet. We have a saxophone, a bass, a guitar, and a singer. That's an interesting mix. The playing is sort of bordering on avant-garde. I've even sat in and played with a legend of avant-garde music, Perry Robinson, a clarinetist, seventy years old now. Stuff is starting to happen. I think I'm more open and more receptive to hearing different styles on the horn. I've even started to play some modern jazz standards, not with all the usual bebop lines, but with whatever I'm hearing, whatever's coming out. I play Coltrane songs. I've done some of that on jobs, but usually parties where nobody's paying any attention.

It's exciting to me. I'm going through a musical evolution. Where it's going to stop, or land, or how long it's going to go on, I don't know. But it feels good to me, and it's exciting. So I always say that Katrina ended life as I knew it. And that's very much true.

But with every ending is a new beginning; with every death there's a new form of existence. You know, you hear those kinds of things, but until you live it, you don't realize how true that is. So I feel like I'm reborn. And in that rebirth almost anything is possible musically.

I'm still recovering, still suffering from Katrina. My house is sitting up there, empty and gutted, nearly five years later. I've gone through major, major emotional hardships. I've had physical complications. I've had logistical nightmares, elderly relatives that I had to care for and that had to take precedence over everything else. I've had many issues, like thousands of New Orleans people, with recovery. Insurance company battles. FEMA. Displacement. Health issues. So many things that have come up that have been roadblocks to complete recovery nearly five years later. But, still, you keep going on.

The music is keeping me going on. I think there's a certain excitement and renewal, in that I'm discovering that there's a whole new me under the rubble of Katrina that hadn't been discovered, or uncovered, before. It's starting to peek through in different ways. It's like finding a mine inside of yourself, inside of your soul, inside of your spirit, and now you're starting to excavate. And you're coming up with jewels. So I'm trying to see how far that will go. It's a great feeling.

# CHARMAINE NEVILLE

Eclectic singer

Leader, Charmaine Neville Band

[ Interviewed January 18, 2013, in the Upper Ninth Ward, New Orleans ]

Charmaine Neville's old house in the Upper Ninth Ward tells the story of much of her life. It's full of art—paintings and sculptural pieces that she's made. Posters and recordings, souvenirs of a life in music, are all around. The kitchen is big, right for a person who loves to cook. Her enthusiastic dogs welcome you, but it's her warmth and hospitality that carry the day. You can't see the high water marks that Katrina left, but you know they're there.

She's a singer, and when it comes to music, her interests and abilities seem pretty much unbounded. Some call her a jazz singer, but she resists that label. In fact, as you'll read below, she resists all labels. She certainly has the classic jazz singer's capacity for messing creatively with songs. With her four-piece band, she holds down a regular Monday night slot at Snug Harbor, the city's premier jazz club. They've been doing that for nearly thirty years. Snug's music calendar lists her as an R&B vocalist, but, like *jazz singer*, the term doesn't really get at what she does, which is to take songs she likes and make them her own. Buy her album, *Before the Storm,* and listen to "Yellow Submarine." From then on, you'll never think the same way about that Beatles composition.

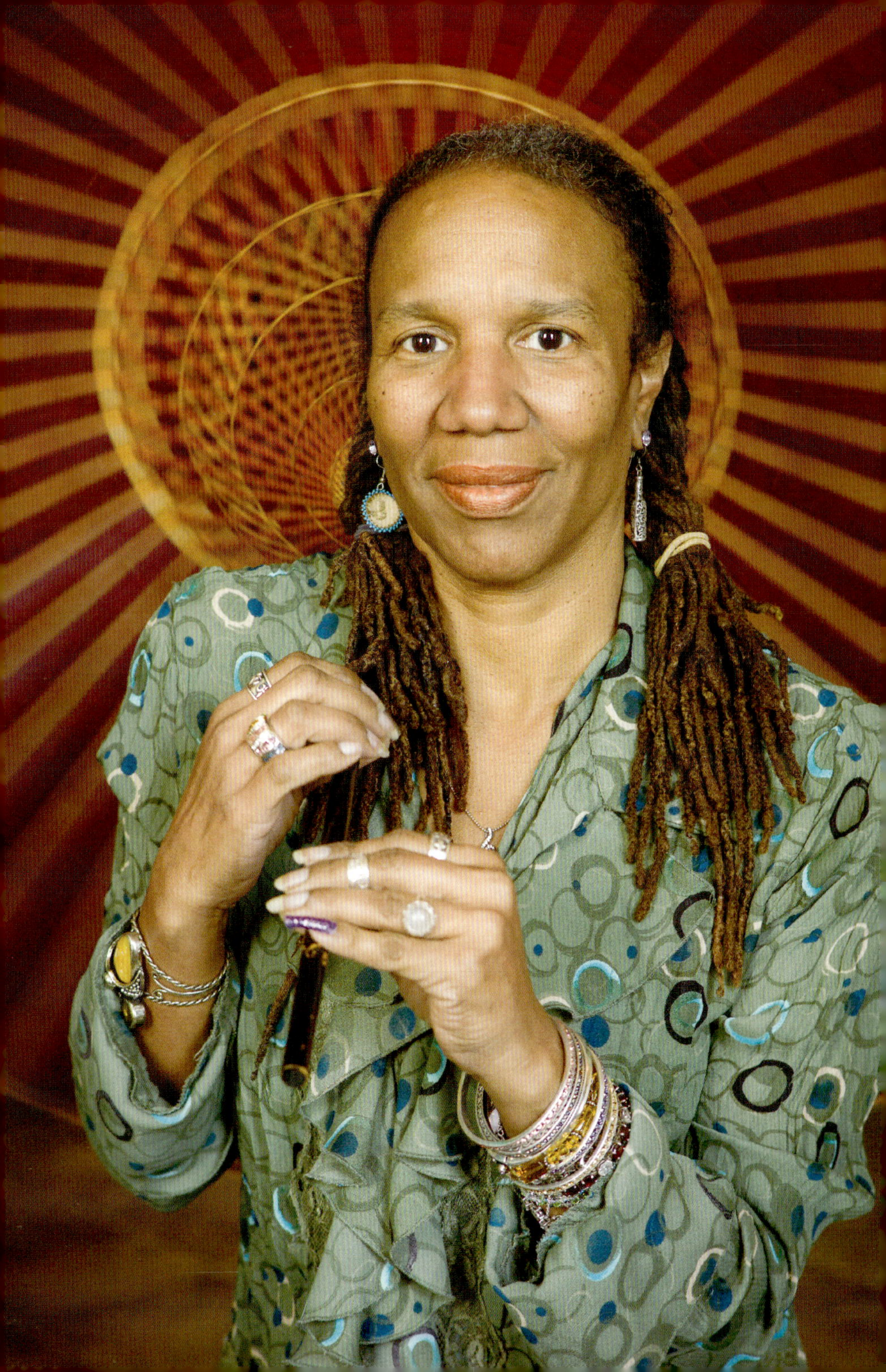

Speaking of the Beatles, there's a wonderful YouTube clip of Charmaine singing "Come Together" at Snug Harbor, surrounded by other Nevilles. Her uncle Cyril is there; Bryson Neville and Gaynielle Neville are on stage, and so is her son, Damion Neville. There is something to the idea of music being in the DNA of certain families in New Orleans, and the Nevilles are the best-known exemplar of that. Her father, saxophonist Charles Neville, performs with his brothers Art, Aaron, and Cyril in one of the city's best-known musical ensembles. Her drummer, Gerald French, comes similarly from a musical dynasty, and her guitarist, the very versatile Detroit Brooks, also comes from a celebrated musical family. Detroit plays the banjo with Dr. Michael White's Original Liberty Jazz Band. When she talks about growing up, she talks about the musical families in the neighborhood, the Lasties and the Barbarins among them.

She lives in the Bywater, in the Upper Ninth Ward, not far from the Lower Ninth Ward where she grew up. When Charmaine was coming up, the Lower Ninth was a place full of vitality, neighborliness, and music. What she has to say about her childhood there is worth thinking about. People looked out for one another, she tells us; people monitored children; music was everywhere. She lived near Fats Domino.

Because of segregation, there were two carnivals, and the Lower Ninth, she says, was fabulous during Mardi Gras. She made her first Indian suit—as one of her father's Uncle Jolly's Wild Tchoupitoulas gang—when she was five. She paraded as a Baby Doll, an African American women's carnival tradition dating to the early 1900s, also a product of segregation. Here she talks about Antoinette K-Doe having revived the tradition.

Today, the Lower Ninth Ward is in physically bad shape thanks to the levee that broke in the Industrial Canal. Parts of it are barren, houses having been destroyed and torn down. The area is rebuilding, with houses going up and new businesses, mostly locally owned, opening. The House of Dance and Feathers, on Tupelo Street, is a museum created by Ronald Lewis commemorating the African American traditions—Mardi Gras Indians, social aid and pleasure clubs, Baby Dolls, and more—from the Lower Ninth. Visit it.

The 2005 storm devastated Charmaine Neville's Bywater neighborhood. Her house was under water; she took refuge on the roof of a nearby school building. Using a flatboat, she helped rescue many people; eventually this led to commandeering a bus to get out. When we talked about the storm in this interview, she found it very difficult. And in recent years, she has been battling health problems. But her faith, her warmth, and her exuberance remain solid and striking. On stage, she's a force of nature, improvising, interacting with her audience, laughing, celebrating her city. Go see her and her terrific band at Snug or the French Quarter Festival or Jazz Fest or anywhere else where you have the opportunity.

## Growing Up in the Ninth

This is the Bywater area, the Upper Ninth. When you get to Poland Avenue it becomes the Lower Nine. That's where I was raised. After Hurricane Betsy, I moved up on this side of the canal, to this general area. I've lived in this house for about twenty-some-odd years. I don't even know how long. Because I'm only twenty-one, you know.

Growing up in the Lower Ninth was fabulous. I mean everybody was a musician. Everybody—people like the Lasties, the Barbarins. Oh my goodness. I could name people forever. James Black lived in the Lower Ninth. Fats Domino lived right down the street from us. Al "Carnival Time" Johnson. Music was everywhere. I could go ahead and tell you millions of names. But that's what the Ninth Ward was about, especially the Lower Ninth Ward. But not just there—the Upper Ninth, too.

It was all kinds of musicians, all kinds of different music. And it never was any one person in the family that played music; it was generations of family members. So if one person played, everybody played. Yeah. The Barbarins—oh boy, what a big family. So many families. And Herlin Riley, one of the baddest drummers in the world. He's from down in the Lower Nine. He comes from down there.

You knew everybody; that's how you grew up. I have to tell people all the time that New Orleans is the biggest little neighborhood in the world. Everybody knew everybody. You knew everybody's mama, their dogs, their cats. And if you did anything, everybody knew what you did. The bus driver would whip you. The mailman would whip you. The policeman would whip you. The winos would whip you. And then you got home, and you got another whipping.

And you knew that you had to speak to everybody. I remember one time I walked past Miss Hattie Mae's house, and I didn't say "Good evening" or "Good afternoon" or whatever. By the time I got home, everybody in the neighborhood knew that I hadn't spoken to her. I got a whipping and had to go back to her house and say "Good evening, Miss Hattie Mae. How you doing?"

That's how we were raised. Everybody looked out for everybody else. You knew if somebody was having problems. Things are different now. Kids, all they worry about is being able to text. And computers. What was a computer? We knew how to play jacks and jump rope. They don't even know what jacks are. Or hopscotch. They don't sit outside and play games anymore.

I'm Catholic. I was raised Catholic. The thing I'm going to tell you is about certain Catholic churches—you ain't going to miss nothing! But I did

go to Baptist churches; I went to synagogue; I went to everything. My best friend was a little Jewish girl, and she taught me how to read Yiddish and Hebrew. I went to her synagogue, and she would come with me to the Catholic church and to the Baptist church. That's just how it was.

I have six sisters and five brothers. No, I'm lying. I have seven sisters and eight brothers, because I have two little brothers now. They're younger than some of my grandchildren. Yeah, my daddy—he says, "It is what it is." I can't say nothing but "Go ahead, keep doing it, as long as you can, do it." Yeah. There's a bunch of us.

He was gone for a while in the Navy. And he was gone, too, because he ended up going to jail. He was in prison for a while. But when he was around, he was around. Yeah. I remember when I first really knew who he was, he was playing the saxophone in the closet. You could hear what he was doing. He was in the closet because he wanted to hear the closeness of what he was doing and be able to practice.

My mother's been gone a long time. It seems like just yesterday, actually. She was good. She was a good singer. Like most people in New Orleans, she was crazy. We're all crazy. But she was a fun person. She had a good comedic side. She was very strict about music and learning what you were supposed to learn. The lady around the corner gave voice lessons; we'd go around there. The man down the street gave drum and cymbal lessons. And the old lady 'round the corner played piano, and you had to go and take piano lessons. Well, you went and did all that. It wasn't like she *made* you—she'd say, "You need to know this." She taught me a lot of things. Yeah. I miss her a lot. And my aunt—her sister—was an opera singer. So, you know, to have those things, the jazz and the opera, and the gospel. It was like, okay, you know what you are going to do.

Four of my little brothers play saxophone. I wonder why. All of my sisters can sing, but they don't. They're all nurses. I was the one who couldn't even stand the sight of blood. But they all can sing. All of them—they have fabulous voices.

It was really phenomenal growing up in the family. Living next door to people like Fats Domino. And people like Al Hirt and Pete Fountain taking you in, and Danny Barker. I used to go and sit on his porch. He would play the banjo and tell all the kids stories, and sing songs. I mean, to grow up like that! It was like, "Where else do I want to live? Nowhere in the world but here." There's lots of places that I love in the world. But this is the best place for me.

**Carnival, Mardi Gras Indians, and Baby Dolls**

I made my first Indian suit when I was five years old, because of my great uncle, Chief Jolly. He taught me how to make patches. He taught me how to make my suits. So I always knew about the Indians. I mean always. It was a part of our culture. I was queen of the Wild Tchoupitoulas.

When I was growing up, living below the canal, in those days there was always two carnivals. There was the white carnival—where you were not allowed, as a black person. And there was, of course, the black carnival. It was the neighborhood carnival. The things that happened were so fabulous. You'd see all these people making suits and costumes. When they went fishing, they'd take fish scales, and use that. Or broken jewelry—make a costume out of that. You know, doing the sewing for the Indians' suits and the feathers and the plumes and everything. So you knew what was going to happen.

And then there were the Baby Dolls. I'm still a Baby Doll—I'm a K-Doe Baby Doll. There's so many different Baby Dolls. But you always knew that who came out first was the Bone Men. They would scare the hell out of us as children, which was their job. You know, "Get up; wake up. It's time, it's Mardi Gras." And then you know when the Bone Men came, who came next was the Baby Dolls. And once the Baby Dolls passed, all you had to do was look in the sky, because the feathers were going to be so high up. "Here they come. I see! Look at that." You'd know that headdresses were coming down the street.

And the prayer—you'd always start with a prayer. Mostly it was about grandmothers and mothers praying that their sons came home, because back in the day, the Indians actually would fight. They actually would fight. Now the fighting is about who's the prettiest, which is better. Many mothers and grandmothers didn't want—"I don't want you to be no Indian. Don't go." But that's what it was. It would be a fight about your neighborhood.

But now it's about who's pretty. And everybody's beautiful. Everybody.

We went through a lot to become what we are. The two things that slave owners hated was Indians and slaves. We were never treated as people. We were treated as property and trash. You were never treated like something that was a real person, a real man or a real woman. So when Mardi Gras came, you could be somebody else. And to be an Indian and black! The Indians were the ones who took us in and treated us like real people. So we pay homage every single year to that. What they did for us is something that we'll never forget. We could never

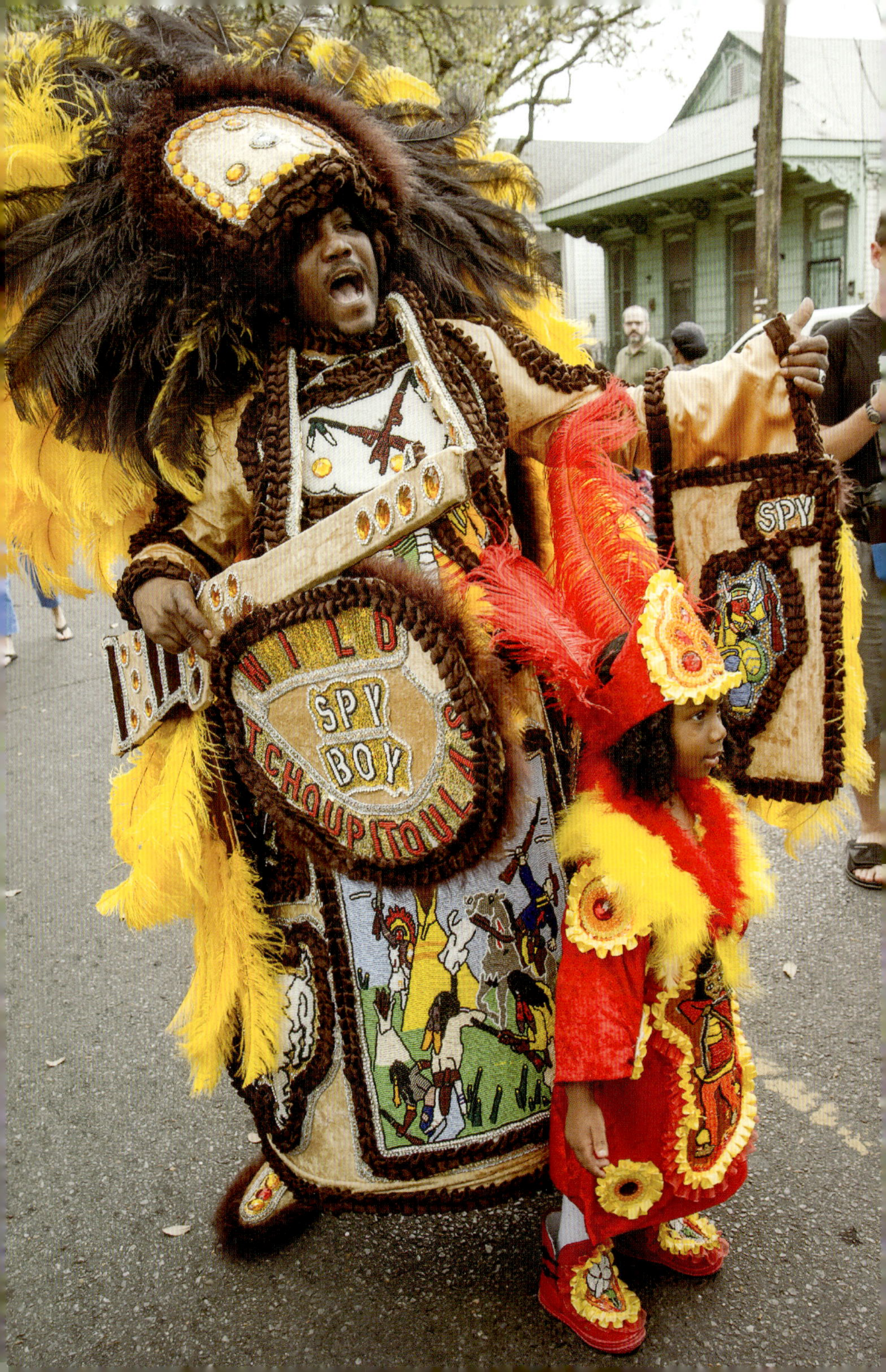

SPY
WILD
SPY
BOY
TCHOUPITOULAS

get away from it. And don't want to. Because without them treating us like real people we would still be nothing. Because that's what slave owners wanted—for us to be nothing. But thank God. Yeah.

So it's an honor. It's an homage. And intermarrying with the Native Americans and there's so much—I've got so much in me. There's Irish in my family. There's French. There's Spanish. There's, oh my goodness, Native American. I think there may even be some German in my family, because a lot of those were slave owners. So that's how it went. The slave owners just took you. Then when you had the child, that was your child. They didn't care. So, if you were Geechee or whatever you were, you still weren't treated like you were somebody. So, we still pay homage to the Indians, because it is a beautiful thing to see them and know that they know what we're doing is to pay homage to them.

There's so many different kinds of baby dolls. Like I say, I'm a K-Doe Baby Doll. But there's the Satin Dolls. There are the Rag Dolls. There are so many dolls. They come from different parts of the city. It just depends on what group you are in and where you come from and what your suit looks like. K-Doe's Dolls, of course, were mostly musicians. But not all of us. There's very few left of the originals, the elders. But she really did a great thing, Antoinette K-Doe did, to bring them back. Because those Baby Dolls had died out. She got a bunch of us together and said "Look—this is what we're going to do. We're going to bring back these Baby Dolls"—and that's how they got named the K-Doe's Baby Dolls. She was just a phenomenal woman. And for her to die on Mardi Gras! We were all downstairs waiting for her to come. She was supposed to fix something on my bonnet and the hem of my dress. We're downstairs waiting on her, four o'clock in the morning so

we can go to the prayer and have the breakfast and everything. She died. We all said, you know, for her to die—she would pick that day to die on. Only Miss K-Doe would do something like that. Her and Ernie, you know, with his wildness. Yeah.

But I remember growing up and people like Ernie K-Doe and Mr. G and Mr. Google Eyes. Placide Bergeron. Oh boy, all kinds of people. The first time that I ever knew what a female impersonator was was Patsy Valdez. Patsy came out with these fans, and I didn't know. I just thought she was just doing a Mardi Gras thing. And somebody say, "That's not a woman. That's a man." I say, "What that mean?" I was a kid. "He's impersonating women." But at Mardi Gras most of the men in the city would go in the closet and get their wives' dresses and makeup and wigs and stuff. They had a krewe that they would all dress in their wives' clothing. So we never thought anything about it. But they weren't female impersonators. That was just a Mardi Gras thing. So when somebody told me about female impersonators, I was like, "You know, they do that all the time at Mardi Gras." "But that's not what we mean." I said "Okay." You know. Yeah.

## Coming to Music

My first memory of music? Wow. Well, I think I do know. In church—singing, at two years old, in church, "Sometimes I Feel Like a Motherless Child." I don't know why that song. But that was the song that I was singing in church that day. I knew from that moment what I was going to do with my whole life, because everybody is saying "You so good," and they clapped. I said, "Oh, I like this." But I mean that's how I grew up—in the church.

I was in the choir, so, of course, I just kept learning more and more and more. In school I would listen to all these different entertainers, people like Blu Lu Barker and Danny Barker. So many people, you'd hear them and you'd learn. I used to go and sneak in clubs and hide under the tablecloths and listen to people and learn songs that way.

On the weekends everybody had a yard party. You would have big party in your front yard or in your back yard, and all the kids were encouraged to sing and dance and play instruments and do stuff, you know, in the family. Then, because they wanted you to go to sleep, the family would give you a little bit of Jax beer in the baby bottle. Then they would do the adult things. I remember waking up one time and hearing everybody laughing so hard. They were all in the garage. They were listening to Redd Foxx albums. So, one day, I went in the garage, and I turned it on, and I was listening, and I was laughing. My mama came outside, and she beat me so bad. She said, "The reason why I'm whipping you is because you were laughing like you knew what you were laughing at." I had no idea what I was laughing at. I was a kid, you know.

But when I got to work with Redd Foxx and people like that, then it was different. I knew. Oh my goodness. But I'll never forget that whipping as long as I live.

That was something that we did all the time. There was always, every weekend, a party where you were encouraged to sing. You were encouraged to dance. You were encouraged to play an instrument. It wasn't just your family, but everybody in the neighborhood was doing parties like that. So you learned from everybody and heard it all. But that's how it went, just from place to place to place, listen to people and learn songs, and then they'd tell you, "Now get out of here." And they'd send you home. "I'm calling your mama and letting them know you coming."

I'd go to places like Concetta's and hide under the table, the Dew Drop Inn and hide under the tablecloths. You heard all kinds of things. Some of the stuff I shouldn't have heard when I was a kid. But that's beside the point—that's how you learn. It was all worth it. The whippings were all worth it, too. Because that made me learn more. I started playing—actually I think I had my first band—when I was fourteen. But my first paying gig, I think I was eight years old. It was at a rodeo. Who was it? She paid me $50 to sing a song with her. Kitty Wells. To sing a song with her. We got on stage; it was a song of hers called "Once a Day." We did that song, and she paid me, and that was the first money I ever got in my life—for anything. That was wonderful. That was an experience, too, because I always loved country and western music.

Any kind of music to me is good music. Country, jazz, gospel. You do it; it's good. And it makes you feel good. That's what music for me is. I know how good I feel, so I want to make other people feel good. That's why I perform—because I want them to feel what I feel.

I love it, even though I'm nervous about being on stage. I hate being on stage and having people look at me. I'm shy. For years I wouldn't even make eye contact because I was saying to myself, "Oh my God, they're looking at me, and I'm going to mess up, and I'm horrible, and why am I doing this?" Still, to this day, I get that feeling. I'm nervous before I go on stage. But when I do that first song, then I'm on. Once I get that first song out of me, then everything is fine. But it takes some time. I don't think it's ever going to leave me. If I ever am not nervous before I go on stage, that's when I know it's time to stop doing what I do. I really know that.

When I was in my teens, my daddy and I had a band together called the Charles Neville Band. I was singing with him, and we were playing hotels and different stuff, all over, everywhere. Also, we went to New York. He was living in New York, in Harlem. We'd go to all of the underground clubs and do stuff there. But then I got my own band; I think I was seventeen. Zigaboo was my drummer. James Booker was the piano player. Sam Henry was the organ player. Oh my goodness, what a band that was.

Then we had a band called the Survivors, which was a really phenomenal band. That was when I started changing and coming into my own—not thinking "I've got to do this song because I like the way Diana Ross did this song," or the way somebody else did that song. I think Diana Ross gave me the best advice ever in my life. She said, "Don't impersonate anybody. Be Charmaine." That's when I started writing my own songs. My father gave me another piece of advice. "If you're not going to be serious, this is a dog-eat-dog business. Don't try it. Because this is not a game." And my mother told me, "Look, just get out there and do it all. Don't be afraid. Do every kind of music that you want to do."

So I had lots of good advice from people. That really motivated me and made me know that I was going to continue. Because you're a kid, and you think, "He gave me a gift, and now I got it." You believe that sometimes; you get a little big-headed. But in New Orleans, you always get right back on your feet. Your feet are always touching the ground, because people will let you know. "You think you're somebody? Well, look, let me show you this." So you can't be big-headed in New Orleans. Not at all.

I think the best tour I ever did in my life was the Diva Tour. I was seventeen. Ella Fitzgerald, Nina Simone, Betty Carter, Phoebe Snow, and I can't remember who else. The band was Dizzy Gillespie, Don Cherry, my father, Baby George, I think, who was the guitar player, Buddy Miles who was the drummer. Lionel Hampton. To be in that company was just phenomenal to me. Betty Carter was the first person I ever heard scat in my life, when I was a little girl. Phenomenal. Stuff like that is once in a lifetime. That was a great tour, and what an honor for me. It was just a few years before Ella Fitzgerald died. It was just fabulous, so wonderful.

Then I discovered people like Alberta Hunter, who was also a phenomenal songstress. I loved all of her stuff, too. She made me write a lot of stuff. I changed her words to "Right Key But the Wrong Keyhole." To be singing that long in life and then retire, and then come back when you're ninety, and still be singing, and have that strong voice. Oh, she was just tremendous. And she never stopped. I think that was the thing. I remember I used to tell people, "Yeah, I'm going to be on a walker, have one tooth, and one little tuft of hair, and I'm still going to be singing." You die on stage. I'm not going to retire. Who retires? Nobody. I mean some people say they retire. And then they come back. Nobody retires.

You get on those tours when somebody calls you, and they say "Come do this." Then you jump at it. You just go. My father had a lot to do with a lot of those early things. But then people would just call me and say, "Can you do this?" Big band leaders would call me and say they're doing this stuff for the homes for the elderly and nursing homes and stuff like that. I would go and do all that stuff, for free. Because when I'm old and in a nursing home, I want somebody to come sing for me. I got a lot of gigs like that. Because when you do stuff like that is when people hear you. And they say "Oh, we could use her on this." That's how a lot of it came about. Yeah. Going to play for the retired nuns or the retired nurses or going to play for the children at the hospital. You know—just anywhere. That's how you get the gigs; people say, "Well, you know, since she did this, let's give her this."

I tell young people all the time, "Do those things because that will help you." "Well, l don't have time." "Yes, you do have time. Think about it. Please think about it, because you never know who's going to hear you at a fundraiser that you're donating your time for. Who's going to be there." Yeah. I still try to continue giving what I can give. I just played last weekend at the retirement facility for the nuns. It was so much fun. Only nuns from New Orleans will get up and second-line. The oldest nun; she's what—ninety-nine or ninety-eight or something like that. She got up, and I said, "Look at you. Out there second-lining." She said, "Yeah," and pulled her handkerchief out. It was so much fun. It really was. But like I say, only here. I think if you went anywhere else and figured that nuns would be doing that—no.

### Race

The thing about the parades was that you were not allowed to go to Canal Street. And that was fine because what was going on there was not really what Carnival was about. In the neighborhood parades the priest from your church could come; the minister from your church could come; your grandma; the nuns; the children. When I got older and went on the other side and went on Canal Street, the stuff that I saw—there was no way. That's why they started leaving that parade and coming into our area. With Zulu. Because Rex hated the fact that everybody would leave and come down to see what Zulu was doing. That's why they decided to incorporate Zulu and make Zulu roll before Rex—so that people would stay to see Rex. You know. Yes indeed.

But you know—I was never a person who really paid attention because of race, because of how I was raised. My mother told me, "Always be courteous and nice to everybody, and embrace everybody, because you're all brothers and sisters, no matter what they look like. No matter where they come from." She'd always say, "Just remember who you are."

I remember when there were three bathrooms—men's, women's, and colored. I remember having to sit in the back. I mean it wasn't that long ago—people act like it was like a hundred years ago that slavery was abolished. No. People say "When are y'all going to get over it?" "Excuse me? That is so stupid." I tell people, "We weren't the first slaves. You've got to think about that. Look at what happened to the Jews. Look at what happened to the Egyptians." We understand. "Well, y'all need to get over it." I say, "You know what—don't talk to me anymore. And then I'll be over it." Yeah.

But racist people are not born that way. They are made that way. So if you're taught to respect life, respect others, respect other people's religions and musics and whatever, then that's how you live your life. You don't worry about it. And enjoy all of the music, because music is the one thing that can change everything that's going on in the world. That's music. I've played in places where I didn't speak the language, but when I'd start playing the music, it didn't matter that I didn't speak the language. Because people would just be like, "Okay. We've got this."

✦ Halloween party revelers, 2014

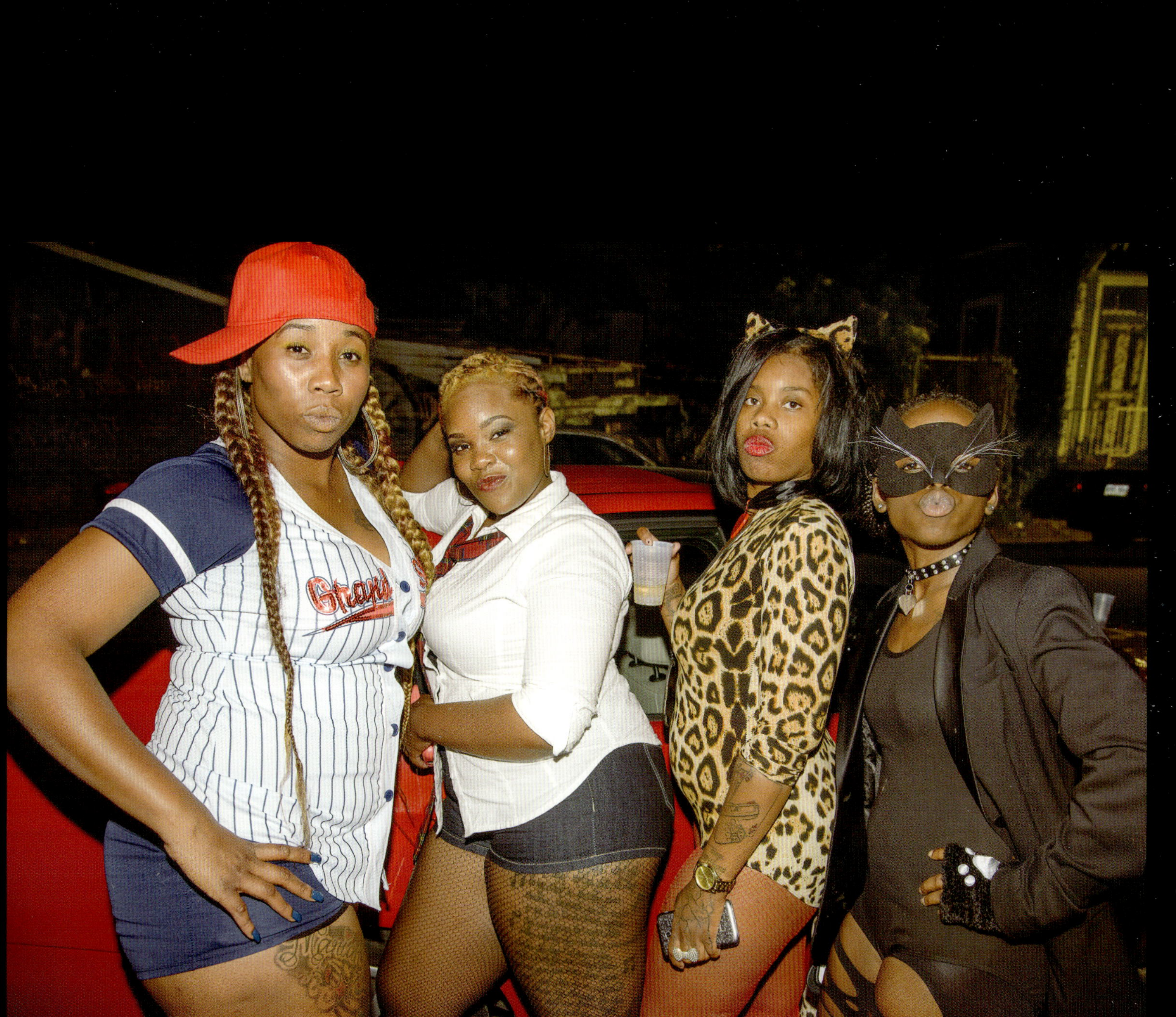

We grew up listening to my grandmother, my great grandmother, and my aunts speak the patois when they didn't want you to know what they were talking about. But you learned. You'd hear that patois enough that you would learn. They'd be talking about people. They didn't want you to know who they were talking about. Like your cousin, Hattie Mae, or Miss Nina down the street—she's getting a divorce. They didn't want you to know stuff like that. So they would start talking in the patois. Yeah. But you learned as you grew up.

**"Established" in Music and Cooking**

I just wanted to sing, so I would do it. If you gave me a gig, I'd be there. That's all it was for me. I never thought about "I'm established." Somebody said that to me one time; they said, "Oh, now that you've made it, and you're established, why do you live in the Ninth Ward?" I said, "What does that mean?" "Well, I think you need to move to a gated community." I said, "Excuse me. And abandon the people I'm trying to show it doesn't matter who you think you are—be who you really are. Leave my neighborhood? And tell these young people, 'Okay get a little something and move out?' No, that's not me." I couldn't believe that she felt that way, that I should abandon who I got this from. No. I could never do that.

So I don't know about being established. I don't know about that. I can't even tell you about that. I mean no, I don't consider myself established, actually.

I've worked every kind of day job there is. I was a waitress in every place in the city. Oh, I'm telling you. I was the first black hostess at the Hyatt Regency when they first opened. I worked at Waterbury's

soda counter on Canal Street. At Walgreens I was a soda jerk. Royal Castle—I worked there. I was the cook, the bouncer, the dishwasher, and the deejay. That was a good job; I loved it. Then I'd go across the street and make the donuts for Tastee Donuts. I worked in different places where I'd serve the food to the elderly. I've done every kind of job.

I learned how to cook from watching people. Pete Fountain taught me things about cooking. Al Hirt taught me things. Fats Domino. You know—everybody. You learn from the Jewish lady around the corner, who taught me how to make Jewish penicillin, and the Italian lady who was down the street, who taught me how to make the best lasagna and spaghetti sauce you ever want to have in your life. The Irish lady who taught me how to make stew—the best stews—and how to make some fabulous desserts. So you learn from the people that are around you. That's what I'm established in—knowing who I am and what I want to do.

I'm not established in anything else. I love to do stuff for other people. My mama used to tell me—we'd be having a picnic on the lake. The whole family. We'd be out there, and I'd go and find the one little kid who was sitting by theirself and nobody was talking to or playing with, and I'd bring them to come and be with us. My mama said, "You. Stray dogs follow you. Cats. You walking down the street, and they stop you and go 'Hey.'" It's true. That's just who I am.

**The Band**

I don't play any instruments in public. That's why I have a band. I play when I'm writing. I play piano. I play a little guitar. I play drums. But only when I'm writing do I play.

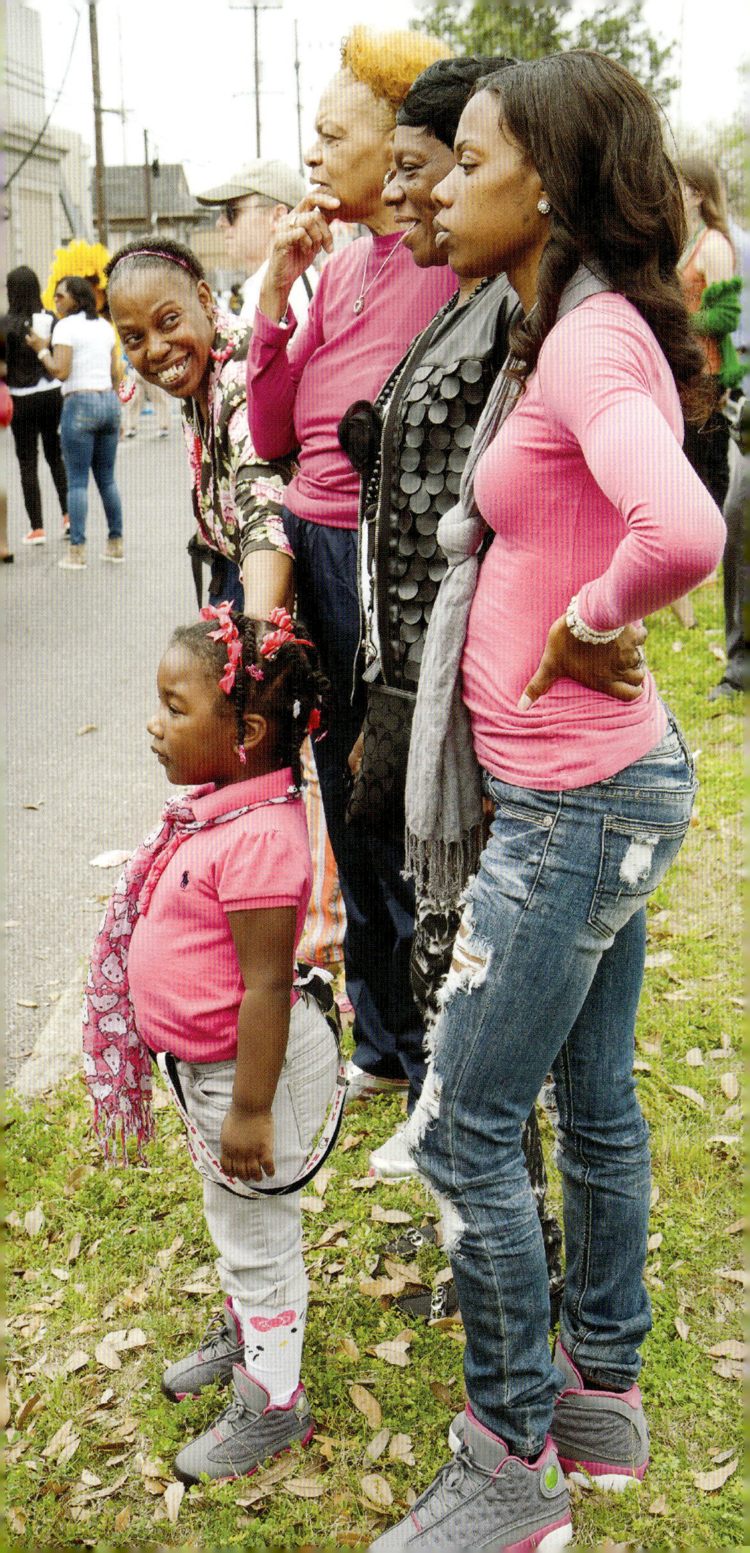

My guys have been with me forever. My piano player, Amasa, has been with me for thirty-some-odd years. The other guys that are in the band—maybe about five or six years. We've been at Snug Harbor—it's been every Monday for I don't know how many years? twenty-five? twenty-eight? I don't know.

If I ever make a set list, my band would die of heart attacks. I've made them a few times, but I never follow them. I'll give them a set list like for Jazz Fest or something—when we did *Austin City Limits*, we had to give them a list. I think that was the only time I ever followed the list. When we do stuff overseas, I'll make a set list out. But I'll make the set list after we do the show. I might tell you I want to do this song, but when I walk on out on that stage, and I see the people, and what I get from those people, that lets me know what my first song is going to be. And my next song. And my next song. Then, after the show, I will write the set list down if I have to give it to the people for BMI or whatever. Then I'll do it. But I never know what I'm going to do until I get out there and feel what I'm going to do. Because it's all in here; it's all inside me. People think that that's strange, but that's just how it is for me. I'm sorry, I cannot say, "Look, we're going to do this song." I get up on stage, and I change my mind, because that's not how I felt at that particular moment. So I never know. And my musicians will look at me and say, "Lord have mercy. Please."

We do have rehearsals. I write stuff, and we write things, and it's good. But then if I don't feel it, then it doesn't happen.

### The Culture

It's endless. In New Orleans, when you hear certain things—it doesn't matter what you're doing, whether you're in the shower washing your hair, in the kitchen cooking, whether you're washing the dog. Whatever you're doing, you jump up and wrap a towel around your head, wrap a towel around, and you run out on your porch. Because you heard it, and you know it's coming down the street. The big bass drum coming down the street. And not just on Mardi Gras day—I'm talking about anytime you hear that, anytime that something is coming. A second line is about to happen. So you jump up, you go outside, you're on your porch in your housecoat, rollers in your hair, whatever.

That's like when the slaves were trying to escape and head to the north, there was a language. I mean if I said to you "eggplant," you know that when I said "eggplant" that means we're getting out of here tonight. But the masters didn't know that. So there was a language. Our language was rhythms. The drums. We didn't all speak the same languages, but the rhythms told the whole story—you knew exactly what was going to happen that day. So when you feel those rhythms coming down the street in your neighborhood, you know what it means.

I grew up with our mayor and his family, as a child. And to see that there's no rapport with the musical community, you know, just hurts me. It really does.

### Music in My Soul

I don't think of myself as a jazz singer, even though sometimes that's how people describe me. Because I'm definitely not. A jazz singer is someone who is totally different from what I am. I am an eclectic singer. I do everything. I can sing jazz. I can sing blues. I can sing country. I can sing gospel. I can sing anything. But I don't ever try to tell people I'm a jazz singer. Because I'm not. Jazz singers are people like Juanita Brooks and Lady BJ. Germaine Bazzle. Those are jazz singers. People, they say, "What kind of singer are you?" I say, "I don't know. I'm fun. That's what I am." And that's who I am.

I love lyrics. I can make up lyrics at the drop of a dime. If I see something or hear something that makes me think about, you know, okay, well look—the sun is out today. It's been raining so much for the last three weeks. That's a whole song—that's what comes to me. It's how you're feeling that particular moment. That's where the music comes from.

I love Prince. I love Michael Jackson. Always, and I got to work with him once in my life—thank you. You hear these things, and that's what makes you want to do it. I wish I had been around when Jimi Hendrix, you know. I was around. But I was a kid. And Janis Joplin—there's so much music. So much. I remember running away because I wanted to go to Woodstock. Yes indeed. I ran away from home, and I said, "I'm going to all that music. I'm going." No. Didn't happen.

One of my uncles was a policeman. And he saw me walking down the street with my little suitcase. "Where you going?" He opened up the suitcase. The only thing I had in there was underwear. Because my mama always told me, "Make sure you have clean underwear." I was going to make it to Woodstock. I wanted to see Janis Joplin. I wanted to see Jimi Hendrix. I wanted to see The Who. I mean, you know, I loved the Beatles. It's funny, people say to me, "How do you like those people?" "What do you mean? They're great musicians. Y'all don't listen." The Beatles—the lyrics, the music. I mean, just everything was phenomenal to me. And I got to play at Woodstock, years later.

But music to me is just in me. It's in my soul. It's in my heart. It's in my feet. It's in every fiber of my being. It's in my fingertips. It's in my hair. It's in my spirit. I feel it.

## Women as Musicians

Musicians tend to not take you seriously because you're a woman. I'll never forget—I fired a musician one time, because he told me, "Huh? Who's the leader of this band? You? I'm not taking no check from you; women can't do nothing for me. You lead this band? I don't want to work . . ." I said, "You don't have to worry about it. You're fired." You know. He said to me, "Women don't even know what music really is. You just up there so you can shake your behind." I say, "What?" I say, "I'll tell you what, then. Don't worry about it. You're fired." "You can't fire me." I say, "Oh, okay. Yeah. Watch."

They really think that you're not really a musician. For years they tried to treat you that way. You're not truly a musician; all you are is a singer. Even the songs that you would write—they would try their hardest to make sure that they didn't play them. "Oh, she wrote that song; let's do something else." So, yeah. That's why I always tell these young singers coming up, "Whatever you do, know what key you sing in; know something about music so that you could be treated as a musician." I don't care; you've got to know. If you come on my set and want to sing a song, and I ask you what key you sing it in, and you say you don't know, you're in trouble. I'll still let you do it. But you have to go to the piano player and hum a little bit to him, and then we'll figure it out. Before you leave the building, I always tell you, "Next time, don't come in here not knowing what key you sing in, because that makes them not respect you. Don't worry about me not respecting you; know that they don't respect you. The musicians are looking at you like, 'Why is she up here, anyway?'" That's sad, to be treated that way. Because regardless of what they may think, you've got it in you. And you just need to learn. Go back to school if you have to.

Of course, there's nothing wrong with knowing all of the fundamentals of music. Nothing's wrong with that. But not knowing how to improvise—there's something wrong with that. I don't care what kind of music—wherever you go in the world and people play, musicians in this city know how to sit in with them and improvise. But other people from other places—I remember in New York somebody said to me, "Oh. You can't sit in with us." I said, "Oh, okay." He say, "Yeah, because we have everything exactly how . . ." "Oh, okay. Alright." So somebody else in the band say, "Come up and do this song." So I got up there, and I improvised, because I didn't know their arrangement. And the other guy was like, "Oh my God." I said, "Yeah, baby. I'm from New Orleans. We know how to do this." And when they come to New Orleans from New York, we're not afraid to let you come up on stage and play with us. We like that. Come on. But that's what it's all about—improvisation. When you've got that, you've got everything.

### Pulling Together

Musicians here pull together to help each other. Always. That goes back to the days when black people were not allowed to be buried or have insurance or own property or own anything. Benevolent societies came forward—that's what it all goes back to. Being a musician is—that's your family. So, your family will always come out and help you. They know—it could be them tomorrow. So they always turn out to help each other. Because that's what it's all about: helping each other and looking out for each other.

My illness is something that I'll be living with for the rest of my life. But God is good, and my doctor, he's phenomenal. So I just continue to take the treatments when I can, and just go for it. I just have to do what I can. I have good days and bad days, just like everybody else. A couple of days ago, if y'all would have called me and said y'all were coming here, I couldn't even get out of the bed—it gets like that. But it is what it is. And I'm only one person. Look at all the people who have it worse than I do. You know. I always have to remind, not just myself, because I know that, but I tell other people to remember that. You think something is wrong with you and that you've got a bad problem. But look at this person. And look at that lady.

### Sons, Grandchildren

My son, Damion, plays bass, drums, guitar, piano, and he's a singer—he's a hell of a singer. But he's also a hip hop artist. He writes raps; he does commercials; he's really a talented young man. My other son, he's in the Navy. He's about to retire, as a matter of fact—a chief petty officer in the Navy. He plays trumpet, and he plays steel pan. He played in the Navy steel band. His sons—my grandsons—they play. And my granddaughter plays guitar and sings. She has the most phenomenal voice. She's in the Navy, too.

I just found out, just recently, that I am a great-grandmother. It's fabulous. She's so beautiful. She looks like everybody in the family. She hasn't learned to talk yet. But she sings. And it's so funny. I mean, not that I'm surprised. But she does sing. So you know, the music has got to keep on going. It'll never stop. Not if I have anything to do with it—it will never stop.

## Making Art

My art is what relaxes me. I might be doing a painting or something, and that helps me think about music as well. It really does. I do art just to relax and because I feel like there's something that can make everything else better. And I think just one of these little pieces might do it. Plus, I want to make money. But you know what—I'm lying. Because most of the time I give these pieces to people for auctions and stuff, fundraisers and things like that. So I never make any money off of them.

I never like any of the stuff that I do, anyway. I think it's all ugly, and who would want to buy that. Of course, my friends tell me, "Yeah, when you're dead." I say, "Well, don't think I don't know that." But that's like Sun Ra. I loved Sun Ra so much. He really was a genius. I'll never forget hearing people talk about him, and the bad things that they would say about him. When he died, then everybody said, "Oh, he was a genius." I'm like, but he was a genius before he died. "Oh, but we didn't know." "How you didn't know?" He was writing stuff like "Elephants on Parade," all those great pieces of music that he did, and you say you didn't know he was a genius? Now that he's dead y'all want to hurry up and buy up all of his stuff?

Don't wait until I'm dead. You know—"Come and get the shit now." Because I can't enjoy it once I'm gone. My lawyer told me just yesterday, "Go in the attic and pull out all of those pieces of art that you have hidden in the attic and think that it's so ugly."

He said, "We're going to liquidate all of that, and I want you to do that." I thought about it—go up in the attic and get all of those paintings I don't want anybody to see? And, you know, it's so funny. Because yesterday I went in the attic, and I found a poster that Ella Fitzgerald and Stevie Wonder had signed.

I've got to get that out of there. I've got to put it in a frame. Oh my God. I was like, "Oh my God; look at this." There's so much stuff up there, though. I need to get it out. I really should. They played together at Jazz Fest. So it was a Jazz Fest poster that they were on. Ella Fitzgerald and Stevie Wonder standing next to each other. And he signed it, and she signed it.

I'm not selling that. Nobody can get that. Oh God. But I've got to hurry up and get it out of there and put it in a frame. Because it's beautiful. But I mean, I fed him, right in this room. Stevie Wonder. Yeah.

## Bill Clinton at Snug Harbor

I fed Bill Clinton, too. He's such a wonderful person. I really like him. I've played many of his birthday parties. He's a sweetheart; he really is. He came to Snug Harbor one night and played saxophone with me.

It was so funny, because I knew he was coming. It was during Mardi Gras, and the Secret Service was everywhere. I told everybody, "Look, we're about to have a very special guest. So I want you all to be on your best behavior. And just don't nobody go crazy." Of course, when I knew he was coming in the door, what song did I decide to do except for "You've Got the Right Key, But You Stuck It in the Wrong Keyhole"? And he came up, and he took the sax, and he played, and he said to me after the set, "Charmaine, I'm going to tell you something." He leaned down, because he's so tall. He leaned down, and he whispered in my ear, "You weren't playing that song for me, were you?" I laughed. He leaned back down, and he said, "Don't play it no more."

So, of course, he stayed for the second set, and you know I did it again. I said, "Yeah; you telling me don't play it no more. Well, the blue dress fits. What can I tell you?" He said, "You know, you are the only person in the world who would talk to me like that." I say, "Hey. It is what it is." He's such a sweetheart, though. And he had such a great personality. I really appreciated him. Not just politically—personally. He was just a fine person. Yeah.

But gosh, thinking about how many different people I've worked with. Wow. I mean I've fed a lot of people.

### The Community

The community has changed somewhat. A lot of the young people of today don't have the same values that we had. It's very unfortunate how many young people don't even know what the inside of a church looks like. I think that has changed a lot of it. Everything has to be passed forward. If you don't pass it forward, then how are those coming behind you going to be able to accumulate anything—any knowledge, any music, anything? That's why with the music, the young people, when they come to a show, I say, "I want you to get up here. Come on. Come see." Because that's a whole part of it. Because that's how I got it—from the older musicians passing it on to me. I want to make sure that I pass it on to those coming up behind me.

There are quite a few things that are right here in New Orleans. One is faith. That's number one. The second is food. Third is knowing the generations of the music and of the culture. And the fourth one is never, ever turning your back and deciding, "Oh, this doesn't matter." We can never do that. If we just turn our back and say, "Oh, this doesn't matter," then it's going to die. It will die. And we can't let that happen. But faith is number one. Yeah.

### The Storm

Katrina interrupted everything. She really did. The bad part of it probably for me was that I knew everything was going to be different. There was no music. That was number one. The kids from across the street—I didn't hear their music. The people in the neighborhood, I didn't hear their music. The only thing I heard was helicopters. And people screaming. It was really horrible. It really was.

I had to stay gone so long because there was just nowhere for the water to go. Nowhere. I couldn't find my house. I didn't know where anything was. I mean to live in a city your whole life and not be able to find where you lived, what street you lived on. And the only thing left in the Lower Ninth Ward was steps.

I had a 145-year-old magnolia tree in my front yard. Katrina took that. That's just something simple that she took. I remember crying the year that my woodpecker came back. And the squirrels. You know, because everything was gone. The birds. Everything was gone. It's funny—people don't think about stuff like that, but those are things that affect you. To not see your neighbors. To not see the squirrels. To not hear the dogs and the cats, or the children playing. All of those things.

Yeah, it was rough. It really was. I think the worst part of it was the response from the government. The nonresponse. Yeah. I wrote a song about that, too,

"The Bushie Man." I did that song at this big conference, and somebody videotaped it. I was never able to do it again, because it broke my heart just to think about what he had done to us. People would ask me to do that song, and I couldn't do it. It just would make me cry. I'll never forget him coming here and saying, "Great job, Brownie." And "We're going to fix all of this." And going down the street here and eating at a friend of mine's restaurant.

People always say, "Oh, they didn't blow the levee. The levee was breached." Bullshit. I was here. I know what they did. I mean when I lived below the canal and Hurricane Betsy came; I know what they did. You heard the explosions. You heard the first one, which was right there at the Industrial Canal. The second one was London Avenue Canal. One was far away, but you could hear the explosion. That was at the 17th Street Canal. You heard all of them.

So you know what they did. It's not like it was the first time that they've done that. Randy Newman wrote that song about they're trying to wash us away. And it's true. But they do it not just to us—if you go all along the Mississippi River, all of the different communities that they have done that to. When the water's coming, the floods are coming. They tell people, "Look, you've got to take everything and get out, because your whole town is going to be underwater." Look how many people they've displaced with that. So it's not like they just do it to us.

I'm getting better about talking about it. But it's something that will never go away. People say, "You're going to get over it." Yeah, right. That's like saying to me, "Well your mom is dead, and you're going to get over it."

# WALTER "WOLFMAN" WASHINGTON

Singer, guitarist, songwriter

Leader, Walter "Wolfman" Washington and the Roadmasters

[ Interviewed January 20, 2013, at Buffa's Bar and Restaurant, Esplanade, New Orleans ]

With his deeply soulful singing and guitar playing, Walter "Wolfman" Washington is a New Orleans musical treasure. His early roots were in gospel, then in R&B and blues. Today, he says, he plays funk and soul. However you characterize his music, you realize there's no one else quite like him. Born in 1943, he's been on the scene for a long time; these days, when you read about him, phrases such as *musical icon* and *guardian of the groove* appear. And New Orleans has an official Walter "Wolfman" Washington day, thanks to a mayoral declaration.

Born Edward Joseph Washington Jr., he mostly grew up in church, singing in the choir. When he was about fifteen, he volunteered to play guitar for a gospel group his friends were forming, the True Love and Soul Gospel Group. Early on, he tuned the guitar to an open chord, which let him play by using just one finger on the fretboard. But then he saw someone play more conventionally, and an uncle helped start him on the path that led to work with Lee Dorsey, Irma Thomas, and Johnny Adams. Speaking of family influence, Guitar Slim (Eddie Jones) and Lightning Slim (Otis V. Hicks) were his uncles. His cousin, Ernie K-Doe, bought him his first electric guitar. A couple of fellow musicians gave him the names he uses today. John Williams, vocalist for Huey Smith and the Clowns, and later the Tick Tocks, and chief of

✦ Walter "Wolfman" Washington at d.b.a., Frenchmen Street

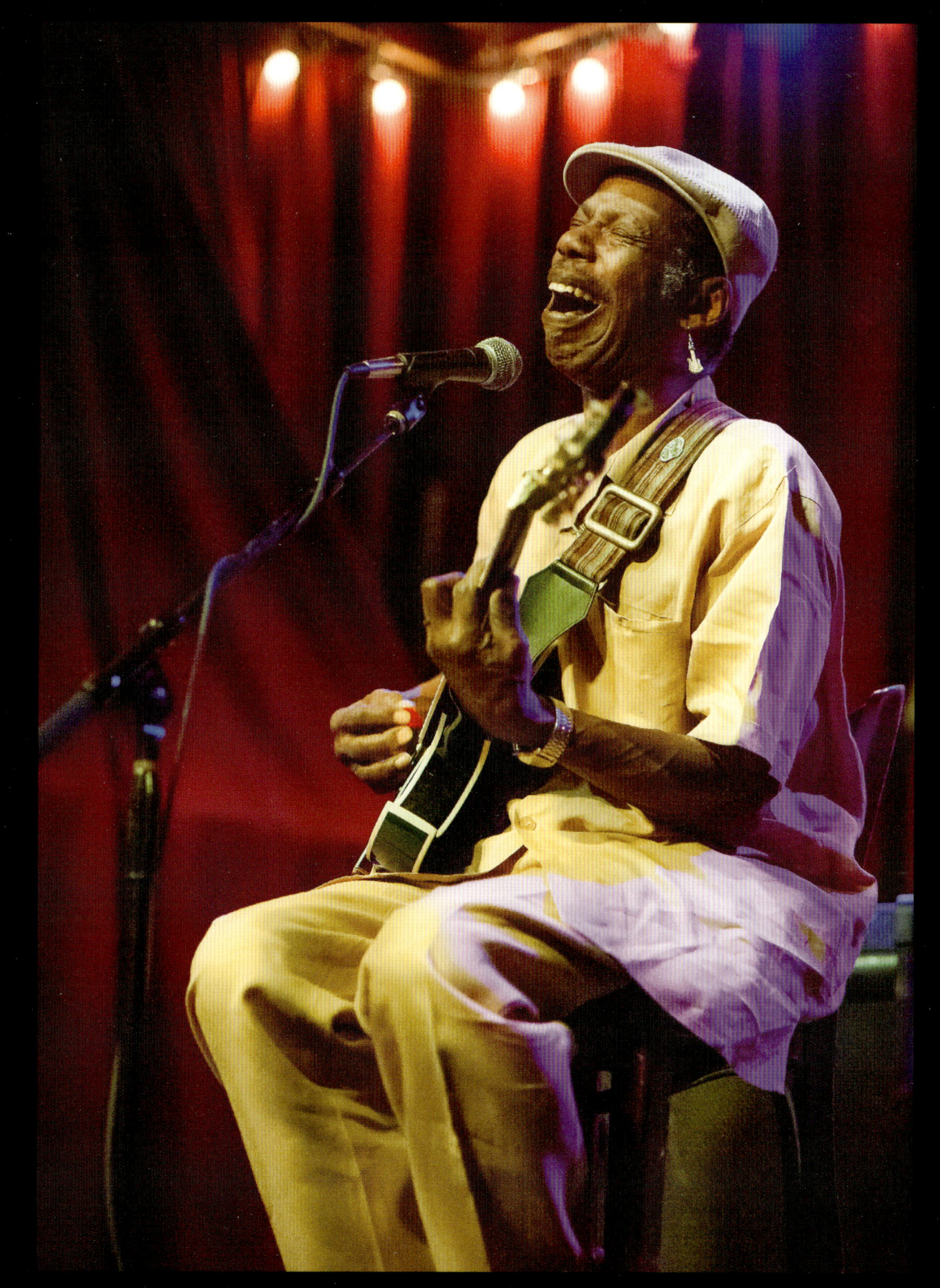

the Apache Hunters, christened him Walter. And David Lastie, saxophone player and member of one of New Orleans's many musical dynasties, gave him "Wolfman."

Walter's first gig on the road was in the early 1960s with New Orleans R&B singer Lee Dorsey, whose "Ride Your Pony" was riding high on the national R&B charts. They were part of a touring R&B show that opened at the Apollo Theater in Harlem. For about two-and-a-half years, Walter played the same two songs as part of the show. He came off the road, determined to stay at home, especially after his mother told him that, thanks to that touring, he had $43,000 in the bank. But then he went to Europe with David and Walter Lastie's group, Taste of New Orleans. And then Irma Thomas needed a guitar player, and off he went again, this time touring more regionally than nationally. In those days, he also led his own bands. It was the All Fools Band in the mid-'60s. Then it was Walter "Wolfman" Washington and Solar System. Now it's Walter "Wolfman" Washington and the Roadmasters.

His twenty-year alliance with vocalist Johnny Adams followed, based for much of that time at Dorothy's Medallion Lounge. Those shows at Dorothy's were legendary. People still talk about first hearing Walter and Johnny there, where large women—shake dancers—clad in very little danced in cages, and where shows started very late and would sometimes go way beyond sunrise. Those were wild nights. His current band, the Roadmasters, began to take shape at Dorothy's. Jack Cruz, his bass player, joined in that period, and his cousin, Wilbert "Junkyard Dog" Albert, was his drummer in those days. Johnny Adams was a superb singer with a remarkable vocal range—from a whisper to a scream. Walter says that he learned a lot about using his voice from Adams.

He released his first album in 1981, on the Hep' Me label, one of perhaps two hundred independent labels in New Orleans from the middle of the twentieth century forward. Senator Jones, who had produced many recordings by Crescent City R&B artists including Johnny Adams, produced it. Before that, Walter had released a single; "Mickey Mouse Boarding House," believe it or not, was the A side. Search YouTube, and you can hear it. A few years later, Rounder producer Scott Billington started a long collaboration with Johnny Adams, producing about nine albums before Adams's death in 1998. Walter played on some of those albums, and in 1986 Rounder released the first of several of his own albums, *Wolf Tracks*, produced by Billington. Since then, he has recorded other albums for Rounder and for other labels, and he has released albums of his own. In the past few years, two records featuring Walter with Joe Crown and Russell Batiste have appeared, and his most recent release with the Roadmasters is a live recording, *Howlin' Live*, done at d.b.a. on Frenchmen Street.

On September 30, 2005, Walter played what some say is the first post-Katrina show in New Orleans, at the Maple Leaf. They used a generator for power; the police and the National Guard closed the show down, citing curfew regulations. These days, Walter "Wolfman" Washington and the Roadmasters play a regular Wednesday night gig at d.b.a., if they're not on the road. Jack Cruz is on bass; Wayne Moreau is his drummer; Jimmy Carpenter wails on the sax. They're often joined by a trumpet player, likely either Antonio Gambrell or Leon "Kid Chocolate" Brown. When they need a substitute drummer, Mike Barrass, who is also in Bruce Daigrepont's band, often fills in—such is the small, complicated world of New Orleans music. Working without a set list, and following Walter's cues, the Roadmasters, are about as tight a musical unit as you'll ever hear. Their Wednesday night shows at d.b.a. are, for me, as good as any music can get. And, playing with Joe Krown on the B3 organ and Russell Batiste on drums, Walter has another regular gig at the Maple Leaf Bar uptown, where the trio has a big following.

In a town known for its horn players and piano players, Walter "Wolfman" Washington is singular. In past years, other New Orleans musicians—Earl King and Snooks Eaglin both come to mind—have also built careers as singers and guitar players, backed by horns in a classic R&B configuration. These days in New Orleans, Walter, who recently celebrated his seventieth birthday, owns that way of making music. "I've damn near played practically all the clubs in New Orleans," he told me, which led to the story he tells here about one owned by Carlos Marcello, New Orleans mafioso. The Wolfman's voice is strong, and his scream, or cry, can send chills down your spine. He still sometimes plays the guitar with his teeth. And he's probably the city's best-dressed musician.

I owe a special note of thanks to Jack Cruz, Walter's bass player, who made this interview possible.

I've had a real interesting, crazy life. Parts of it have been rough. But I had fun, though. I've really had fun.

## Early Days

I was born and raised on Derbigny, between First and Second. It was segregated at that time—wasn't too many places to go, you know. But we had a park that we played in.

I mostly grew up in church—at New Home Missionary Baptist Church, in the choir, with my mom and them. I wanted to sing more, and so what I did was—I must have been about fifteen years old, and some of the cats in the neighborhood wanted to form a spiritual group. But at that time, all the spiritual groups had guitar players and stuff like that. And nobody in the group wanted to play guitar. So I decided I would do it.

I was listening to the Soul Stirrers, and I was listening to B.B. King, Bobby Blue Bland. When I was a baby, Mama would put the radio on and put them on, and she could do her housework all day long, just be listening to the radio. So that's how I really got into the music. I loved it.

There's a funny story. I have an adopted sister. She stays in Baton Rouge. See, my mama didn't want to have no children. So she adopted Shirley. My daddy was in the service. He came home on furlough and caught her. So, you know, she said she never wanted to have no more children.

That's all he wanted to do—go into the service. When he got out, that's when he started being a playboy. I mean everywhere. He was the first one to actually encourage me to play music.

His name was Edward. There was three of us. His daddy was named Edward Washington. He was named Edward Washington. I'm named Edward Washington. My middle name is Joseph. Edward Joseph Washington, Junior the Third—that's my name. They called me Junior.

My nickname was "WaWa." John Williams—you remember Huey Smith and the Clowns? Well, they left Huey Smith and formed their own little thing called the TickTocks. When I told John, "My nickname is WaWa," he said, "No man, it ain't going to work." I said, "Well, my first name is Edward." "No, that isn't going to work either. Okay—Walter."

David Lastie gave me the name "Wolfman." The Lastie brothers—I was traveling with them. I would always find one of the guitar players; whoever it is, I'd go jump on him. We'd battle and stuff. Because David would say "Wolf." I'd wolf at them fast. So he started calling me Wolfman. That's how I got Walter "Wolfman" Washington. Mama told me "Don't lose Washington, now." I said, "No, I ain't going give up Washington. I'm going to keep that."

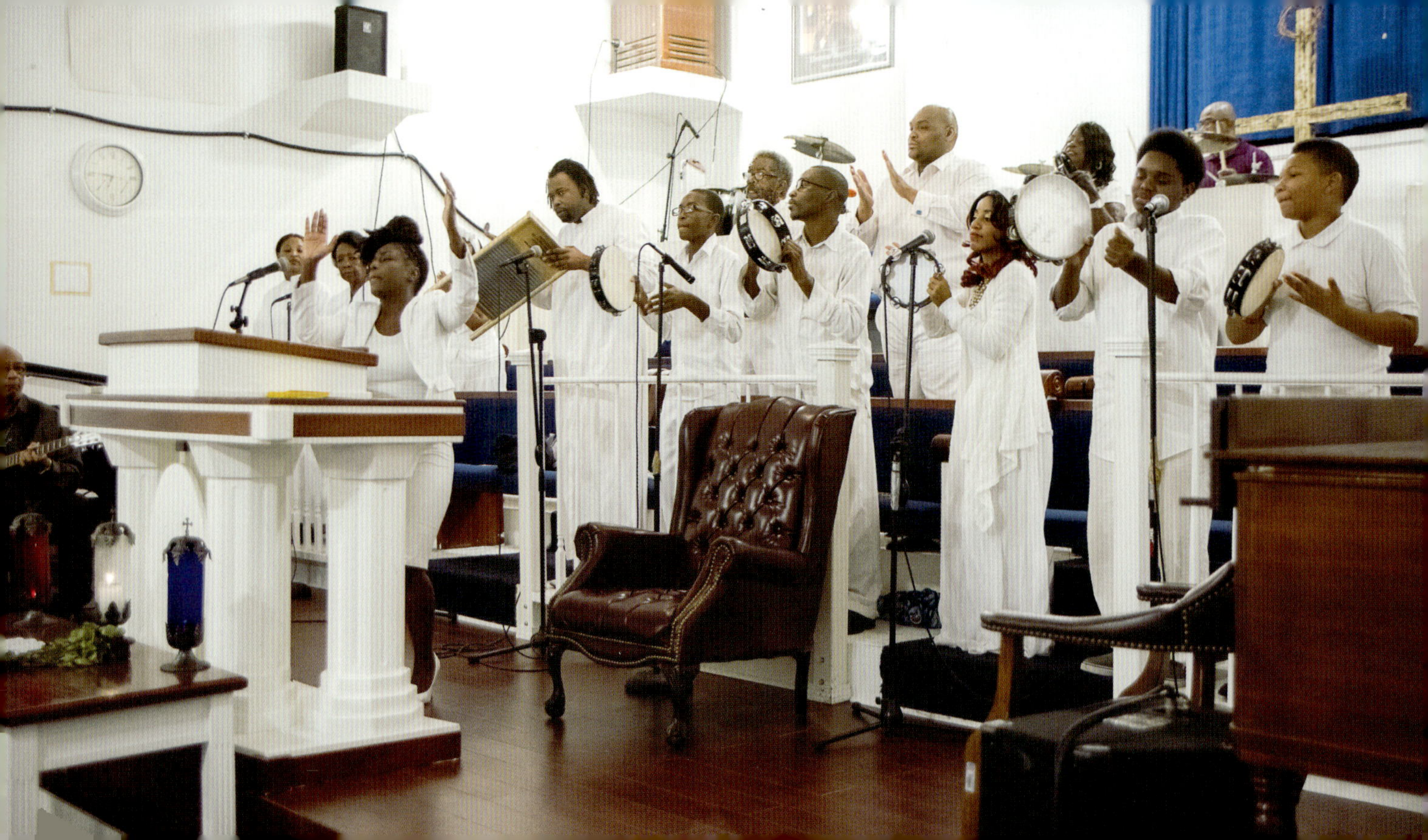

## Learning the Guitar

My cousin played. Guitar Slim, Lightning Slim—they was my uncles. And Ernie K-Doe was my first cousin. He was the one that really got me started. He bought me my first electric guitar, a Gibson. I've still got my old amp, the first amp I ever had—a Rickenbacker amp. It had one speaker. Man. And it still plays good. Still plays good. I bring it on gigs sometimes.

I started playing with one finger. I knew how to tune it to a regular chord—just an open-string chord. And it just so happens that one of my uncles had a regular guitar. So I would take it and try to play it. It kind of went good for a while. And then what happened was we was invited to go to WBOK radio station and sing, because one of my uncles had a group called the Zion Travelers. They let us come down, and we started singing. We sung about two songs. But they had this guitar player who was playing with all his fingers. I mean, he was flying! I sat there, and I watched him—for about an hour, just watched him, looking at his fingers, seeing how he put them. I went home and was going to try the same thing—it didn't sound right. So another one of my uncles, he told me, "Look, Junior, you've got your guitar tuned wrong." He showed me how to tune it. Oh man, he showed me that, and I started trying it with my fingers, I said, "Oh, yeah, I like this!" So I started like that.

## Day Jobs

I've washed cars. I've worked in a grocery store. I've hauled bricks. I've laid bricks. I've done poured concrete. I did all that because I didn't want to go back to school. Mama told me, "If you don't want to go to school, you've got to get a job." You know, getting up at 6 o'clock in the morning wasn't cool. It wasn't cool. Then, when I got this job working in a grocery store, all I had to do was stack the shelves and wash the owner's car. When I was done, I'd take my guitar; I'd go sit in the yard in the back and play it. He caught me back there, playing. "Look, you either going to be playing music or you're going to work. Which one do you want to do?" I said, "You can have this job. I'm gone. I don't want this." So that's my last day job. Last.

## Lee Dorsey

It just so happens that Lee Dorsey had come in town, and he was looking for a guitar player. I didn't know but three chords. He told me, "That's all you need to know is three chords. You're not going to be soloing a lot." I said, "Okay, I'll try it." So, my very first professional gig was in New York City. After a while, I started meeting all these different cats, different guitar players. They were showing me this and showing me that. But I just couldn't learn it right. What I would have to do is go home and practice. After a while, I felt I could play.

They had at least about ten different artists. Lee was one of the headliners. Joe Tex was the other headliner, when he had the song "Skinny Legs and All" out. Lee had "Ride Your Pony" at that time. And I did those two songs, "Ride Your Pony" and "Coal Mine," for two years and six months. That's the only two songs we had to do. It wasn't like playing a whole hour and all, like we do now. We'd do two songs and that was it. I loved it. Didn't have to stay on the stage too long.

We played at the Apollo Theater. All the artists were staying at the Theresa Hotel, right down the street from there. To look at all them lights and all that—I had never seen that many lights before in my life. I didn't sleep for the two weeks we was there. What they did was, you'd go there for a week and you'd rehearse. Then the next week you do the shows. It was fun.

I knew all the cats that was in Joe Tex's band, because when I was working we'd go on the weekends to Thibodaux and play at the Sugar Bowl. And they would be playing there at that time. I could have gone on the road with them, because that's when Joe Tex wanted to take the band on the road. But I was scared to leave home. I didn't want to go. Then when I did go to the house, that's when Lee asked my mama could I go on the road with him. Come to find out we all met up at the same place. So I had fun with the boys.

Lee only traveled at that time with three pieces—bass, guitar, and drums. Six months before I left, that's when he wanted a big band. That's when he had like five horns. No keyboards—five horns, bass, guitar, and drums. That was fun for a while, until we went to Chicago. That's what made me say "I quit." Because at that time it was snowing—we had to dig our way in and dig our way out. I said, "No, I can't take this snow. This isn't going to work." So I came home. I didn't want stay out there no longer.

I played on the road with Lee for like two years and six months. We came home like three times. The longest we stayed home was like a week. Then we'd go back on the road. So the third time I came home, I asked my mom, "I said, Mom"—because I was sending all my money home. I was living on like a hundred dollars a week. So when I come home the third time, I asked, I said, "Mom, how much money I done saved?" She said, "Well, look, Junior. You're not getting it, but I'll tell you what you made." I said, "Well how much?" She said, "You got $43,000 in the bank." I said, "Well, I'm not going back on the road no more. I'm going to stay home."

That was during the time that Sam Cooke started singing rock and roll. And then Aretha changed and started singing rock and roll. That was during that time. Johnnie Taylor started singing—he had been with the Highway QCs. And so, you know—to me it was like, okay, big change coming. I had fun. I really did.

## Irma Thomas

I was home for like a month. Then Irma Thomas wanted to get a band. So I helped her get her band started—the Tornados, her first band. I stayed with her for like two years. That was another big hunk of money that I made. Then I decided I want to go off on my own.

With Irma, we didn't stay out long. We'd go out on the weekend and come back. She didn't travel too far. The furthest Irma traveled was Tampa, Florida.

That was the last gig I played with her. We were playing with, what was his name? Anyway he was on the show, and Irma—they put us in the barracks, Army barracks. And his band was staying in a hotel. So when we went to the gig that night, we were passing his dressing room, and he had all—I mean, full of women in the dressing room. So I told the cats, I said, "Look brother, we going to bring them girls home. We ain't going to let them stay." Man, when we got through, all Irma had to do was walk across the stage. That's all she did. Well she sung, but when she walked across that stage we had already lit it up. So all she had to do was walk. When we got ready to leave, they had women all over. They had so many women that they forgot I was in there. They had left me at the theater. So when they got to the hotel, the drummer turned, said, "Hey man, Walter's still back at the club." So they came back and got me. I've had fun, really.


**Johnny Adams**

It just so happens that they were looking for a house band at the Dew Drop, on LaSalle Street. And Johnny Adams, he came to my mama and said, "I'd like Junior to play at the Dew Drop with me." I went there, and I started meeting all these different artists coming through there. So, when Lee Dorsey decided he wanted to go back on the road, I said, "Well, I might go back on the road; I don't know."

Johnny wanted to go back on the road, too. So what I did was I went on the road with Johnny. I played with Johnny for almost for fifteen years. That cat would find clubs, man, back in the woods. I mean you wouldn't know how to get there. I didn't know nothing about it. We'd go back in the woods, there, little place. Man, they had so many people there. I said, "How in the world they can find this place?" I played a lot of those little clubs with Johnny.

I played at Dorothy's Medallion Lounge with Johnny for like eight years. Oh man. They had the girls in the cage, dancing. It was a dark place. All they had was lights behind the bar. But in the rest of the club you had a little candle on the table. We would play, and the girls would be dancing in the cage. Everybody would come in there; they'd say the only person they wanted to watch dance was Big Linda.

Dorothy and Pop owned a lot of property, so they gave me an apartment across the street. Pop would come and wake me up around ten o'clock. I'd go over there and help him stock the place, and help him in keeping things straight, and stuff. That was a nice gig for just hanging out, you know. But I had fun there, too.

The thing about Dorothy is like if Johnny had a gig early that night, and the gig got cancelled or something like that, and Dorothy would have a band playing—she would knock them off and let us play. Because we were the house band. They could be coming in and just setting up, I'd call her and say, "Look, Dorothy, the gig is cancelled." "Oh, boys, y'all quit—the band is coming in." Yeah, I worked for her for like eight years.

And they had this other club. I worked there for like seven years. We would start at like ten o'clock at night and probably wouldn't get off until like seven thirty, eight in the morning. Why? Because they had all different musicians coming through, and they'd be wanting to sit in. Sometimes they wouldn't even close. That was a nice club.

When you're having fun, doing something you like, it's easy. You know, you don't have no pressure. Just playing and stuff. And by the time I was doing that I was kind of good, you know.


**The Roadmasters**

I decided I wanted to form my own band. That's when I formed the Roadmasters. The Roadmasters been formed now for something like twenty-six years. Actually, my bass player's been with me just that long.

Before the Roadmasters, I had one called the Solar System. I had another one called the Mighty Men. Actually, they were just a three-piece band. When I got the Roadmasters, that's when I added horns. I had like three horns. That was my favorite band. Oh yeah. That was the only band I was able to go to Europe with.

Jack's got his own band. Wayne's got his own band. Jimmy has his own band. And my trumpet player, he's got his own band. But my band, they check in with me before they do anything else. Yeah, they check in with me. What I do, I send out a list of gigs we have each month. That way they know not to book a gig on such and such a date. But when I had my three horns, nobody was married. We could stay out there as long as we wanted.

I do a lot of gigs with Joe Krown. But with my band I don't do too much traveling anymore, because all of them have got jobs, families, and stuff. They can't really travel like I would to travel. I'm home most of the time. I love it, too.

### Playing Europe

We played Europe for like five years. I was playing Europe so much I had apartments in different countries. But what I would do, when I knew I wasn't coming back there for a while, I rented it out, let somebody stay in it until I got back. The best fun I had was when I went to Holland. It was playing the North Sea Jazz Fest. That was the funniest.

I had never been to Europe at that time—that was my first trip going over there. We was playing in Holland. I had never been to one of the coffee shops over there. So, I'm in this coffee shop, and they had this dude that lit up a joint about this long. He didn't have no light, so he was standing in the door. This policeman was passing by—he turned around and asked the policeman, "You got a light?" The policeman, looked at him, took out a match—I said, "Man,

this is where I want to be. Yeah, this is where I want to be."

So I fooled around there, experimenting. We were there for like three days. First two days, I just stayed in the hotel room. That third day, we had to work. And, man, we went to the place. We were up there just jamming. All of a sudden I got sick, in the middle of a song. So I told David, "Finish soloing; I got to go to the bathroom." When I came back he had the crowd going—everybody moving. So I thought, "Now how am I going to get back up on that stage without distracting him?" Something told me, "Why don't you just crawl to your guitar?" So, like on my hands and knees, I crossed to my guitar. Well, I have never seen so many people hollering and screaming, and all I could hear was David saying, "Get 'em, Wolf. Get 'em, Wolf." That was my best fun.

I went downstairs that next day, and all these cats—Lou Rawls—all these cats, they're sitting in the lobby drinking coffee. "Come over here, Wolf; come over here." I knew I had to come back. So when I got my band together, I brought them back over there. That was fun.

### Recording

I started recording right after I left Irma. It just so happened that this cat, Senator Jones, he got me a recording thing. My first song was "Mickey Mouse Boarding House." The first song I ever recorded. That got me started with recording. That was a single. And then after that, when I formed the Roadmasters, that's when Scott Billington, with Rounder, said, "Hey man, I want to record you." So he recorded me. That's when I really started. That was a treat for me. Oh man. I've had fun doing this stuff.

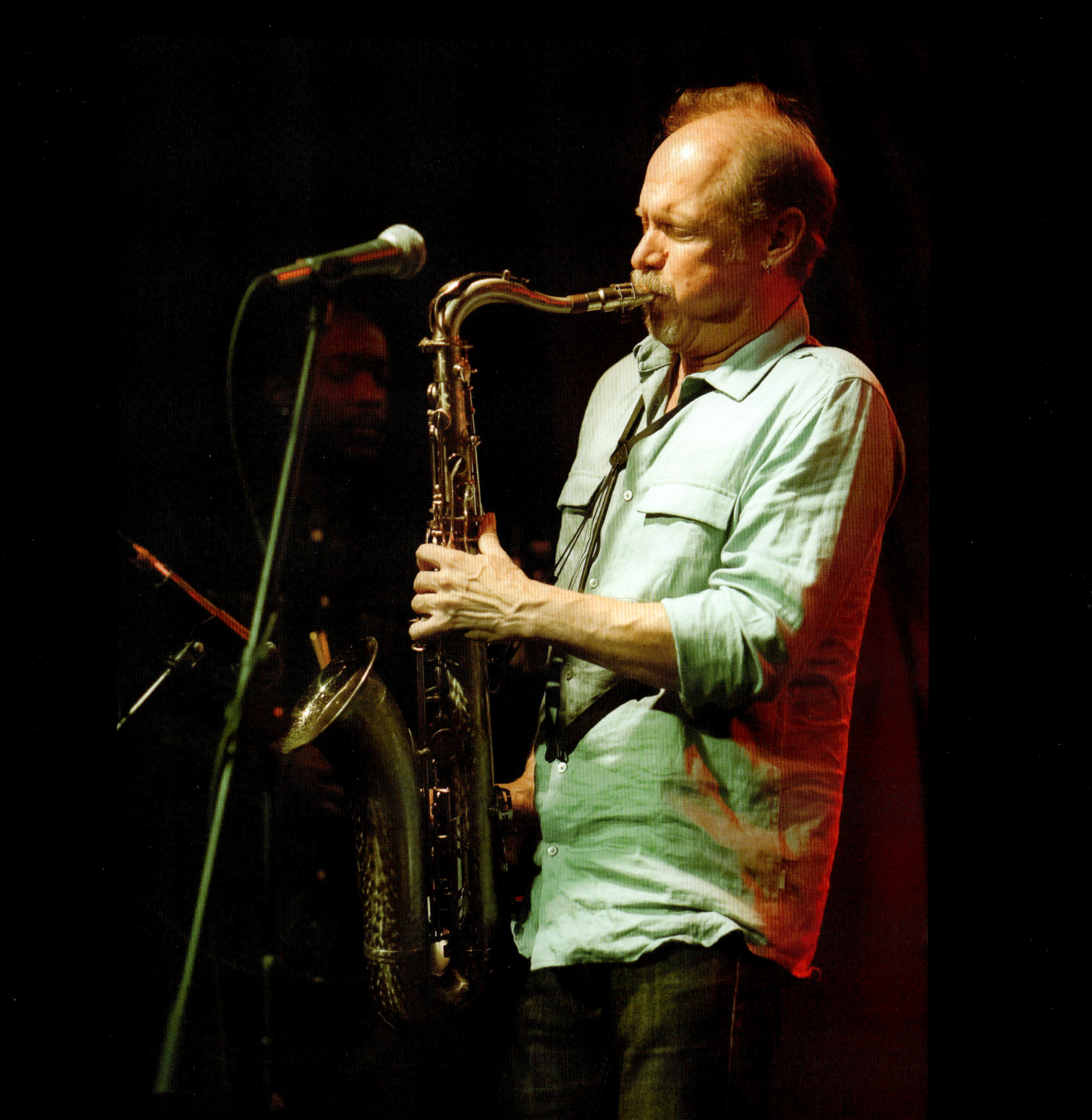

## Guitar, Band Arrangements, Singing

When I was playing with David Lastie and them, it was just bass, guitar, and sax. And we was playing this club called the Off Limits. They had a keyboard in there. We would start like three o'clock in the morning—from three to seven in the morning. During that time all these different keyboard players would come. And they'd say, "Don't do that, man; you're not playing right. Play something like this. Play something like that." So I started listening to how they was forming their chords on the keyboard and how they're moving their little fingers. I said, "I can do that." Then I started figuring out really how they was doing that.

They taught me that this little finger on the left hand is a dangerous thing. That little finger is a dangerous thing. And I started playing keyboard chords instead of guitar chords. So I developed that, and kept on until I got it to the point where I could do that. Most of your guitar players that are really good play scales. I don't play scales. I just play what I hear in my head.

I try to play as close to the horns as possible without losing the bass player. That's why I don't play like a regular guitar player would play. I try to play more full sound than just a half sound. I been like that all along.

Do I read music? No. I don't know how to read nothing. They put some dots in front of me, I say "No." Now if they write the chord changes—say "Play this chord or that chord," I know how to do that. But to read dots, no. I tried. Don't think I didn't try. I took vocal music up in school. It was easy for me to sing and hear different stuff. But basically I didn't take no lessons. When I play solos, that just what I be thinking and hearing in my mind.

I do the band arrangements. See, my tenor player writes; he can read. So what I do, I just tell them what I hear and they write it down. Now me and my bass player, I just show him the chords, the notes that he's got to play, because I play bass a little bit myself. So I show him how I would like the bass to go and he'll play that. Now my drummer, he teaches music. He's a drum teacher. So it's easy for him. And my first drummer, Junkyard Dog, Wilbert Arnold, he taught him stuff before he even started teaching. So he actually studied under Wilbert. That's why it's easy for him to find where I'm going and how to get there. I'm enjoying all that. Really enjoying it.

I always did sing, but when I formed the Roadmasters, that's when I started singing in public. When I was with Lee Dorsey, I didn't sing. When I was with Johnny I didn't sing. With Irma I didn't sing either. They always had someone else to sing; I wasn't ready for that. I was always being shy. That's why when I sing I close my eyes. I can't look at anybody.

But I always was a singer. I did go to school and was in vocal music—Miss Lawrence and the choir at school. She would take some of the kids sometimes and show them different stuff that they need to think about: how to use your voice; how to hear what you're doing. So it was kind of easy for me learn a little bit more. Then when I got with Johnny, Johnny started showing me different stuff about how to utilize my voice and that stuff. It really was fun learning.

I like singing, too. But I'm trying to do something that's different; whatever I'm soloing, I just solo and sing with it. Once I get it to the point where I can go anywhere I want it, well it's going to be good. But right now I just got to take my time and study it. I'm working on. Oh yeah, I'm working on it.

I started writing when I got with Rounder. That's when I started writing my own material. Now I've had—Dr. John, he wrote a song for me. And Anita Baker, she wrote a song for me, her writers. But most of the stuff I write myself. I just love it. But you see, I'm the type of person, say for instance, what I would write would be something that has bugged me for a long time. You know—if I keep hearing it, over and over again, okay, it must be a song. So I'm going to write it down. And eventually it turns out to be. But I have to really feel something about it. You know, they got some people who can just write anything, any time. I can't do that. It's got to be on my mind for a while. Then I'll put it down.

**The Scene Changes**

After I went to Europe, that's when everything changed. It was more integrated. I was playing so many clubs; I was working like seven nights a week. It got to the point I had to cut it down. I wasn't able to go nowhere; you know, I'd be working. When I'd get off, I'd be too tired to do anything else.

And the boys started getting married, having children. They couldn't really travel and go anywhere, so I had to slow it down. I've damn near played practically all the clubs in New Orleans. That's when they had different bands in different clubs. But now you don't have that many clubs that have bands. Mostly you have clubs that have a band in the back on the weekends. They've got clubs now that are so small they really can't have bands. They had bands back in them days, back in the '80s and '90s and stuff. It was fun. That's where the fun was. But then they started this nonsmoking thing, and that kind of cut out a lot of the clubs; they wouldn't have bands.

I have played thirty-seven weddings. And, would you believe, all of them are still married. I had one couple that came in at the Maple Leaf, "Do you remember us? You played our wedding. We broke up—but we got back together." I said, "Good, good." If I'm not mistaken, I think I'm playing their anniversary in April. Yeah, I'm playing their anniversary. But all those people that I played at their wedding, they're still married. They come to a club and holler at me.

**Katrina**

In my neighborhood, all the houses on my side of the block is high. Now, on the other side of the block, they're low. When Katrina came, trust me, me and my wife, we said, "We're not going to leave." We figured that it ain't going to be much. You know. Everybody talk about, "We going leave; we going to leave; we leaving." There was nobody in that neighborhood but me, my wife, and my dog. Come to find out they had a couple of old people that was staying around the corner; they didn't leave either.

A friend of ours had a boat. He'd come around and pick up garbage. We had two cooks—one that worked at Igor's and one that works at this restaurant around the corner from us. They'd taken this thing on the porch, you know, where you barbecue and stuff; we had steaks. They were cooking steaks. I had at least about eight fifths of Jack Daniels, umpteen cases of beer. And what my wife was doing, she was cooking on a wok. We had one of those little things you cook with. And we were feeding the old people. They'd come around and pick up their food. We stayed there twelve days after Katrina, until the water went down.

I had put my car across the street. The water came about this much from the bumper, from getting inside

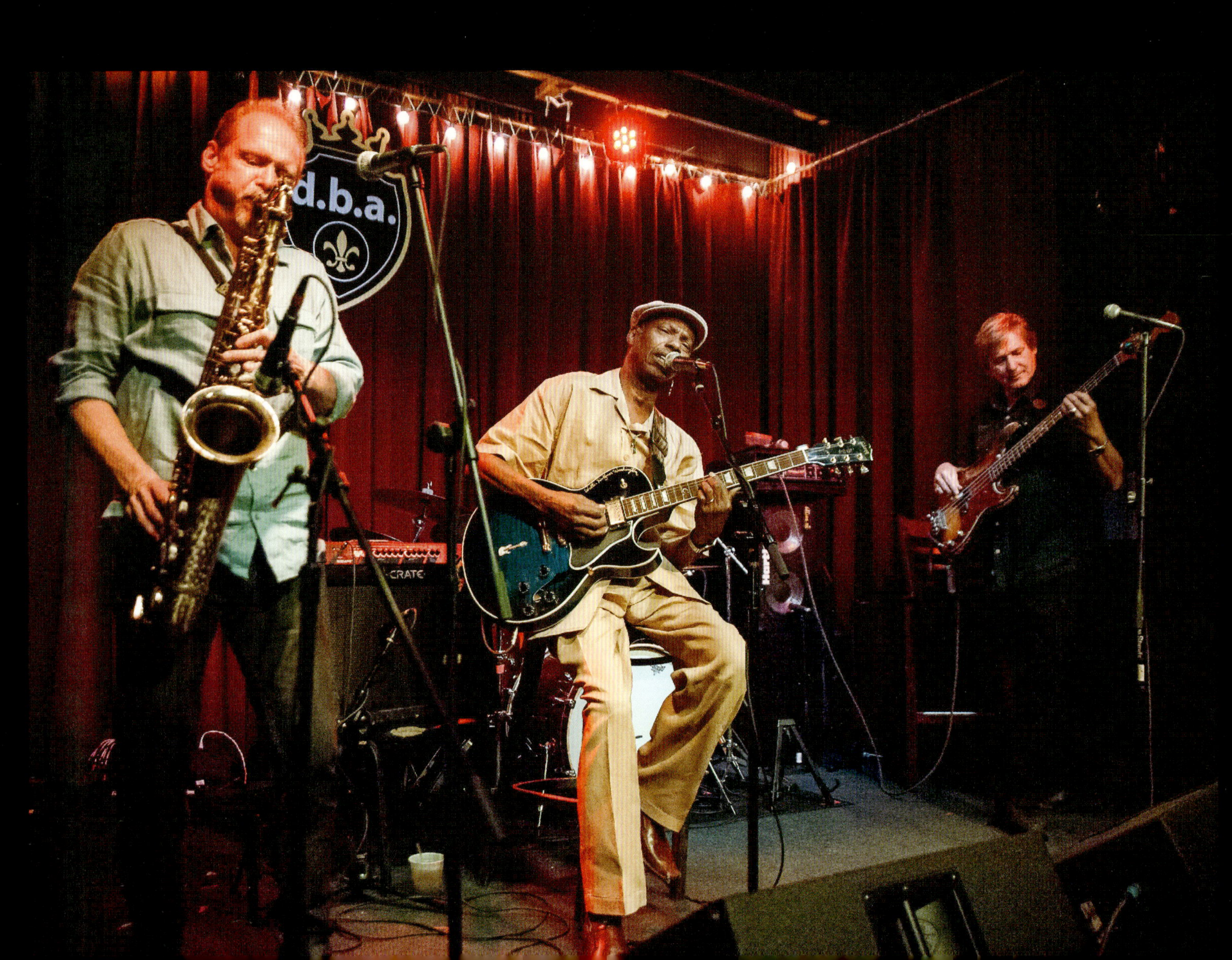

the car. I had a stick; I'd go out and wade in the water, just to see how high it was getting. That Thursday we got ready to leave, because we went up to Ohio. What we did was we went out the day before we got ready to leave, and cleared a path to Claiborne Street so we could get up on the bridge and get out. We were the last ones to leave our neighborhood and the first ones to come back to the neighborhood.

The only reason I came back was because Hank at the Maple Leaf, he called me, said, "Look man, I'm going to start some music. You want to come back and play?"

The curfew was six o'clock. We had to get back in New Orleans before 6, because they had it all blocked off. Man, that night that place was packed with TV cameras and people and stuff. Then about twelve o'clock, that's when the police came and told us, "Y'all got to close down." So Hank said, "Why? There's nobody here but us." They said, "You can go to one." So that next week, we played again. We had five generators. It looked like the club had never closed. Hank stayed there the whole time. He had a sawed-off shotgun, sitting up on the steps up on the balcony, just in case anybody wanted to break in to the club. Oh yeah. I had fun during Katrina.

### Clubs

Yeah, so they got a lot of clubs. A lot of bands in this city. But basically they got a few new bands just starting out. Most of the old cats, old bands, they mostly is traveling now.

I don't ever want to work on Bourbon Street no more. I worked down there for like two years. At that time Carlos Marcello had the clubs that I was working at. And that was fun. I had fun there. We would play like three hours; then another band would come and play six hours. Then we would play three more hours. Now where we made our money down there was he would have a meeting. And he would put everybody out of the club. He would just tell the band, "Y'all play." And this cat would go to the bathroom at least five times during the meeting. And each time he would go the bathroom he would drop $400 in the tip jar. Each time. Sometimes I had so much money I didn't need to cash my check. After he left, I quit. I didn't want to work down there no more because they started this thing where you get, it's like $25 a set. I don't want to do that. I don't want to do that.

I got out of the union a long time ago. At that time they wasn't giving you anything. If anything, they'd take; they wasn't giving nothing. So I just got out. I'd rather just be freelancing. Other cats, they'll tell you the union don't do nothing for you. I don't see why they got it. They take your money. Then they knock you off gigs. If the club is not in the union, and all that stuff—so I say I don't want to do it.

In New Orleans you have a variety of different types of music. If you're somewhere else, everybody's playing the same style of music. Here you can play any style you want to play in—as long as you do it good. And you get recognized for that. And, trust me, they do recognize New Orleans musicians. They do recognize it. That's why I'm so glad I'm from here. I wouldn't want to stay nowhere else. They got people saying, "Man, you can't find no work in New Orleans." I say, "If you come here, they got more work than anywhere else." You can get a gig anywhere. All you got to do is be good enough, you know, to perform.

**"Basically It's Just Funk and Soul"**

Funk and soul, yeah. I don't think I'm blues; I don't play blues much. Now when I first started playing music I did do a lot of blues—when I first got my band together. I stopped that. I wanted to do more funk. Basically, it's just funk and soul.


**"I'm Going to Keep On Doing This . . ."**

Until the Lord say I can't. I don't plan on quitting right now. I think I might be playing for a while. I've been playing professional since nineteen. I'm sixty-nine now. I don't want to stop. No, I would know nothing else to do. It's all I know is playing music. I'm not that good at fixing things around the house. I've always had fun playing music. I'd rather play music than anything. Yeah, I don't want to stop.

# BRUCE DAIGREPONT

Cajun singer, accordionist, composer
Leader, Bruce Daigrepont Cajun Band

[ Interviewed July 23, 2011, in Lowell, Massachusetts ]

Cajun music is rooted in southwestern Louisiana. It is primarily the product of the complicated resettlement of Acadian people—seventeenth-century settlers from France—after their mid-eighteenth-century expulsion from the Canadian Maritimes, Quebec, and Maine by the British. The music is French, because of *Le Grand Dérangement*, but its story is not the same as the French history of New Orleans—it's about different people, different times, different cultures. But in recent decades, Cajun music and cuisine have come to be associated, to some degree, with New Orleans, in addition to the Louisiana region that can claim to be its birthplace.

For me, at least until recently, this New Orleans connection has always seemed to be more a product of marketing than what amounts to a cultural truth. That is, I thought that what Cajun music was being played in the Crescent City must have been more a tourist thing than something rooted there. But I was wrong.

Bruce Daigrepont taught me otherwise. It turns out that, as is often the case, the historical and cultural facts are more complicated than they first appear. Bruce, a masterful singer, accordion player, and composer, leads a world-class Cajun band in New Orleans. He grew up in the city, the

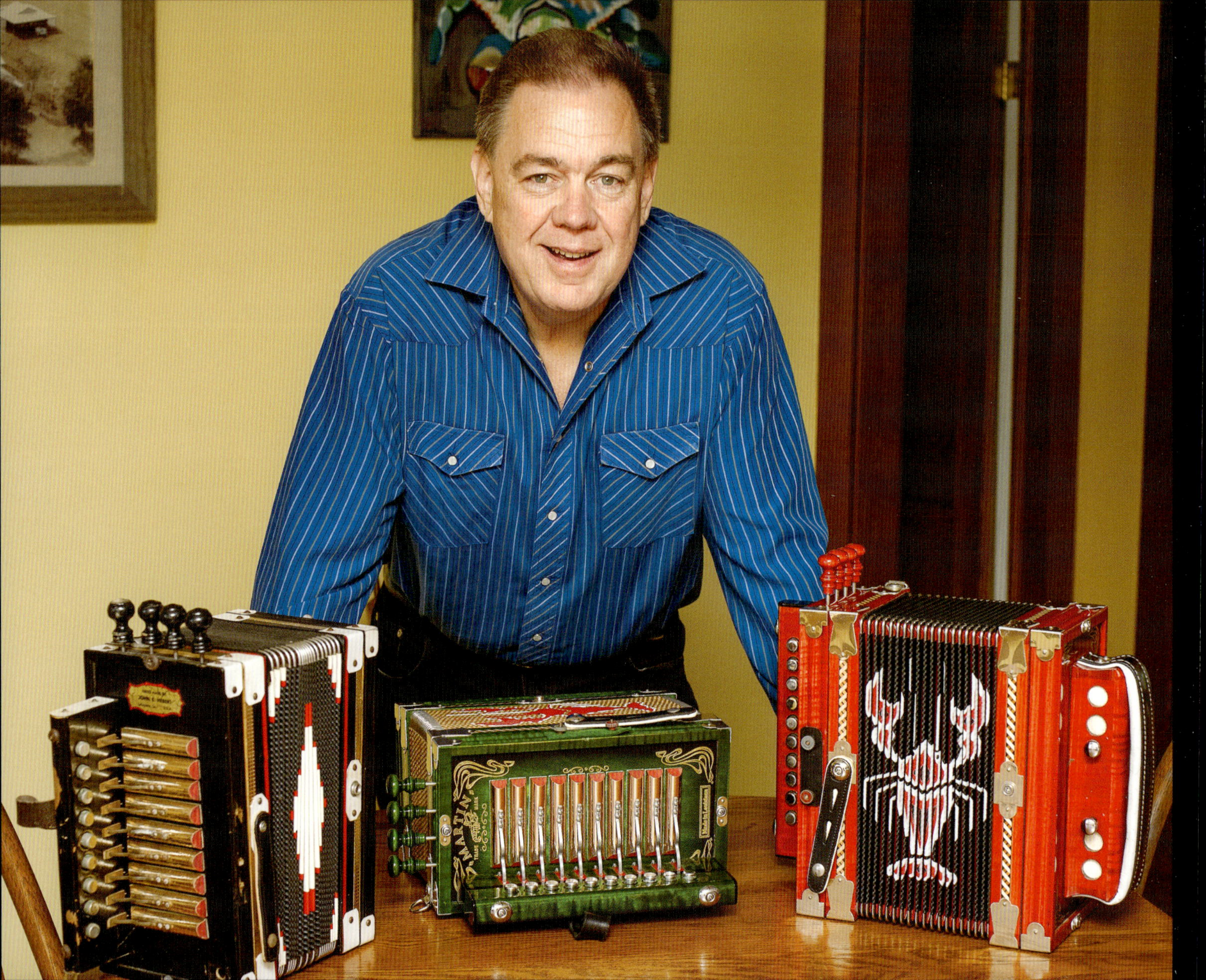

child of French-speaking parents who moved there from the country, his father motivated by experiencing the Great Depression in rural Louisiana. Born in 1958, Bruce was part of an urban network where Cajun music and country music were part of life. He started playing music at five. The guitar was first, followed by the five-string banjo. As a teenager, he played in a bluegrass band. But then, like many other children of people who move from the country to the city, he discovered his cultural roots. For Bruce, this was thanks to a visit to a festival of Acadian music, in Lafayette, Louisiana, a hotbed of Cajun and zydeco music. What is now known as the Festival de Musique Acadienne changed his life. As he relates here, he went home from that event and told his parents that from then on he would speak French, and French only, at home. And he bought an accordion, the instrument at the center of the Cajun music tradition. This was within a year or two of the national explosion of interest in Cajun food, especially as interpreted by Paul Prudhomme in his New Orleans restaurant. The Cajun cultural revival was gaining momentum, both in southwest Louisiana, and, to some degree, in New Orleans. Likewise, zydeco music—a music developed by black Creoles from southwestern Louisiana, often sung in French, often featuring the accordion in one form or another—is also part of the public sphere in New Orleans. You find it in clubs—especially Rock 'n' Bowl (which combines a bowling alley, a large stage, and a dance floor) and at Jazz Fest.

In this interview, Bruce talks about what amounts to an émigré community in the New Orleans area. He grew up listening to Allen Fontenot. A deejay on local radio, fiddler, bandleader, and promoter, Fontenot, who died in 2013, was, like Bruce, rooted in the country but located in the city. There were others with similar stories, such as Wilson Touchet, who moved to New Orleans from southwestern Louisiana in 1967 and who played at a restaurant in New Orleans for eighteen years. You could hear the music on local radio. You could dance to it in venues in the greater New Orleans area.

So, all the pieces were there—a "native-born" community of Acadians who moved to the city, a groundswell of interest in the culture—especially the music—in southwestern Louisiana, and a growing popular association of Cajun culture with New Orleans, propelled in part by culinary developments. Within months of buying that first accordion, Bruce was playing on stage in New Orleans and beyond, representing his culture. And represent his culture is what he does today, with passion, commitment, pride, and unmistakable pleasure.

In this interview, Bruce relates that history. He takes us into the present, talking about touring in France and Canada, about occupying the unusual position of being not so much from New Orleans musically but not so much from southwestern Louisiana in his personal history, and about making it as a musician in the city. For decades he has played a Sunday afternoon dance, usually at the famous club Tipitina's—named for one of Professor Longhair's enduring classics—building a community of mostly local dancers who follow his band. He plays private and corporate events and festivals. He reluctantly admitted to me, although not during this interview, that he sometimes plays on Bourbon Street, where the tourists are. His interest in his own culture is enthusiastic and devoted, and with him in the lead, Gina Forsyth on fiddle, Mike Barras on drums, and Jim Markway on bass, the Bruce Daigrepont Band makes some of the very best Cajun music you can hear—anywhere. And despite his telling me that he might not record again, Bruce's album *Jamais de la Vie* has since come out, recorded in Denmark, featuring him playing and singing some of the compositions he talks about in this interview.


## Cajun Music in New Orleans

I play Cajun music; I play the music of southwest Louisiana, and that's my heritage. And yet I'm based



---

✦ Bruce Daigrepont at home, Metairie

in New Orleans. I don't feel that I'm part of the inner circle in southwest Louisiana, in Acadiana. I mean people respect me. They like my music. But I don't feel like I'm part of the clique, so to speak—the inner circle. And I'm not part of New Orleans's inner circle either. I haven't been in the *Treme* series—I'm not in the inner circle with the whole New Orleans music scene. Because they see me as somebody from southwest Louisiana. But I think I'm respected in both places. I'm kind of like an independent.

I guess to some degree I'm why people have started to associate Cajun music with New Orleans. Before me there was Allen Fontenot, who was from Ville Platte, Louisiana. His band was all French-speaking Cajuns from Ville Platte, Church Point. There was a fellow from Marksville that played with him. They were all from different little towns, and they were all first-language French-speakers. They played in the New Orleans area in the '60s and '70s. Even to this day I guess they might occasionally play gigs. But they're getting up in age.

But what Allen Fontenot did, he would have Cajun radio shows in New Orleans. He started out at WSHO, which was the local country station in the 1960s and '70s. He would do a French Cajun program. I guess it was on weekends. I remember we would listen to it when I was growing up. His program was bilingual. He'd speak French awhile; he'd speak English; he'd go back and forth. The majority of people in his age group would go back and forth from French to English, naturally, without thinking about it. If my mother was to talk to you, and I'd ask her five minutes later was she speaking French or English, she couldn't tell me. You know, they would just very naturally go back and forth. So Allen did a bilingual radio program with all the old Cajun music at WSHO. Then when WWOZ came in, which is the

community station, around 1980, he went there. I think by that time WSHO was probably finished as a country music station.

Allen had a place called the Cajun Bandstand close to the airport in New Orleans. I remember going there when I was in high school. And we would dance. He'd play Cajun for a little while; then he'd play country. He'd mix it up. He'd play a French song. and then he'd play "Please Release Me." That would kind of aggravate me—I always wanted to hear Cajun music. I wasn't there to go listen to three or four country songs in a row.

So Allen Fontenot was there. I think he made the first inroads with Cajun music. The one thing that was different between myself and Allen is that Allen was way out at the edge of the suburbs. He was close to the airport. He'd do dances at St. Rose and Kenner. The vast majority of his audience were French-speaking Cajuns from the French-speaking parts of Louisiana. And they were older people.

When I started playing, about thirty years ago, about 1980 or so, we brought the music into Uptown New Orleans. We played every Thursday night at the Maple Leaf bar for five-and-a-half years or so. When I started playing with my band, Bouree, on Thursday nights at the Maple Leaf Bar, it was the only time on a regular basis that you could hear Cajun music in the city of New Orleans, not in the fringe of the suburbs, but actually in the city. We were very inexperienced, but we had a lot of spirit and a lot of fun. We were learning. And we gave it our all, you know.

I did that for five-and-a-half years, and then I went to Tipitina's after that. I've been doing that on Sundays since 1986. So if I add the two together, I've played a weekly dance for thirty years in the same part of town. Maple Leaf to Tipitina's is not more than maybe a mile or two apart, a couple of miles, maybe two or three. The crowd just followed me from Maple Leaf to Tipitina's. So I've had really a thirty-year run of a weekly dance.

I don't know if any younger people are doing that anymore. I know Walter Mouton did over forty years at La Poussiere, in Breaux Bridge, Louisiana. He just retired, I think, at the end of last year. He had started in the 1960s—every Saturday night. He hardly ever traveled. I think there was one festival in upstate New York that he'd go to every year, but other than that he had no desire to leave home. He had another job, but he would play Saturday nights at La Poussiere in Breaux Bridge for forty-plus years.

I wasn't working a day job. I finished college in 1980. Of all things, I got a degree in accounting. I've never worked in accounting. I don't think it's something I would enjoy. If I didn't play music I'm not quite sure what I would do. I just got out of school; I was playing the regular dance on Thursday nights at the Maple Leaf. I was living at home with my parents, and we got along great. I just kept playing the music, and it evolved, and it grew. You know, I'm not a wealthy man by any means, but I've been able to do decently. I do find that it's dropped in recent years; it's not what it once was. I would not advise a young person to go and just do that. You have no health benefits. You've got to buy your own health insurance.

I think there was a peak period of interest for our music, the Cajun and zydeco thing, maybe in the '80s and the '90s. In the early '90s and the '80s, the movie *The Big Easy* came out. That was a big push. I think it started dropping toward the latter part of the '90s. It's just my opinion. Once again, I'm not part of any system. I don't have a booking agent. I've had no promotion in my career. Everything I've done is word of mouth. So I don't know what the other people

experience. But I think it's slowed down, probably somewhat for everybody. I really do. I think that live music in general is not what it once was.

## Growing Up in New Orleans

I was actually born in New Orleans. It's kind of a confusing thing, because people see me playing Cajun French music and say, "Where're you from?" I try to give them what I think is the best answer. I say, "I'm from New Orleans. My family is from around Marksville, which is the northernmost French-speaking town in the state of Louisiana. It's at the top of the Cajun triangle." If I just say "New Orleans," I could be Italian; I could be of any descent. I'm pure French. My father's side, my mother's side— all the way back. I don't have anything but French in my veins. And part of Avoyelles Parish, where we were from—there's a lot of pure French people there. Some other parts of Acadiana, I think they had maybe more Spanish and German influence and so forth. Avoyelles had a pretty heavy dose of French in there. Not to say that there wasn't maybe a few Spanish names in there. You know, a lot of Cajun musicians don't have French names—Steve Riley, Dennis McGee, and so forth. So, obviously they had some ancestor that came into Louisiana and married the French girls, and so forth. I don't think there was as much of that where we were from. I think it was more straight French.

My parents got married in 1954. My father had a connection to New Orleans because he had an aunt and uncle who had moved to New Orleans, I guess when he was a child, in the 1920s. And my father's father had a store, so they weren't dirt poor. They actually had a little car. Most of the people in the country did not have a car. So my dad was not raised dirt poor like most people. They would, once a year or whatever it was, take a trip from the Marksville area to New Orleans to visit an aunt and uncle who had moved to New Orleans from the country. He would tell me about that. Today it's about a three-hour drive. Back in the late 1920s he remembered it being about fourteen hours. And I used to love to hear his stories. It was all gravel roads; they weren't paved. All the roads followed the rivers. You know, rivers curve like a snake. He said they would get several flats, like that was a common occurrence, to get flat tires. Also, there were no bridges. So they would have to cross ferries at the Atchafalaya River and the Mississippi. He said it was like a fourteen-hour thing. I loved listening to those stories that he would tell me. And I remember pretty well what they would experience; I'd try to imagine what it was like.

I grew up knowing my heritage. My mother and father spoke French at home. They moved to New Orleans—let's see, got married in 1954, and, like I say, my dad had a connection to New Orleans because he had an aunt and uncle that he had visited as a child. Now my mother's family had never really been to New Orleans. They didn't have so much of the connection. I guess they were a little poorer, farmers. And my father's sister and her husband, they were both from the country, but they had moved to New Orleans. They came to New Orleans to get a job. And back in those days, unless you farmed or had a store, you wouldn't stay in the country. My father, growing up during the Depression, he had seen so many people lose their land that he decided that he never wanted to farm.

So they came to New Orleans, and I was born a few years after. I feel like—I tell you what; I feel like I got good exposure to both the country and the city. And

I feel very thankful for that. Because we moved in an old part of the city, right off Canal Street. I grew up in a little half-double, right off Canal Street, in Mid-City. I grew up with a corner grocery right across the street. Everybody knew everybody. If you wanted to play, you just walked out the door, and there was more boys in that neighborhood. My dad always said we had enough for two full baseball teams that lived within about a block from each other. And we were all within about two years of each other in age. So, you were never bored.

Something I really appreciated: we had the corner grocery. And then at nighttime our mothers, during the summer, would come out and sit on the porches at night. So if they sat out until ten o'clock at night, we played outside until ten o'clock at night. If they stayed out until eleven, we played until eleven. Every night people would sit on the porch and visit. That's something you don't see anymore. So that was part of living in an old city neighborhood that I really felt was special.

And, of course, we would go up to the country all the time—my mother and father and all my people were from there, going back to the 1700s. I was very close to my mother's parents. They were still farming when I was a boy. I used to love to go stay with them on the farm. In early years they grew cotton, and my grandpa always grew sweet potatoes. In the last years—and I remember this better—they were truck farming. They would grow okra, purple hull beans, crowder peas. They would put all that on the back of the porch in crates. I remember going out in the field and picking all this stuff. My grandpa had a two-row Farmall tractor when I was a kid. Before that he plowed with a mule. But I don't remember that. Then when it come time to harvest, they picked everything by hand. My grandmother worked just as hard as any man in the fields. She lived to 103; she died in 2007 with a full mind and had great health all her life. But she worked—it must have been hard. Picked cotton during the day and then go cook all the meals, wash the clothes.

I remember they would load up the back of their pickup truck, and they would go to Alexandria, which was the nearest city, about thirty miles away. We'd go in the neighborhoods, and we'd sell out of the back of the truck. I feel like that was a very special thing for me. I was very close them. They were very affectionate people. They loved to joke. They loved people; they loved music. And during the wintertimes they'd butcher a pig—they called it a *boucherie*. I remember lots of boucheries at my grandparents'.

Having caught the tail end of that era, I think I had a better connection to playing these old songs than if I had never seen that. I really feel—if I was maybe eight, ten years younger I would have missed that. And if I was a little younger than that, I would have been maybe more influenced by cable TV and shopping malls. So that to me was a vital experience—that I feel a connection to the old songs. I also knew a lot of my great aunts and uncles. They were all still living, and they were all farmers. I remember visiting lots of sets of great aunts and uncles back in the country.

**Becoming a Musician**

I was born in 1958. I started playing this music when I was around twenty-one years old, really playing the Cajun music. But suddenly—you know, when I started playing Dennis McGee was still living, Mr. Sadie Courville was still living. They would still sometimes go play. Of course Bois Sec Ardoin was still living. He just recently passed away. I'm trying to think who else. Octa Clark and Dewey Balfa was still living. Nathan Abshire was still living. Aldus Roger. All these people. We were the young upstarts learning the music. But suddenly, you kind of just turn, and you say, "Man, all these people are gone." Suddenly you just look, and you say, "I'm going to be one of the older guys." It happens kind of fast, you know. I mean you still got D. L. Menard and Walter Mouton, a handful. But there's not too many ahead of my generation. It's kind of strange. I'll go play music somewhere, and sometimes people call me "Mr. Bruce." Sometimes they're only like ten years younger than me. We always joke about this. Barry Ancelet, a Cajun folklorist who's known me for thirty years, whenever he introduces the band he always will say that I'm a young musician. Because in his mind I'm one of the young guys. My band always laughs at that. They say, "Man, when are you going to quit being one of the young musicians in the music? You've been playing thirty years." So we kind of laugh at that, whenever Barry introduces me in some capacity. I guess he's still thinking of me as that twenty-something-year-old kid he knew.

I probably would have never played music had it not been for my father. He was born in 1921, and he got a guitar as a boy and taught himself to play. And at what he did, he was pretty good. He never played on stage. It was always just something at home, in the family. But he learned to play Jimmie Rodgers songs, and then the Carter Family songs. He played those sort of songs very well. He wasn't a singer. Couldn't carry a tune. But he would play the guitar, and he'd get somebody else to sing. And when he played music as a boy, I think. He had a friend, Herman Lachney, along with his cousin, Lee Guillot, and they would play fiddle and guitars.

As a result, when I was five years old, Santa Claus brought me a guitar. And I started. My father tuned the guitar in an open tuning, and he made a bar for me, like a dobro. And of course he wouldn't say the word, "fret." He called it a *frate*. I guess that's maybe the way Cajuns thought of it. He said, you're in G, he said, "If you go to the fifth *frate* you're in C. If you go two more, you're in D." It wasn't until later on that I heard people call it a *fret* instead of a *frate*. The first song I think I remember him teaching me was "I'm Thinking Tonight of My Blue Eyes," who went sailing far over the sea. So, I started playing the guitar like that when I was five, six, seven. Eventually I learned to make the chords and started playing. I'd sing sometimes. I've got tapes of some of that. Sometimes I sounded pretty good; sometimes I sounded bad. It wasn't consistently good. A lot of times at nighttime, my father would piddle around with his instruments in that little half-double we lived in. It was a shotgun half-double a few blocks off Canal Street.

My parents had taken a trip to the Smoky Mountains at some point, and they grew up listening to the Grand Ole Opry. My father loved Grandpa Jones. So he learned to frail a five-string banjo. And he'd play the harmonica and just different things. Based on that, we started going to a music show in the '60s called the South Louisiana Hayride. It wasn't the one in Shreveport; that was the Louisiana Hayride. This was a smaller version in Ponchatoula, Louisiana, called the South Louisiana Hayride. Every Saturday night it had Grand Ole Opry singers. We'd go, I don't know how often, but we'd go every month or two, whatever. We'd go to the shows. As a child I saw Porter Wagoner and Dolly Parton, George Jones and Tammy Wynette and Ernest Tubb—a long list. Lester Flatt, Earl Scruggs. It was really nice, because people would bring their families. And you were

right there with them. It wasn't like going to some big arena today, and you've got to spend a hundred dollars for a ticket or whatever. So we would go to these country shows at the South Louisiana Hayride. There was a bluegrass band playing there that lived in south Louisiana, and there was a five-string banjo player named Mr. Jim Burkhammer. We went and talked to Mr. Jim—my dad did. And he said, "Would you teach us to play the five-string banjo?" He said, "Come on over." They lived on the River Road in Kenner in a little cabin, basically. They'd hunt rabbits right behind the house.

We'd go to their house, and you could hear the music playing when you were pulling up. They were always picking. They were always playing music, I guess something like the Darling Family on *Andy Griffith*. It was interesting—Mr. Jim was not originally from Louisiana, because five-string banjo players are not common in south Louisiana. He was from West Virginia, and his wife was a Houma Indian from close to the Gulf of Mexico, around Dulac, Louisiana. And she spoke French.

We would go every so often. Mr. Jim didn't want any money. I think my dad eventually got him to accept four dollars for a lesson. My dad and I started taking lessons, but I left him in the dirt pretty quick, and he gave up. So I started picking the five-string banjo, and I got pretty good. I look at that as a special experience, because it was so interesting to go there. A man from West Virginia; his wife was a Houma Indian; my parents would speak French with his wife. We would get there, let's say seven o'clock. He'd sit as long as it took. There was no, "This is a thirty-minute lesson; this is an hour lesson." He'd sit with me until he taught me a certain song. Very patient. His son, Billy Burkhammer, was about my age, and he was a good flat-top guitar picker, at ten years old. After the lessons we'd have this jam session, and musicians would come by and stop. We'd leave there sometimes at three o'clock in the morning. That was a real special experience. I didn't so much realize it at the time, but, you know, West Virginia, Houma Indian, the music 'til three o'clock in the morning, the fact that he sat with me and taught me from the heart. He wasn't about making money. It was very special.

I'm still answering the question of how I started on the accordion. Okay. I went from playing the guitar to a five-string banjo. I got pretty good; I never reached my full potential because my heart was never totally in it. But when I was about fifteen, sixteen, seventeen, I played with a little bluegrass band called Luke Thompson and the Green Valley Cut-ups. I played at the Maple Leaf Bar in 1974. I did that for a couple of years. And I started writing songs when I was pretty young, started out writing in English on the guitar. Maybe a handful of them were pretty good. Most of them were just a kid's song, you know.

## French Consciousness

Then, in the latter part of the '70s—1978, I want to say—I went to the Festival des Acadienne, in Lafayette. It was the third or fourth festival, and the theme that year was *les jeunes continue*—the young people continue with the music. I was dating a girl, and her sister took us there, visiting in Carencro, Louisiana. The first band I saw was Jambalaya, and I'm very good friends with Terry Huval, and that whole band. We'd been friends for years. Terry was like two years older than me, so we were basically the same age group. For the first time, I saw people my age playing Cajun music. Prior to that I would have thought of Cajun music as more the music of my grandparents.

Even my parents' generation had gone more towards country music. And, man o'mighty—that experience totally changed my life.

I didn't know it at the time, but in those days the festival was run by CODOFIL—Council for the Development of French in Louisiana. All the announcements were in French. Entirely. It hadn't been like that for years. Barry Ancelet still speaks French, but many of the other people had kind of let it go. When I play that festival, even though I haven't played it now in almost ten years, I always make all the announcements in French, because that's the way it was when I first went there. There's a few people that think the way I do. But what happened is that as more and more tourists have come—and then there's a lot of young people that play the music that can't speak French anymore—it's gotten to be more and more in English.

But anyway, I went there the first year. All the announcements were in French. All the vendors spoke French. I was thrilled. I'd go around, and I'd order my beer in French—*"une bière."* And I spoke kind of a crooked French. I wasn't fluent like the older people. But it was all in my head, hearing it all the time. Any older people at that festival in lawn chairs, I'd go strike up a conversation with them in French. I was always interested in French, from when I was boy, a kid. I came home from that festival—I saw a lot of younger musicians. I saw Jambalaya. I saw Tim Broussard. I saw the Sam Brothers 5, which was a great little zydeco group. I haven't heard of them in years and years. And Robert Jardell with Nathan Abshire.

So I saw all these young groups playing, and I went home, told my mother all about it. I told her in French. I said *"Asteur en allant on va parler juste en français,"* which means from now on we're going to speak only French. And I was determined to become

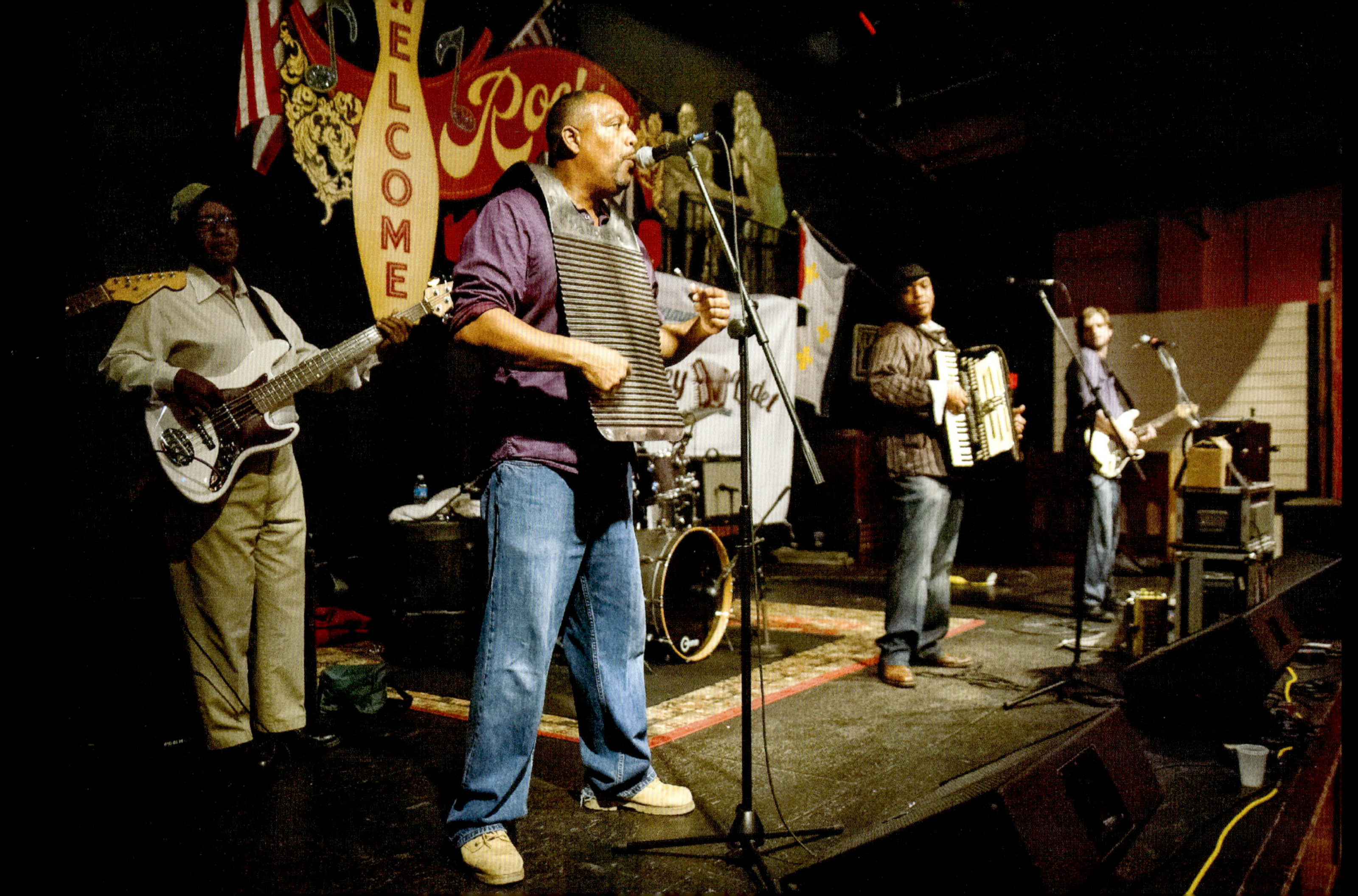
WELCOME
Rock

a better French-speaker. When I think about it, by today's standards I speak French very well. I'd say I'm one of the more fluent people. It's really odd, because by the standards of forty years ago I'd speak it so-so. I can't speak French like the older people did. Their vocabulary was much larger. But as time has gone on, the people that do speak French generally aren't as fluent as the older people were. I'd say by today's standards I speak it very well. By the standards of when I was growing up—mediocre. Anyway, I knew at that time I wanted to get an accordion. Of course I'd been listening for years to Allen Fontenot. I'd wake up on a Sunday morning—eventually as I got a little older, I'd wake up with a hangover. And I'd smell that pork roast in the oven my dad was cooking, and Allen Fontenot on the radio. I wanted an accordion.

It took me about a year before I actually got one. The first accordion I went and got was from Mr. John Hebert, who lived right in the city of Lafayette. He was about the age of my grandparents, probably born like 1906 or something like that. He was very nice with us. My parents came with me. They always supported my music. And we were real close. I remember coming home from John Hebert's house with my first accordion. My dad was driving and my mother in the front seat. I was in the back seat, trying to figure out how to play the accordion, from Lafayette to New Orleans. And by the time I got to New Orleans I had found the notes to the song *Bayou Pon Pon*, which was the first tune that had come to my head. I was like twenty, twenty-one years old.

### Making a Career, Representing a Culture



I didn't plan on making this a career. But things moved very fast for me. I found a friend who had a band called Laissez Faire and were doing some Cajun music. They were playing on Bourbon Street. It was a short-lived group. I made good friends with the fiddle player. His name was Seymour Richard.

I got the accordion in September. By January, Laissez Faire was calling me on stage to play songs. I had been playing for three months or something. In April, six months after I got my first accordion, I played my first dance. Wilson Touchet was the accordion player, and he was having oral surgery. They warned me two weeks ahead. They said, "Bruce, Wilson could be out April 3" or whatever. "You've got to play the dance." So I had to learn not only to play about thirty songs but also had to learn to sing them, because I had to front the band. That's a whole different thing. I fronted the band and played and sang about thirty songs I had learned in a couple weeks. Seymour would come to my mom and dad's house every day, and we'd sit in the back yard. He was like my coach—about ten years older than me. Somehow I pulled that dance through. I guess I did okay. That was in April. And in July I had my own band, called Bouree, like the card game. Nine months earlier I had never picked up an accordion, and here I had a band. Then Seymour dismantled his band and came and joined my band to play the fiddle. Sadly, Seymour Richard was killed a couple of months later, on Labor Day weekend 1980, while coming to the aid of stranded motorists on the highway.

One year after that, July of 1981, we were sent to Quebec City to represent Cajun music at a festival. That's where I met Barry Ancelet. He was there, and we hung out and talked. Zachary Richard was up there. We had a jam session with him one night. To think that I had been playing less than two years! Here I was representing the music there. I was very fortunate. I don't know how it happened. We were

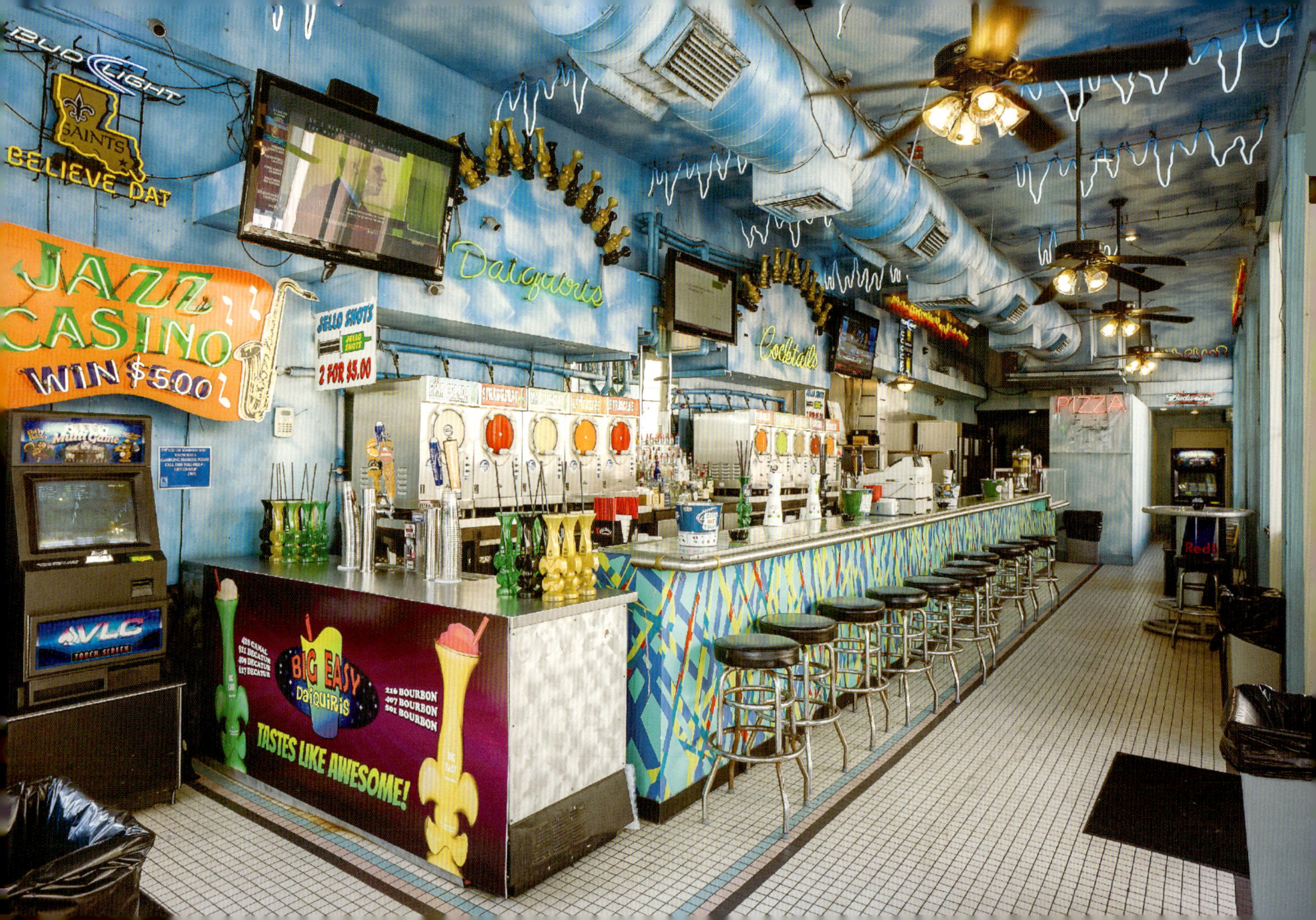

BUD LIGHT
SAINTS
BELIEVE DAT
JAZZ CASINO
WIN $500
JELLO SHOTS
2 FOR $5.00
Daiquiris
Cocktails
PIZZA
Multi Game
VLC
TORCH SCREEN
BIG EASY
DAIQUIRIS
TASTES LIKE AWESOME!
216 BOURBON
407 BOURBON
501 BOURBON
Budweiser

green, but we played hard. We gave everything we had. I was fortunate that this whole thing progressed kind of fast for me.

I've always felt—I'll say this over and over—when we get on stage, we represent our whole culture. We're not just playing for ourselves. We represent the French Cajun people of south Louisiana, every time we get on stage. I've always felt that to be very important. And I like to try to present it in an intelligent way—to inform people and to have fun. But also, you know, I'm not interested in singing gimmicky songs; I want to play songs of intelligence.

## Recording

I made four albums for Rounder. That's the only ones I've made. I haven't recorded in eleven years. I want to record again. When I made that last album, I felt a little discouraged. Sales were down. My first album was the best seller. My second dropped a little bit. The third one dropped, and the fourth. I have found out that's pretty common—I'm not the only person.

After I made that last recording, which was called *Paradis*, in 1999, I just felt a little discouraged. You know, you can listen to the radio, not that I listen—I never listen anymore, only once in a while driving in my car. You can write a really intelligent song, and it may not get much airplay. Yet you can write something really goofy, and they're going to play the heck out of it. So I was a little discouraged. I said, "Really, who cares if I record anymore?" I mean it's really not that important, in a sense. I just felt like not many people were that interested in what I did. And the computer thing came in, you know, people could take anything off of a computer, so they don't have to buy it. Recording was something I was spending way too much on for the return I got. I have a family—you never can seem to make enough money to support a family, you know, with three kids. So I just thought to myself I may not record again, maybe never, or for at least a long time.

But as the years have gone on, I definitely want to record again. I've got a lot of good songs that have never been documented, that we play with my band. Some I've never shown my band. I have no aspirations of anything. When I record again, it is what it is. It may be ignored. A lot of people say, "Oh, you know there's a category now for the Grammys. You could win a Grammy. You need to jump on the bandwagon." I don't care about that. That's not important. If I won a Grammy, that would be great. But that's not what motivates me. What motivates me is I want to document the band that I have—Gina Forsyth on fiddle, Jim Markway on bass, and Mike Barras on drums. I have great musicians playing with me. I think we have a great sound, and I feel like I have some great songs that, if something happened to me, would be lost. I don't have the lyrics written down anywhere or anything. I want to document what I've done. And that's all there is to it.

There's not much money in it. There's not going to be any big sales or anything. And I'm at a point in my personal life, I've got so many things going on, I don't have time to make a record now. I lost my parents two years ago in a car accident, and I'm still dealing with their house. I've got to fix it up, and I'm going to try to see about getting that rented out at some point. So I can't make a record right now. I've got so much weight on my shoulders that I couldn't think about it. But I have the songs. I really have enough good songs for a few good albums. Of course, I could record old songs. But I have—I think I wrote down in a notebook, I've got about a good twenty-five or more original French songs that I have never put on an album yet or recorded. And I think they're all good songs. It's just a matter of eventually recording again.

**New Orleans Audiences**

The audience in New Orleans? When I started, I would say they were kind of like the ex-hippies. You know. Most of them were a little bit older than me. I was in my early twenties. I guess the average age was around thirty. That would be my guess. Then the World's Fair came to New Orleans in 1984, and we played a lot at the fair, plus a lot of great Cajun music came to the fair, all the time. And that totally mainstreamed the audience. It broadened the audience from what it was before.

Today's audience—well some of those original hippies that kind of follow the band now are about sixty years old. Back in the early days I think a lot of them, you know, went out late at night and so forth. Now it's just more like regular working people. A lot of divorced people come. They like to try to meet somebody on the dance floor. Sometimes it gets like a soap opera out there, but I'm too busy concentrating on what I do to pay much attention to it, because when I'm playing and singing I try to put my whole body—my heart and soul—into what I'm doing. I guess the crowd is getting older. We survive at Tipitina's; I'll say that. It's been twenty-four years on Sundays since 1986. You've got to keep drawing some new people, because it will die out.

I used to play a dance on the West Bank of New Orleans, at the Four Columns, in Marrero, Louisiana. For quite a few years I played one Tuesday night a month. That dance lasted fifteen years. It was mostly all older people, a lot of French-speaking Cajuns who'd come to that dance. They had to suspend the dance because the original group of people were dying off, and it just got too small. So you got to keep getting new people coming, or it will die.

We've been able to do that at Tipitina's. We're not breaking records like we did when I first started. But we hold our own, and we've outlasted so many other people. The whole dance was my idea. I'm the one that called Tipitina's; I suggested doing a Cajun fais do do dance on a Sunday, like we do. After that, many other places in the area copied us and tried to do Sunday dances with Cajun music. They had a big corporate place called Mudbug's—huge, huge place. They put a lot of money into it, and they would give away so much food. They had offered me to play there. I'd have had to quit Tipitina's. I thought about it, but I said, "Tipitina's is a tradition. I'm not going to leave." And Mudbug's came in, and for a few years it was a hot spot. I mean they'd lure people there with free crawfish, free steak dinners. They got some friends of mine to play the music. I think Waylon Thibodeaux and his band played there. But it didn't last. And as soon as the crowd started dipping, the big corporate place drops them. They could have gone to another venue, or whatever, you know. But many other places have come and gone—Bayou Barn—and they all copied us on Sundays. We've outlasted all of them.

That's the only real regular gig. I play conventions, I play festivals, weddings. I wish I had more opportunity to play. I've never gotten a booking agent with the intent of traveling a lot, although I have played in Europe twenty times and Canada about forty times. Maybe I could have gone that route, but I chose not to, many years ago. I do appreciate the fact that I'm home with my kids quite a bit. I'm at their ballgames and stuff; I'm not somewhere on the road playing music. But I'd like to play a little bit more; I need to play a little bit more. It's gotten slower, it seems, as the years have gone on.

At our gig on a Sunday at Tipitina's, we do get some tourists there, but we have a very strong local following. I would say 80 percent of the crowd are local people. 20 percent will be tourists from anywheres in the world. What I think makes our dance at Tipitina's very special is that our regular dancers who come there, the people that come all the time, they open their arms to anybody who comes in there and welcome them. They go talk to them. They get them dancing. I've been at some dances where people were more cliquish and the outsiders might come watch more. I think we have some of the friendliest group of people. They make everybody feel at home when they come through the doors at Tipitina's. But most of our crowd, the majority, are local people.

There are a lot of tourists—there's a place on Bourbon Street now, Tropical Isle Bayou Club, where they play Cajun music. There's a little guy that I must have given thirty accordion lessons to, who has a band. His name's Lance Caruso, and he's got a band called T'Canaille. They play on Bourbon Street. I think Brandon Moreau is playing on Bourbon Street. I don't know how many people are playing. All those people play for tourists. I'm the one that plays more for the locals. The tourists that do come to see us make an effort to come there, because it's not in the French Quarter. It's not like you walking up and down the street with a beer in your hand and all of a sudden you hear an accordion. You have to make an effort to go there.

Who else is playing in the area? We had Kermit Venable for many years, but he passed away. Kermit Venable was one of the most knowledgeable people about Cajun music and music in general. He was very knowledgeable. He died like four years ago or something. So I don't know how many people are playing the music. I don't know if Allen Fontenot—he might play once or twice a year. There's me. There's Lance and his band. Now my cousins are playing—my cousin Michael Dupuy and his boy Cameron, who is twelve, is really picking up the accordion. I mean he's got all the ability in the world. He can sit and play that accordion and play with the grown men now. He's really good. And my cousin Michael is a very good singer; he's got a very good voice. So they play some, and also Michael plays with Lance. There's John Dowden, a young guy that plays the fiddle. He's a good little fiddle player. And of course there's my band, Gina and I. I heard Wilson Touchet moved back to the country. He was from St. Martinville but he was playing in New Orleans for a long time. I'm trying to think.

There might be some more that I don't know about. There's a lot of people that don't play in public. They'll tell you, "Oh, I've got an accordion I play at home." You know, that kind of thing. But there's not too many of us. And then there's some that come on Bourbon Street—like Nolan Cormier was there for years, and his sons. But I don't think they're there anymore. Jimmy Thibodeaux played for years on Bourbon Street. I think he lived in New Orleans. I don't know if he's there anymore, because I don't go much on Bourbon Street. Jimmy Thibodeaux's an excellent player. Oh—there's one other person that lives in New Orleans I almost forgot: David Doucet from BeauSoleil. David lives in New Orleans, and I know he plays on Monday nights at the Columns Hotel. We say we're going to go one day, but I have never gone. Maybe one day when my kids are grown I'll get out more. So you've got to count David in there; he's in New Orleans, too.

## Canada

I've played a lot in the Canadian Maritimes. I'll tell you where I've had the most success—southern New Brunswick. I've played up in northern New Brunswick, too, at Caraquet and all those places. Nova Scotia, the southwest part, La Baie Saint Marie, the heaviest Acadian part. And Chéticamp, up in the north. I guess I've played in French Canada like maybe forty times in my career.

It's one of the greatest experiences that I had playing the music. I'll tell you how the whole thing started. I was at Barry Ancelet's party, where he makes a *cochon de lait*, every January. This is like 1989 to '90. I started drinking a few beers with a fellow named Jean Frigault, who is from Tracadie, New Brunswick. We're drinking and we're talking, and he's telling me how much he likes my songs and the music I play and so forth. He says, "The people back home have got to hear to your music." He said, "They would love your songs. They would love your songs." So after we were drinking together, he takes one of my recordings and sends it to a fellow named Ronnie Bourgeois in Halifax, who was working for the government of Nova Scotia.

Ronnie loved it; he loved the songs. The next thing I know he's inviting us to play Grand-Pré, Nova Scotia, where the Acadians were exiled from. So we started going. From that point on, in the last twenty years I don't know how many times I've been up there to play festivals and so forth. We started going there every year, at least once a year. It would expand—you know it might have started in Nova Scotia, and we didn't maybe play New Brunswick right away, but a year or two later, the next summer, went there. Prince Edward Island and so forth.

Then in 1995, after I had been there three or four times, we went to Bouctouche, New Brunswick. I was worn out. I took a nap in the afternoon in my hotel room. We'd been traveling a long time. My phone rings, "Bonjour, Bruce." It's the security people. They wanted to know if I wanted barricades in front of the stage that night. We were playing in the Forum, which is the hockey arena of Bouctouche, New Brunswick. It holds, I think, close to two thousand people. They wanted to know if I wanted barricades in front of the stage. I started laughing. "Barricades?" I said, "We don't need barricades."

Well, we got there that night, and the place was packed. I mean people standing shoulder to shoulder, like a rock concert. We get up on the stage, and they start screaming like it was the Beatles or something. So we start our first song. They turn those fog machines on. They had a bunch of fog machines. We started laughing. We couldn't even see each other on stage with all the fog up there. And of course they had a big spotlight, like a big rock concert and everything. I started singing my songs, the songs that I had written, not the traditional Cajun songs but songs that I had written in the Cajun style—the people started singing them. They knew them word for word. And not just the choruses. They knew the verses. We all looked at each other, the band and I. By this time I guess the fog had subsided, because we started looking at each other. Our eyes were this big. I'd look at the drummer, and we were all like, we were in shock. We were totally in shock that the people knew these songs. I didn't know anything about it.

Obviously, what happened was they started playing these songs on the radio, and the local musicians started playing them. Because later on I would go to festivals, and I'd hear my songs being played in the distance by all kinds of French Canadian bands. Not just traditional bands—sometimes it would be a rock band. They'd be playing my songs. Or a country French band. And based on that, first thing you know, the general population knew a lot of my songs. It was just like standards. I didn't know anything about it.

If you really think about it, for something to become popular like that, usually it takes a lot of promotion—some kind of concerted effort by a group of people who say, "We've got to promote the hell out of this." There was no concerted effort. It just started with me and Jean drinking at Barry Ancelet's party, when you really think about it. And then it grew. There was no promotion or anything like that. And the other thing that was strange about it—they could not even buy my CDs. I talked to Rounder, and they said, "Oh, we distribute in Canada." Well, if somebody wants to drive three and a half hours to Halifax, he might find one Bruce Daigrepont CD in the best record shop in town. Or maybe in Montreal there's a couple of copies, which is eight hours away or whatever. But these songs became so popular among the population up there, like standards, and they couldn't even buy the recordings. It really totally baffles me—there's nothing that makes sense about it.

So that was one of my greatest experiences. I did get this on film. It's somewhere in an evacuation box. Ken David was playing the bass with me. Ken's been a regular with the Jambalaya Band for years, and he did a lot of playing with me, too. His son, Thomas, who is now in the Pine Leaf Boys. Thomas was there with the band that night. He was ten years old. And I remember thinking "We've got to get this on film. This is unbelievable. People will not believe this." And I'm thinking, "Of all times to have ten-year-old boy to

film." Well, he did a pretty job. I got a film, and when I got home I showed that to my parents. I mean it would bring tears to your eyes to see that. Because, you know, we basically play for English-speaking people. To actually go where people can actually appreciate the words to the songs, and sing them, you know. That is extremely special to me.

We went back seven, eight years in a row, and played in that hockey arena, and sold it out every year. I still go up there and play festivals. And I make a lot of TV shows up there, where they know my songs. It's national television, and I've done quite a bit of great productions up there, that I'm very proud of. And most people in Louisiana have never seen them. I've got a collection of them at home, VHS and DVD, but nobody's ever hardly seen them, except my family. And the people in Canada. Some good stuff.

### France

Another greatest experience for me—I mean I've done the standard things. I played at Lincoln Center back years ago, several times. In Wolf Trap, the New Orleans Jazz and Heritage Festival, and all those things are tremendous. But another great experience I had with the music was in 2005. We were playing in France, and I had a family that came and waited to talk to me, way after the gig. They waited and they waited. Finally when I was finished we talked. They said, "Bruce," they told me in French, "We think we are related to you. We have a home named *Aigrepont*." They were descendants of the females of the family. The name *Daigrepont* no longer exists in France. They told me later on that the last male died in 1905. But they had this home near Moulin, right in the center of France, that was built in 1640. They wanted me to go visit it; they found me on the Internet.

So we went in 2006, and we played music over there with the band. My fifth cousins in France, or whatever they are, picked us up at the airport. I spent a week with them. We spent three nights in the home that my ancestors built in 1640. I was the first person that actually has the name that went to that house in a hundred-plus years. Isn't that interesting? I can imagine when they found me it must have been like finding life on another planet or something. The father said he suspected there was one of our people that had gone to Louisiana. And I think that Daigrepont got to Louisiana in the 1780s, I believe. They knew exactly how we were related. To show how close the family came to dying out—the name—the original was named Jean Jacques D'Aigrepont. He was one of three brothers who were officers in the French military. He had one son that was born when he was fifty-four years old, and he died a year later. That one son was named Pierre. Pierre had eleven children: the eleventh was born when he was fifty, and he was my father's grandfather. And then from there there's more of us now. But it's not a lot of generations. And the fact that one generation was fifty years, another was fifty-four—so it's a little bit close generation-wise, even though it goes back to the 1780s or somewhere up in there, 1790. But I would never ever had experienced that had I not played Cajun music.

# IRMA THOMAS

Singer

Leader, Irma Thomas and the Professionals

[ Interviewed October 8, 2013, in New Orleans East ]

Her crown may have been lost in the flood, but Irma Thomas will always be "The Soul Queen of New Orleans." In her early seventies she's regal, gracious, and strong. Her voice has, if anything, gotten even better in its fullness, richness, and nuance. Among New Orleans musicians, she's royalty.

Born February 18, 1941, in Pontachoula, Louisiana, Irma says that she never knew a time when music wasn't part of her life. When she was a child, singing, at home and in church, was just part of what you did. The radio—much more local then than now—was often on, playing blues and gospel. She began singing in clubs when she was sixteen, asking the house band if she could sit in. A year or two later, she was being paid to sing with the house bands, sometimes sitting in while waitressing in the club. In fact, she lost a waitressing job because the manager thought she was spending too much time singing.

Tommy Ridgley, who led one of those bands, helped her get a recording deal with the Ron label, and when she was nineteen, her first Ron recording, "(You Can Have My Husband) But Don't Mess with My Man," was number 22 on the *Billboard* rhythm and blues chart. That wasn't her first record, though. As she relates here, the first was a recording

99

of her school song, done in New Orleans's most famous studio, for use on the school p.a. every morning. I can't find any evidence that "The McDonogh 41 School Song" has ever been re-released. What a treat it would be to hear that track now. Irma's Ron recordings were followed by releases on the Minit label, produced by Allen Toussaint. Minit was acquired by Imperial, and she continued to chart with releases such as "Wish Someone Would Care" and "Time Is on My Side," which the Rolling Stones covered pretty much note for note. She went on to be associated with other labels, including Chess and Atlantic, not always happily. Making records that were played on the radio helped her early in her career, especially with getting gigs around New Orleans. But most of her work was on the road. That's still the case, although her appearances at Jazz Fest are, for many, among the highlights of that huge event.

With more than fifty years in the business, she's seen considerable change. The regional record labels she began on are long gone. The world of touring is very different from what it once was. The significance of being from New Orleans has changed as well. In her early career, no one promoted her as a New Orleans musician. Because in those days so much of America's music was being recorded in New Orleans, she surmises, there might have been no reason or advantage in being promoted as a New Orleans singer. All of that, of course, is different now.

Not only was New Orleans not an identifier in the first part of her career, but race seems to have factored in differently, at least in her particular case. She says that because the practice was not to picture African American artists on album covers, early fans, especially adolescents in New Orleans, sometimes were surprised to learn that she isn't white. Another ramification of not appearing on album covers, she says, was that some artists had doubles touring, claiming to be them. That wasn't her experience. Tours, too, were different in the early years of her career. Eight or more acts would appear in a theater as part of a package, doing three or four shows a day, playing to largely African American audiences. Now of course, she is a headliner, selective about where she'll perform. And her audiences are mostly white.

There's a 1964 clip of her singing and being interviewed on *American Bandstand* available on YouTube (http://www.youtube.com/watch?v=9bfzxVEwHXs). Take a look. Then listen to her sing one of my favorites, "River Is Waiting," on her 2008 Rounder release, *Simply Grand*. In 1964 she sounds a bit like Nancy Wilson, one of her favorites. She seems a bit ill at ease or inexperienced during the *Bandstand* interview with Dick Clark. Forty-four years separate the two performances, and what's abundantly clear is how rich her voice has become, how much more confidence she has, how, as a mature artist, she's become a true American master. In fact, a few years ago, National Public Radio designated her as one of their 50 Great Voices of the recording era.

It can't always have been easy for Irma Thomas. Early parenthood and divorce are chronicled in many of biographical entries about her. But she has made her way through life with impressive determination. She left school early, but later she earned her GED. In her fifties, she went to college, earning a degree in business at Delgado Community College. On Delgado's City Park campus, the Irma Thomas Center for W.I.S.E. Women opened in 2007. W.I.S.E. stands for Women in Search of Excellence; Irma helped create and continues to support that center. When I asked her if it was challenging being a woman in the music business, she answered that she's always demanded, and gotten, respect. The idea of *respect* runs through our conversation, and it's clear that this matters a great deal to her.

Now, of course, she is one of the small top tier of New Orleans musicians who represent the city to audiences around the world. Globally, New Orleans has had a direct claim on jazz for many years; the recognition of its importance in other genres is a newer, more musically inclusive notion. Irma Thomas's career spans those two ideas of New Orleans music.

✦ Irma Thomas at home, New Orleans East

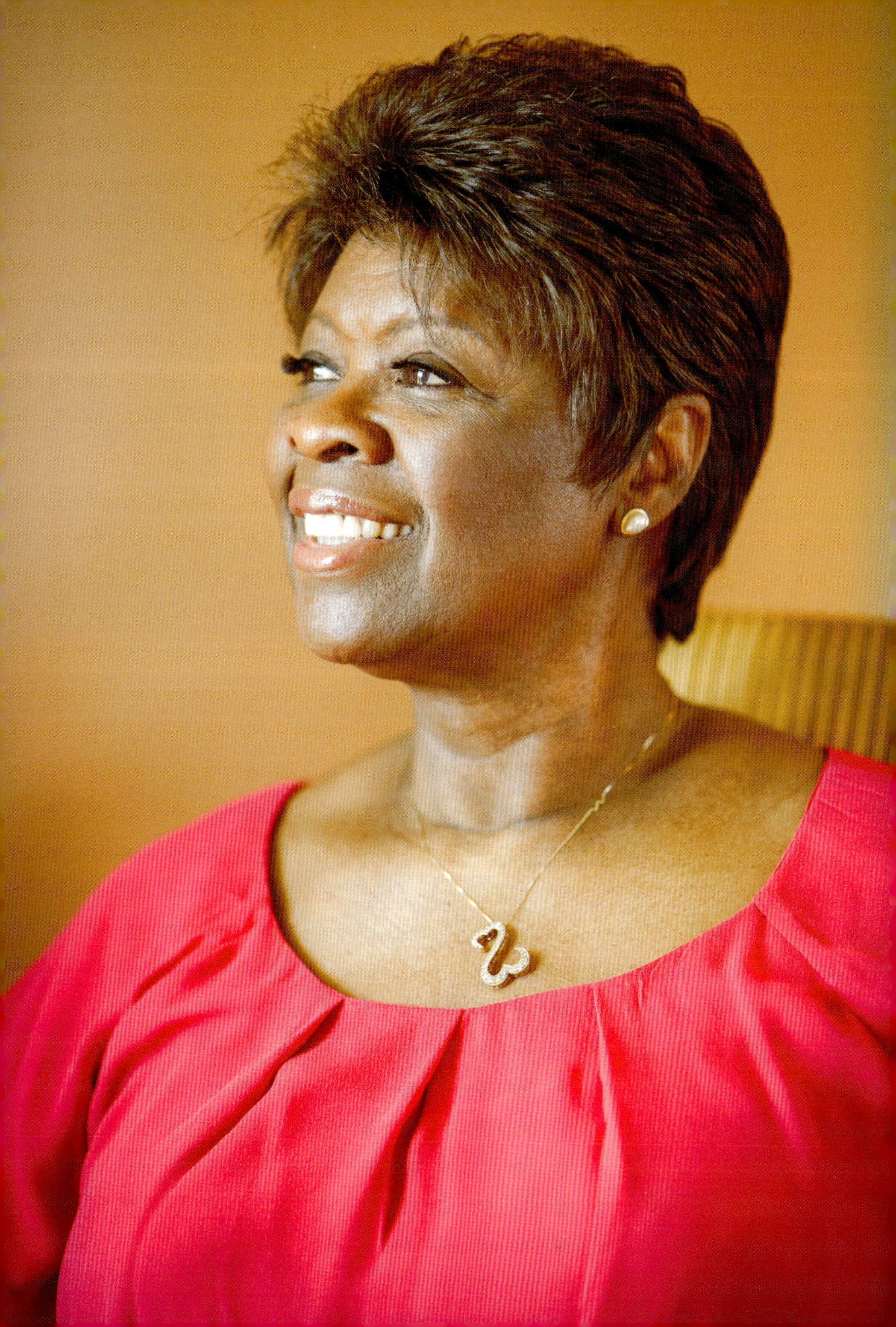

Part of that change has to do with Rounder Records. I won't repeat here what Scott Billington tells us in his interview about working with Irma. But Rounder's belief in the importance and commercial viability of a number of important New Orleans musicians, starting in the mid-1980s, clearly opened a new stage in Irma Thomas's career, just as it was helping the world appreciate the manifold musical contributions of the city and its artists. It's often the case that musicians who have early success live out their careers on the basis of those younger days. Not so Irma Thomas, who continues to grow, finding songs that fit her age and this era.

Today, Irma and her husband, Emile Jackson, who is also her manager, live in a comfortable, ample house in New Orleans East. Visiting them in 2013, it was hard to visualize 2005, when the levee broke and much of New Orleans East flooded. The interior of their house, their home for more than thirty years, was destroyed. But it, and New Orleans, are home, she says, and, even as she stayed elsewhere when the neighborhood was unlivable, for Irma Thomas life elsewhere holds little appeal or interest. The soul queen believes in her city.

## Roots

I've only been around since mud.

I was born in Ponchatoula, about sixty miles away from here. My mama hatched me in Ponchatoula, but we ended up in New Orleans, with, I guess, a bunch of other places in between. My parents were like gypsies. They were all over the place.

We lived in the Uptown section of New Orleans, the area which is now called Simon Bolivar. There's a high-rise center there now. But it used to be a very vibrant neighborhood. My parents lived in the back of a place called the Vogue Hotel that also had rooms for rent. At the time, my mom was working for Southern Bell Telephone Company. And my dad was working for a steel company. So both were employed, and they stayed with those jobs for many years. In fact, my dad stayed on one job for twenty-four years, and then when the company moved he didn't want to go back to the country. So he went to the riverfront and stayed out there about twenty-some-odd years as well.

I lived here with my parents from infancy until I was maybe four or five, and then they were having difficulty finding someone to sit me after I became school age, because they worked. And they had an incident that happened with the lady who they had left me with. She gave me some bad food, and it made me sick. So my dad got paranoid. He took me to live with his mom in Greensburg, Louisiana. I must have been about five at the time. She died the same year that he took me out there. So I wound up living with his sister, who at the time had three or four kids. I stayed in Greensburg, Louisiana, until I was nine years old. And then back to New Orleans. I've been living in New Orleans ever since, with the exception of the time that I moved as an adult to California. But other than that, this has been home.

When I came back to New Orleans, we lived in—I guess they call it the Garden District—Felicity Street, a block or two off of St. Charles Avenue, between Oretha Castle Haley Boulevard and St. Charles Avenue. I grew up in that area. Then we moved in an area called Zion City. The Zion Harmonizers—I think that's where they got their name as a group from that area. I lived right there until I moved out on my own.

Zion City today, it's pretty much depleted. A lot of the houses and people who lived there did not come back after Katrina. There's a church called James Chapel Baptist Church that's buying up a lot of the properties and using them for parking lots and what have you. The block where I was raised and lived before I moved out on my own is no longer a block of houses. It's a house here and there, and the rest is a parking lot. It looks like a ghost town.

## Early Memories of Music

I can't remember when I didn't have music around me. That was just the way things were. I mean even when we lived in the country, we self-entertained, singing around the house and on Sundays at church, and after church on the front porch, or "gallery," as they used to call it. It was always music in the family, both religious music and whatever was available on the radio. We didn't think of it as something that was necessary—just something that took place as a part of our everyday life.

In fact, I think about that now, and I laugh, because living in the country, they didn't have electricity. They had lamps and a battery-operated radio, which didn't get used until evenings when my aunt used to listen to whatever it was she used to listen to in the evenings and on Sundays. We would listen to whatever music was available on Sundays—for about a couple of hours, because she didn't want to use up all her battery.

We would listen to what was available, which wasn't very much, because you had a choice between either the blues music, or you had—they didn't call it country music—they called it hillbilly music. And that was your choices. When I moved to New Orleans, music was more vibrant here, more alive, and had a lot more variety. My dad used to play a lot of the early B.B. King, Lightnin' Hopkins, and folk like that. And on the radio you had several choices of various music genres. So music was all around, all the time.

In my early days brass bands were only around for special occasions such as celebrating a social and pleasure club's anniversary or a part of someone's funeral procession. They weren't as prevalent as they are today. You had them regularly, because there wasn't a week that didn't go by that somebody wasn't celebrating something. But you didn't have as much of it as you have now. A lot of the younger kids are hooking onto the music, which is a good thing. It's keeping it going. But as a kid, I can only remember special occasions. Of course, during the Mardi Gras season there were a lot of bands, brass and school bands, that were available. But you didn't have a lot of clubs that had brass bands in them. You had clubs that featured either R&B music or whatever the venue was presenting.

I can't remember when I wasn't singing out of the house. I sang at church, at school. It was just a part of what I did. I was in the church choir. Ironically, it wasn't until I was grown that I realized that the church that my father attended was not a Baptist church. We had church like Baptist churches— we had a choir, we sang the old hymns. But it was a Methodist church. As I became of age and made a decision on my own, I got baptized Baptist. So that's what I participate in. But I've always had religion in my life, from a wee baby on up. And it's still a big part of my life.

When I moved back to the city, they had a lot of gospel programs on the radio. You got your gospel programs in the early part of the morning. Sometimes you would get one in the late afternoons; then you had the late-night DJs who would sometimes play some gospel in the beginning of their shows. Then they would end up playing the blues—whatever the

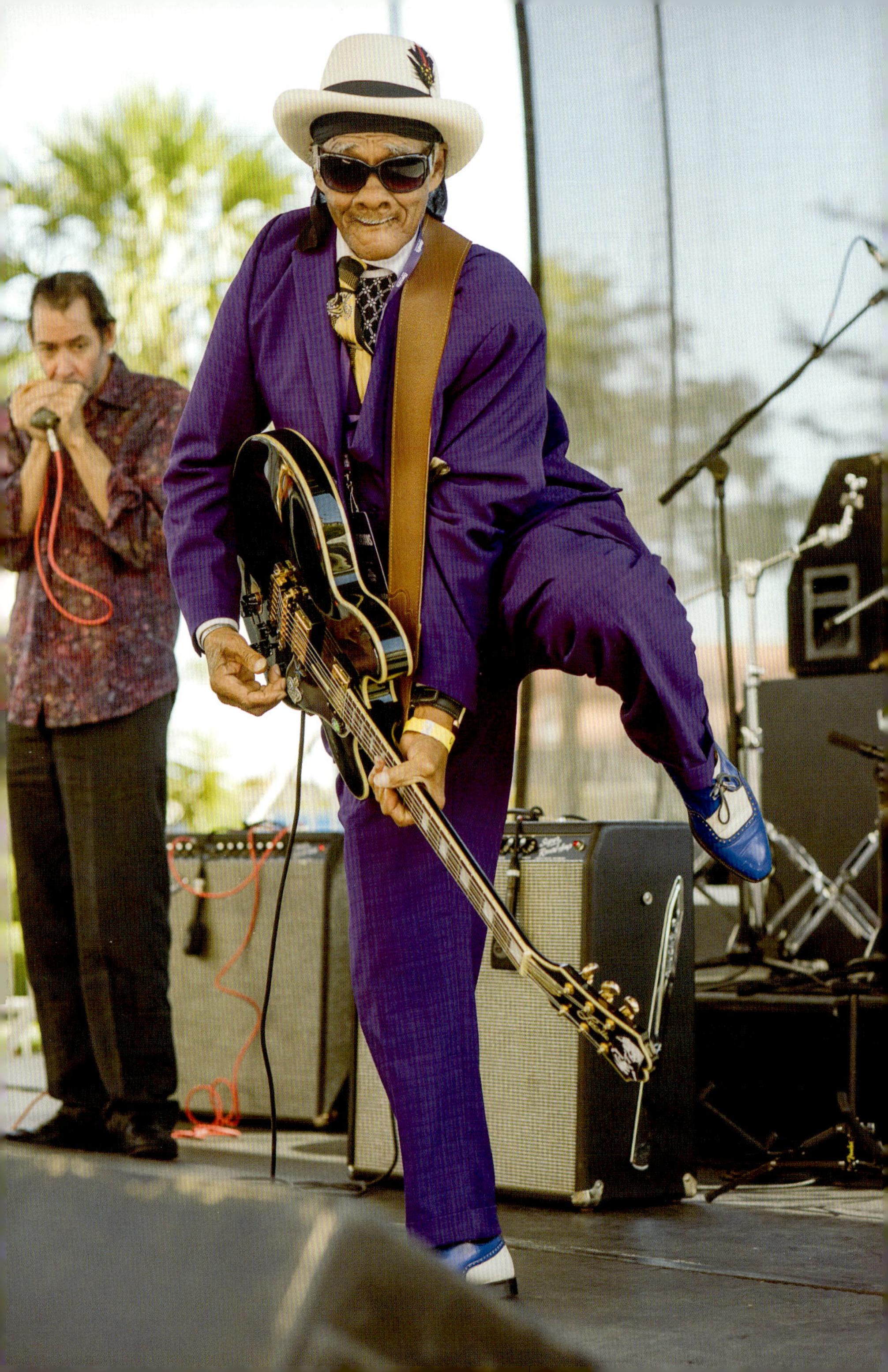

popular music of that time was. But they both were always around on the radio. And in those days we had a lot of local DJs, and the stations were owned by a lot of local owners. So you had a lot of the local music, as well, being played regularly.

Now half the owners don't even live in the state, let alone in the city. And they don't really particularly care whether the local entertainers' music gets played or not. That's truly a shame. There's so much good talent here, but aside from the college radio stations and WWOZ, you would not know that they existed. If it's not on the playlist, it doesn't get played. And even though we have a lot of entertainers here in this city who are Grammy winners, you still don't hear their music on the Clear Channel radio stations.

**Starting in Clubs**

I had been singing in and out of clubs since I was sixteen. It was something you did. You enjoyed it. I was a mom, so I was an adult, per se, and I could go in a club and listen to the music. If I felt like singing, I would ask the band—whatever band was the house band at the club—could I sing, and they would let me. But to get paid for it—I didn't start getting paid for it until I was, I guess, about seventeen or eighteen years old.

I'd sing whatever was popular at the time that I liked. Probably something I've heard on the radio. Ironically, most people who were in the business at the time were listening to pretty much the same stations that I was. So, I didn't have to have a rehearsal or anything. It was just a matter of getting a key that I could do it in. I'd have to sing a little bit in the key that I thought I could sing it in, and they'd pick it up, and we'd do the song.

You have to start somewhere. After you get practicing and on the job, eventually you learn.

The only one that I really spent any time performing in was the Dew Drop. Aside from the Dew Drop Inn, the other clubs were like one-nighters where I got hired for one night, and then I would play somewhere else. After I had made a recording, I did most of my singing on the road.

The Dew Drop was a very classy club. It was the number one black club in the South. Anyone who was anyone of any caliber, that had any hit records, that was black, played the Dew Drop when they came through the city. If they didn't play the Dew Drop, there was a place called the ILA Hall, which was a black union hall. You could get maybe 1,500 people in it, and they would do performances there. In fact, a lot of whites used to go to the Dew Drop. They wouldn't really sneak in, but they would get in there, because we didn't care. We weren't hung up on what color you were. If you wanted to be in there, you came in. But it was a segregated time, so they would probably have to be aware that they might be arrested for being somewhere they wasn't supposed to be. Nevertheless, they would come. And some big stars have spent some time in the Dew Drop.

The entertainment was good. In the Dew Drop you had whoever the featured person was, and there was an emcee there who went by the name of Patsy Vidalia, who was a female impersonator. Patsy Vidalia put on a show first and also introduced the other acts on the show that night. There was another emcee who used to be there, called Google Eyes, who had some records of his own, who did real well back in the mid-'50s and '60s, as well. So you had some really classy entertainment that came through the Dew Drop. And of course I was blessed enough to have played there several weeks at a time. A lot of

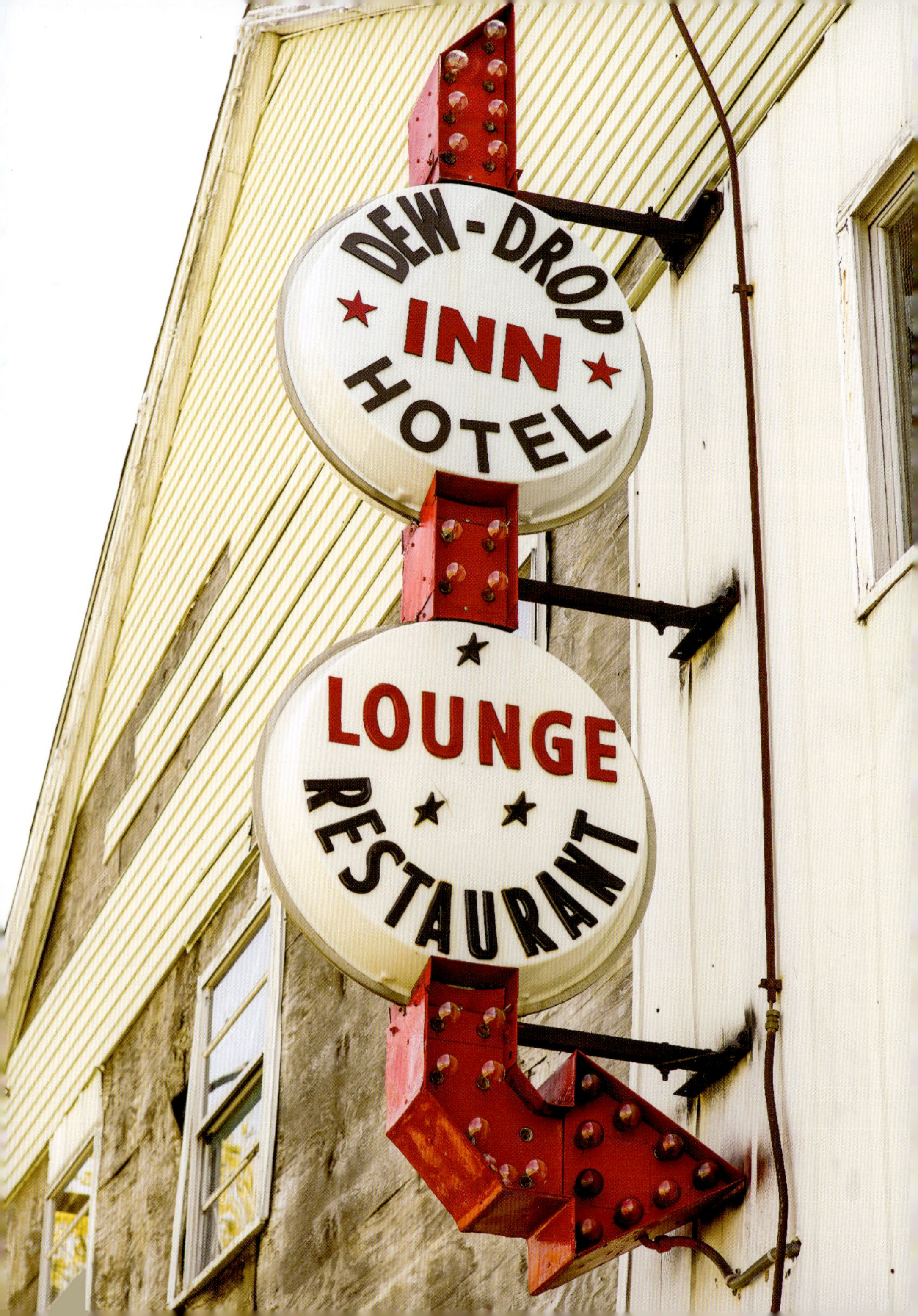

DEW-DROP
INN
HOTEL
LOUNGE
RESTAURANT

the other locals who had records out, or who were good talent that didn't necessarily have a record out, also played the Dew Drop. If you were a good talent and a good entertainer, Mr. Painia would hire you.

## Singing Locally in the Sixties

I didn't do a lot locally until I would say the early '60s, mid-'60s. Radio stations used to do promotions for the schools. They would have the schools write in, and the school that did the most write-ins would get a band at their gym for that Friday evening. It would be their pep rallies or something like that. We got hired through that situation oftentimes. So, you got a chance to get out there quite a bit. In fact, from some of my early recordings, after I switched labels, they were being played on the stations, and they thought I was white.

I had done "Don't Mess with My Man," on the Ron label. Then I switched from Ron label to Minit. The first release on Minit was called "Cry On." It stayed on the radio quite a while. I think the flip side of "Cry On" was "I Did My Part." That got played a lot. Then, right after that, they released a song called "It's Raining." Well, between those three songs, my songs stayed in the loop of radio airplay—I had like the number one, two, and three songs in their charts for weeks at a time. Then the kids, the white kids, started requesting the song, and then when they would ask for a band they started asking for Irma Thomas. It didn't matter—once they discovered that I was not white, it didn't matter to them. They wanted to hear what they wanted to hear. So, I could be considered a crossover artist before they called it crossover. And a lot of those kids from then are still my fans today.

Most of the time it would be dances in the school gym. They called them sock hops back then. And fortunately, around the city of New Orleans, there were a lot of places where they did shows geared to the teenagers, to give them someplace to go, to be able to have fun and enjoy the music as well as opposed to going into a night club.

And we had places like the Metairie Lodge, Germania Hall, F&M Patio, for the kids, for young adults. They could come in these places because there were no drinks being served. Except for F&M Patio—that was for those who were older who could drink. A lot of time they brought their own, anyway. But there were a lot of venues that was geared toward the younger people, so they would have somewhere to go and have fun.

Making those early records sure did help my career. Because when you're on the radio, people know that you exist. And of course you would get bookings from that. But once again, I didn't do a lot of entertainment in New Orleans, even though I played the Dew Drop and some school venues; I did a lot of my work on the road—like I still do.

## Soul Queen

I was just Irma Thomas back then. The "Soul Queen" didn't come until the '80s. Wilbert, the drummer that was in the band that my husband and I put together at the time, didn't want to introduce me as the "singing grandma." So he came up with the "Soul Queen of New Orleans." He started calling me that. He's deceased now; he died with cancer. Then they made it official in 1989—the mayor, which was Barthelemy at the time, and another gentleman who was very into the cultural aspects of the city. His

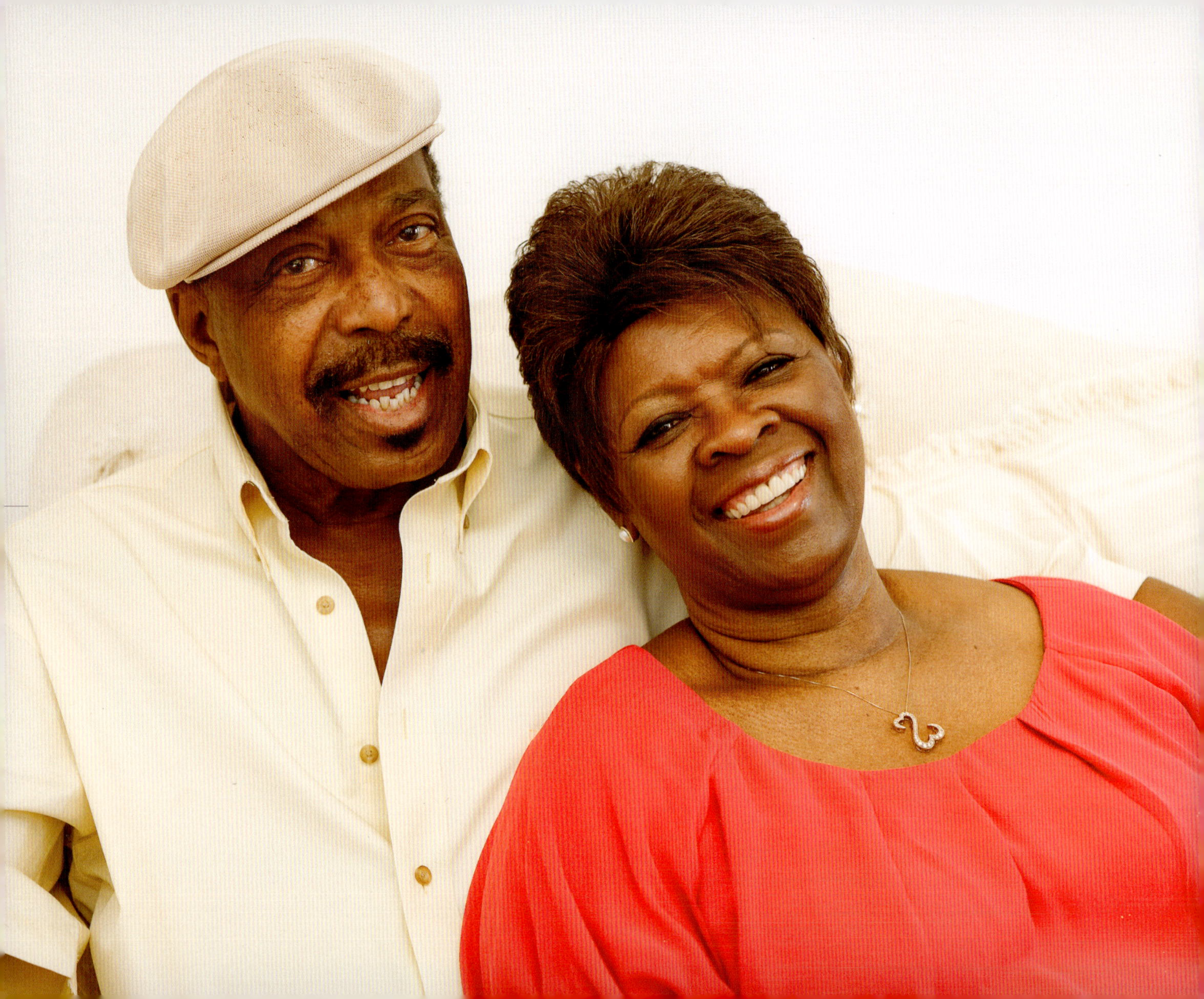

name was Kalamu ya Salaam. I think he was working with the Jazz and Heritage Foundation, and he wanted to make it official. So, he put together the whole night. And the mayor came up, and they made it official. So I'm now the official "Soul Queen of New Orleans."

Of course, the crown got washed away in the flood. But, yeah—the whole nine yards. They literally crowned me the "Soul Queen of New Orleans."

**Early Days on the Road**

It didn't really matter to people where you were from. I was being introduced as the artist whose records at that time were popular on the radio. And so I was Irma Thomas. It wasn't so much a big deal in terms of introducing me as a New Orleans artist. They didn't so much connect you with a city as much as they do now. They tend to do it more now in recent years than they did back then. The people wanted to hear the song. They couldn't care if you were from around the corner. If it was their favorite song, and you were the artist who performed it—fine.

The one good thing about the early stages of my career—I didn't have to worry about having a body double out there. Like a lot of groups who had—there were three or four different Drifters and four or five different groups of the same name. There were the phony groups, of course, and then the original groups. The reason for that was because in the early days of music, because of segregation, a lot of black artists' pictures were never on their album covers. So that gave the possibility—in fact it happened—where, if they sounded like the record, groups could go out there and perform as that group. They had an artist who, maybe there was another guy or girl in another city who sounded like that particular singer—they would go out and be that singer. But until they started putting the picture on the covers of the albums, they didn't know who the original person was. I think because of all of the phoniness that was going on out there, they decided, "Well, we better start putting the original pictures on there, so people will know who the original persons were." But, fortunately, I didn't have that problem. I don't think anybody wanted to be me.

You know, hindsight is twenty-twenty. To me, I was making a lot of money compared to what I was making before. Okay. So you can't really blame any particular person for that. When you go from $4 a night to $50 a night, that's a big jump. And you learn to live with that. Although I could have been making $50,000—who knows? I don't know. And I'm really not angry with anyone, because I didn't have any management—I was self-managing. When you don't know your head from a hole in the ground, you do what you know is best for you. I don't really regret any of it, to be honest with you.

I mean there were a lot of things probably could have changed or would have been better for whatever reason. If I would have had that kind of management, who knew the business, but by the same token that don't mean that that person was going to be honest with me. Some years later, I did have a manager who wasn't honest with me. And because of my husband, who I'm married to now, who saw through him, my eyes were opened to what his shenanigans were. He's no longer my manager.

Every now and then I'll hear one of my early records on the radio, and I say, "Oh, I sound so young." Which I was. I was. As you get older, either your voice will get better or worse. And I'm blessed mine got better.

I mean, I had gotten turned down for a couple of auditions, so my head wasn't swollen because I thought I was so great. Because I had been refused a couple of times on auditions. Yeah.

A lot of the early tours that I did wasn't so much of a touring revue, but you played in theaters where there were at least eight acts on a show, and you did three or four shows a day at those theaters. That's the way they did it then. Depending on where your record was in the charts, you were either a headliner or you were somewhere in the top three or four. But all the acts that were on the show had records in the charts. So you were among pretty tough entertainment there. But we weren't so much in competition with each other. We were all out there doing what we knew how to do and enjoying it, making whatever it was we were making. Yeah.

I never toured with Lee Dorsey. Most of my gigs with Lee Dorsey were shows that were here in New Orleans. But that only happened maybe once or twice, even though I knew Lee Dorsey very well. Lee Dorsey was a nut, but he was a real nice guy. He cared more about being a mechanic than he did singing.

I don't know if people were in those days so much concerned with a sound that came out of New Orleans, because back in those days everything came out of New Orleans. Ninety-five percent of the recordings that were recorded was recorded here in New Orleans. We must have had, what, seven or eight major record labels here back in the '40s, '50s, and '60s. So a lot of the music that was recorded was recorded here in New Orleans. And came out of New Orleans. I don't think until last, what, twenty, thirty years, that people was making that difference between the music genres out of this area. Granted, now, you could tell if the drummer was from New Orleans or not. Because all of the drummers out of New Orleans got hired out by major artists and played behind major artists until they got too old to play. They had this distinct ability to play those second line beats, with those extra beats in it, that was a thing that came natural to the drummers out of New Orleans. But it wasn't until recent years that they started making that distinction—"That's a New Orleans record," or "That's an artist from New Orleans." I don't think it made any difference for me because half the time folks didn't know where I was from. It wasn't that big of a deal.

## McDonogh 41 Song, Minit, and Cosimo's Studios

My very first recording, I did record in Cosimo's studio on Rampart Street—it was the McDonogh School 41 song. I was a student at McDonogh 41 and the young man, Henry Carbo, and I were students at the school, and we recorded the school song at the studio on Rampart Street. It was just a school song to be played at the song every morning. When they opened up the school day at the school they played the song. As opposed to us getting on the mic singing it every day, they decided to record it, and it got played until the record wore out. It was being played long after we had left McDonogh 41. But when I became a recording artist professionally, all of my records were done at the Governor Nicholls studio with Cosimo.

When they started the Minit label and they were auditioning singers for the label, they turned me down. So I didn't come on board with Minit until after I had recorded "Don't Mess with My Man." And then Allen Toussaint was the producer, of course, for that label here, and that's when he wrote and produced the songs that I did on the Minit label at that time. Up until he went into the service. All of those records were done at Cosimo's. The studio that they were using at the time that I came on board was the one that was on Governor Nicholls Street. That would be the second one.

### The Club Scene

We don't have a curfew here. There's no law on the books saying you got to close your club at two o'clock. The only law that they changed, you cannot walk down the street with a bottle of liquor in your hand. It has to be in a go-cup. But there is no law saying you have to close your club at two o'clock. If you want to stay open twenty-four hours, you can stay open twenty-four hours.

There was a club here in New Orleans East on Chef Menteur Highway called the Safari. It's no longer there because the bridge is there now. When Danny White and the Cavaliers was there, I used to do shows with them, and we would get off at two o'clock in the morning. Then we would head to the French Quarter and do another two shows from two thirty until seven a.m. I did it a couple of times. But after that I said, "No, I can't take this." I couldn't do it anymore. I just couldn't take the long hours.

I mean you had entertainment all night long. I don't know how many of them still do, but I do know that if clubs have customers in there who are spending money, they don't close the doors. They just clean up around them.

Some people still play for tips, if that's what they want to play for. But I mean that's their choice. It's not forced upon them. I mean, you go into a club, and he tells you, "I'm not paying you; you play for tips." If you feel you're going to make the money, that's your choice. It's not a thing where you have to do it. You don't have to play for tips if you don't want to play for tips. That's their choice. I don't play for tips. Never did. That was my choice.

There's a lot of clubs in the French Quarter that the musicians are playing for tips. And they play practically all night long to make a decent salary, if you want to call it that. But that wasn't a choice I wanted. Even when I played down there with Danny White and the Cavaliers, we didn't play for tips.

### Demanding Respect

That comes up a lot in interviews that I do. "Was it tough being a woman?" Compared to what? What do they mean, "Was it tough being a woman?" I'm a woman. What's tough about being a woman?

You got respect if you demanded it, yes. If you didn't demand it, no, you didn't get it. And I've always demanded respect. I've never had a problem with anybody mistreating me in any way. Even during the segregated times, when they had these instances where the white patrons would call you names and make demands, I never went through that. The one time I did, I rebelled, and it got straightened out. I didn't go to jail, and I didn't get beat up. I demanded that, "Okay, if I'm going to come here and entertain you, you're going to respect me as a person. Period. I don't have to do this. Even though I may need to do it because it's financially my job, but I don't need to take your disrespect, and then I'm going to come in, laugh and grin and try to entertain you? No."

When that happened they realized that I wasn't going to take it, and they stopped. So when you demand respect, you get respect, even in segregated times. When you showed that you wanted respect—that you didn't have to come out there and do that—then you got the respect that you asked for. Yeah.

The end of segregation didn't affect me, because I was already playing white clubs and white audiences. It never really made that big a deal in my career, because I was playing both audiences at that time. That's why I say I was crossed over long before they called it *crossover*. I've always had a larger white audience than I've had a black audience. And so, that's the way my career has been.

But when it comes to, you know, comparing it to what, I mean what they may be alluding to is that oftentimes they found that female artists didn't get the accolades or pay that male artists were getting. But that was because they didn't demand it. Most times we never knew what the male artists were getting. So how can you say you weren't getting paid—you were getting paid what you said and that you demanded. So whether or not it was as much as male artists got, or less, who knows. But the industry in general, when it came to female workers on what we call lay jobs, no, they were never paid equally. And they're still fighting to get paid equally. So that's an ongoing thing. But in terms of was it harder or not harder for a female as an entertainer, you got what you demanded. If you didn't demand respect, then you didn't get respect.

### Rounder Records

Rounder came in around, I want to say, late '85, '86. To be honest with you, I didn't know Rounder Records existed.

I was in between labels. I really wasn't seeking a recording label, and I don't how Rounder found out about me. I guess from being at Jazz Fest, because I had been playing Jazz Fest every year from 1974—even before I had moved back to the city I had been part of the Jazz Fest lineup. And Scott Billington actually came to the house, here, and talked with my husband and I about being a part of the Rounder label. And we've been a part of the Rounder label ever since.

What I appreciated with the Rounder label, Scott would always come and talk with my husband and I about whatever project that he had in mind. He would run it by us and get our opinion of it and what we thought before he would move forward with it. And the respect that he gave me as an artist, and my husband as my husband and manager, I appreciated it. Because at least he was not trying to take over and to just push anything on us that we weren't comfortable with. We still have that same working relationship, even though they've changed hands a couple of times since my last recording.

Rounder is the label that really took care of the mature artist who had been in the business for a long time and had not gotten any kind of national recognition the way they should have. I mean, I'd had some national coverage, but nothing of the magnitude of some others out there. And these were artists who had great voices. Johnny Adams—when they say "the singing canary," that was not a falsified title. He could sing. As we say in the country, he could *sing*. And he had such a beautiful personality—to have not been known nationally. So, when Rounder came along and recorded Johnny, Johnny started getting the recognition and being in areas where he had not toured before. And people realized that here was a guy who could sing.

They had a second Johnny Adams, by the way, in California, which I busted. Because I told him, I said,

"No, you're not the real thing." But Johnny was the real McCoy. And he was a very pleasant gentleman. It was because of Rounder that he did some European tours. He was just getting the recognition he deserved at the time of his death. But they came to New Orleans, and they were recording artists of that caliber, who had been around—great entertainers with great voices who had never really been put on wax and had never gotten that recognition in other countries. Rounder would send stuff to Europe and what-have-you.

The first album that I had with Rounder won an award in Europe. I wasn't aware that it had, but it did. When I got over there, then I realized that it had won an award. So, yeah—they reintroduced me to Europe. I had been to Europe in the '60s, but they reintroduced me to Europe along with Johnny Adams, Walter Washington, who went over there several times and got to be well known and liked. And you know, the Europeans just eat you up. In fact, they told me about musicians who was on recording sessions that I didn't even remember the names of. Rounder reintroduced us to that situation, and a younger audience as well.

**Changes in the Industry**

The music industry in general is going through some radical changes now. I mean I'm getting letters and emails and phone calls where—I have a seven-piece band. And invariably they will ask me, "Well, can you come with four pieces? Can you come with five pieces?" "No. You want Irma Thomas and her show, you want Irma Thomas with what she comes with." If you can't afford it, then I just don't work.

I've worked with no less than six musicians in my entire time in my career—I've always had at least five or six musicians on stage. When I work with other people's bands, whatever they have was their business. But the band that my husband put together for me, it's always been at least six musicians—we've always carried at least two horns. For a while we carried one, but then we realized when you're doing rhythm and blues, most true rhythm and blues bands have at least two horns—a trumpet and a sax of some kind. And so that's the kind of music I've been doing for these last fifty-some-odd years. Why would I want to go with less? You know. It just makes no sense. I have seven musicians. If your space does not accommodate me, don't book me.

Or if your budget doesn't—don't book me. I can't ask seven guys to be loyal to me if I'm not going to be loyal to them. And that's my mindset. I mean, I've missed a lot of work because I've refused to come with less musicians. I mean, the guys would probably not be angry. They would probably understand. But most of these guys been with me for over twenty years. I find it a slap in the face that all of a sudden I'm getting work and they want me to show up with just five. To me, that's not rhythm and blues anyway. I don't want to use a synthesizer horn, in lieu of a real, true trumpet player or saxophone player. To me, that's not the true music. Because all those little glitches and little mistakes that happens on the stage, that's part of the ambiance of the music. You don't get that when you have this stuff on the keyboard. It's not the same.

I'm not a clubber. I don't go out a lot. So there may be a whole lot going on out there I may not be aware of. I do know that, overall, the music scene has changed in terms of recording albums and releasing CDs, albums on CDs, and getting them purchased the way people used to buy music. The only generation, I think, that's still buying that way would be those of us who are now in our late '50s, '60s, and

'70s, who still prefer having that solid piece of something our hands that we can put on when we want to—not having to download it off of some situation on the Internet. But a lot of music now is out there on the Internet, and they're fighting with the people in Congress, although Congress got a whole other thing going on. But anyway they're fighting for us to get paid for that, because a lot of stuff that is being downloaded, the artists are not getting paid for. So I think they came to some negotiations on getting that resolved. I don't know if it's completed as of yet, but that's going to make a difference. And it has made a difference, in how record companies look at artists in terms of producing them and promotion. A lot of artists who are coming on board now come with the whole package already done, and the record company either chooses or not chooses to accept the total package and connect their label to it, or the artist is just doing it on their own and putting it out there. But it's a whole 'nother scene now. It's not so much going into the studio and coming up with just a good solid recording; it has to have a theme of some kind.

My last couple of CDs had to have a theme. I mean, "Simply Grand" was a theme—I did songs with all these various great piano players. They did another one; they released one called my fiftieth anniversary, the fifty years I've been in the business. Everything has to have a theme now. What happened to just going into the studio, getting some great songs, recording them, and putting them out there? I don't get it.

It really has changed drastically, and I don't know if it's a good thing or not.

### We're All Getting Older

Some of the guys in the band use charts because we're all getting older. And even me—I even carry my lyrics to songs that I've recorded in the past, because oftentimes we play venues where the people will ask for songs I haven't sung in four or five years, maybe even longer. I remember them musically, but lyrically I may forget a few lines here and there. So I have an iPad now. And most of my lyrics are in the iPad. I don't hide it. I've recently bought a stand that hooks onto a mic stand. I need that. I'm not twenty anymore. This brain don't retain like it used to. And I don't pretend about it. I mean, you know, it is what it is. You keep waking up, you get older, some things you're going to remember, some things you won't.

People are not dumb. They are aware that we are a world of aging people. And you learn through that aging process that some things don't come the way it used to. You're not any worse off; you're just slowing down a bit. And some things function differently now. I embrace it, you know. Because there's always the alternative.

I was never a smoker or drinker. The only thing that I find that I must do if I have a tour where I'm going to be out there for more than seven days, say up to two weeks—I have to have at least one day off during that week to relax and really rest. Because the tireder I get, my vocals get tired. That's with anything. And that even from when I was younger. That was one of the things I learned the hard way—that if you're going to be doing a tour out there, one day of the week you need to be off. Period. You need that rest. And so if it's a two-week span, and I'm only doing one show, I can get by. But if I'm doing two shows a night, I need a night off. At least one; a minimum of one night off. But other than that, I don't do anything special. I just try to get as much sleep as I can when I'm working. I don't eat within five hours of a gig, because my digestive system is slower. And I'm not like opera singers—I can't eat a full meal and walk out there on that stage and sing. I can do it, but

I would be limited as to my ability to get the breath that I need to hold the notes that I want to hold. So I have my little routine, that I just don't eat within five hours of a gig. Now, I might eat like a horse when I get through. But I'm mindful of those little things that I know are necessary for me to give the performance that I want to give.

So I embrace the aging process, because I think it's a wonderful thing. Because there are things I know now that I didn't know then. If I had known them then, I probably would be a totally different person.

## Choosing Songs

I've always chose songs from storyline. Most of my songs have good storylines. I look for songs that have both a good storyline and a great melody to it. Because I have to live with that.

## The Lion's Den

My husband had a club that I performed in, the Lion's Den. It started out as a rehearsal place, and it got to be popular, so we started charging admission. We said, "We can make some money with this." It lasted up until Katrina, when we just decided we didn't want to be club owners anymore.

The club started in the late '80s. We had it like about twenty-five, twenty-six years or so. It was a long time. In fact, at the time Katrina hit, we didn't want to be in the club business anymore. We were trying to sell the business. Because we had employees, we didn't want to close it down. We were doing pretty decent. We wasn't making beaucoup money, but we had our regulars who would come there every day and make their demands on what they wanted to eat.

But it was a friendly situation, so when Katrina came along, we just decided, you know what—I don't think we need to go back into this. Because then I got busy, right after Katrina—I mean everybody who knew what had happened to New Orleans, a lot of the New Orleans artists got a lot of work right after that. Because they were trying to help us get back on our feet. So we wouldn't have had time to really spend taking care of a club. The other side of that was we didn't have any employees that we knew of that could really be trusted to leave that situation behind and be on the road as much as we were on the road at the time. So we just decided no more club business.

I miss it to some extent. It kept me up on my lyrics, because I was singing them more often. But other than that, I don't miss the hassles of being in the business. No. Because it is a twenty-four-hour situation. Even though we didn't always stay open twenty-four hours. But there were some occasions we stayed open twenty-four hours, and trust me—we felt it the next day. But we had good customers. We had people who would come, would sit, and get comfortable, and wouldn't go home. You know—if you were there and spending your money, why would we want to put you out? You came to have a good time, and you're having a good time. Why would I want to tell you it's time to go? For what? Whenever you're ready, you go. And we've had some customers come in and say, "Do we have to leave now?" "No. If you're having a good time and spending your money, have a drink. Enjoy yourself."

## Katrina

We weren't here. We had a job, and it shows you irony—that's why I have strong faith. The irony of it. The only job we had for the month of August took us out of the city. We were in Austin, Texas. We left for the gig that Friday morning. And when we left, the storm was still out there in the Gulf, and it hadn't shown any direct directions as to where it was going to go. So we just assumed, "Okay, we'll go and play our gig, and come back. And then if we still have to prepare for the storm, we will." Well, consequently, the storm made up its mind while we were gone, and the only clothing we had was what we had taken with us for that weekend. We were scheduled to return that Saturday. It didn't happen. We couldn't get back. In fact, we didn't get back into the state of Louisiana until the week after the storm. And the rest is history.

We got back, and we stayed with relatives until we were able to find a place of our own. We wound up buying a house in Gonzales, my husband's hometown. At an astronomical price. But you do what you have to do. We were there for a couple of years—we got back into our home here in New Orleans in 2007. We still have the house, because we would never get out of it what we paid for it. So we just decided to keep it.

Ironically, we had just sent the last payment for our New Orleans house the week before the storm. We had six or seven feet of water in here. The water stayed in this house for three weeks. So by the time my husband was able to come in to look at it, the walls had disintegrated. You could stand here in the front room and see all the way to the backyard. We weren't able to put anything up or to salvage—there was nothing. Everything was the way it was.

And, you know, the force of the water was just astronomical, what water can do inside of a building. I used to have a wall unit in my den. Part of it was in here in the front of the house. Another part was somewhere else. I had an étagère case, with the

crown and other awards that I had won, on the wall. We never did find that. None of that stuff was ever recovered. The refrigerator that sits in the corner between the countertop and the wall, the refrigerator was face down in the middle of the floor by the bay window. So, you don't know what the force of the water can do. In the bedroom, ironically, the remote control was on the mattress—we watch TV in the bedroom—the mattress rose up and settled back down. And the couch that was in here, it just rose up and settled back down. The remote was still on the armrest. So, it's just weird how different things reacted to the water within.

I've been living in this city you could say practically all of my life. And we've experienced some really rough weather over those years. I was here as a child in 1947, or was it '46, before they started naming them. In fact, they named that storm—after the storm had left, they decided to call it Audrey, I believe. I was in New Orleans at that time. Then, of course, we've had Betsy, which is another storm. Camille affected the city, but not in the way it affected the Gulf Coast. So we're accustomed to being surrounded by, or within, a hurricane at some point in your life or another.

I still don't say Katrina was the cause of the flooding. It was lack of government supervision that caused the flooding. Because where that levee broke, they had just replaced a bridge on the Old Hammond Highway. Next to that, where they were doing that construction, is a levee. And you're driving pylons in the ground to support the structure of the bridge. And you didn't take the time to check the levee. It was weakened. And that's where that water came in initially. Now, there was another break here downtown here in the Industrial Canal, but that happened because of a barge that was not tied down. So we had two breaks and water was coming in from two directions. But, of course, Katrina got blamed.

But that's the first time we've ever had any flooding. I mean I've lived in this house thirty-one years now. And we had never had any flooding. The street got a little water in it, but we never had any that actually came into the house.

### "It's Home"

People used to ask us, "Why are you moving back?" Why not? It's home. You know. I mean, that storm didn't do us anything; it was the after-effects of what happened that did the damage.

It's home. It's where I grew up. It's where I got my roots. This is the place where I'm comfortable. If you know what home represents to you, then you understand when I say it's home. It's your comfort zone. It's where you're comfortable at. Even though I lived away for six years, where did I wind up? Back in New Orleans. It's my comfort zone.

Unlike a lot of people I could have probably made a stay in California, probably would have gotten along pretty good with it. But I would have eventually ended up back in New Orleans. No matter whether I'd gotten married or not, I probably would have eventually wound up back. Because there was a difference in the atmosphere of the total living situation. I mean I was okay—I had a home, I had a car, I was okay. I had a job. In fact, I had two jobs, because I was working weekends doing singing and doing my Montgomery Ward thing. But it wasn't New Orleans—meaning that camaraderie, that close neighborly atmosphere that you have here they don't have anywhere else.

We have a lot of new people who moved in, and they've gotten infected. So, evidently whatever it is here—it's either in the water or in the food—but when you move here you become a part of that situation. In fact, that's what has drawn a lot of the younger, and not so much younger, but the newer people who moved to New Orleans since Katrina, who've decided to make this home. It's that—that's what made them want to be here. When people say, "Well, what is it?" We don't know what it is, but whatever it is, we've had people who I know personally—there's a lady who came to the Lion's Den. I think her first time was in the early '90s. She came down to Mardi Gras. And she came by the club, and we were doing shows there—I think I did one show and then we decided to stop because people wouldn't come in until after the parade, and by that time everybody was tired; so we stopped doing them. But then she came back again, for Jazz and Heritage Festival. Well, then, instead of going home after the Jazz and Heritage Festival to stay, she went home and got a U-Haul truck, and the next thing we know, she was living here. And she said, "I don't know what it is, but I had to come back. I needed to live here."

When you grow up somewhere, you're influenced by your surroundings. And that's just a normal progression. You never think about it as a person living here and growing up, you never think about how much it has affected you. It's just what it is. You know—your neighborhood is part of you are, and the things that happen to you in your neighborhood is a part of your growth. So, it's just what it is.

So whatever it is that draws people here—the only thing I can say is that we don't know strangers. It's like you come to New Orleans and you can actually get some directions that make sense. You know, we give you landmarks, tell you how to get to where you're going. Most people have invited people to dinner and have a drink together. If you're in a bar and talking, you may get offered a drink, and they may tell you the spots that they like. It's that openness to make you feel comfortable here that I think draws a lot of people back. And the neighborhoods are just different. I mean there are folk who live in Chicago that don't know what their neighbors' names are. But here we know at least one or two of your neighbors by name. Now we may not learn them all, but we know them by looks; we know that that's our neighbor. I'm terrible with names. But I do know my neighbors. I know the folk who live in my neighborhood. And when they need help we gather together as neighbors to help each other when we can. And that's the way the city is—the city as a whole. We've helped other cities, and cities have helped us. But it has always been the norm for New Orleans as opposed to other cities who in recent years are discovering what it is like to need somebody's help. That's always been the way for New Orleans. It's always been that way. They call it "the Big Easy"—it's not so much that it's easy, it's just the way, and who, we are.

# BRAZELLA BRISCOE

Gospel singer

President and tenor voice, Zion Harmonizers

[ Interviewed October 5, 2013, in the Bywater, New Orleans ]

In March 2014, the Zion Harmonizers celebrated their seventy-fifth anniversary as a group, first with an event at the Joy Theater on Canal Street, then at the Ephesus Church on Delachaise Street. Almost certainly New Orleans's longest-running gospel group, the Zion Harmonizers have, since their beginning, been devoted to the sacred. For decades, too, they've successfully negotiated their way between the sacred and the secular, performing at venues such as Jazz Fest and the House of Blues—not an easy task for a gospel group.

They began in 1939, taking their name from the Zion City neighborhood, a small section in Mid-City. According to the New Zion City Preservation Association's website, "From the 1900s to the 1980s, Zion City was a self-sustaining neighborhood, with restaurants, sweet shops, grocery stores, fruit and vegetable stands, fresh chickens, barber shops, beauty salons, seamstresses, mechanic shops, carpenters, coin-operated laundry, barrooms. We had a community park and even a law office." Like many other New Orleans neighborhoods, it was also a musical incubator. Irma Thomas lived there for a time. And there, in the 1930s, Alberta French Johnson formed the Southern Harps, a celebrated all-woman group that patterned their close harmonies on the

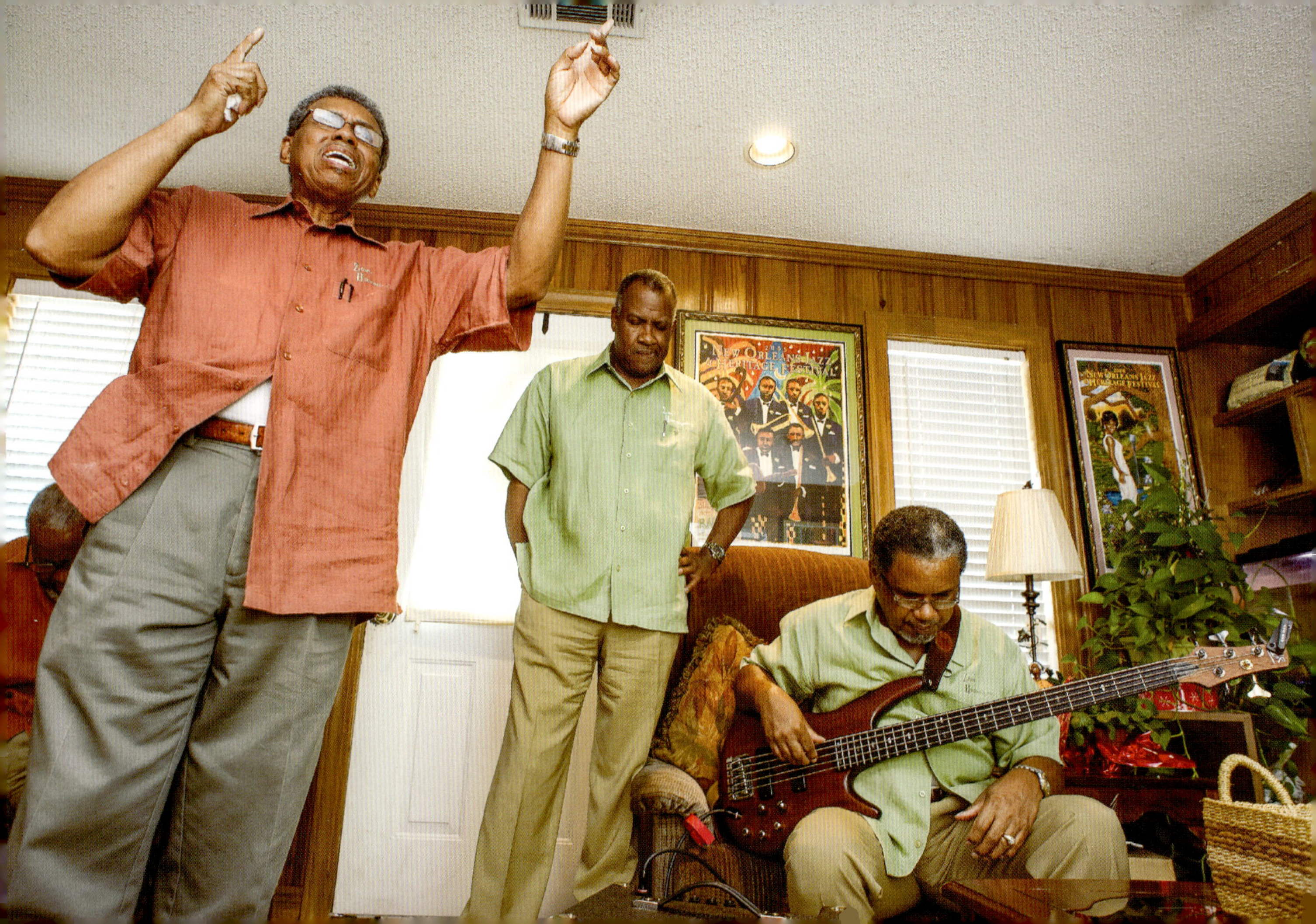

male quartet sound that was growing in popularity in black music, both sacred and secular. In 1939 a group of young men (including Johnson's nephew Benjamin Maxon) who enjoyed street-corner harmonizing became the Zion Harmonizers; for years, they opened shows for the Southern Harps. Maxon left the group in 1948 to devote himself to preaching. At that point, Sherman Washington, who had joined the Harmonizers in 1942, when he was fifteen, took over as the group's leader. Washington led the Zion Harmonizers for nearly seventy years, until his death in 2011.

In an interesting twist, Benjamin Maxon's brother, Joe Maxon, formed another gospel group in 1947, calling it the Zion City Harmonizers. With the brothers Chuck and Chick Carbo as members, that group later performed gospel music as the Delta Southernaires. Then, in 1953, Cosimo Matassa convinced them to cross over to the secular side. The Delta Southernaires became the Spiders, and they had a number of successful records, including "I Didn't Want to Do It," which reached number 3 on national R&B charts in 1954. The original Zion Harmonizers remained on the sacred side, and that's where they locate themselves today.

Sherman Washington was a pillar of New Orleans's gospel music community. In 1956 he began a long run spinning gospel discs and announcing programs on local radio, first on WMRY and then on WYLD (940 AM—"We're WYLD for Jesus!"). When the New Orleans Jazz and Heritage Festival began in Congo Square in 1970, the Zion Harmonizers performed, thanks to his initiative. Washington and his group became fixtures at that festival: he convinced the organizers to create, and have him program, the Gospel Tent, an annual showcase for New Orleans groups. For many visitors the Gospel Tent is Jazz Fest's peak experience, despite the international popular music stars who perform elsewhere on the festival grounds.

Following Washington's death, Brazella Briscoe, who had been a member for about a quarter of a century, singing tenor, became the Zion Harmonizers' president and leader. Gracious, committed, devout, and enthusiastic, Briscoe invited Gary and me to a Saturday afternoon rehearsal. Hosted by Shirley Washington, Sherman's widow, the group continues to practice at the house in Boutte where they rehearsed for many years. There, dressed in color-coordinated linen shirts, the Harmonizers worked on arrangements of songs such as "People Get Ready," led by Briscoe's sweet tenor. They discussed upcoming performances and enjoyed each other's company. It was a privilege to be there.

Later that afternoon, Brazella Briscoe came to the Bywater apartment where we were staying, and I did this interview. Briscoe talks about the group's history and his experience first as a member, then as the leader. Born in 1948, he grew up in Gretna, across the river from New Orleans, and he loved gospel music. He cites the Dixie Hummingbirds, who began in Greenville, South Carolina, and the Zion Harmonizers as two of his favorite groups on the radio. He was singing with another group when Nolan Washington, Sherman's younger brother, also a Zion Harmonizer, invited him to join. With the group, he has toured Europe, performed for years at a weekly gospel brunch at the New Orleans branch of the House of Blues, performed at Jazz Fest and other festivals. All the while, though, the churches, many of them small, at home have been their mainstay.

A fine documentary film, *By and By: New Orleans Gospel at the Crossroads,* looks at black gospel in New Orleans, focusing on another quartet, the Electrifying Crown Seekers. What it shows is happening in many black communities. Not surprisingly, the world of African American gospel has changed considerably since 1939. In the 1930s quartets singing tight harmony would "wreck the house" in neighborhood churches. Some groups, notably the Golden Gate Quartet, achieved national prominence. That old quartet style has endured, but newer forms of gospel music have threatened to supplant it. Charismatic soloists and choir leaders such as Andrae Crouch, what is called urban/contemporary gospel, and other more recent forms, often deeply influenced by (and sounding pretty much identical to) contemporary forms of African American popular music, are very much in fashion. There's an irony in the fact that much of today's African American gospel music sounds like contemporary popular music, because, historically, much of American popular music is itself derived from or influenced by African American gospel music. Add to that the fact that Katrina displaced many of the Zion Harmonizers' and other quartets' traditional constituents, inner-city black New Orleanians who were unable to return home after the storm. In *By and By*, one singer estimates that before Katrina there were thirty or forty gospel quartets in New Orleans. Now, he says, there are perhaps fifteen. In that context, the singing of the Zion Harmonizers, and their very long run in New Orleans, makes them a national treasure. But they keep on keeping on. In March 2014 they released a CD, *Bringing in the Sheaves*, their first in about fifteen years. As Brazella Briscoe says, let's look forward to their hundredth anniversary.

## Origins

I'm the leader and the president of the Zion Harmonizers. The group was organized back in 1939 by the late pastor Benjamin Maxon. I believe he stayed with the group about two or three years. I think Pastor Maxon and the rest were around sixteen, seventeen years old—they started as a childhood group. There was a neighborhood, I'm told, called Zion City, in the Gert Town section of New Orleans. So the name actually came from the city itself, or the suburb, called Zion City. That's how it started.

Pastor Maxon's aunt was Miss Alberta Johnson. She had the Southern Harps. That was her group. She taught them to harmonize. They'd go to her house and rehearse, and they got pretty good. And

they started opening up programs for her, and they started to do a little traveling with her.

I'm told after about maybe three or four years Pastor Maxon went into the ministry and turned the group over to Sherman Washington. Sherman Washington was here from that time until the time of his death, which was about two years ago, in 2011. Sherman was here for about seventy years. Dearly beloved and dearly missed. His one constant request of me was to keep it going. And by the grace of God, we're going to do that. We enjoy every moment of it.

I am told that Sherman was about seventeen years old. The story is he was working at Higgins Shipyard along with Pastor Benjamin Maxon, who worked there also. And one day at lunch they started a conversation. Pastor Maxon told him that he had a group and they sang, and invited Sherman. And he went. Sherman just loved it. It was love at first sight, I guess. He stayed there from that time until the time of his death.

Sherman's father was a Baptist minister. Morning Star Baptist Church, in Thibodaux, Louisiana, was his father's church. So he came from a real religious background. He also had his brother, Nolan Washington, who sang with him for quite a while too, until the time of his death.

I know there was another group here, and they were Zion City Harmonizers, too. One of their members was Joe Maxon, Pastor Benjamin Maxon's brother. So, maybe they just ventured off from the Zion City Harmonizers. I think Sherman might have changed the name, left the "City" out. I heard Sherman kind of mention about changing the name. Maybe it went from the Zion City to just the Zion Harmonizers. The other group went on to sing, I think, kind of rock 'n' roll, or that type of music. Then Joe Maxon came back to our group. I know he was



✦ Zion Harmonizers rehearsal, Boutte, Louisiana

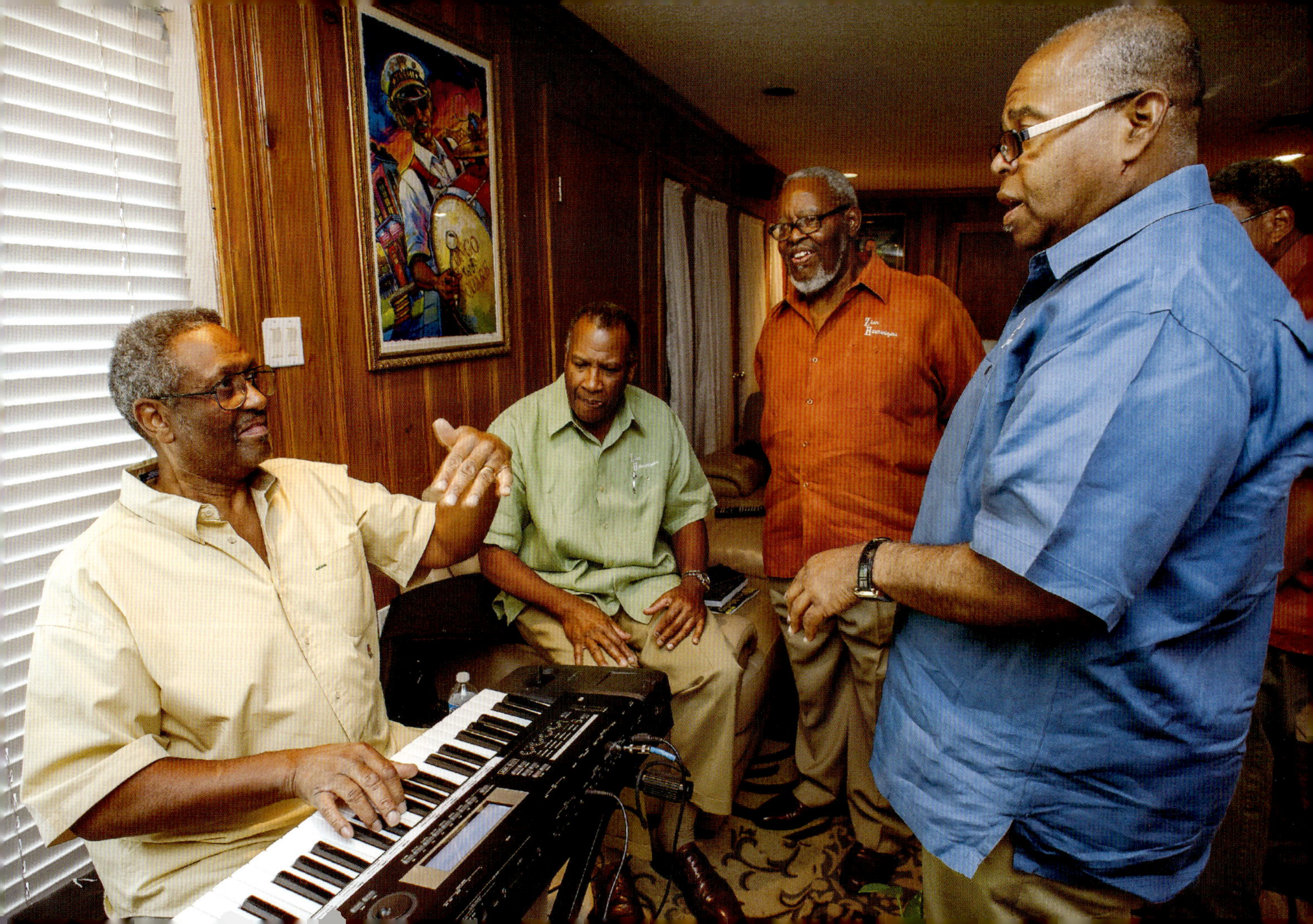

with Sherman for quite a while, even after Sherman took over. I think he's actually the only original one living. He's still living somewhere with his daughter. I heard him sing about maybe five, six years ago. Beautiful voice. Beautiful tenor. So, hopefully, he's still alive; I think he is.

Next year will be our seventy-fifth year, anniversary. And that's a long time. That's a feat. We've had some wonderful times, and we've seen some wonderful places. They tell me there are some old photographs, and I need to start getting some together. We do miss Sherman. But we've got to continue on.

And to still be singing four-part harmony—that's exceptional. Because for some reason or another the bass line is not written into today's music. I don't know any gospel groups, not locally, for sure, that has a bass in it. That's gone. But we just love it. Man, when you put that bottom in, it's different.

## Family and Musical Background

I was born in 1948, July 20. Next year, I'll be sixty-six, and I'm going to get my social security. But I'll still be doing something. I drive eighteen-wheelers and stuff like that.

I'm from Gretna, right across the river. I was born in good old Charity Hospital. Everybody was born at Charity. I had always sang. My mother had a beautiful voice. My uncles could all play some type of instrument. One could play guitar and accordion. But they tell me that their mother, my grandmother, was a music teacher. I never met her—never met any of my grandparents. No grandfather, no grandmother on either side. They were all deceased—which I find strange. You hardly find anybody that never met any of their grandparents. But that was the case.

There were seven of us—four boys, three girls. My brother was the oldest; I was the second-oldest. My mother died of childbirth with my youngest brother. He was born May the first; she died May the 18th. My father raised us all, except him; he was just a newborn, and he couldn't handle him. His sister raised him.

My dad did several things. He was a carpenter by trade. But he could do a lot of other stuff. He could do plumbing; he could do concrete work. So, as far as building a house, he could do the whole thing—plumbing and all. You don't see that anymore, you know. But he was a carpenter by trade. He also worked for a fellow that had a milk distributorship, or whatever you call it—Borden's. They used to go load the trucks. Then they'd go to the ice house, and they'd load the ice on it. Wasn't no refrigerated trucks, back then. Good old ice. He worked there for years.

My dad was nine years older than my mother. The story he told me, he met her when she was seventeen. She had lived on this side of the river. We had an aunt that lives on Chestnut Street. She had two brothers that were living in Gretna, and when they were ill, she came to see about them. And my dad met her. And that was it. But it was still ten years before my oldest brother was born. They prayed for children; couldn't get nothing. And then when we started coming, we started coming—boom!

## "We Always Loved Gospel Music"

We always loved gospel music. My dad would always play gospel music. And we would hear these groups on the radio, and we would sort of imitate them. We could always hear the Dixie Hummingbirds and the Zion Harmonizers. My brother would say, "Well, I'm a Zion Harmonizer." And I would say, "Well, I'm a

✦ Procession, Sunday service at Ebenezer Baptist Church, S. Claiborne Avenue

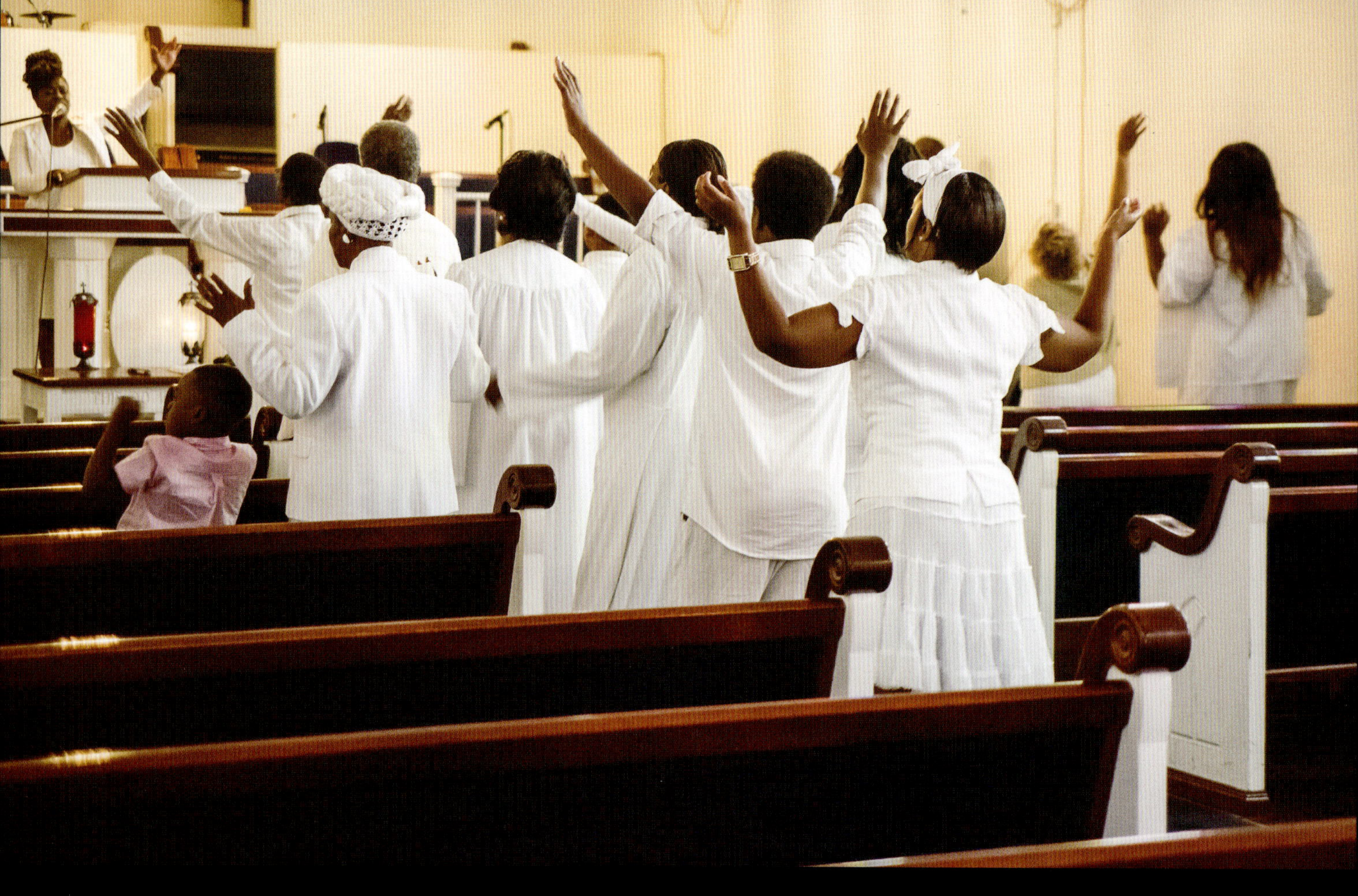

Dixie Hummingbird." Or vice versa. Never knowing, never having the slightest iota that one day I would actually be a member of the Zion Harmonizers.

I was Baptist—my mother used to belong to a church, and she would take us. We would go to church—every Sunday morning we had to go to church. We had to go to Sunday school. Reverend Ballantine was the pastor's name. My mother would see that we'd go. And then she would go to her church sometimes. So, I did grow up in church.

I had met Pastor Benjamin Maxon several times because he was a pastor. His church was right, even to this day, on Jackson Avenue. So we used to go to his church quite a bit and sing. And sometimes he would come out and talk with us, and every once in a while he would sing a little song with us.

My dad hardly went to church. But he studied his Bible. He knew the Bible. My mother and him was married so long, like I said, before we were born, ten years, and then after seven children, she died. And he started to drink. He still raised us, took care of us. Had some friends who would help us out, you know. But he would always—we discussed the Bible. He would tell us things about Job and about Paul and Agrippa. He was a studious fellow. His dad was a professor at Southern University, an architect. Man, he used to show us his tools—protractors, and all of that. But my dad, he finished ninth grade. But he could read. And he had books, books, books. So there was nothing that you could talk about that he couldn't hold a good conversation with you, a knowledgeable conversation.

Then I met a fellow; he was singing gospel. He worked at a flower nursery across the street from my house. We became friends. He could cook; he'd bring food from his house, cook real good. And I would go, and he would give us some of his lunch, and some of the food—corn bread and stuff. So we became friends, and he was singing in a gospel quartet. And then my dad started letting me go stay with him sometimes, you know, back and forth, back home, and to his house. He started singing. When I got nineteen, he started joining little groups of young fellows. Then he brought me in to sing with them. And I've just been singing ever since, you know.

### "I've Done a Little Bit of Everything"

I've done a little bit of everything. I started out driving heavy equipment—bulldozers and front-end loaders, motor patrols, oil distributors. I worked for the City of New Orleans for fifteen years. But I really wanted—my daddy always had a truck, but not to a large degree, like eighteen-wheelers. He would have straight trucks with stake bodies and stuff like that. On the side, he would haul rags and aluminum, and metals, and all that kind of stuff—paper. I always liked being around trucks.

So around 1982, I bought my own truck. Never had been on the road. Never had been away from home a lot. Not at all, really. When I got opportunity to buy one, my wife said, "Why don't you go try it? Drive for somebody. You may not even like it." Well, at that time, I didn't want to hear anything. Next thing she know, a $66,300 truck was sitting in front of the house. Brand spanking new. And lo and behold, after about two weeks I realized I had made a grave mistake. I should have taken her advice, but I didn't. They saw me coming. I was green and young, willing to pay more for the truck than I should have paid— paid more for the down payment than I should have paid. And I think they just thought they would get this money and eventually take it from me, and then

let somebody have it for little or nothing. Because it's a tax write-off, and insurance going to pay it, make it good. So everybody would be happy—except me.

## Becoming a Zion Harmonizer

About twenty-six years ago, I was with another group, and we had a radio broadcast every Saturday morning. The Zion Harmonizers were about to go abroad. They were going to Switzerland. So they came down and, you know, we would go to each other's broadcasts and just to make a few announcements. Nolan Washington, Sherman's brother, came, and we let him make some announcements. And me just joking, I said, "Hey man, why don't you let Bowie stay home?" Howard Bowie was their first tenor—oh, he knew music. He was taught from an early age, classical and what have you. I said, "Why don't you let Bowie stay home, and I'll go sing tenor?" And we had a laugh.

When I finished my broadcast, I went outside, and Nolan was still there waiting. I was surprised. I thought he left. He said, "I need to talk to you." He said, "Man, why don't you come and sing with us? We'd love to have you." I said, "Oh man, I can't sing with y'all. I don't know the chords and stuff like that." He said, "Man, we can teach you."

I kind of thought about it, you know, and I said, "All right."

So, they went over to Switzerland, and the tenor singer that they had—I think he sang second tenor—he died over in Switzerland. They had to ship his body back. So after the wake and the funeral, I went to my first rehearsal with them in September. I think it was September the 7th. That's when I actually got with them. And they began to teach me.

I came with them just before their fiftieth anniversary. I think I was here six months before their fiftieth anniversary. Sherman was here. Nolan, his brother, was here. Howard Bowie was here. There was a fellow named Louis Jones, from Thibodaux. Nolan knew him and got him to come sing bass. He was here. We had a guitar player named Willie Williams, plays a lot like Howard Carroll with the Dixie Hummingbirds. He really could play chords and notes; he was gifted. So he was here, and he kind of was instrumental in bringing me here, also.

So that was my initial meeting with the older ones.

## Singing God's Praises around the World

I can't think of anything in the world that I would rather be doing than singing God's praises. I just love it. I just love it. And we've been to a lot of places. We've been to Rome, Italy. We opened up in Rimini, Italy, for José Carreras. Yeah. They wanted us to come. I think we sent them about four or five CDs, and they picked the songs that they wanted us to sing. We didn't know why. But they said, "Okay, I want you to open with this song; I want you to do this; I want you to peak; and then I want you to bring it back down." And we found out later that if they had let us sing like we wanted, man, José, wouldn't have been happy. Because there were a lot of young people. They wanted the Zion Harmonizers. The Zion Harmonizers! I have some pictures of that. They wanted the Zion Harmonizers, when it was time to get off the stage. So José went on his jet, came in, did his little concert, got his money, got back on his jet, and gone. But we had a wonderful time.

We've sang in some cathedrals that would knock your eyeballs out. Chandeliers big as this room.

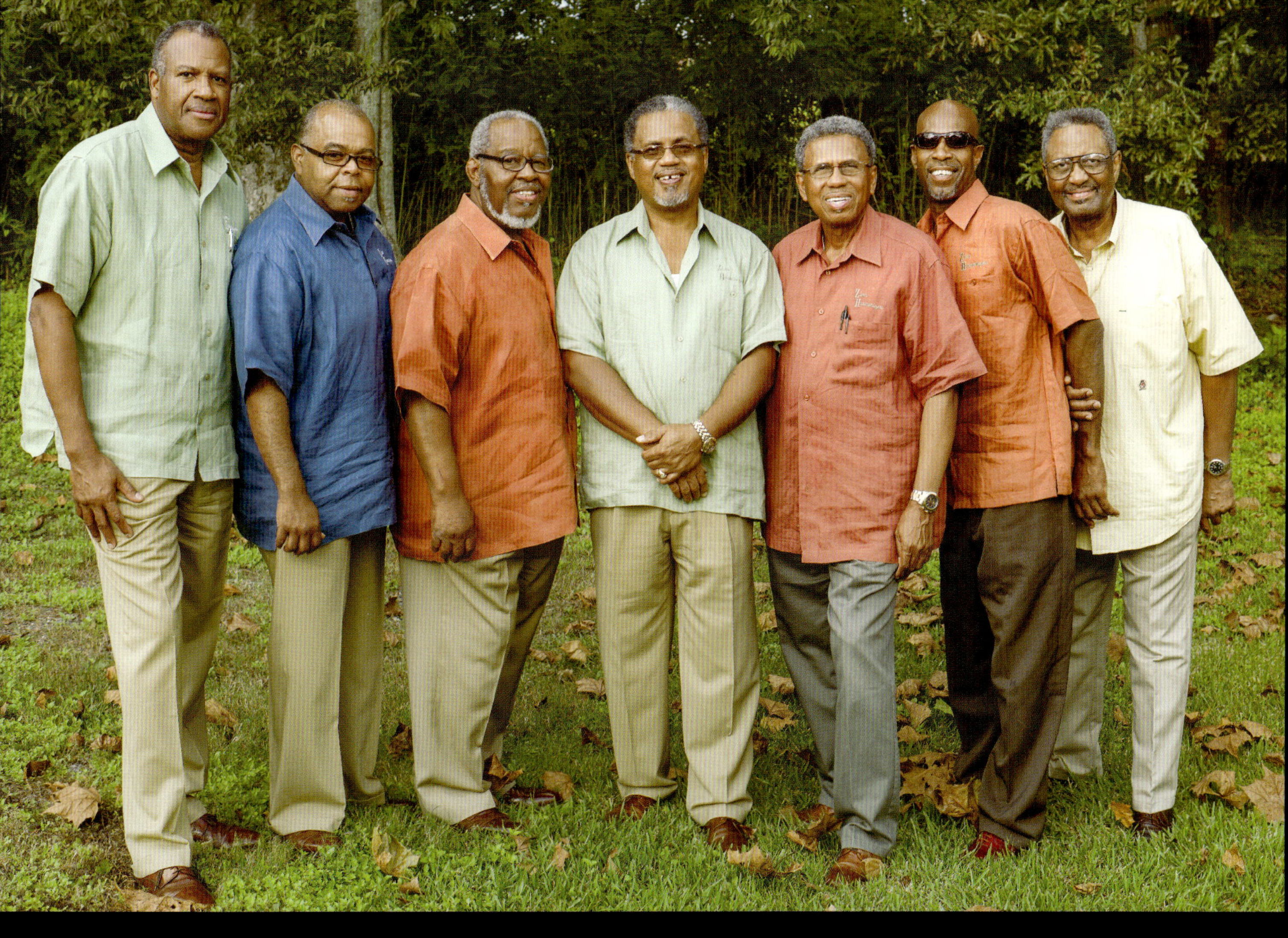



⚜ The Zion Harmonizers outside
the late Sherman Washington's
house, Boutte, Louisiana

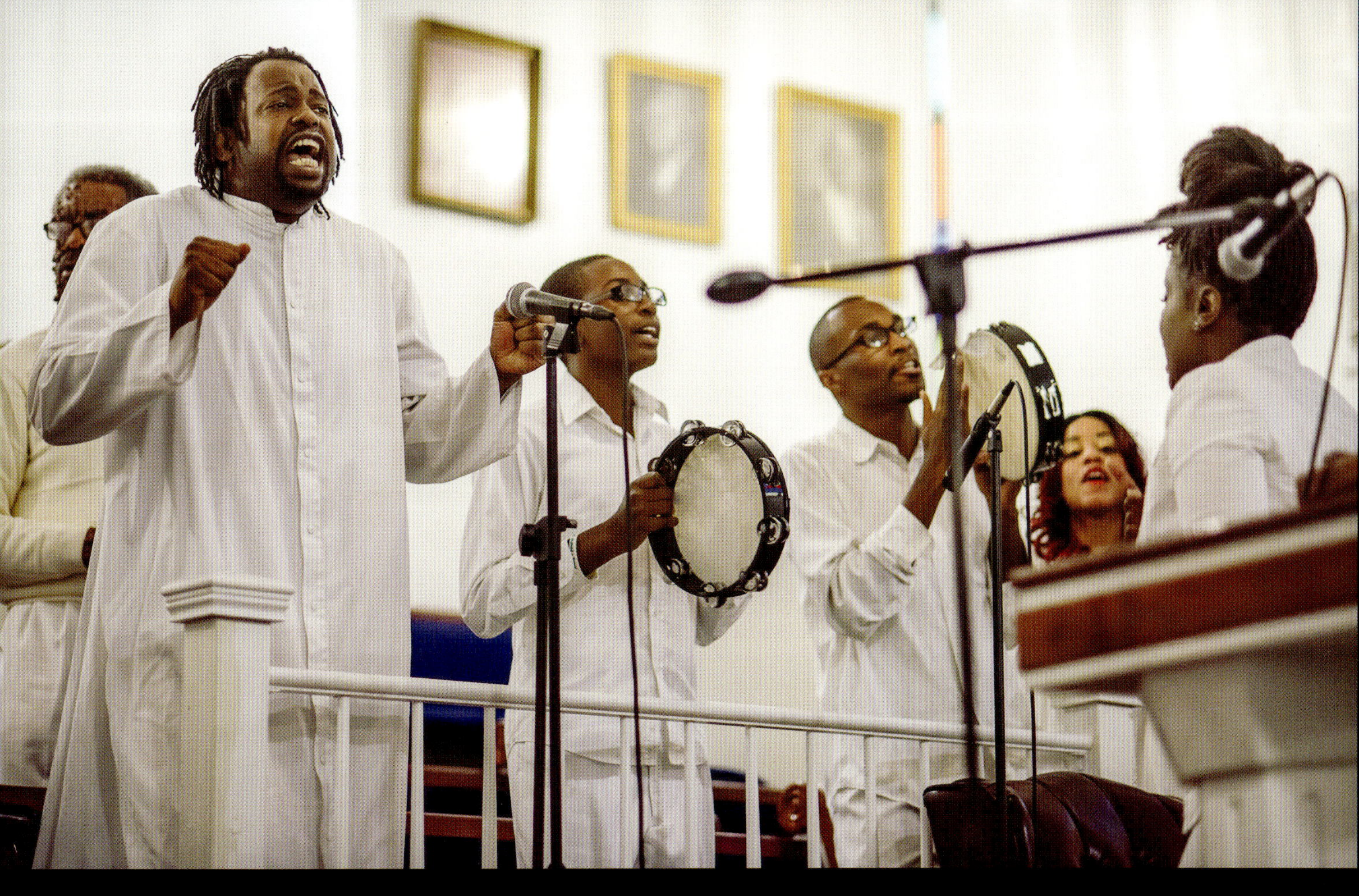



Choir, Ebenezer Baptist
Church, S. Claiborne Avenue

We've seen a lot of things. You know that castle that they show on Walt Disney, Disney World? We've been there. Beautiful place.

But we've seen a lot of things. We sang for the president of Heineken beer. Let's see; was it Amsterdam, Rotterdam? I think it was Amsterdam. A promoter we know brought us over there. We went over there, and we sang one show. It's all they wanted us to do—one show. They treated us like kings, man. Everything paid. It was the same thing when we went to Rimini. Beautiful hotels. But everything is different. They don't do like we do in New Orleans, in the United States. Tear down. They don't demolish; they just re-do. Yeah. They don't tear nothing down. Very seldom do you see them blow up something and stuff like that. But they'll just remodel them. But some beautiful places.

In New Orleans, mostly we sing in churches. We did the House of Blues for around twenty-two years—gospel brunch. We started that. We were there from day one. In fact, we were the only gospel group they had. April was our last show we did.

Man, I've had chances to see places that I never would have seen in my life. We went to Austria, right next to Germany, and we sang for a convent. Man, you talk about creepy. Oh, Lord. Beautiful, quiet— you can hear yourself think. And when we sang in the auditorium—they didn't want any music. We couldn't play the music; we had to sing *a cappella*. But there was a piano, a baby grand, I think. And so our drummer, he's a pianist also. He would just go there, hitting a key, and we'd get our note. And, boy, the acoustics was so great. Two stories; you just had to sing above a whisper, and the music permeated the whole place. Boy, we loved it. Everybody loved it. We only stayed there like the night before

and the night after. Oh man. They tell me that one of the bishops or something, his skull was buried underneath the church, the foundation, you know. And man, we all had our own rooms. So it wasn't like we roomed together. And man, I'm sitting there on the bed, and I could hear—something fall. My pants would fall off the rack. Now, I don't believe in ghosts—well, I believe in the Holy Ghost—and I do know that there are ghosts, like Satan. But I said, "Man, all this noise going on here; I can't wait 'til the morning comes." When the morning come, we took a few pictures with the pastor and left.

We've been on the autobahn in Germany. Man, you can flat out—whatever that car can do. We had a little Volkswagen; we could get it up to about 85, that's all we could do. People passing us like we were standing still. So, we had our own driver assigned to us, took us all over.

We went to a place. Sherman was there; his brother, Nolan, was there; Bowie; me, Louis Jones, our bass singer; our drummer; guitar player. So in our contract, they always put that they had to give us two meals a day. And so when we got to this promoter, he had a big old bag of po' boy sandwiches, you know. So Nolan said, "What's that?" "Well, that's your lunch." I mean it looked just as dry as could be. Nolan say, "No, man. I can't eat that." He said, "Our contract says we're supposed to have two meals a day." He said, "Well, I got the contract here. But it don't say what I have to feed you. It just say I have to . . ." So you know what Nolan said? He said, "I don't think I can sing tonight. I feel real bad. I'm sick. We got to cancel this. I won't be able to do this concert tonight." "Wait a minute!" the promoter said. He took us across the street to, boy, a mega-restaurant. And we had everything—we got anything we wanted.

## The New Orleans Sound

We have a unique sound here. And the Zion Harmonizers has a sound I don't hear any other group. There was one group that used to, I think, sing—you know, they all sang four-part harmony back then. And that was the Messianic Kings. And I still know some of the fellows. The three boys are still living. The sister died. But they kind of crossed over, and they played secular music and different stuff. The oldest brother, he still plays gospel. But they still do some things, you know.

But the New Orleans sound is unique. The Zion Harmonizers sound is unique. A lot of people have kind of moved away from our sound. But we love it. And we've had countless opportunities to sing crossover music. A lot of big hotels, we sang at restaurants. And they want us to come in and sing, and then, well, "Do you all know this song? What about this song?" Say, "Yeah, we know it. But we choose to sing gospel." And we might do a folk song or two. But it's nothing way out, blatant; no, God's been too good to us. We may not ever get rich. But we can be happy. And that's how we look at it.

## Katrina

Katrina was a wakeup call—at least it should have been to most people. It was a sobering factor in our lives. My wife went through Betsy forty years prior to Katrina. She lived down here, right across Industrial Canal. She moved down from Mississippi when she was about five, six years old, with her parents. When Betsy came, the warning was to get out. You might know the story that they broke the levee, dynamited the levee, to keep the poor people from St. Bernard from drowning, but they let the people in New Orleans drown. The water came in. And water came over the rooftops. So many friends drowned down there.

Ever since then, whenever a major hurricane came, we had to go. My wife has the majority of our photos packed up in big old Tupperware drums and stuff. Every time we had to leave, we had to take the pictures. And, man, they were heavy. I had to load this stuff in the car. Go back home; take it out. Load it back in the car. It's still packed up today. But we were able to save a lot of our pictures.

So, here comes Katrina. So, we boarded up the houses. I wanted to leave. I told my wife "I want to get out." My wife wanted to get out—she called me home, and she said, "We need to get out of here." We was at a program at my church, right down in St. Bernard Parish. The winds were blowing pretty good. She said, "We need to get out of here right now." So I said, "Okay, let's get out." Went home, I turned the television on, and usually in the Gulf you'll see a little red circle. But this time that red circle engulfed the whole Gulf! I said, "Oh, yeah. We got to get out of here. Let's go now!" She said, "We got to board up the windows." I said, "Board up nothing. We got to get out of here." "Oh, no."

So I had to go buy plywood and board up all the windows, spend all that money, all that kind of stuff. We didn't know. We thought a day or two, we'd be back home. It took us seven and a half hours to get to Baton Rouge. Seven and a half hours. Got to Baton Rouge—couldn't go any further. I'm tired. So we said we'll try it again, so we're trying to get to Houston, because my daughter lives in Houston. We tried to get to Houston. So we left, went a little further, we got, what, about another fifty miles, not quite fifty, around another forty miles to Breaux Bridge, so tired I couldn't pull anymore. We hunkered down there. The news came on. "Well, the worst is passed, and everything is looking good. We passed all the major damage; things looking good. Everybody should be able to go back home within three or four days." So I said, "Well, that's great." Then I heard, "wait, no—the walls been breached. And the water is coming in.

Man, they sabotaged that. Nothing in the world. You know, you can lie to man. You can't lie to God. The Bible says we stand accountable for every deed we've ever committed. A lot of people drowned, lost their lives. I don't know if you remember, but the federal government wanted to buy a lot of houses around Industrial Canal. We were right around Industrial Canal. They wanted to widen the locks. Well, the people had their little homes, and they didn't want to sell them. "Look, man—we're home-owners. We don't want to sell." So, they weren't able to widen the locks. But I think when Katrina came, that was a number one opportunity to breach that wall. A big old barge came through the wall. What in the world? A barge? For the evacuation, was nothing supposed to be in that channel. But you know with all this going on, man, with his greed, scheming and thinking. I believe with all my heart, and if I'm wrong, Lord forgive me, and we know they dynamited it for Betsy. I think they did the same thing again. They blew that wall. But anyhow, I try to let judgment be with God. I don't want to judge. I have my beliefs. I've got too much sense to accuse anybody. But I really believe, with all my heart, it was sabotaged.

They say we had about twelve feet of water. But I knew we had more, because I built a metal building before Katrina. It was 16 feet to the peak. And it was 50 feet long and 34 feet wide. Because, like I say, I'm in the trucking business. So I wanted something big enough I can pull my truck inside and work on my equipment out of the weather. I fixed my own tires and whatever I had to do. I'd pull inside and do it. I built it like 12 inches above the curb. Which was pretty good. I thought. But when we went for the permit, the city came and said, "Oh, no. You got to raise it up another 12 inches." So, it was 24 inches above the curb, and 16 feet to the peak. And the water came up on that building, my metal building—the water came up about a foot and a half from the peak.

A friend of mine, little young fellow, he was in there. He said, man, he got in water around his ankles, so he went in the kitchen to get a drink of water, and said before he knew it, water was up to his neck. When they broke that levee. So he had to swim out. And he said, "Mr. Briscoe, when I swam out," he said, "I didn't see a house nowhere. The only thing I saw was the top of your metal building." Now this was 16 feet plus another two feet. You're talking about 18 feet. So I knew it had to be at least 16 and a half feet. That's in the Lower Ninth Ward, on Delery Street.

So after Katrina, when all the contractors came in, Shaw, out of Baton Rouge, came in with equipment, and the federal government was pumping money to them hand over fist. They were paying people $3,500 just to come out with a little blue tarp and nail it on your house. You can get a tarp for about five or six dollars. You might spend $6 for nails, and you come put that, and you making $3500. And you know that's not going to last longer than a snowball in hell.

But I learned that God was trying to tell us something. Katrina was a wakeup call.

My daddy was always a person who worked and generated things. You know, if you work and you don't accumulate nothing, you're working in vain. I didn't throw my money away, but I bought equipment. Beautiful equipment. Heavy equipment. Anything I needed to do, I'd go buy that piece of equipment.

But anyhow, I think it was devastating that Katrina came. But like I say, I have to be careful. God didn't send it. You know, God has a permissive will, and he has a divine will. His divine will is that none should perish, but all should come to repentance. And ask for forgiveness, and be saved. But he has a permissive will, like with Job. It wasn't God's will that Job suffer like he did. But he had to prove a point. Katrina was not God's divine will. It was his permissive will. But it should have been a wake-up call.

So, that's my take on Katrina. I think it was a needed and necessary thing, to try to wake up some of God's people. It wasn't good. The Bible says all things work together for good, for them that love the Lord, to them that are the called according to his purpose. It didn't say everything was good. But it says it all works together for good. And that's my take on Katrina.

### Will there be a Hundredth Anniversary?

God willing. I'm going to be sixty-six. Now, Sherman was about eighty-seven years old, I think. He was bedridden for the last four. So when we'd come to his house to rehearse, he'd be in the room. Boy, if we'd miss a note—"Hey! Somebody missed that note!" He could hear it, you know. And he loved it. He would perk up. Oh, man, he would perk up. And so, if God is willing, who knows? I would love to be here. I don't ever want to be here when I'm in the way, where I'm a burden. But if I'm still useful, I want to be here.

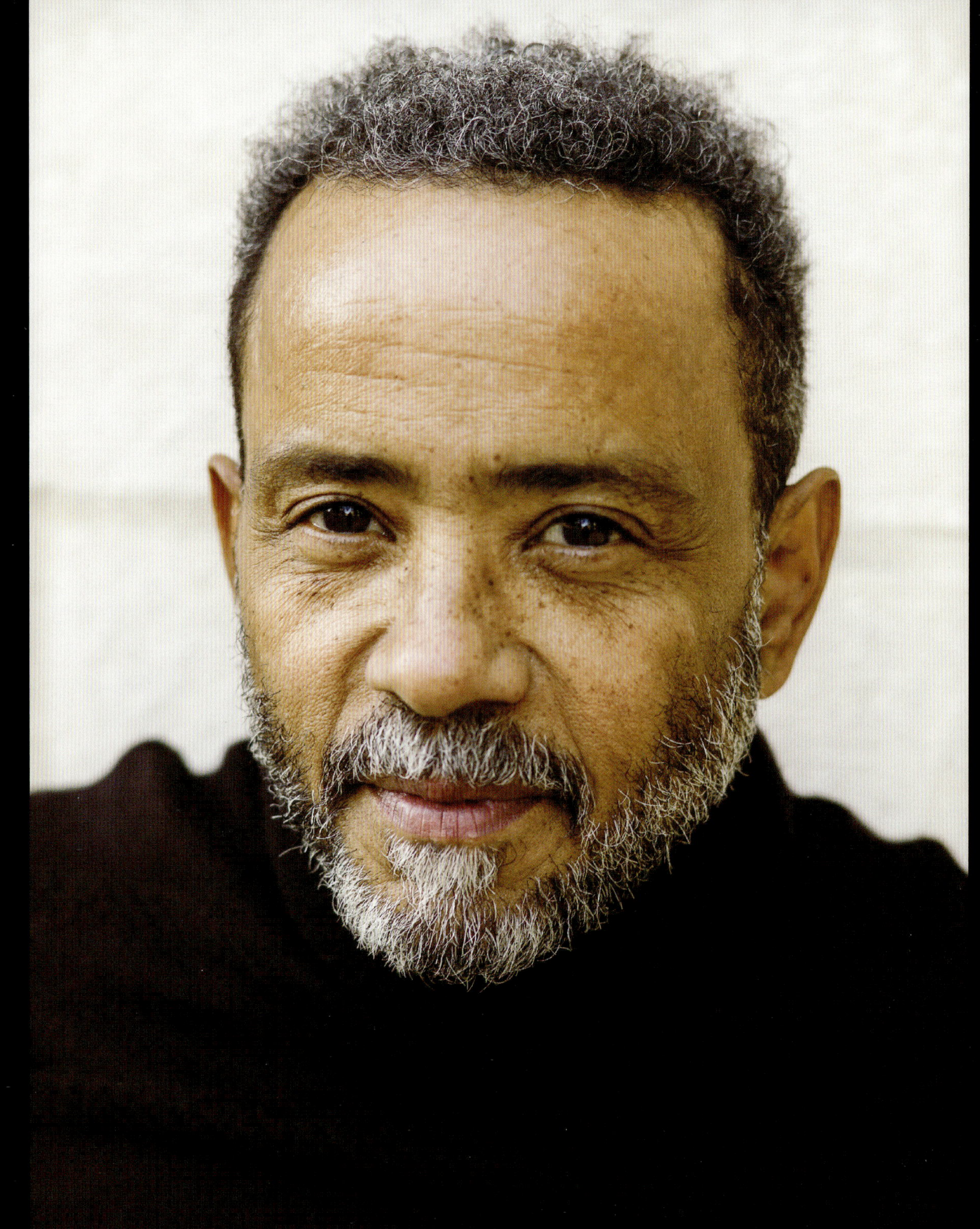

# JOHN BOUTTÉ

Singer

[ Interviewed January 17, 2013, in Uptown, New Orleans ]

At the very last minute, I wasn't sure this interview would happen. I'd contacted John Boutté, asking about doing an interview. His response was gracious, and we set a time to meet at a café one evening. Early on the day of the interview I discovered that the café would be closed that night. There ensued a set of phone calls and a search for another quiet café that would be open. To complicate things more, it turns out that John was recuperating from surgery. Prospects looked grim. Then John asked where my partner, folklorist Jeannie Thomas, and I were staying, and he offered to come to us. That evening, he came Uptown to the house of our friends and hosts, Tamarin Hennebury and Steve Armbruster. So Jeannie and I had the good fortune to sit at the dining room table with John Boutté, a bottle of wine, and a recorder, talking for a couple of hours. Two days later, we saw him at *Offbeat* magazine's Best of the Beat awards ceremony, where he was named, not for the first time—and more than likely not the last—best male vocalist in the world of New Orleans music.

And what a vocalist he is. Although some describe him as a jazz singer, he says he doesn't like classification. His voice is like velvet—simultaneously smooth and textured. He

✤ John Boutté

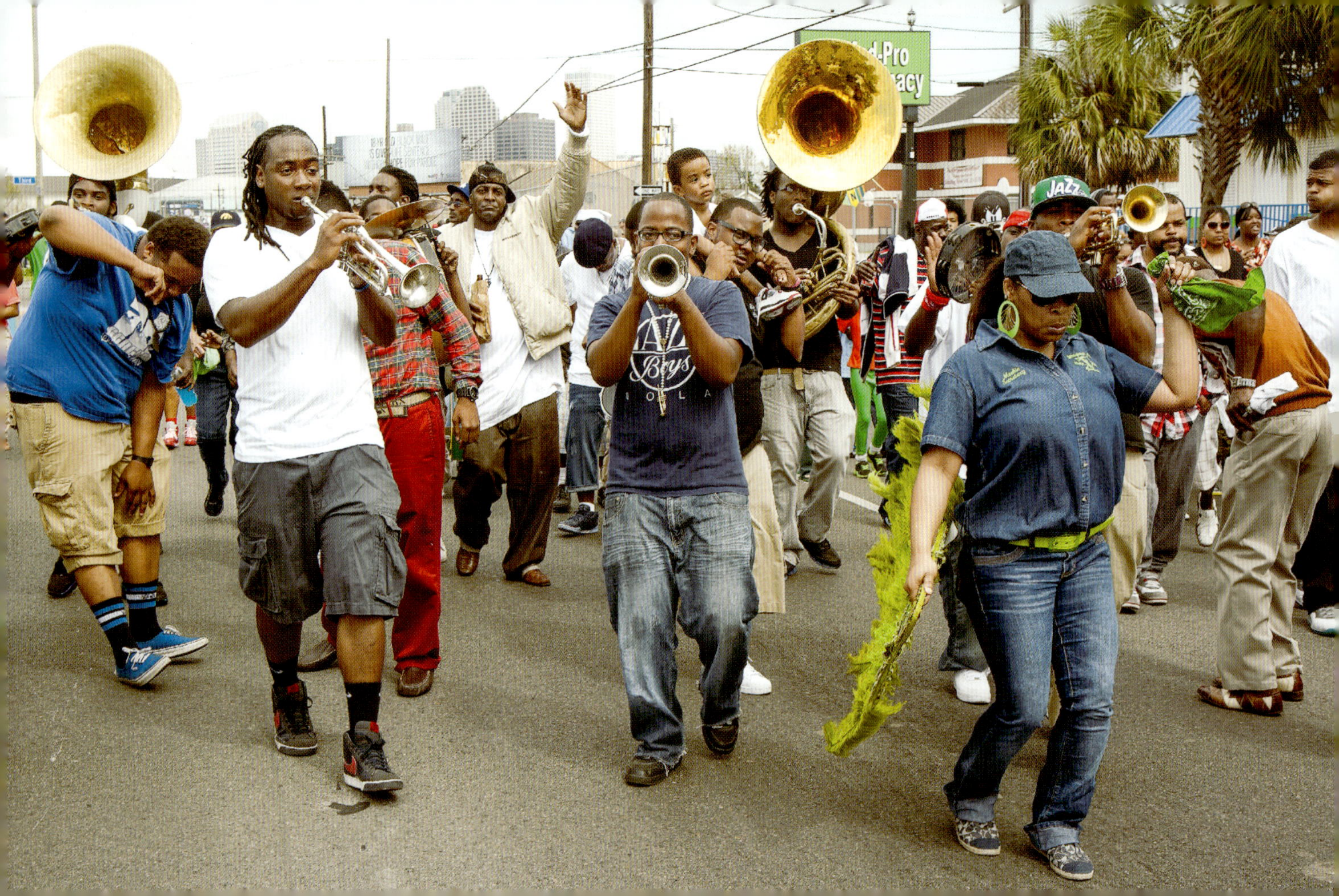

can push it to the edge: listen to his angry post-Katrina live recording at Jazz Fest of Randy Newman's "Louisiana 1927." You can hear that online on the Threadhead Records (whose motto is "rebuilding New Orleans one song at a time") website (http://www.threadheadrecords.com/2008/04/27/john-boutte-louisana-1927/). He can break your heart; listen to him sing Annie Lennox's song "Why." The fact is, John Boutté can sing pretty much anything, and no matter what, he'll get you. His performance of his own composition, "Treme Song," is probably his best known. Inspired by a funeral procession passing in front of his house, he wrote the song from life experience, capturing everyday scenes from his neighborhood. The producers of the HBO series *Treme* used it as the program's theme song. As he says in this interview, the song changed his life. It also became a standard part of many performers' repertoires. You hear it all over town.

> Hangin' in the Treme
> Watchin' people sashay
> Past my steps
> By my porch
> In front of my door
>
> Church bells are ringin'
> Choirs are singing
> While the preachers groan
> And the sisters moan
> In a blessed tone

John Boutté was born in 1958 in one of the few black-owned hospitals in the country. A Seventh Ward child, he was part of a large family. Music was all around—it was "like grass growing," he told us. Brass bands and school marching bands walked the streets; people harmonized on street corners; famous musicians lived nearby; churches rocked on Sundays. At eight, he began playing the cornet, and even before then he knew he loved to sing. And, of course, Stevie Wonder, Sam Cooke, Aretha, Ray Charles, and Marvin Gaye were on the radio. Not surprisingly, other family members have also made their mark in music. Lillian, his sister, is a well-known gospel and jazz singer. Their nieces Tricia Boutté (Teedy) and Tanya E. Boutté are singers, too.

To my mind, John had the best possible situation for becoming a musician—superb local music at his doorstep and lots of family support, combined with full access to the music that was shaping a generation across the country and beyond. Pay attention when he talks here about all the musicians in his neighborhood and in his life. He ranges from the Barbarins—Paul, the influential pre-big-band-era drummer, and Lucien, the celebrated trombonist who plays with everyone from Dr. Michael White to Harry Connick Jr.—to Earl Palmer, the R&B and rock 'n' roll drummer who may be the most recorded session drummer in history. John's is also a quintessential New Orleans story in which deeply creative local cultural traditions lie at the base of a singular and distinctive voice.

As a singer, John Boutté has crafted a comfortable career. These days, perhaps because of the financial benefits of having written a television series theme song, he doesn't leave New Orleans much, only occasionally venturing elsewhere for a gig or short tour. His Saturday gigs at d.b.a. on Frenchmen Street are where you're most likely to find him, although he can sometimes be spotted wheeling around town on his bicycle.

As John tells us here, he majored in business at Xavier University. Then he went into the U.S. Army, where he managed a company of 360 men—not as challenging, he says, as managing his band, though. After he left the military, he used his college education and went into banking. Then came a chance encounter in New Orleans with Stevie Wonder, who told him he had a "signature voice." Wonder encouraged him to become a full-time singer. John Boutté left his banking career behind the next day, and from that moment on he seems never to have looked back. That was a very good thing for the world of New Orleans music.

✦ Parade, Uptown Super Sunday

You know what? I'm a singer. I'm a singer, man. I don't like to put labels on it.

## Family and the Seventh Ward

I was born on the corner of LaSalle and Louisiana, down the block from the Dew Drop Inn, at Flint-Goodridge Hospital, November 3, 1958, at 6:31, the eighth child of Gloria and George Boutté. Although my mother promised her doctor, who was also a cousin of ours, that she was going to stop having kids when she had a boy that looked just like her, she had two more after me. They were Catholic—what would you expect?

I'll put them in order: Lolette, Anthony, Lynnette, Lillian, Lorna, Lita, Emanuel, John, Lenora, and Peter. Back then, people would have big families. And I tell you, they taught us to love each other so much. With that comes, inevitably, having to say goodbye. Right? So the last one standing, man, you got to figure they're going to bury nine siblings. I'm fifty-four, and we all get along. It would be one thing if we didn't get along. We all do.

I've got one sister living in Europe. That's Lillian. Teedy's my niece. Everybody thinks Teedy's my sister. Her mother is the oldest sibling in the family—that's Lolette. But she's not a sister.

My parents were great. My mom—basically, she raised ten kids. She was a logistician, man. She was a chef. She was a nurse. She was a psychologist. She was a doctor. She was everything. She's ninety years old; she's still alive. And she's still smart and beautiful, very wise—an opinionated Scorpio like her favorite son. She was a beautician also. She did study to be beautician. And in her late years, she also worked for Frank Minyard, in the coroner's office,

dealing with people with mental issues. And here's a kick—she never had any kind of degree in psychology. But when she started working for Dr. Frank, my mother could always read through who was nuts and who wasn't. Because you know—you got ten kids, you know who's lying and who's not lying.

My father was a great guy. He came from a long line of carpenters, and he was a master carpenter himself. He built the home that our mother raised us in. He worked for the post office, but beyond that he was a golfer, a fisherman, just a great provider, man. Incredible. I mean who can have ten kids and walk in every day from work and have a gift for those ten kids every day—whether it was a piece of gum or whatever—just something? We all waited for him to come home. He'd come, and the house would be like—can you imagine—radios would be going, TVs would be going, kids going, noises and everything, dogs. And when he hit the front door, the first thing he'd say, "God damn it!" Everything would stop, you know. We had one dog, Junior; he broke so many screen doors, because my dad would come in and do that. He was a yellow German shepherd; he'd pee on the floor and run out. And Mom was like, "George, you can't do that."

So we had a real, real, real excellent upbringing. And the Seventh Ward of New Orleans was gorgeous back then. It was really a community. People owned their homes. They took pride in themselves. It's changed, man, changed so immensely. I started seeing a change when they brought the interstate in, right through the heart of that community. And we can go back to other reasons. You know—I am from the South, right?

Crack just wiped out a generation. The war on drugs—it's just been devastating for that community. It's funny because my older sisters' boyfriends, those guys didn't come back from Vietnam; the ones that did come back, they were really out of their gourd, you know. So that changed a lot. I think that changed not only my community but America in general. But I could see it clearly in my neighborhood.

### "I Was Surrounded by Music"

As a young kid I was surrounded by music. I had Mr. Jack Willis, the trumpet player, who lived on Roman. Next to him was Mr. Ferdinand, incredible clarinet player. Around the corner from him was Mr. Picoult, who wrote the "Purple Rose of Cairo." The Barbarins, the two brothers, Paul and Lucien, great old guys, man—they lived on New Orleans Street, not far from my mother's home, where I grew up. Next door, Mr. Glass. He was the oldest bass drummer in the world—in the *Guinness Book of World Records*, for the oldest playing drummer. He played with the Eureka Band. He was playing with Louis Armstrong and everybody else. You had Danny Barker. My dad used to cut Louis Cottrell's hair. My brother married the grand-nephew of Sidney Bechet, who also lived half a block from my grandmother. Papa Celestin used to play barbecues in my other aunt's yard, on Annette Street. So, yeah, we were immersed with music, everywhere.

But those Creoles had an idea. It's okay if you can play music. That's nice. You're talented. But you better have a real job. It was only acceptable if you had another job or a craft. So that was always one of the things that they stressed. I always got, "Well, you need something to fall back on." And I realized, man, if you're falling back, you're headed in the wrong direction. So I just threw that out the door. I don't regret my education, the years I spent as a banker, logistician,

the Army, etc. It's all been good for me. But sometimes I wonder what would have happened if I would have jumped out of the gate swinging as a singer and a musician. But no regrets. I'm in a good spot.

My first instrument was a cornet. I got that when I was eight years old, and I started reading music at eight. The public school system was just littered with incredible teachers. They had great music programs. They had great music teachers. I remember in junior high school, Mr. William Houston the first. He would get cards from Duke Ellington, Count Basie; they would stop in and check on the band. We were kids, but what did we know? That was the scene. And my high school teacher was very strict on tone—she didn't want you "screaming no high notes." That was out of the question. If you couldn't hit an altissimo C or whatever without tone, you understand—"You better not let it come out of that horn." So, yeah, we had some incredible teachers.

It was the cornet because my grand aunt next door had a cornet. An old cornet, man, just like one that Pops would have. It was a beautiful instrument. Man, I loved that horn. I loved the smell of the horn. I loved the way it felt in your hands. I was just proud of being able to play. That was the start of my formal musical career.

Before that, I loved singing. As a kid in school, you always sang. They taught you all little ditties. I would drive my sisters crazy, man, very patriotically singing, "We love our flag, our beautiful flag. The red, the white, the blue." And just repeat it and repeat it and repeat it. They would scream and say "Make him stop." I'd say, wow—so this has power. I didn't have to swing a punch. I wish I could remember some of those melodies I would sing to my dog. You know, kids, when nobody's around. I wasn't like someone would say I was talking to the dog—I was singing

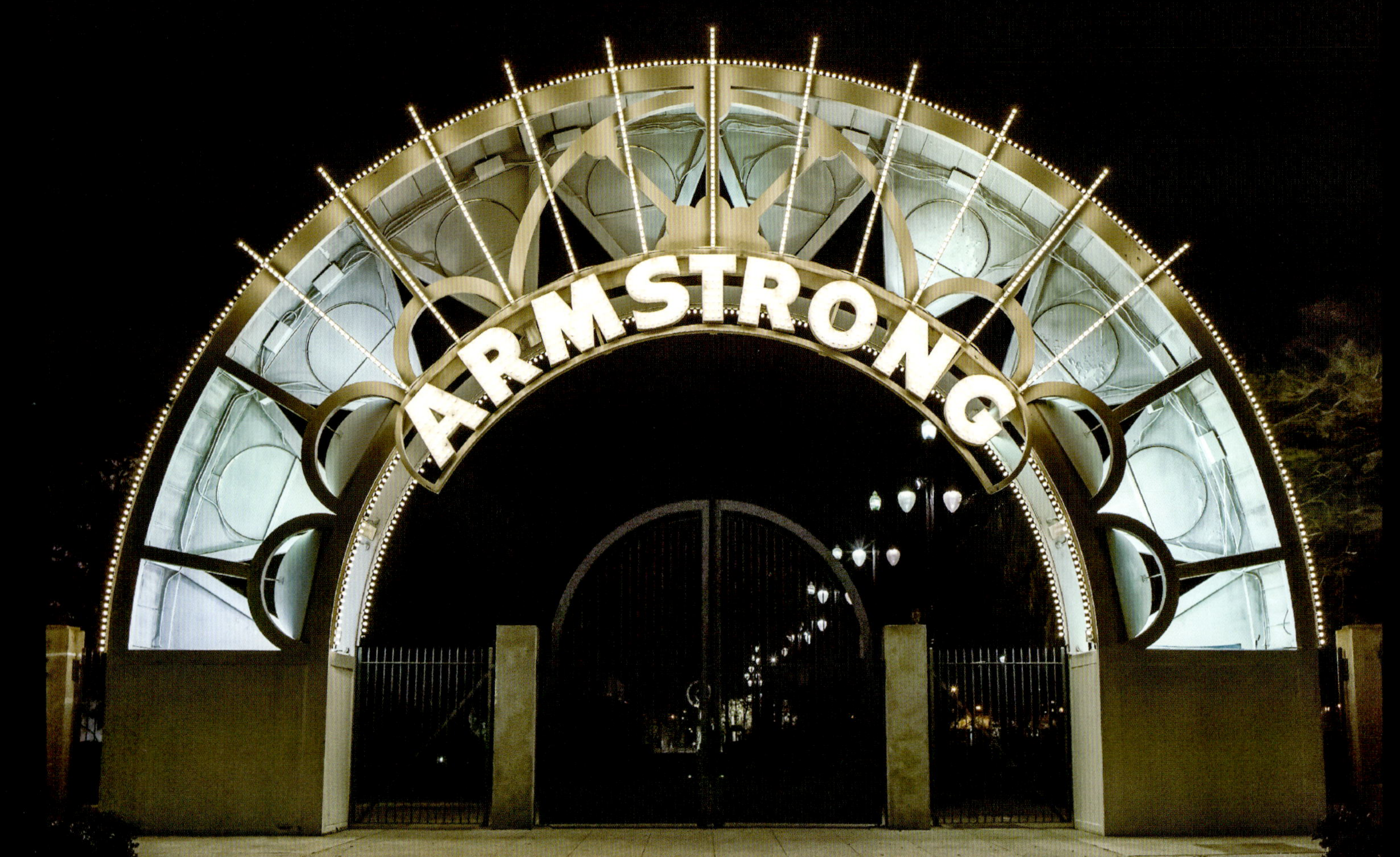

ARMSTRONG

to the dog. The dog wasn't singing to me. Yeah, you know, I think about those things.

The church? I was Catholic—so they weren't having none of that. Actually, they did have pretty good music. They'd break out the guitars every now and then. It was like John Denver—you know what I'm saying. Oh yeah—now we rocking, baby.

But just beyond me, around the corner, adjacent to the house where I grew up, was a sanctified church. So, they would be rocking. They would be rocking so loud, man, let me tell you. You'd hear the organs, the tambourines. Every now and then I'd get a glimpse of the sisters, doing the alligator on the floor. You know what I'm saying? Then, when I was seventeen and I was in college, I actually kind of started playing for a little storefront church on Galvez Street. And let me tell you, my grand aunts and those hardcore Catholics were not happy about that. Let me tell you.

And I did a lot of singing with vocal groups. Some guys go out and shoot hoops. My friends went out and sang harmonies. We were always literally looking for echo. I couldn't wait to get off school and get with these guys and make just beautiful harmonies.

We'd sing everything from any of the old doo-wop tunes to Sam Cooke and the Soul Stirrers, which I really loved, because I got to do Sam's part. We had this kid, man, he fell, a victim to the drugs. But he had the most incredible bass, this guy. When you've got a vocal group, that's what sets it. If you've got a real bass singer your harmonies are just so well-rounded. You've got the intonation right. He was just an incredible natural. I'd just love hearing that guy sing. I think we used to call ourselves Spirit, or something like that. It's funny, because I was reading an article about Aaron Neville today, and I remember we used to do talent shows. And he was like doing the same thing; he'd be on the same little bill.

These little clubs, trying to make fifty bucks at a talent show.

Aaron used to get his hair cut in my grandmother's kitchen. My sister, as a senior, would cut his hair. I've worked with Ivan; I've recorded with Ivan. All of those guys are good. I can't believe that Art is seventy-five. My mom's ninety-five—that's only fifteen years younger.

Nobody even thought about it. It was just like grass growing. It was everywhere. I realized later on that people from Europe took notice. The old guys who were living around my neighborhood—my first trip to Europe, these guys were legends. I had no idea that they were held in such high esteem in Europe. And they just came back to their humble beginnings at home and just hung out. But in Europe these guys would fill auditoriums and stadiums all the time. And you just never knew what they were up to. I remember I did a trip, and I was on a tour bus with this old guy in Switzerland. I guess this was about the early '90s. He was sitting next to me, and he was just telling me stories. He was talking about being in Switzerland. I asked him, "When was your first time in Switzerland?" It was like 1929. I was like, "What!?" I mean this guy was playing jazz in 1929 in Europe. Right? That just blew my mind. You know, I thought I was hip. It was Doc Cheatham, man.

### Starting to Play

I started playing the piano before college, about seventeen. We always had a piano in the house. My grandfather taught us how to play "Salty Dog." We all knew how to play "Salty Dog." That was necessary. But then when I was in college and I was doing the singing, the a cappella stuff. A friend of mine's from Buffalo, who had won a Debussy award to get a scholarship down here, right, at Xavier; I heard him play the piano in the auditorium one day. I was just mesmerized. He actually taught me how to do my first scale, properly, right, on the piano. Otherwise, I used to do it all by ear.

Then later on in my freshman year I took piano at Xavier, and I studied classical piano—Mozart, Bach, Debussy, Chopin. I was so good at picking it up by ear. My teacher would say, "No, no, no. You're not reading." But, yeah, that's when I started playing a little piano.

I also played the organ and piano when I was in the military, when I got out of college. Because while I was in the military, dealing with the church kept me in the music. So I volunteered to play piano at the services.

I was really fortunate to travel Europe with my sister and my brother-in-law, and also incredible New Orleans musicians. All the greatest drummers out of New Orleans, I've had the good pleasure of playing with, man—all these old cats. Back in the '80s, when I got out of service, before they had the University of New Orleans program, the youngest guy in my band was fifty-four years old. There was no young cats playing jazz. I remember when I first saw Brian Blade playing with the first crop of kids from UNO, at Café Brasil. They had these incredible young lions up there playing. It was wonderful. That was the first crop of really young guys that I saw. Because it wasn't hip. Everybody wanted to play electric guitar; horns were out, jazz in particular. I think Danny Barker was a part of that resurgence, and the fact that we just don't let things go here. We're hoarders.

At Xavier, I studied economics and business. And music was my extracurricular activity. And I worked forty hours a week at the morgue. Yes, can you believe that?

## Becoming a Singer

I knew that from the start—I wanted to sing, ever since I was a little a kid. I knew I wanted to sing; I wanted to do music.

When I was working as a banker, back in 1986 or '87, Stevie Wonder was in town, getting his first honorary doctorate in human letters from my alma mater, Xavier. My friend, Tim Francis, whose father was the president of Xavier, called me up. Tim happened to be dating one of Stevie's background singers. I didn't know that Tim was Stevie's publishing lawyer also. So he called me and asked me if he could use my DX7 keyboard. I said, "You don't play a DX7, man. No." He said, "Man, look, bring it up here." So I brought it up to the hotel room. Long story short: he calls me and tells me to come pick it up. And I was furious. Because I brought it up, and now he's saying come pick it up. I'm thinking, "The guy's cheeky, man. I'm going to give him a piece of my mind." When I get up there, lo and behold, I hear music through the door. I say, "It can't be." I knocked on the door. And who's sitting right where I put the piano? Stevie Wonder.

I spent the day with him. Begged him to take me with him. He told me he couldn't do it. But he did tell me I had something special. He said I had a "signature voice." I'd never heard that term. He was basically saying I sound like me; I didn't sound like anyone else. So I said, "Well, take me with you." He said, "No, I can't do it." I said, "What do I have to do?" And he left me with these two words: *patience* and *determination*.

I quit my banking job the next day. Because of this, I was so excited I forgot to shave. Subsequently, my boss called me on the carpet and said, "Go home and shave." I said, "Really?" So, I went home, fixed me a mint julep, sat on my veranda, in my hammock. And the phone rang. It was him. He said, "Where are you?" I said, "I'm home. This is my two-week notice." Everybody thought I'd lost my mind. I said, "Nope. Just found it."

My sister called that afternoon. She was in Europe. I told her, I said, "You need some help? Give me a ticket; I'll come over and help you out." She got me a ticket, and I was riding around with her, basically driving her car, setting up the sound system, being the roadie guy for all these incredible old jazz guys. Sitting at their feet and learning from them. They started bringing me up to do cameo performances. That led to like, "Two songs is not getting it for me." I wanted to do my own thing. So, later, I broke off and came back home and started with my own band.

I played the Storyville Club that was owned by Taylor Hackford at the time. And who was in the audience but Earl Palmer. And Earl Palmer sat in for the whole set. I mean, I tell you, I've had experiences like that. Incredible, man. And I used to play Molly's at the Market. I played Café Brasil. I started some of the first music there and some of the first music at d.b.a. on Frenchmen. Every now and then Snug Harbor would let me in. So, yeah, and I hustled, man. Whenever there was something for me to do, I'd do it. You know, if they wanted me to be grand marshal, I did that. I remember one gig I did—I was a fake photographer for a TV convention that comes in. Oprah Winfrey and all these guys were coming in in their limousines. And I made $200 to have an empty camera with a flash—to act like I was really concerned that they were here, shooting pictures while they getting out of the limousine. I realized, don't believe the hype.

Yeah, I did whatever I could to keep my foot in the entertainment industry at the time. In fact somebody brought me some pictures from way back, when I first started. I was doing a show—I was "Mr. Fixit" in some kind of show about Storyville that ran at Le Petit Theater. So I did all kind of things to try to get into the music industry.

And then I started summering up in Mackinac Island. I did that for almost eight years, which was kind of cool because I knew it was a good spot for me to make a few dollars—not much—but it was a retreat, away from New Orleans. Good air. Riding a bike every day. It was like rehab for three months out of the year. I'd come back refreshed. And I couldn't stand the smell of cars. I wanted to smell horse manure. That's what you smell—horse manure and hay and fresh air and pine. And you don't realize—actually when you got off the island you started smelling carbon from the cars. Once you'd get to Detroit you could hardly breathe. You'd get back to New Orleans—oh my God—you'd want to wear a mask or something. But good air and just good exercise, singing with the house band. It was like a cruise ship that never moved. Singing to the blue-haired Republican ladies who thought I was the sweetest *kleiner gemütlich Neger*—that's German for cute black guy.

Stevie was right. Yeah, you've got to do it. You have to have patience. It can't be just handed to you. And, you know, lots of times I sit back and I question my ability. Who doesn't? And there's times where I listen to something and I think, "Oh my God; is that me?" And it's true—sometimes I suck. Then there's times when I can say, "My God; that's me." That is incredible, man.

## Singing

I sing very emotionally—I think you have to emote yourself to sing. That's part of being a good singer. You just can't come out there like a cold fish. You might hit the right notes, but you have to have some kind of spirituality, emotion in there to connect. That's hard to get sometimes. You really have to focus to get there.

I remember once someone interviewing me asked, "Why did you cry? I saw you had tears." I'm like, "That's a dumb question." I thought about what Ben Webster had said. He said, "I cry because I sound so good." But sometimes there are certain words that are so powerful to sing—if you don't well up inside, I think you have a disconnect there. There's just some lyrics that make you do that.

Some of my favorite lyricists are Annie Lennox, some of the modern guys who I hope to get a chance to see—Leonard Cohen. There's also a lot of older lyricists that wrote incredibly beautiful things. "Lush Life"—Billy Strayhorn wrote that at seventeen. Seventeen. What does a boy from Harlem know about that kind of scene? At seventeen.

Annie Lennox. You know what? Her song "Why," when I recorded it for my record initially, I ran out crying like a baby. The lyrics finally hit me, and I literally ran out of the studio into the rest room so no one would see me lose it. I had to get my composure; you know what I'm saying? Because it just—I connected with it. And the lyrics all of a sudden became so real to me. She's a hell of a lyricist. Her "A Thousand Beautiful Things" is gorgeous. It's another gorgeous song.

So, for me, lyrics are number one. And then the melody. Some melodies can be very simple, but the lyrics—I love lyrics.

There's so much music, man. That's one of the reasons I think I really wanted to get into it—it's a never-ending story. And it's all been done before. We're all just plagiarizing. You know, you tell me something that ain't been done.

## Katrina

These days not much excites me. Actually, that's not true. Music excites me. But it's not many things that can give you the shock value. It's like, what's going to come next? Because I've had some experiences since the levee failure in New Orleans, I mean, that were epic.

The first thing I would say is coming back and finding no music. And trying to get it started again. It was like trying to start a fire without matches in the damp. But we got it going. And just to watch the whole thing evolve from a city that was totally brown—I mean brown. It would have been a bad commercial for UPS. To see how in the clubs there was nobody there. In singing to just a few people—the faithful and the people who just had to come out. I mean, I felt like I was the psychiatrist. Because people would come, and they would lay it all down at my feet every weekend.

And there were no kids. There were no kids here. But the parents that did have kids that were too young to be in school, they didn't want a babysitter, so they would bring their kids to the show. It was just beautiful, man. I saw women come in from two months pregnant to where the kids are running around the joint. You know what I'm saying? In that whole time I watched them grow up, and then to the point that the clubs started saying, "No kids in the club." I watched that whole turnaround.

⚜ John Boutté in Armstrong Park

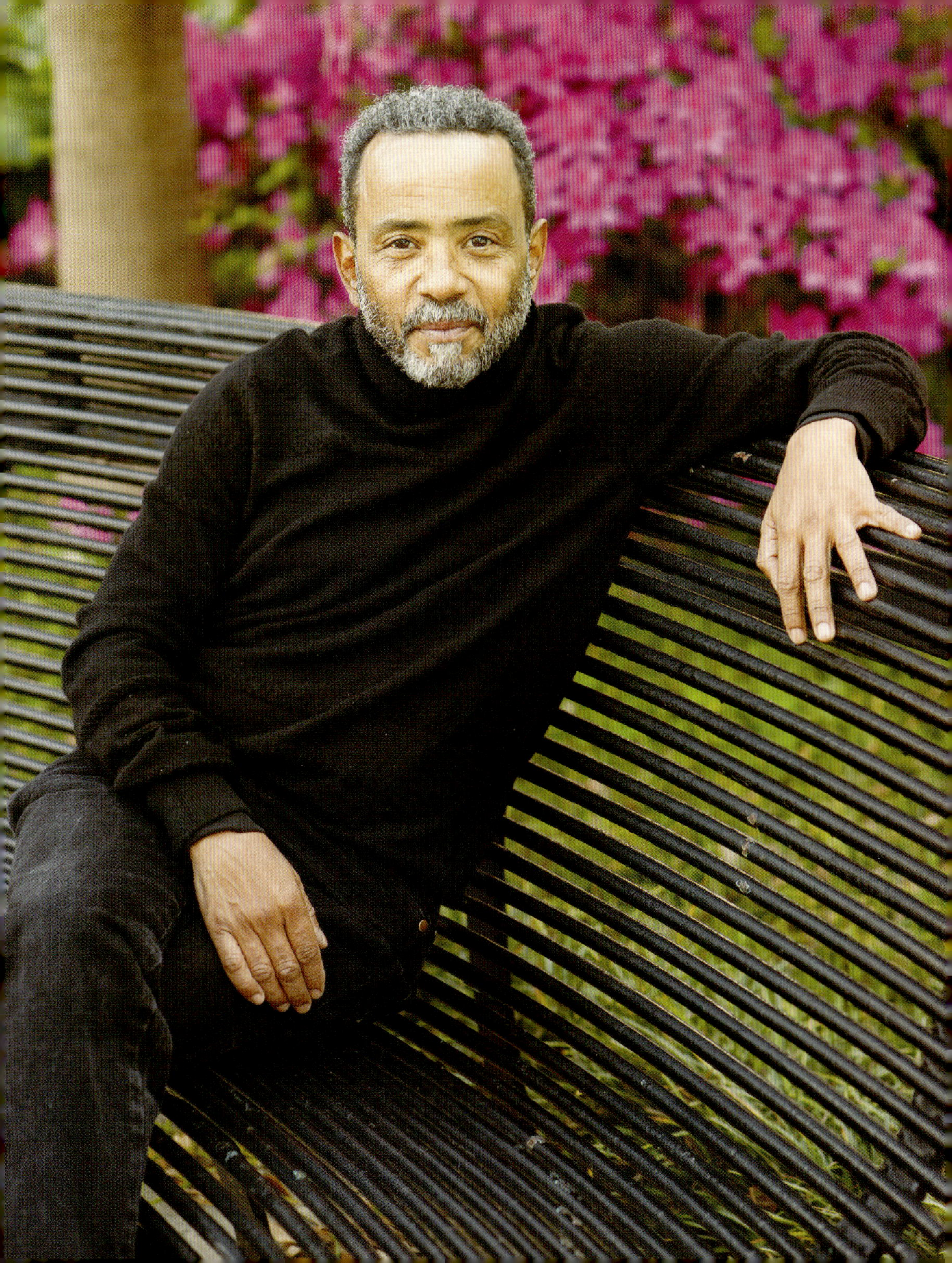

It was all locals at that time, literally all locals. Now that I can't tell you who's in the audience. There's one or two people I know.

I absolutely knew the music was going to come back. I was hell-bent on that. I was in Brazil when the levees failed. In an interview there, they asked me why would I come back to New Orleans. I said, "Because my ancestors' bones are there, and that's my home." Then I started singing Louis Armstrong's, he didn't write it, but "You'll Never Walk Alone." You know:

> When you walk through a storm
> Keep your head up high
> And don't be afraid . . .

I started singing that a cappella in the airport. To the cameras, because I know they can't understand English, but they'll understand music. And you know what? As I rode to the airport and had to pass through the favelas in São Paulo, that put everything in perspective. I said, okay, New Orleans is flooded, but that water's going to subside, and we're going to be able to get back at it. These guys are stuck in the sewage. And I felt more sorry for them than I felt for myself.

I've never owned a house, so I didn't have one to lose. I've never used my GI Bill. I just never looked at it as something I really desired. Because the people who had stuff; I didn't need a house to say, "oh, what I've got." Because you never own a home. I mean the truth is the bank owns it. You don't. You start paying. Or it owns you. And even if you pay it off you still have to pay taxes. So you have to have income generating. You never own it. That's an illusion, man. You know, that's a big illusion. You don't own anything.

I feel like I own my songs and my music. People would say, "What did you lose?" I'd say, "I didn't lose anything because I had my music, and my songs were here." I saw my friends who had stuff—oh God, man, it was like a veil pulled over them. Because they lost their stuff, and they identified through their stuff. I could give a damn about stuff. I've got friends with stuff. You know, I'll play with their stuff. I know they've got so much stuff sometimes that they're tired of their stuff. They get bored with their stuff. They want some people to help them play with it. That sounds like a song: "Don't Play with My Stuff" or "Come Help Me Play with My Stuff."

No, man. What I got, they can't take that away from me. And nothing in life is secure. It can turn on a dime. I can tell you that right now. The fact is that I was the only one able to come back who wasn't shattered—I was shattered emotionally, but I wasn't shattered financially. I was able to lend a hand and say, "Okay, I'm going to help you guys out. I don't own anything. But I can be here, because you guys got real jobs."

## HBO's *Treme*

So, it's really funny how that turned around. I always knew because I wrote songs, and songs have an indefinite shelf life. I couldn't really relate that to my family; they'd say, "You don't have a 402k, you don't have this or that." I'd say, "I've got songs." Guess what? I came back from Katrina, started traveling the world, telling people about the plight in New Orleans, etc., etc., trying to get guys back here, bringing my band back.

And then along comes HBO with the *Treme*. And they grabbed my song from nowhere, man, and changed my life.

I wrote the song just how a song is supposed to be written. It's got to be written from your heart and

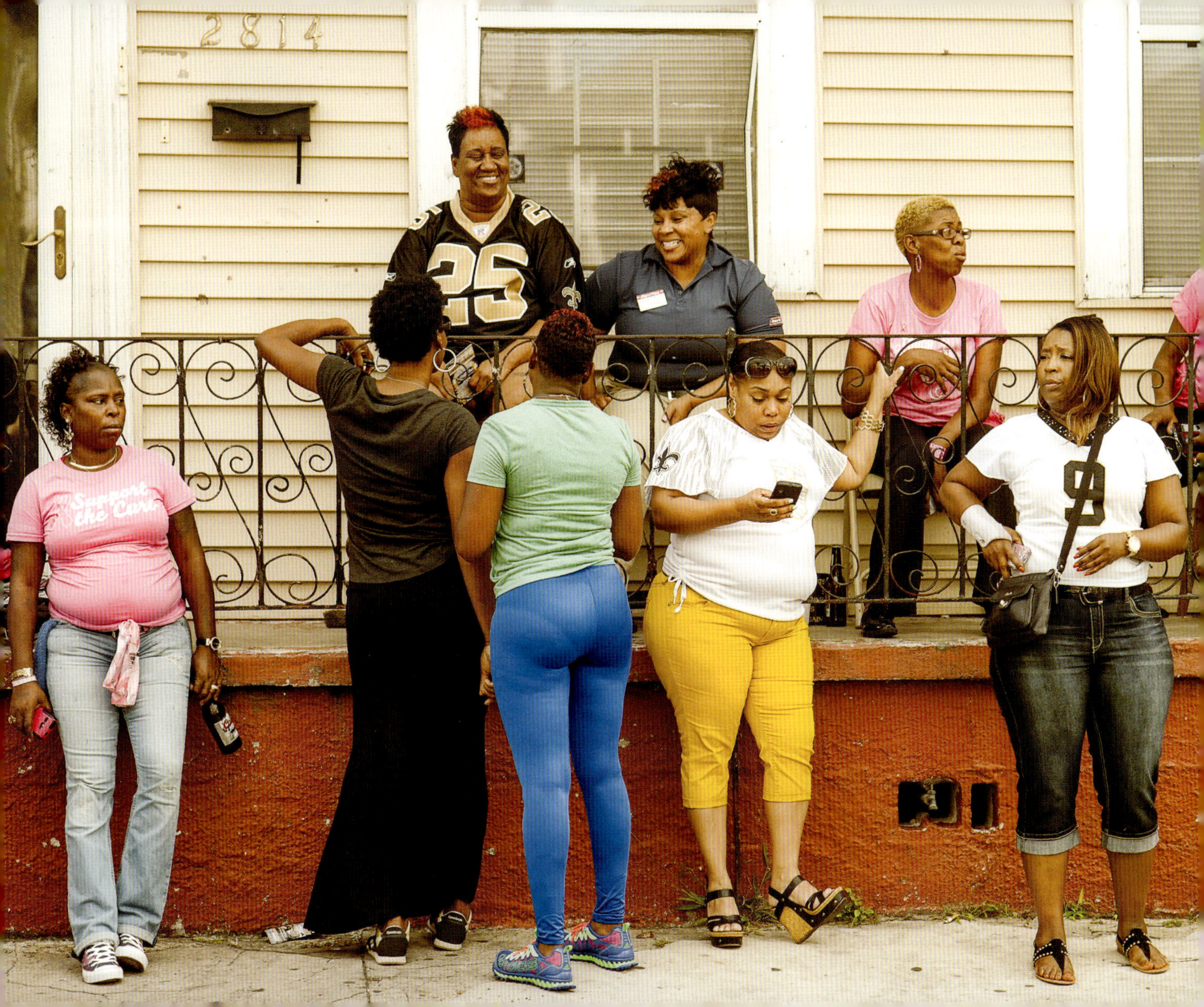

about an experience that you've had. You can't be just making things up. It's got to be from the heart and true. And you've got to believe in it. And it's got to have a little hook. And what's more hooky than a blues line? I sat down and in one take, just right at the piano, man. I sat there and did the clave, the little bass line and the chords on the piano that was right in front, as I walked off my step. The lyrics just flowed, just like that. Then I just forgot about it, until I was recording, and somebody said, "You need one more song." And everybody thought that it was so silly, a silly song.

But it's got legs.

I have no idea how HBO found it. You know what? A writer friend of mine did a documentary about the Treme. And Lolis asked me could he use it. I said, "Sure, man." You know, that's my neighborhood. "Absolutely." And I had people telling me, "Well, how much money you got?" I'm like, "It's none of your business." But I didn't care about the money. They could have used it for free. I didn't care. It's my song. I own the masters. I said, "You can do whatever you want with it. If it's going to put a good light on the history." But they still gave me—they gave me about two or three hundred dollars, whatever it was. And I was like, "Cool." I was satisfied.

But now—I asked the program's music supervisor—and I don't know if he ever gave me a clear answer—where he heard it. One of the reasons he said they used it was because—and I never realized this—is that it's all about New Orleans. It's a moment in New Orleans. It's so New Orleans. And it never says "New Orleans." It never says anything about the French Quarters, the paddlewheels, Jackson Square. It never says any of that. Of course, I had tried to analyze it, and I was, you know, using my marketing knowledge that sex and death were the two things that sell. Because those are the two things that most people live their entire lives, and the whole thing is an enigma to them. They never figure out sex or death. They go to the grave confused about both. And my opening lines in the "Treme Song" are "Hanging in the Treme / Watching people sashay."

Now, I meant like we're hitting it, sitting here hanging. You know, congregating. But "hanging" could also evoke in your mind, subconsciously, a lynching, which would bring up death. "Watching people sashay" is an act of like voyeurism or watching somebody walk sexy. So I hit death and sex in the first two lines, right? That's my analysis of it. Believe me, when I was writing it, that's not what I was doing. I was telling them what I was doing. I'm "hanging in the Treme," and I was watching people sashay past my steps, by my porch, in front of my door. That's exactly what was happening. And the church bells were ringing. And etcetera. So, if you want to call that songwriting, I did it.

I need a couple of more like that.

## Money

My business training has helped me. Because the legalities of the business, I was always interested in songwriter ownership—who owns what, what's a collaboration—and publishing. If I wanted to really make money, I could *really* make money. Money's easy; love is hard. I tell people that all the time. You can get money. Money's common. Love is rare.

I've seen real love in my life. And I've seen lots of money, and I've seen it not bring people happiness. I've seen it bring them misery. I did realize that I couldn't afford a factory. I couldn't afford the raw materials to build widgets or whatever. I didn't have the collateral that a bank would lend me the money if I did have an idea. But what I did have—I had my head, I had my music, and if I had a little food in my stomach but not enough food in my stomach, I had the incentive to write.

And I realized that once you write something, some of the richest people in the world are publishers, and they control everything. So, when you wonder who runs thing—turn on your television or open a newspaper, and that will tell you exactly. Because information runs things. And these are the guys—they're the publishers. So that kind of tweaked my interest. These guys are just getting stories, and they're selling these stories. And they're making millions a day. And people writing songs—all you need is one to hit.

But money, I've never really ran after it, never worried about it. I don't know, you get to a certain age, and I don't worry about it. I never have. Never did. Never have. I just wanted the music.

Most important to me is the music. I like doing art. I like seeing where I can move people. When I have a really good show, and I see people who are really touched by it—I mean recently I've had people come up to me and say that they had a partner, a wife or a husband, who was dying, and on their death bed they were playing my record. To me that's so humbling, man. You have no idea.

**Culture Wars**

We had some struggles getting Frenchmen Street started, believe me. I've seen the cops coming, raiding the joint, with horses and beating people down. You would swear it was the 1960s, my dear. We were just out playing music. You'd wonder why. Who didn't get paid off. That's what it boiled down to.

And they still kick them in the teeth, man. They still kick them in the teeth. I'm not going to name this guy, but I was working for this gentleman who happened to be on a committee for renaming the airport. He was against naming it Louis Armstrong International. And I'm like "Who is better known than him?" I was so upset that I decided I'm not playing his club. So he called me, he wanted me to play. "What's going on?" he said. I said, "I understand that you abstained from voting to name the airport after Louis Armstrong." He said, "You know, Louis Armstrong left New Orleans." I said, "He couldn't eat at your father's restaurant. You understand? What would you have done?"

So, you know, that's the mentality that people have. And there's no question in my mind that I play for the rich and the bourgeois. But I do it at my leisure, not theirs. That's one thing I can tell you. Because you know what, if they say, "We can get somebody else," I say, "You sure can. But you won't get John Boutté." Because there's only one.

And who doesn't work for somebody that's rich or bourgeois? The thing is that sometimes art is relegated to that corner. No, no, no. I'm not using no back doors, and I'm not doing none of that shit. No, my friend. I'm walking through that front door. And if I want a drink, I'll have a drink. And by the way, I'm not going to eat anything. You know why? Because I eat before I come to work. I don't come here to eat your food. I'm a very good cook. I don't go to work hungry. I don't care what kind of hors d'oeuvres you have there. Believe me, I've had the best of the best. You can only eat one meal at a time. So, your fancy champagnes and whatever—there's not many events that I've been to, that I've worked at, where I would be fighting for the food. I'm so sorry, you know— "You keep that cheese plate." But there are some

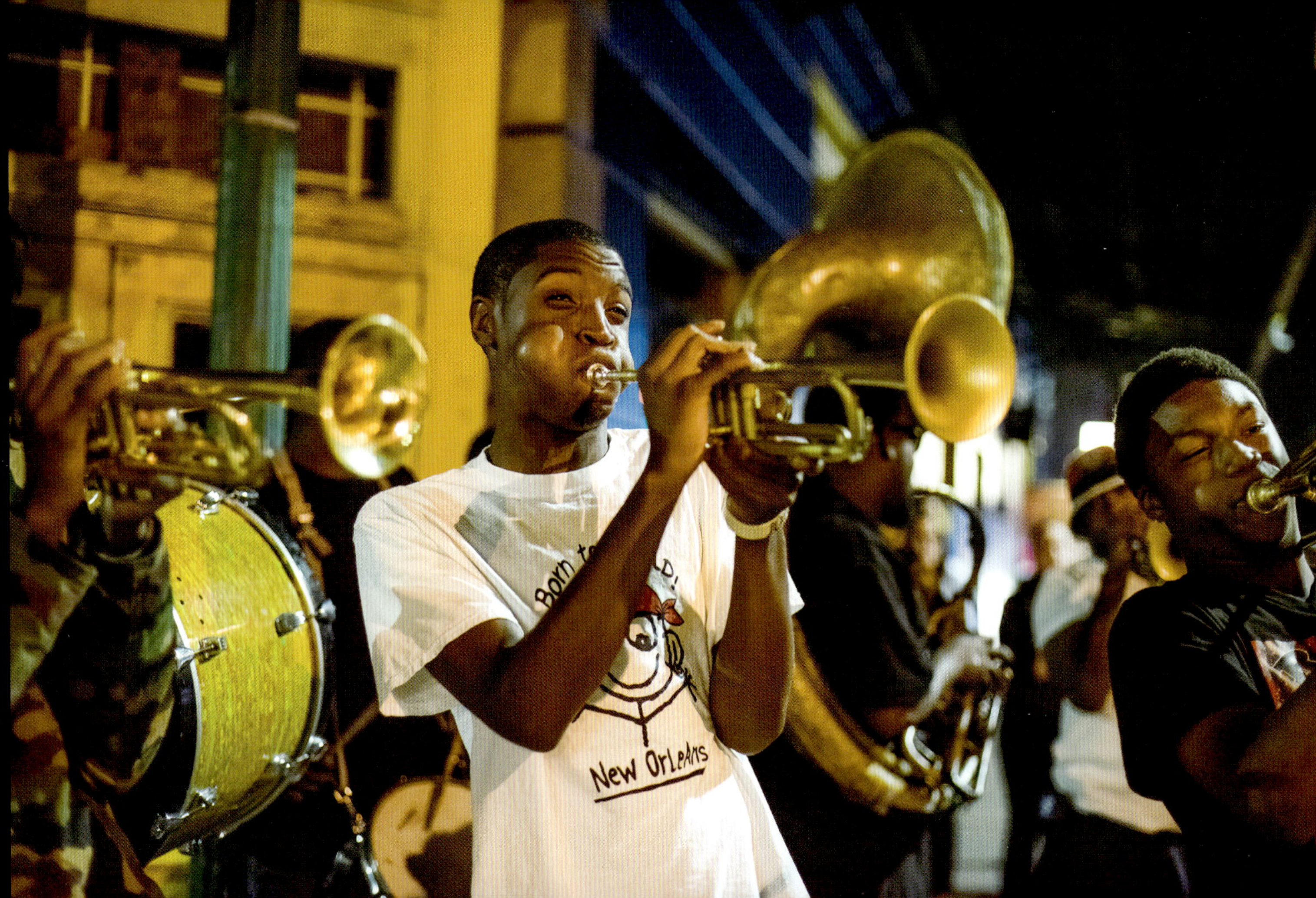
Born to...
New Orleans

private things that I've been to where they've treated me extremely well.

Last year the Indians were prepared; they actually had lawyers marching with them. But once again, man, I mean come on. You know. What's up with that?

The cops cannot stop guys loitering in front of my house on a building that they don't live in, you understand. They won't stop and say, "Hey—if I see your asses sitting on this porch, I know you don't live here, and you don't pay rent here. The house isn't abandoned. If I see you loitering on somebody's private property, you're going to jail." They just ride past them. You understand what I'm saying? Hence you get the guys sitting, and they start dealing drugs and everything else. But come on man, how simple is that? You see a bunch of guys sitting on a porch, you pull them over and say, "Move your asses." But they're scared. They won't do it. They ride right past them. So, what are you going to do?

Tourists? I think they miss the origins of it all. Right? And why these traditions got started. And what was really behind it all. All they see is, like, getting dressed up. And they don't realize that the Mardi Gras Indians—this was a protest. Some people say it started because of the Wild Bill shows, right? But that's not totally true. That may have influenced it, like all pop culture at the time influenced things. But it was basically the Indians and the slaves, because a lot of slaves escaped to Indian tribes. And 80 percent of the African Americans in America south of the Mason-Dixon line have American Indian blood. So it was like keeping their heritage. You know—like look at me. Right?

And down here in New Orleans, we're still very close to our heritage. Sometimes it's like you can't see the forest for the trees, because you're living with it. Then you have to want to know where it's coming from, and research it. It's not always given to you.

I've heard stories about why do people shake the handkerchiefs. You know why? There was a law, because the octoroons and the quadroons and the Creoles—there were certain women that they couldn't tell whether they were black or white. Right? They were *passé blanc*. But the way they could tell, they passed a law saying black women, or anyone with Negro blood—which means everybody in the frikkin city in the United States, for that matter. I mean, come on, we all come from Lucy. So they had to have a *tignon*, like a headwrap, on the head. And during the second lines, in defiance, because they had so many people out there at the funerals, the women would take the tignon off and swing it in the air. And the cops—what would they do? They got all those folks; you know, they're overpowered. So it was a defiance. People wonder why they swing those rags. That's the story I got.

**These Days**

These days I am mostly working close to home, because my mom's ninety years old, and I'm basically watching out for her. I find myself recording her stories now. Because she's really old school. She's smart, and she's still got it in her head. Her biggest fear is that one of her kids is going to die before she does. Any parent's fear, I guess. And she's always having dreams now, man. She's telling me about her dreams about kids. She says, "I was trying to get shoes for Pete and Lenore and had to get their books." But what are you going to dream about, you raise ten kids?

So the rumors are that I'm afraid of flying. Or I'm not well. All the rumors. Guess what—I've got more miles than you can shake a stick at, my friend. And I can jump on my bicycle on a Saturday night and go on Frenchmen Street—a ten-minute leisurely ride. Don't get dressed up if I don't want to. And I have a packed house of people waiting for me every Saturday night, when I want to. If they can make it that easy for me, and financially come up with the same kind of money, I'll say, "Well, maybe I'll go." But now I don't see the need of having to jump on a plane, risking life and limb, and the indignity of people sending me through x-ray machines and checking all my orifices. It's changed completely. Sorry—I don't see the allure in flying any more. It's a pain in the ass. A royal pain in the ass.

My last record was with incredible guys, incredible songs. And of course, I didn't even put one advertisement out for it last year. And I'm a Grammy member, but I never even submitted it for a Grammy because I don't want to have to go through that. It's like how many Facebook friends can you have to vote for you? Is it the music or is it your ability to campaign? So, c'est la vie. I could have probably paid $5,000 to a publicist and they'd have been spreading it all around. I kept that money instead.

My band? Basically I have a guitar player who I stick with, Christopher Todd Duke. And, yeah, I do have a steady band, man. Loren Pickford. Wendell Brunious. Nobu Osaki, my bass player. Mark McGrain is my trombone player. But Todd and I have been playing for over twenty years. I've seen him through at least six girlfriends and a wife.

I love it, because when we're on the road, he gets in his hotel room, I get in mine, he doesn't bother me, I don't bother him. We're just great traveling partners, man. We get together; we work on music. We get together, we have a drink, laugh, when things are done. He don't complain. It's hard to have a band on the road. I found it harder to manage six people than it was to manage a company of 360 in the army. Because you have the personal relationships with six that you won't have with 360. And you've got to stroke everybody.

I've got to go. I'm usually in bed at nine.

# CHRISTIE JOURDAIN

Snare drummer

Leader, Original Pinettes Brass Band

# JANINE WATERS

Tuba player

Original Pinettes Brass Band

[ Interviewed October 7, 2013, outside a coffee shop on Esplanade, New Orleans ]

Not even three weeks after Gary and I met Christie Jourdain and Janine Waters at a CC Coffee House on Esplanade, the Original Pinettes Brass Band—New Orleans' first and only all-woman brass band—won the Red Bull *Street Kings* competition, simultaneously demonstrating their mastery of the form and calling into question the gendered title of the contest. They won a New York recording session produced by two New Orleans luminaries—horn-player Trombone Shorty and hip hop producer Mannie Fresh. With judging by Trombone Shorty, Kermit Ruffins, and others, the Pinettes triumphed over the New Breed Brass Band, TBC (the To Be Continued Brass Band) and the New Creations Brass Band. Their victory may augur further change in a music scene that has experienced considerable transformation and growth in recent years.

Brass bands have marched and paraded in the streets of New Orleans since before the start of the twentieth century. Military bands preceded them, as was the case in many American locales. But in the twentieth century New Orleans added jazz to what was already an exuberant African American culture of public musical display. The synthesis created a new form of marching music, using brass instruments,

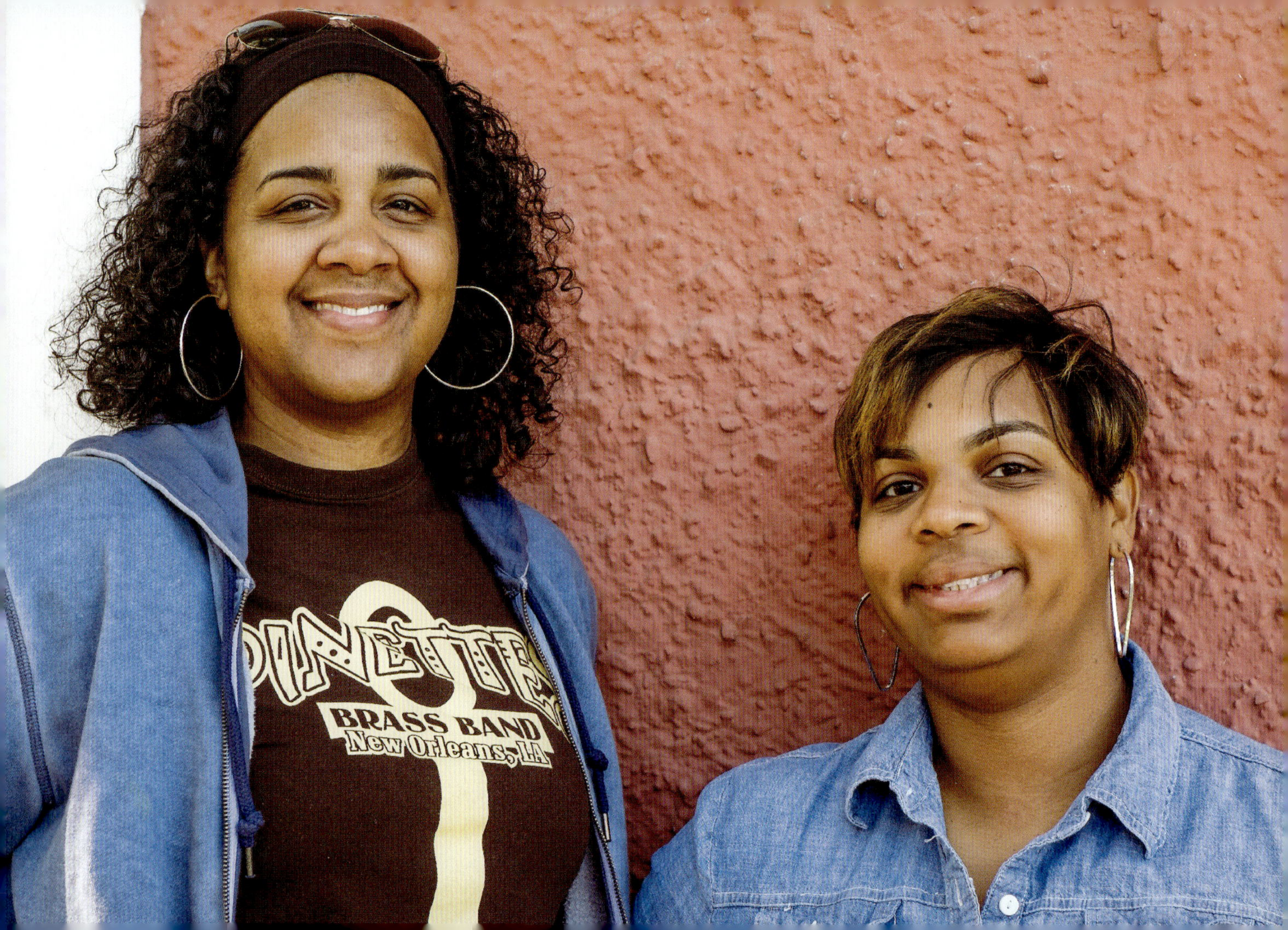

PINETTES
BRASS BAND
New Orleans, LA

strongly inflected by black aesthetics. The results were glorious.

In the early years, New Orleans brass bands dressed in uniforms; they played arrangements of religious and secular music, marching as part of funeral processions and second line parades. By the late 1960s, there was concern that these traditions were not being taken up by younger people. Danny Barker, guitarist, banjo-player, jazz musician, and cultural advocate, responded by creating the Fairview Baptist Church Marching Band in 1970. The revival of the form is often attributed to Barker's group, which had a remarkably distinguished list of alumni (see the Dr. Michael White interview in this volume).

Revival is often a form of transformation; perhaps unsurprisingly, the pace of change picked up in the aftermath of Barker's ensemble. The genealogy is clear, at least for part of the time. The Dirty Dozen Brass Band, established in 1977, added bebop and funk, and then their music took them around the world. Next, the Rebirth Brass Band, established in 1983, pushed the limits with other forms of jazz, lots of funk, and some hip hop, bringing the music to a worldwide audience.

Today, the city's brass band scene is jumping. Bands run the gamut from the uniformed, traditionalist ensembles to the groups that incorporate many kinds of popular music influences, both in their music and in the ways they present themselves. Brass bands play funerals and second lines; they perform in clubs; some tour the world, playing festivals, concert halls, and clubs. In New Orleans, many young kids, so I'm told, want to play the trumpet, where in other cities it would probably be the guitar.

Dramatic change and growth notwithstanding, the ten-piece Original Pinettes Brass Band are still pioneers. In this conversation, Christie Jourdain, band leader and drummer, and her good friend Janine Waters, the band's tuba player, talk about the group's roots in a high school marching band under the tutelage of band director Jeffrey Herbert, who

also played with the Pinstripe Jazz Band. They tell us about their early encounters with the music, both citing Rebirth's influence. They talk about the challenges of leading complicated lives, about the beauty of their friendships, and about being a singular band.

And they are singular, making their way in their own way. Unlike virtually every other brass band, the Original Pinettes don't play second-line parades—Christie says they simply don't have the volume, the strength. That cuts out what is a major source of income for many other bands, and it means they have to make it in the very competitive, and often not very remunerative, world of clubs and at private gigs. On the other hand, they've not been plagued by the violence and misfortune that have hit many of the other brass bands so hard. And now they are royalty, the Red Bull Street Kings. They'd prefer Street *Queens*.


### Roots


**Christie:**

My name is Christie Jourdain, and I am the leader and snare drum player for the Original Pinettes Brass Band. I'm from New Orleans East, the eastern part of the city. My parents were from the downtown area, Sixth Ward, Seventh Ward, where a lot of the second lines pass through. So, I guess it just was in me. My mom was a singer. She liked to sing in a choir. My oldest sister, and my uncle, my aunts, were in a choir in high school. But as far as anybody actually playing music, I think I'm probably the first one.

My dad, right now he's supervisor at River Parish Disposal Company. And he's also a mechanic. My mom, she's retired. But she worked for the city for twenty-plus years. I have two sisters. One is out in Houston; she's been in Houston since the '90s. And my little sister, she's here. But she's pretty much family-oriented—kids, husbands. I'm the middle one, the middle girl. I'm the only one that does music full time besides goes to school.

Church? Oh, yeah. Actually, I started out at St. Luke's Cathedral. I went to elementary school there. Then I went over to Goritti. My trumpet player, her mom does a choir over at St. Peter Claver, which is a church in the Treme area, Sixth Ward. It's real popular. And I think they kind of baited me in, because they're just natural. So, yeah, I try to get to that Saturday mass every time I can.

I'm studying music business at Delgado Community College. So it's fun. It's a challenge. I'm taking a recording engineering class, and it gets to be challenging. I would love to stay in the music industry, if I don't continue to do brass band music. I would love for the band to press on. We're getting old. We range from ages seventeen, eighteen to thirty-eight.

As far as the business aspect, my classes do help. Music is probably 15–20 percent—the other 80 percent is all paperwork. We even had to fight over the name before. It's crazy. So you just have to be careful. When members want to leave or split out, you just have to be real careful. You have to know the business part of that. And that thing—the business side of it—is ongoing. You never going to know enough. So, I'm learning every single day.

There's something called Super Sunday, and I remember my first time going there in like fourth, fifth grade. I just fell in love with it. My dad had a Rebirth tape. I think it was when they changed their name to Rebirth Brass Band. Because the first time I think they were called Rebirth Jazz Band. I think it was called *Feel Like Funkin' it Up*. That tape; I must have played it until it popped. And that's when I knew what I wanted to do. Because I was an '80s baby; I listened to a lot of Madonna, Bruce Springsteen, Sheila E., Prince. And I played in marching band as I got into high school. But it was different watching musicians play brass band music. That was a good challenge that I wanted to do, but I'd never think I would still be doing it years later.

I started playing drum out in the marching band at St. Mary's Academy, like 1991. That's so much different from brass band music because in marching band we're taught what to play, we're taught how to play, versus second-line music is just improvising. And you may have a unit in marching band, like six to eight members, on one line doing the same things. In brass band music, we stick to the chord, but everybody does their own thing.

**Janine:**

I'm Janine Waters, and I'm the tuba player with the Pinettes Brass Band. I'm from Downtown, the Seventh Ward. My grandfather, Albert Waters, is a musician. My great-grandfather played with Preservation Hall, Tuxedo. So, I guess it is in me.

I'm working on my bachelor's in criminal justice. I'll be done in December. I'll probably start working on my master's—in emergency management or homeland security or something of that sort. But in the meantime, I'll still be here, playing music and working on another degree, and wherever it takes me.


## Jeffrey Herbert and the Original Pinettes Brass Band

**Janine:**

A guy by the name of Jeffrey Herbert started Original Pinettes Brass Band. He was the band director at St. Mary's, back in the early '90s. He was actually a member of the Pinstripe Brass Band. He started the band for the girls, to make some extra money. You know, with parents paying tuition and everything—people wanted money in their pocket, you know, their own money. So he started the band.

When he started the band it was like sixteen members—it was like a mini marching band. From there members came and went. Once you graduated from St. Mary's Academy you were no longer in the band. He would just find somebody to replace whoever graduated. That's actually how I got into the band, because the tuba player that was before me graduated from St. Mary's, and he asked me to step in and be the tuba player.

**Christie:**

He did everything for them. I mean from what time to be there, telling them what to wear, how to play. They were real sheltered. They were real uniform.

**Janine:**

I believe the members of the band came up with the name, but he gave them a little push in that direction, maybe. It was like a collective idea. When they first started, Mr. Herbert told them what to play. A lot of them didn't really know much about brass band. They didn't listen to it. This band, now—a lot of us came up listening to brass band. We came up going to second lines. We came up around it, in the areas we grew up in. So, like I say, because they didn't really know much about it, it was just like a mini marching band, basically. Because they were told what to play, how to play.

Like I said, he was with Pinstripe, so they knew a lot of people around the city and had different connections. So, if nothing else, the band played Jazz Fest every single year. The Pinettes have played Jazz Fest every single year. If we have no other gig, it will be Jazz Fest; you'll see the Pinettes at Jazz Fest.

**Being an All-Female Band**

**Janine:**

I think it's a challenge being an all-woman band not simply because they don't want us to play this music. But when we first started, they were looking at us like, "Oh, they're just girls." I mean, we couldn't even get a guy to come and sit in on our sets, even to come to our gigs. Now it's like they line up at the side door or outside the door, and ask, "Can I come; can I come?" So it's changed dramatically.

It's just a challenge staying there and going up the ladder, because we're in a male-dominated world. Any female who's in a male-dominated world is trying to get the respect, keep it, and continue to get it.

**Christie:**

We're mothers, wives, and at the end of the day we want to take this to another level. A lot of people have their own reason why they're into the music. But we're into it because we love it. We're the first, but we don't want to be the only all-female brass band. There's people that say that they're all-female bands, but they're not brass bands. Not brass bands.

We are the only all-female brass band. That's what makes it so hard. Like when some of us go off for maternity leave, surgery, personal issues, it's hard to get an alternate. It looks easy, but it is a hundred percent not easy. We work hard for this. We work so hard. We've been running a band since like 2000, you know, by ourselves. Everything we basically get, we earn it. We go get it ourselves.

Oh man. Just to organize a rehearsal. Just to get everybody on the same page. We work via text, so every single one of the ten of us have something different going on. You have people that's working, you have people with kids, you have people on this side of town, on that side of town. And it's hard—to get everybody out at one time, to get a rehearsal to start on time. To possibly try that two, three times out of the week. Then you know, to get to a gig, and have to go to several gigs.

Plus all my band members don't just play with the Original Pinettes. One member, she just played a gig with the Hot 8, at the Vaso, last minute. So we can gig from possibly that morning until the next morning. My trumpet player plays with different bands. She plays at the church. My saxophone player, she did a performance with this show that's called *How Sweet the Sound*, a gospel show. And actually won. So she's going to Los Angeles to compete for the finalist, winner. So, it just doesn't stop. It keeps going.

**The Brass Band Scene**

**Christie:**

I tell you, there are so many brass bands in New Orleans now—when you guys leave this week, they'll have another one. They'll have another one. But it's crazy because they don't understand how serious it is and the purpose for it. Some of these guys get together just to make a quick dollar. But those guys like Rebirth—you have New Birth, Treme Brass Band, Dirty Dozen—those guys play from their heart. But they had to do it—they were supporting their families. They were doing that because they were trying to support their families. They just got

great along the way, doing it. So, no telling how many brass bands you'll have by the end of the year. It's just crazy now.

**Janine:**

The music has evolved. We've evolved a lot over the years.

A lot of us look to Rebirth as an influence, because they were the only brass band that we knew, coming up. They were great in our eyes. So it was, why not follow the best if you're going to follow somebody?

**Christie:**

Definitely. Before Rebirth came in and did their thing, it was traditional jazz, not so much up-tempo. So when they came in, the first time I saw them— well, it was the first tape, called *Rebirth Jazz Band*— they were kind of pulling the traditional to funky. By the time they came out with their second tape—at the time it was tapes, it was cassettes—they had just switched the game, they just was like, "We respect where it comes from, but this is what we're doing." And when they did that—I mean, there was the Stooges, Hot 8, New Birth, the Little Rascals—there were so many bands that started to form under that type of style. And then from then on the brass bands just started to come. Us as well.

**Our Livelihood**

**Christie:**

This is our livelihood. This is what we do. It's just what we wake up to, to try to get more gigs, try to get out there in the world, because people here still don't know we exist.

✤ The Original Pinettes Brass Band at Bullet's Sports Bar, Seventh Ward

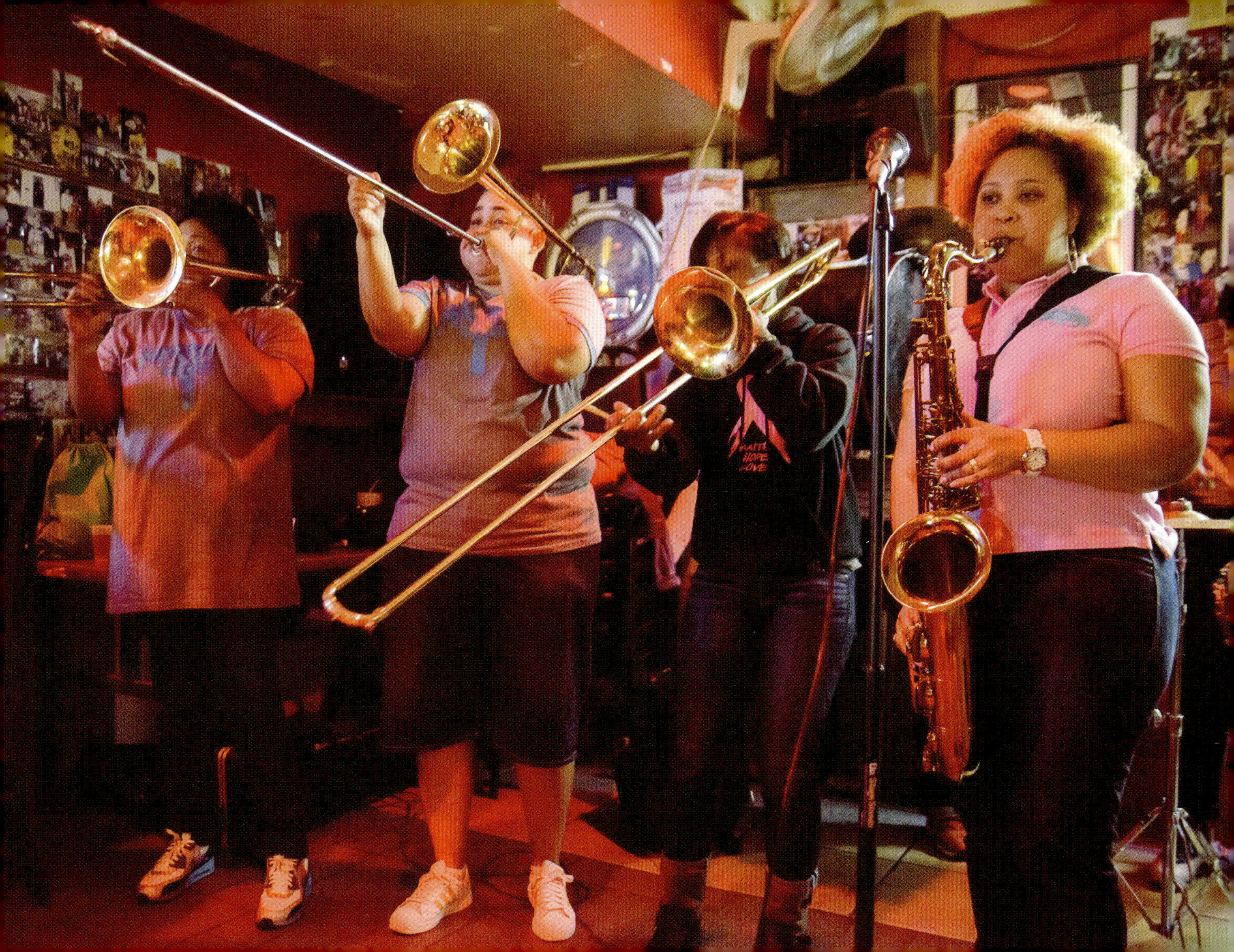

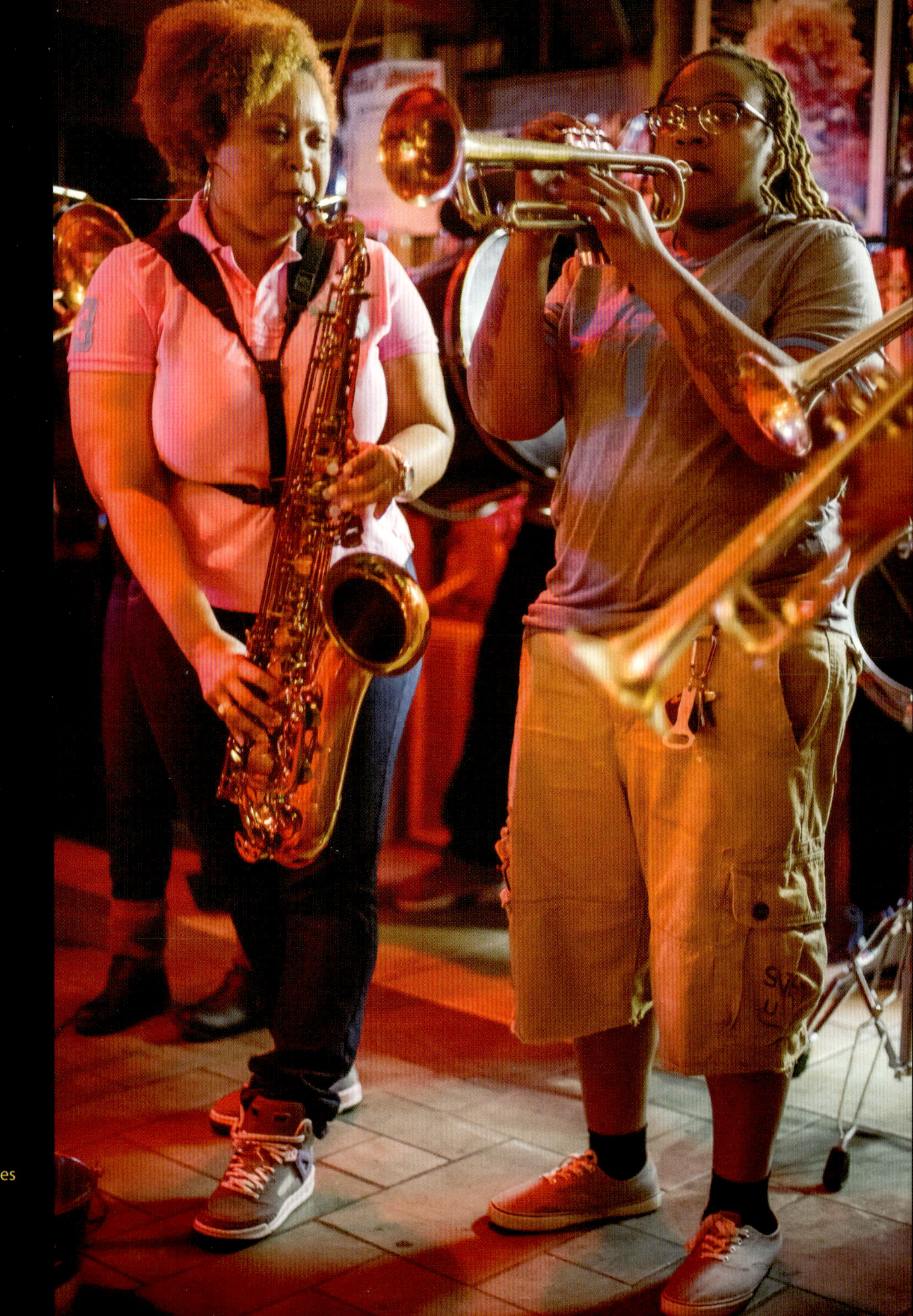

The Original Pinettes
Brass Band at Bullet's
Sports Bar

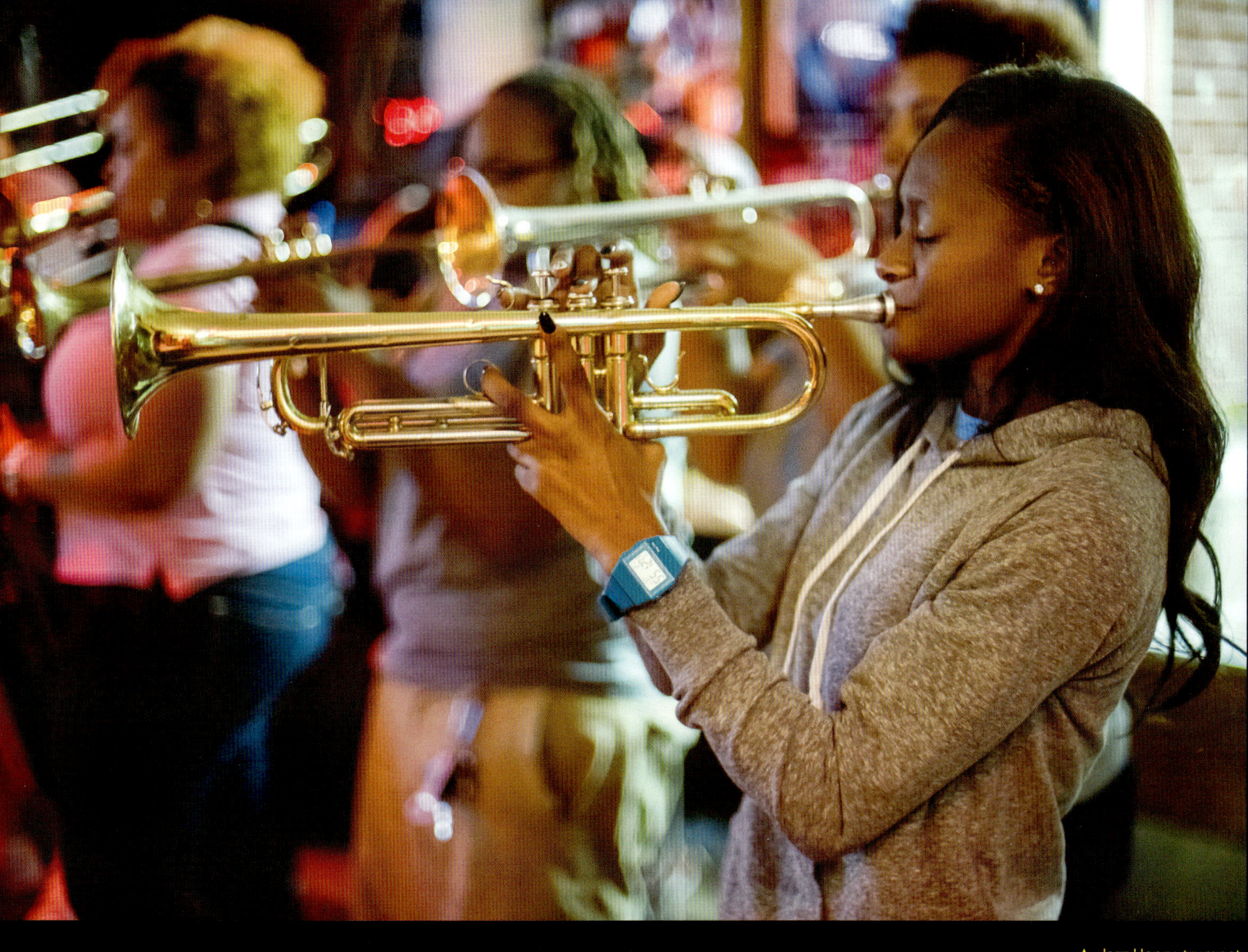

✦ Jazz Henry, trumpet
player with the Original
Pinettes Brass Band

We play the traditional music, too. I think pretty much every brass band has their own repertoire of what they do, because some gigs only require—I mean at Preservation Hall, you can't go in there and just be funky. No. So you know, that's different. Some gigs we do for the churches and some of the old Treme heads, that's all they want to hear. So you have to know your traditional and play what they want to hear.

Second lines? I'm going to be honest. I don't really think that we have the volume to make it. You know, those guys come, they be like fifteen to sixteen members. We only have ten. And that's not to say that we'll have ten members. Because we're not able to quit our jobs. We're not able to have a babysitter to watch our kids. And some of my girls' jobs are in the church that Sunday morning, doing three or four services. Or they'll play at their church and then go to another church. So it's just not feasible for us. It's really not. I have much respect for it, but no—we have to prepare for the next day. Some of those guys do second lines and go to another club and play. But we haven't broke the barrier yet to quit our jobs and take this show on the road.

We manage ourselves—we do everything pretty much for ourselves. I mean we had a few people to help us. Trombone Shorty helped us out, Phil Frazier from Rebirth Brass Band, Bo Dollis Jr. We're grateful just for the help we get. It may be a little help for someone; it's major help for us.

## Katrina

**Janine:**
I was a 911 operator at the time. So I actually had to report to work. We usually call each other—if a hurricane is coming, we'll call each other. "Where you going? What are you doing?" So we know where you're going or whatever.

I remember it like it was yesterday. I was actually on the phone with Christie, and she was like, "What you going to do? You going or . . ." And I'm like, "No, I'm going to just go to work and make this double overtime, and my check going to be nice. I'm going to be alright." My mom was in here packing clothes for me. I ended up in Dallas and in Arlington, and then I moved to Houston, where Christie's family was.

Two other girls were running the band, and they were actually back in New Orleans, and they were not doing anything. And we were like "Everybody's playing. All the brass bands are playing; they're traveling. We're the only ones not doing anything." She was like, "We just not going to do this." And I was like, "If you want to run a band, try running a band, I'll help you. But I'm not running no band." And she was like, "Okay." And from that day one, whatever she needed help with, whatever she needed me to do, all she has to do is call, text, whatever, and I'm on it, no problem.

**Christie:**
That's basically what it was. I didn't leave at first. And then I was like "I'm going to Houston," because I have family out there. And just like she said—we tried to, you know. I have family out there, but to just know what was going on, it was hard to have a bright side of anything. Once we got over that hump; it was Janine and me and the bass drummer. We were all in Houston. Cassandra was in school. She had her kids. So she really was more busy, and her thing was when Janine came to me and said, "Look, if you'll run it,

I'll help as much as I can." She was like "I'm aboard. Whatever the gig, whatever you need, I'll be there. Just tell me." And I kid you not. We were like, can you girls get us some gigs? So what happened was so crazy; we probably came home for a few gigs, not many, but we spent money, more than we were making, to come play.

Then it got to point where we had no front row, and we didn't know what to think. And Trombone Shorty came up to me and said, "What's the problem? What's wrong?" "We just going to pitch in the towel; I don't know how to build." And he said, "We'll help y'all. I don't want y'all to fail. We'll help y'all." So it was us three; me and Janine moved back home. And keep in mind, every brass band was working. Not only were they working; they were giving money, they were giving instruments, their bills were getting paid, their home—households—was getting paid. We didn't get anything. We tried to get some funding, some help for instruments. It took months to get a $500 card from MusiCares to prove that we were even a band. And then when they gave us the money, it was like, "Now, shoo. Go on."

Some bands were like, "Are you serious? We're turning down gigs. We can't even do it." And we probably had three gigs since 2005 to 2007, six, whatever it was. So we went on and moved back home. When I started to run the band, the other members was in it, but their heart wasn't in it, and they decided to vanish. So we built it up again from three members to ten. That's what I was telling you when I said it looks easy. And we had members come and go until clear up until two months ago. Come and go, and come and go. Because they see the fame, and then they get excited about it, but this band I have now is so humble and so modest.

## The Pinettes Sound, Growing Popularity

**Christie:**

In the brass band, a lot of us either do cover songs, which is songs on the radio, or take another brass band original and play it. It's really hard—this is just my opinion—it's really hard to get an original out in the brass band world, because you have to make the crowd want it. You can have an original for five years, and if the crowd not feeling it, just throw it out. And that's just how I go.

As far as originals, my saxophone player, Natasha Harris, and myself, we do a lot of original pieces, and we bring it back to the band. And I kid you not; this band going to play it. Everybody's just like, "Cool; let's just play it." Now if they're not feeling it, we take a vote and we'll throw it out. But they'll take it, and they'll own it, and then that's it. We have one called "Get a Life," that's on our CD that we sell, and the original here, called "Ain't No City." We're just paying homage to our city—what we're known for. Our football team, New Orleans Saints, the second line, and the Indians. You know, just letting people know—the food, the fun. There's no city like this one.

And now that, and our other original, "Get a Life," are being requested.

**Janine:**

By other bands.

**Christie:**

It's crazy. Like Janine said before, bands wouldn't even come see us. Now they come, and I'm like, "You guys have a gig?" "No. We come to see y'all." "Really?" And they standing on the side of the stage with their

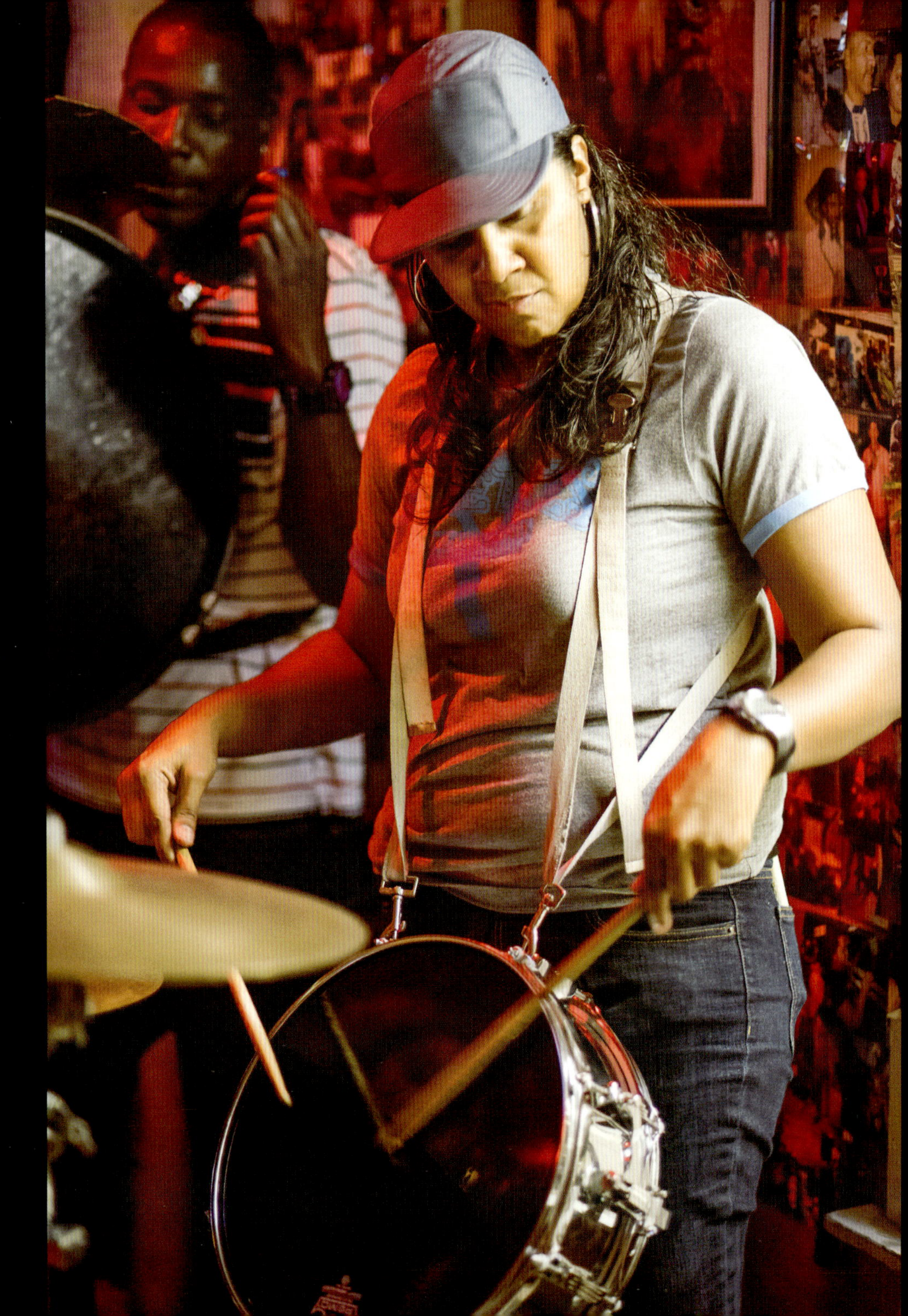

instruments, and like "Can I get on?" And I'm like, "Yes! You want my drum?" Because they never came to see us. And we never even can pack a house up. Never. Uncle Benny, with Treme—he even tried. "Come on; we going to put you opening for us." You know, he even had us over at the Candlelight. I love him. He's great. So, they try. They try to help us. And like she said, now it's different. They come now. But at one point, they didn't care what we were doing. There was even one time Walter, with the Stooges, came up us. They had something called a blowout, brass band blowout, in the House of Blues, and he looked at me and said, "Why are you all not in it?" And we was like, "They don't call us." He say, "You know what? It's a shame. We going to have to take this to the board, because I don't even want to be a part of it, if they're not even asking you." So there's a lot of people in the brass band world that is rooting for us. And a lot of them know now we're not afraid to compete.

**Red Bull Street Kings**

**Christie:**

There's this big competition coming up October 26. Red Bull. They did it two years ago, and we submitted our information, but we got rejected. I was kind of upset. But I went out there, and when I went out there, I have to be honest and say we were not ready.

This was a competition like no other. This was like a miniature Mardi Gras Day. And this year out of what—fifteen, sixteen, nineteen, or however many bands submitted—we were chosen to perform against three other bands. So we're just really focusing on that. Out of the four bands that march in, we want to be the one to march out.


✦ Christie Jourdain in performance with the Original Pinettes Brass Band, Bullet's Sports Bar

It's not going to be easy. My main thing is—if we don't win—to gain respect. I know they're coming out there to see what we can do or if we even have what it takes to get respect. Yeah, it's a whole different thing.

If you win, you get, I don't know how much money. But you get a contract—you get to record a CD. They fly you out—I don't know if it's New York or California. Fly you out in December. And you get to record with any producer that you want.

We're working real hard. Real hard. The chemistry is there. We're trying to get the fear out, the anxiety, the nervousness. We're just trying to get all that out. Once we get that out, I think we'll be okay. Once we get relaxed, it will be fine. Because we only going to be ourselves.

We going to try. We going to pull every trick we have out the bag. It doesn't matter. We say, "We may not win, but they going to know we was in the battle." It's just a whole different band here.

**"We're not blood related; we're love related"**

**Christie:**

My slogan for the band is, "We're not blood related; we're love related." Because I've been knowing these girls since forever. And the age difference is so far apart, but we still can sit around and hang with each other. Christen each other's kids. Be in each other's weddings. I mean even on the off days, they'll just come over to my house, and our kids get along well, and talk about band stuff, not band stuff, ideas we have, our next move. Life. We cry on each other's shoulder. I mean we lift each other up. Whatever it is.

I'm not going to sit up here and tell you every day is sunshine. But we'll get into it, and just be upset

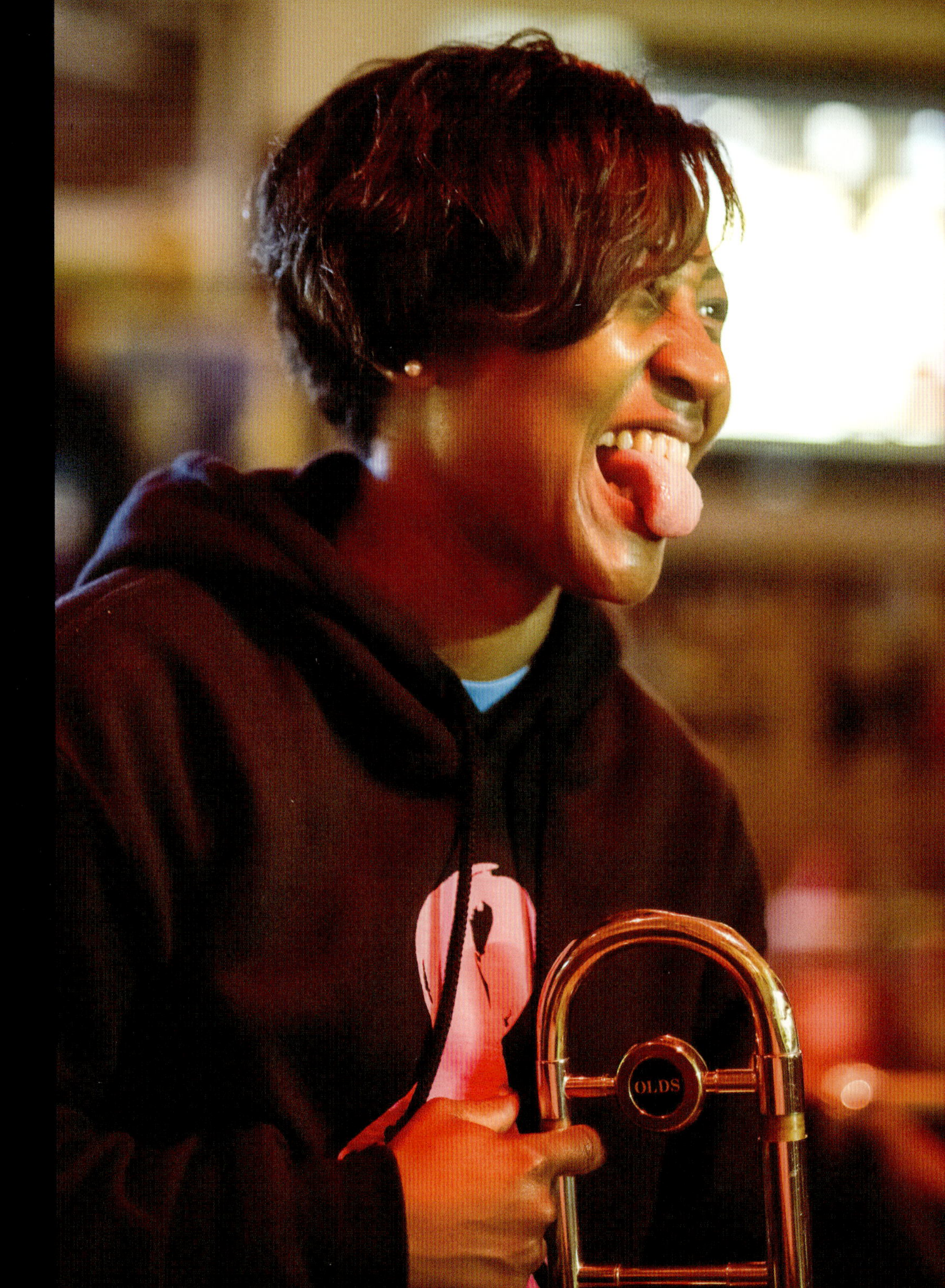



The Original
Pinettes Brass
Band at Bullet's
Sports Bar

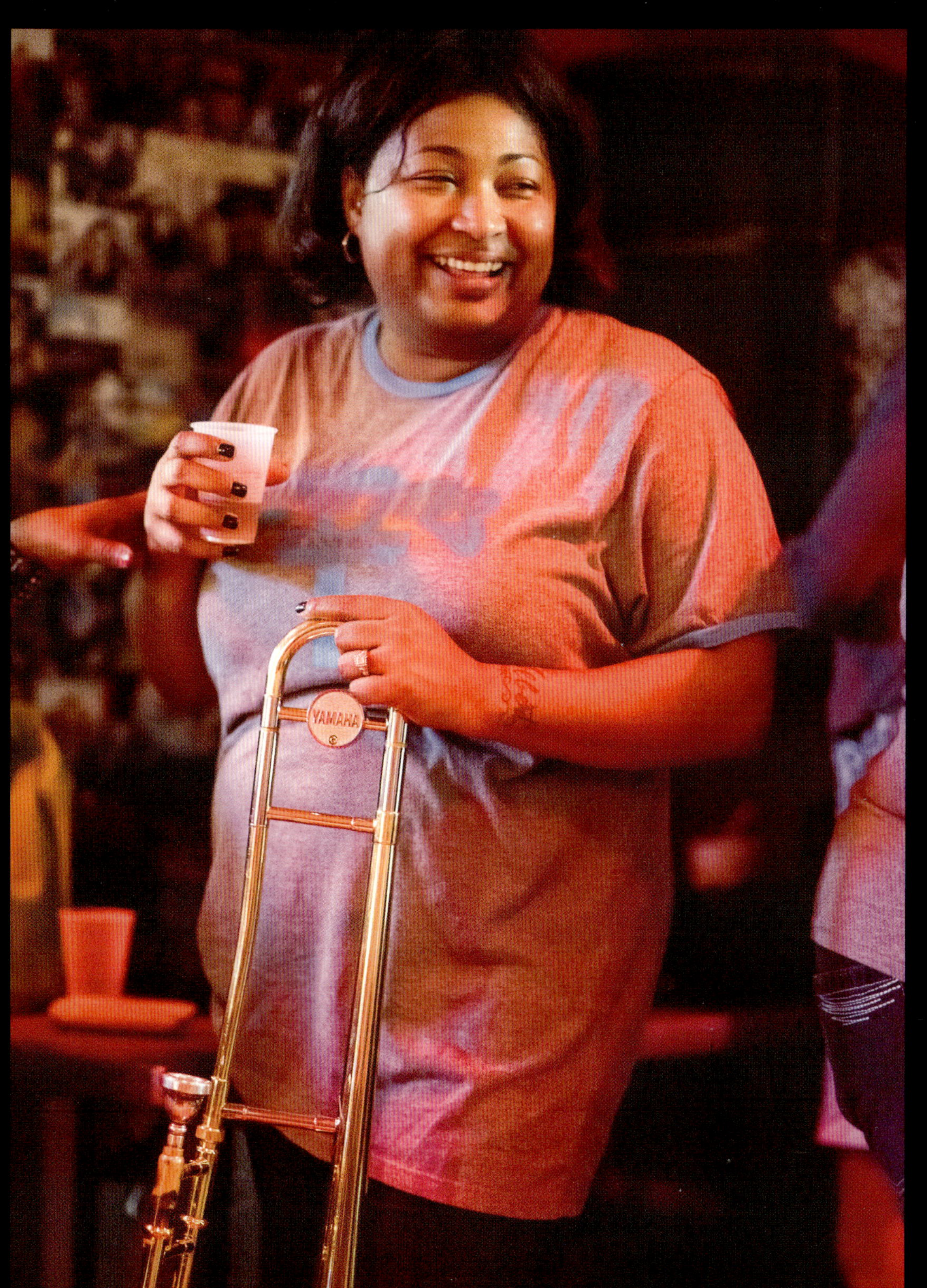



⚜ The Original
Pinettes Brass
Band at Bullet's
Sports Bar

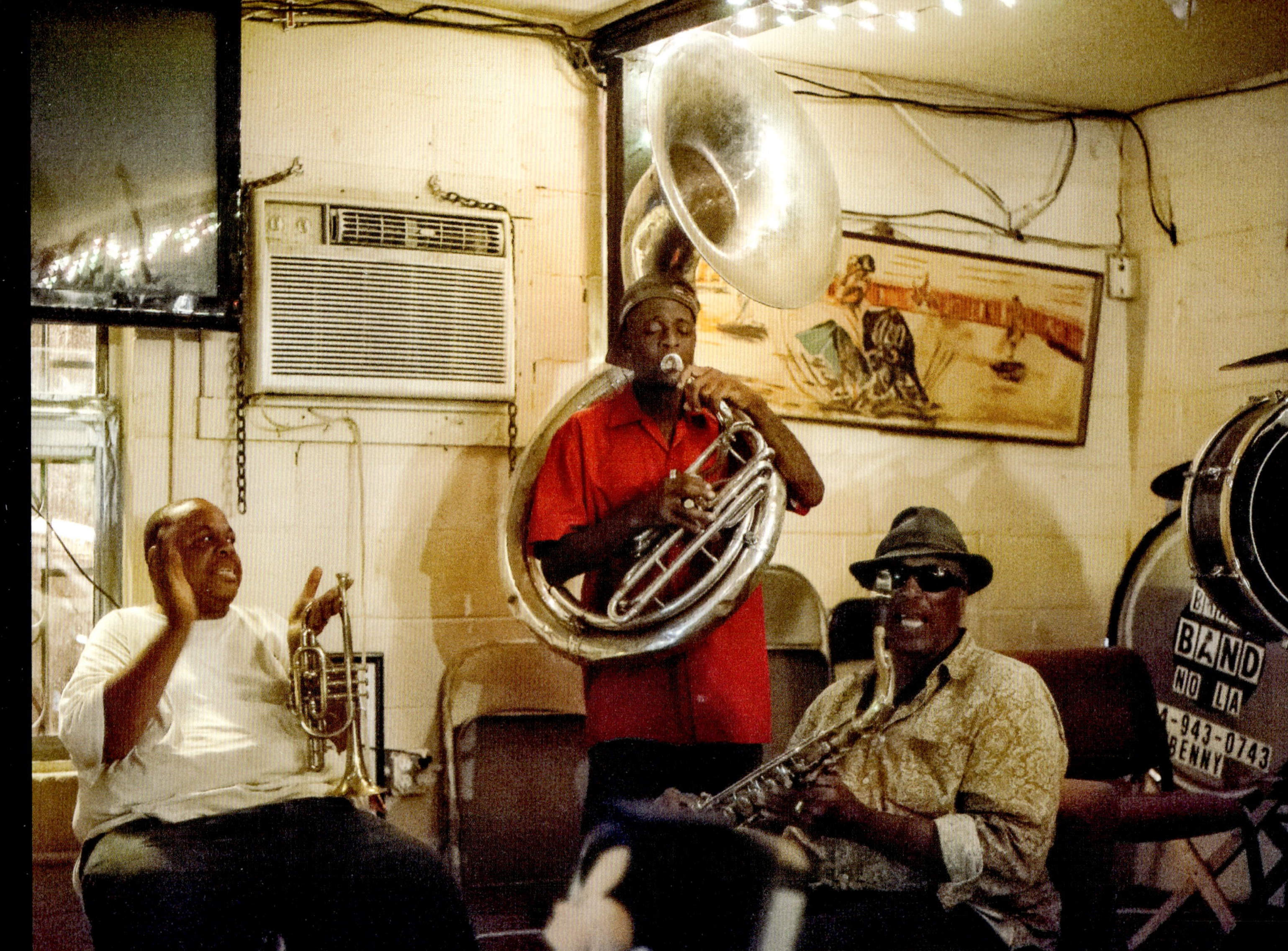
BAND
NO LA
4-943-0743
BENNY

with each other. By the time practice is over, we'll be like, "Hey y'all, want to see another band; want something to eat; want to go get a drink?" My trumpet player asked was it real. She was like, "What do you mean? Do you all like really hang with each other?" She was new to the band. She was like, "What you mean? Y'all really get along like that? Or are y'all just hanging like that so people can see y'all?" She really didn't understand it. And I had to explain that to her. "Those guys play their gig, and they go about their business. You don't really see too many other bands hang together like we do. And it's genuine. It's genuine. There's nothing phony about it. It doesn't matter if I live in this part of the city and they live in that part of the city; we go and get each other." We really have a family friendship thing here. It's real. It's really real.

We've never lost any band members to death or anything. We're blessed in that. We have our personal health issues, but it's nothing like Terrell, from the Hot 8; you know he lost his legs. Hot 8 experienced a lot. A lot of their members dead. Their tuba player went down.

So, it's nothing like those guys. We're blessed. We're just trying to take what we have and just get it out to the world. If the world's not dancing to what we're doing, then we're not doing our job.

⚖ Treme Brass Band at the
Candlelight Lounge, Treme

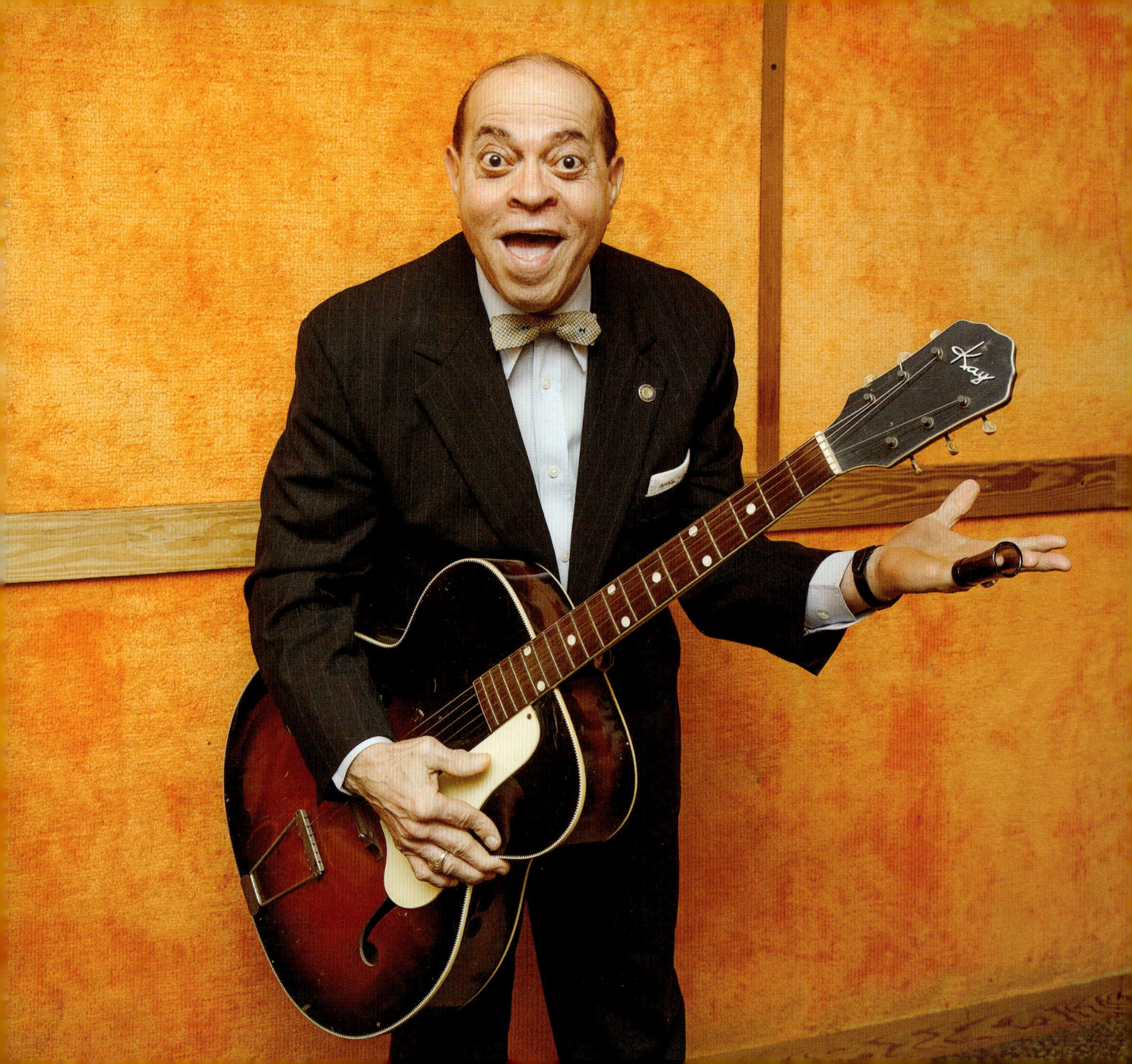

Kay

# DEACON JOHN MOORE

Singer, guitarist

Leader, Deacon John and the Ivories

[ Interviewed January 18, 2013, at his studio and home in Uptown New Orleans ]

When we knocked on Deacon John Moore's door, he opened it wearing a shirt with a nametag over the pocket—something along the lines of a mechanic's shirt. But the name wasn't his. I mentioned this to a mutual friend who told me a story. So many people recognize Deacon John, so the story goes, that a minor disguise helps him run his errands. Like many other stories, it might or might not be true. But it's believable. Deacon John Moore has made a career out of playing for private functions around New Orleans—weddings, proms, fraternity parties, Carnival balls, and the like—and he's been at it so long that he's a

well-known figure around town. And, uncredited, his guitar playing helped propel many hit recordings that came out of New Orleans.

Born in 1941, John Moore was one of thirteen children. His mother, who had graduated as valedictorian from Xavier, majored in music. She played the piano and sang in church. He sang in the choir. And then he discovered the guitar. Here he describes himself as mostly self-taught, and he talks about the powerful pull of the rhythm and blues he heard on the radio. That led to singing and playing in a number of bands, starting around seventh or eighth grade.

✦ Deacon John Moore at home, Uptown

As he matured as a musician, but still a young man, he realized that he couldn't base his career on live gigs alone.

Good fortune intervened. He was playing at the Dew Drop Inn, where his group often performed before national acts took the stage. One night, Allen Toussaint came in and invited him to play guitar on a recording session at Cosimo Matassa's studio. As an opportunity, this was as good as it could get—Toussaint the legendary producer, songwriter, and musician, and Matassa's studio the source of a huge number of influential R&B and rock 'n' roll recordings. As Deacon relates here, the next night he was in the studio playing guitar on Ernie K-Doe's "There's a Will, There's a Way." And he played on many of the records, hits and otherwise, that originated in Matassa's J&M Studio. Those records helped define the popular music of the '50s and '60s. Uncredited, as is typically the case for session players, he can be heard on any number of classic recordings, including Lee Dorsey's "Working in a Coal Mine" and "Ride Your Pony" and Aaron Neville's signature 1966 recording, "Tell It Like It Is." He played, he estimates, on about 95 percent of the recordings that came out of that studio, and he worked with other legendary New Orleans producers Wardell Quezergue, Harold Battiste, Eddie Bo, and Dave Bartholomew. So, in New Orleans, you can hire someone who helped define the role of the guitar in American popular music to play at your daughter's wedding.

He also developed his talent as a singer, building on his experience in church. It seems that he can sing just about anything, which is an important ability for someone who makes his living playing mostly at private events. In his home studio, bundles of charts sit on music stands, and it's clear that he's serious about being ready for any request. "Whatever you want, Deacon John has it," says his website. Hire Deacon John and the Ivories, and what you get is Deacon on guitar and vocals, and a band that includes keyboard, drums, bass, guitar, alto and tenor saxes, trumpet, trombone, and two female vocalists.

Musically, he's a local hero, and he has the awards to prove that. He is a member of both the Louisiana Music Hall of Fame and the Louisiana Blues Hall of Fame. New Orleans music publications *Gambit* and *Offbeat* have both honored him repeatedly. In 2010 *Offbeat* gave him its Lifetime Achievement Award. His website (deaconjohnandtheivories.com) has a very long list of those honors. And in another form of homage, in 2006 fellow musicians elected him president of the New Orleans chapter—Local 174-496—of the American Federation of Musicians. It's worth pondering the fact that he's the first African American president of that chapter, which serves a city long celebrated for the musical creativity of its black residents. He speaks here about what the union does for its members, and he paints a bleak picture of aspects of the music business, locally and globally.

A gifted performer, Deacon John has also had roles in films and commercials, and, as he says here, he looks forward to more of those. He has the presence and persona to do that kind of work. And, as he says here, film and TV people like his smile. The producers of HBO's *Treme* cast him in the show's first season, where he played Danny Nelson, the trombone mentor for Wendell Pierce's character, Antoine Batiste. Danny Nelson didn't survive the first year, and, unfortunately, while the national audience got to see Deacon as an actor, they didn't have the opportunity to see him in all his glory, as a performer. You can have that experience, though, if you search out a copy of the 2002 concert DVD *Deacon John's Jump Blues*, which documents a celebratory concert, headlined by Deacon and featuring a twenty-piece orchestra. It's worth finding.

All this is not to say that life has always been easy for Deacon John. He tells us that he was born into poverty in a racist world. He speaks frankly about the ongoing challenges of traversing the color line and about the ambiguities of being identified as Creole in New Orleans. And despite his celebrity in New Orleans, he's very aware that his musical contributions have not brought him national and international

✤ Sheet music in Deacon John's studio

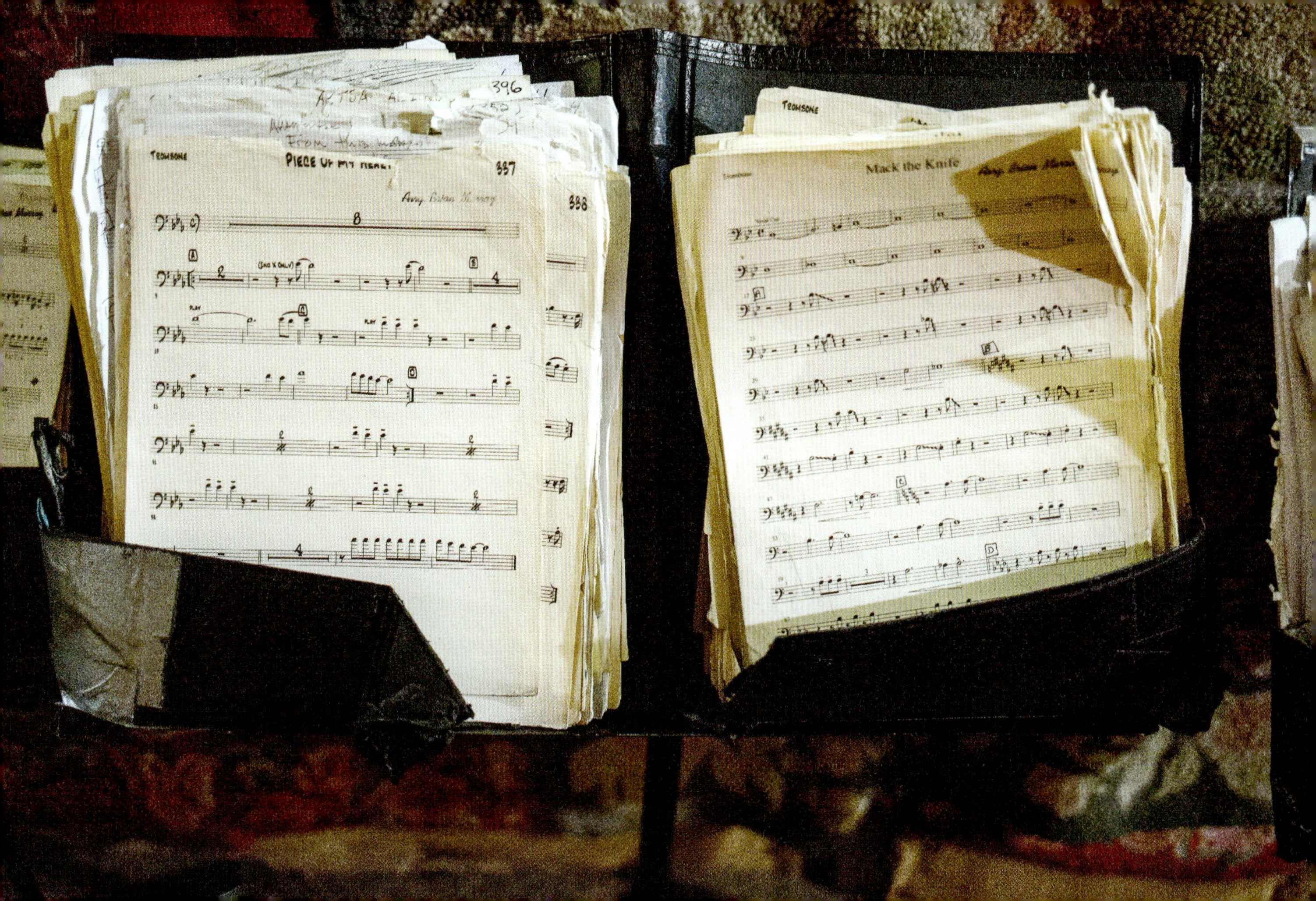

Trombone
PIECE OF MY HEART
337
338
Arr. Brian Murray
Trombone
Mack the Knife
Arr. Brian Murray
TROMBONE

fame. But the charisma is there, along with a blend of playfulness and dignity, and a strong sense of personal accomplishment. He wishes, he told us with tears in his eyes, that his mother had lived long enough to see what he became.

Thanks for thinking of me. I'm not one of the big stars, you know. I'm not in no Rock and Roll Hall of Fame. I've known a lot of the New Orleans musicians—the legendary ones—because I've played on a lot of their recordings.

## Coming up in the Eighth Ward

I was born downtown in the Eighth Ward, which is very close to the Seventh Ward, where Jelly Roll Morton was born. And he's high yellow, just like me.

I was raised amidst poverty and racism. My parents had thirteen children. I'm number five. I was named after my maternal grandfather, John Boudreau. He was a musician also. He played the banjo. And my mother played the piano. She was the valedictorian of Xavier University, the first graduating class. She was a music major and also taught school. She directed church choirs, and she also sang. We always had a piano around the house.

My mother was a very, very devout Catholic. That's why she had thirteen children. They didn't believe in birth control. She said, "I'll just have as many as God sends." And he kept on sending them.

My daddy, you couldn't tell him "No." That was one of the few pleasures he had in life. Seven boys and six girls in a little half of a shotgun double. It was quite a challenge for my parents to raise all those children. I don't know how they did it. But they did.

My father dropped out of school at eighth grade to help his father with the ice and charcoal business.

This was before the invention of the gas stove and the refrigerator. They had a fairly lucrative business in the Uptown area of New Orleans, delivering ice and charcoal. Of course, they were wiped out with the invention of the refrigerator and the gas stove. But my father continued to persevere, and he was subject to a life of hard labor because he didn't have any educational skills. Of course, my parents were married during the Great Depression, so to make matters worse, they were trying to raise kids in the Great Depression.

I wasn't born until '41, so I'm the war baby. One thing my parents did was instill in us a love for music and education. Most of my brothers and sisters are college graduates and have really excelled in their endeavors in life.

## Families and Music

Music talent, in my opinion, is largely a genetic thing. People are just born into music. Of course there are exceptions to the rule. But if you look around New Orleans, you see most of the musicians come from musical families. You see the Neville Brothers. All their kids, their grandchildren—they all turned out to be musicians. Look at the Marsalis family. Look at the Joseph family, all trombone players. Look at the Brunious family, all trumpet players. The father, the son, the grandchildren, they're all trumpet players. And you look at the Adams family, they're all string players—the mother played piano, and the sons, one of them played drums, one of them played bass, and other one played guitar—Justin Adams, a very famous and accomplished guitar player. He was very active in the New Orleans recording scene back in the '50s. Justin Adams was the guitar player on a lot of the great hits that came out of New Orleans during the '50s. Hits like "Just a Dream," with Jimmy Clanton. Some of the early Huey Smith recordings.

So, in New Orleans, just like other places in the country, musicians come from musical families. I got it from my mother's side of the family. Her father was a musician. She was a musician. My oldest sister played the viola and violin. I have a younger sister that's a percussionist. And I have two brothers who play bongos and conga drums. They played in my band at various time periods when I was coming up as a musician and bandleader.

We have a lot of musicians in the family. I have four brothers who play the guitar. One brother plays in the band with me. He plays bass—acoustic bass, electric bass. He's also a very proficient guitar player. He can play better than me.

His name is Charles Moore. I had already left the house, so I had no influence on his development as a guitar player. I just came home one day, and he was sitting down and playing. I say, "God damn! Where this dude come from?" I was just totally amazed at the level of his musicianship at such an early age. He grew up under the tutelage of my second-oldest brother, one down from me—Raymond Moore, who played classical guitar by ear. Charles was just gifted; he just was born with it.

Also, the show goes on, because I have a niece that sings with band now. She also plays saxophone, and she plays piano. She's a vocal music major who just graduated from UNO. And of course there's my brother who plays the electric bass and the guitar. He plays with a lot of other bands besides me. But to make a living you can't just play with one band anymore, unless you're playing with Wynton Marsalis or Dr. John or somebody that tours a lot.

## "I'm Primarily a Self-Taught Musician"

So I got a kind of genetic predisposition to music. At a very early age, my mother recognized that I had a talent for singing. Because I'm kind of like an entertainer—I'm a singer and a guitarist. I guess I excel more at singing than in my guitar playing.

Of course, there's a lot of dispute about that. Some people think I'm a better guitar player than I'm a singer. But I know I can sing better than I can play guitar, because I know myself by now.

I'm primarily a self-taught musician. I just kind of picked up the guitar and listened to songs on records and got little instruction books from the local music stores and sat down and just spent a lot of time teaching myself how to play. But my singing ability came early in life. My mother said she knew I was going to be a singer because she said I was the one who cried the loudest. And to solidify her beliefs about me becoming a singer, she adhered to the old Creole superstition that if you cut a child's nails under the fig tree, he will grow up to be a singer. And that's exactly what she did. Sure enough, I grew up to be a singer.

She recognized my singing ability at an early age. She used to play the piano and get me to sing for her friends. Of course, I was real shy—I had no faith in myself as a singer. Then she put me in the boys choir at school. I was kind of like, "Ooh, no." Because you had to wear all those gowns and stuff, and all the kids were calling you sissies. You know, it wasn't a very masculine thing to do to be a choirboy. If you wanted to have the masculine job, you got to be the altar boy. Because he gets to drink the priest's wine and hang out with the priests. So, anyway, I had to endure all of that, because my mother made me join the choir. She say, "You have such a beautiful voice, a gift from God, and you supposed to share this with the world."

I learned a lot singing in the choir, because we had a good choir director who showed us how to sing correctly, from the diaphragm. That was some of the best vocal training that I had, and I got it at a very early age. So, when I became a professional singer I already knew how to sing, technically.

And she used to put me in talent shows. Of course, I'd always win. She knew how to pick out the right songs for a little boy.

But, anyway, she'd get me to sing for her friends, and she'd play the piano. She would pick out songs that were kind of mature for a kid my age—songs like "Because," the perennial wedding song, with all the high notes. Then she'd pick out some little country and western songs sometimes, like Hank Williams's "Hey, Good Lookin.'" I also had an aunt on my father's side—my father's sister taught dancing. She taught toe tap and ballet. She had the first Creole dance school in New Orleans, and she taught some of the famous Creole families in New Orleans. Of course, she taught several of us—my younger brother and some of my older sisters.

Of course, I was the perfect opening act for the dancing school revues. I was a little kid in short pants. My mother would play the piano, and I would come out on stage singing—did my little bow, and people would throw money at me. Whoa. That was a mind-blowing experience.

You've got to remember I came from a real poor family. My mother couldn't work. And she had a college degree. So my father was the breadwinner. We had a lot of help from the nuns and the priests, who just adored my mother because she was such a devout Catholic. So we got the benefit of having a free parochial school education. Of course, we did a little work after school—erasing the blackboard. I sang in the choir. Several of my brothers were altar

boys. I was the one who had to stay after school for choir practice, and we had all these religious celebrations that I had to do, like funerals and weddings.

Getting back to my early tutelage as a musician, I taught myself how to play the guitar. But when I was coming up singing as a little boy, I was so shy. My mother used to make me sing for her friends, until one day one of her friends gave me a silver dime, and said, "Oh, son, you sound so good. Here." A silver dime! That was like a hundred dollars back in those days, in the '40s. That's when I found out you could get paid for singing.

That made quite an impression. So she didn't have any problems getting me to sing after that. And then that was ameliorated by me singing in the dancing school revues, because people would throw money on the stage—pennies and nickels. The only other money that we could get of our own, we had to work for it. As a child I used to cut grass, and make kites and sell them, and repair bicycles. I had a little job working at a grocery store, doing stocking, deliveries. And I used to deliver prescriptions for a drugstore when I was in high school.

I was blessed with brains, because I had a scholarship to go to one of the best boys high schools in the city. That was St. Augustine, the Purple Knights. I had a four-year academic scholarship. During my high school years is when I started playing the guitar. When my sisters had to go to the high school dances, they needed a quote-unquote *chaperone*, because my mother was unable to do that. She had too many children. So she sent me. I used to park myself right in front of the stage. I would just sit there, transfixed, all night, and look at the musicians.

I would focus primarily on the guitar players. I got to hear some of the really great guitarists that were playing in the popular high school bands when my older sisters were attending high school—like Art Neville and the Hawkettes, Allen Toussaint and the Flamingos, Dave Bartholomew, and Snooks Eaglin. So I got to see all the bad cats. I would just sit there, transfixed, right in front of the stage, watching the guitar players. And all of a sudden, I wanted a guitar, too. So I saved up my little money, and my older sister who played violin and viola, took me to a pawn shop, and that's where I bought my first guitar.

I just kind of taught myself from listening to various recordings. I had another challenge, because my mama didn't like rock 'n' roll. My mother would mop the floors and sing the arias from operas. She knew all of *La Traviata*; she knew all the great classics, because she studied that when she was going to Xavier University. She knew all the church songs, too. And she loved popular music; we used to listen to some of the pop music on the radio—Doris Day and Sinatra and all of the great people that came out during the '40s.

### Rock 'n' Roll, Blues, R&B

But, me, I liked rock 'n' roll. Well, it wasn't called rock 'n' roll then; it was rhythm and blues—blues music, and R&B. The phrase *rock 'n' roll* didn't come into existence until sometime in the '50s when Alan Freed, the famous disc jockey involved in payola— he's the one who coined the phrase, *rock 'n' roll*. He observed the undulations and gyrations of the hips and the buttocks of the people that were dancing. And he said, "Looks like they're rocking and rolling when they dance to that kind of music." The phrase just caught on, and it's been that way ever since.

I came up during the great period of rock 'n' roll, the early '50s, late '40s. I didn't have a record player

around the house, but my cousins who lived next door did. They'd buy these 78 records, and I could hear through the walls. They were playing, "I want to do it, do the chicken with you." And all the popular songs, like "Work with Me Annie," "Annie Had a Baby."

My mama didn't want me to listen to that stuff. When she heard Shirley and Lee, she said, "Ooh, that woman sound like a cat on a hot tin roof. Turn that stuff off." So to listen to rhythm and blues, I bought myself a crystal radio with headphones. I'd wait until they'd go to sleep that night, and I'd pull out my little headphones, and I'd tune in to WLAC in Nashville, Tennessee. Or I'd tune into Del Rio, Texas, with Wolfman Jack.

So I got my early education of rhythm and blues and blues music. Back then they called it *race music*, and it couldn't get played on mainstream radio. You had to know the stations to listen to to get Big Maybelle and Chuck Berry and Little Richard, Howling Wolf, and Muddy Waters, and stuff like that. Man, I just couldn't get enough of it. I would get my guitar, and I'd try to play along. That's what inspired me to play—I got hooked on rhythm and blues and blues music.

### Early Bands

I started singing in a little band when I was in like seventh and eighth grade, when I was singing in the choir. Some of my friends had organized a little rhythm and blues band, and they were playing all the hit records and playing little dances and talent shows. So, I decided, I'm going to see if I can get in with them. We were all friends in school.

So I started singing with the band. They had two singers, me and another guy. We would sing all of the

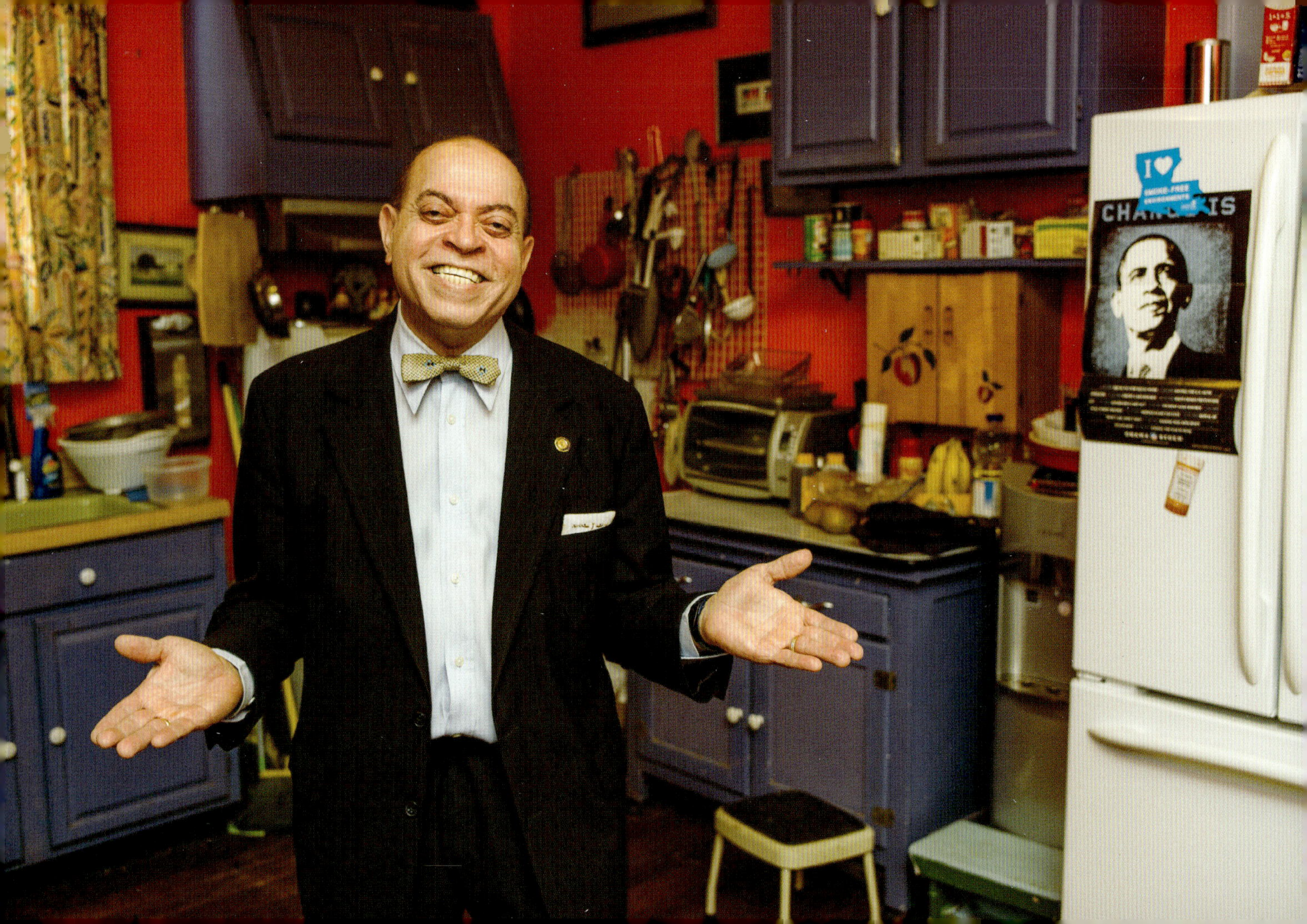

I ♥ SMOKE-FREE ENVIRONMENTS
CHAMPIONS
OBAMA BIDEN

big hits, like Lloyd Price, "Lawdy Miss Clawdy," and we'd sing Little Richard, "Lucille," "Tutti Frutti," Fats Domino, "I'm Walkin'," Chuck Berry with "Johnny B. Goode"—all the great hits. Chuck Berry started out as a blues musician, before he crossed over into rhythm and blues. He had his own unique brand of R&B, because he infused country music and blues music, and just like him, Little Richard's formula was, he would amalgamate gospel music and blues music. And he came up with all the screams and yells from the church. It was Fats Domino who combined the polyrhythmic and syncopated music of New Orleans and the Caribbean with the junco blues element.

So that was the music of my generation. I cut my teeth on playing those kind of songs. But being in New Orleans, it was kind of hard to get a gig unless you played a variety of music. So I had to learn some jazz, too, like "The Saints Go Marching In," "Bourbon Street," and various New Orleans jazz songs. And then I hung around the musicians who could play. They showed me, gave me pointers on the guitar, people like Roy Montrell, Justin Adams.

I started playing with various pickup bands. Somebody'd call, say "Hey, what you doing tonight? I got a gig for you. I'm going to come pick you up." So they pick you up, and they go pick up the bass player and the drummer, and they all get into a car and roll out to the gig. That was the days before PA systems. All you did was plug the mic into your guitar amplifier, and that was it. You had to have at least one horn, a strong tenor man, because all the hit records had tenor saxophone solos in them. The guitars were primarily a rhythm instrument until they broke loose on some of the stuff. But as the years progressed, the guitar players became the kings. People didn't want to hear all that blowing anymore; they wanted to hear somebody on the guitar.

There's more to my story, but primarily that's how I developed my talent as a guitarist and a singer—from singing in the church choirs and then playing in all these pickup bands as a guitar player. I found out early on that I could get more gigs if I could play and sing. They'd jump over a hundred guitar players to get to one that could sing—kill two birds with one stone. So I was a very popular musician, playing in all the pickup bands. The one I played with the most was a band called the Ivories. They were mostly fellows of my own age, from high school. We played a lot of the fraternities, and we played a lot of picnics, and we played a lot of carnival balls for black people. And then we crossed over to start playing for white people in the fraternity and sorority parties and dances.

Then our popularity spread. I hate to say it, but it was primarily because of me, because I was the front man. The leader was the drummer, but I was the guy out in front, singing and entertaining the people. During that time era, you had to have a front man. Like every band was called Danny and the Juniors, Danny White and the Cavaliers, Sugar Boy and the Cane Cutters. You had to have an *and* attached to the guy who was fronting the band. That was the way things were back in those days.

When the band broke up, I took the helm and hired some other players, and retained the name, the Ivories. I didn't have a professional name then. I was just John Moore, or Red, or whatever nickname attached to me. So everybody looked at me, saying, "What we going to call him?" We were sitting around at a rehearsal, and everybody was putting names in the hat.

The drummer was much older than us, and he played with Roy Brown, Professor Longhair; he also was a trumpet player. We were just all tossing names around, because before that I was just John, the guitar player. All of a sudden, he saying, "Let's call him Deacon Jones." And everybody just fell out laughing. "Yeah, let's call him Deacon Jones. He look like a deacon." I started crying. I said, "Man, don't call me Deacon Jones." I said, "We wouldn't never get nowhere, because they think we got a gospel group. We won't never get no gigs. They ain't going to play our records on the radio. Everybody going to think we're a gospel group!" Everybody just fell out laughing. And they said, "Yeah, I like that—that name's going to stick. Ain't nobody else got a name like that." I found out that Deacon Jones was some mythological character that was talked about in a song that Roy Brown did, "Good Rockin' Tonight." You remember the line that says

> Deacon Jones, Elder Brown, two of the slickest cats in
>     town.
> They'll be there, just wait and see.
> Rockin' and a stompin' at the jamboree.
> I heard the news; there's good rockin' tonight.

I didn't know that at the time, but I found out later that during the era that I came up, when I first organized a band, most of the singers had some kind of preaching quality to their songs. Like James Brown, Ray Charles—he was the high priest, you know. And during their songs, they would do some preaching—like Solomon Burke. Ray Charles, especially—he would take you to church in a minute. "Let's see all the hands of the good Christians in the building." Now, he'd do, "If you've ever been in love with somebody that didn't love you, let me hear you say 'Yeah.' Hit me!"

We had all kinds of gigs. We would back up a troupe of female impersonators sometimes. We'd play at the Dew Drop for floor shows. And we played the carnival balls and picnics, all kinds of miscellaneous engagements. That's where I came up. During those days you couldn't really make it as a musician unless you had a well-rounded education, and you could play a waltz, you could play jazz, you could play R&B. You had to do it all. Most of the musicians from my era grew up having to play a huge variety of music.

Over the years, I've looked back, and I've said, "The only thing I can brag about is I was able to make a living from playing music." I've never had a day job. That makes me the envy of all the musicians—that I could make it without getting a job.

I never had any hit records. I had a little regional record, "Many Rivers to Cross." But throughout my career I've never had chart-busting records, toured the country, played all these foreign countries, all these festivals all over the country and the world. But I was able to make a living just playing music.

**A Session Musician**

And I just didn't do gigs. I found out early on that you can't just do gigs. So I did other things through the years. The first big break I had was playing on recording sessions. I was playing at the Dew Drop one night; in walks Allen Toussaint. He just walked right up to me while I was playing on stage, and he said, "I like the way you play. Would you like to come in the studio and make some records?" Man, you can't imagine the exhilarating feeling that has when somebody like that invites you to play on recording sessions.

So I seized the opportunity. The next night I was in the studio, playing on Ernie K-Doe's "There's a Will, There's a Way." And I played on the early Lee

Dorsey recordings. I was an accessible musician, because many of the studio musicians, guitar players, they were constantly touring with Fats Domino, some of the prominent bands. They would be on tour. Me being mostly a local musician, they could get me like that. "What you doing tomorrow night?" Boom. "I ain't doing nothing." "Come on down the studio. We got a session on Lee Dorsey; we got one on Irma Thomas; we got one on Professor Longhair." I played on a lot of the hit records that came out of New Orleans back in the late '50s, early '60s.

That's when I became of age—when I was doing recording sessions I was in my early twenties. That's a big thrill for a kid, you know, to be playing on records. You get in the studio, and then all of a sudden you hear them on the radio. "Hey, that's me playing on that!"

We mostly played from charts. Some people, they'd just have head sessions; they'd just run the song down to you, tell you, "You know what to do. Just do what you got to do." And some people, like Allen, well, he was more strict. Everything he wrote, he had the music for. He would write out all the parts. I got to hanging around his house, and I saw all the artists come in, that hang at his house. We'd go over some of the stuff that we had to record the next day. I could see all these artists coming in and out his house all day long.

One of my favorite stories, you know—Chris Kenner knocks on the door. Chris Kenner. He had a French bread wrapper; it was all crumbled up. He unfolds it, and he had the lyrics to "Land of a Thousand Dances" written on it. And he started singing it, and Allen got on the piano and turned the tape recorder on, trying to get his key. Chris was one of the few artists that Allen didn't write for. Chris had his own stuff. Most of the artists that Allen recorded,

he was the songwriter also—like for Ernie K-Doe, Irma Thomas.

I was real fortunate that he chose me to be the guitar player on most of the recordings—the early Aaron Neville stuff, stuff on Minit Records. Later on when Allen got out of the service, he resumed his recording career with Marshall Sehorn, and they started producing even more records. But the style of music had changed; the guitars were the king then. So he would hire two, three guitar players. During that period the piano playing was really sparse, because he had to let the guitars stick out. Before that, the guitars was in the back seat. Allen played the piano, and the piano was dominant in all the recordings that he produced back in that early seminal period when he started working for Minit Records and Instant Records, producing hits like "Mother-in-Law," "Fortune Teller," "Lipstick Traces," "It's Raining." I was the guitar player on just about 95 percent of all those songs that were recorded back then. I would call it the ghost guitar player, because nobody knew the musicians who played on the record, except the producers and the bandleaders—whoever happened to be in the studio knew who played on the records, the artists.

I had a popular band in town at the same time. Many of the artists we recorded would play on the shows with my band, because I was the guitar player, and I knew the songs. They would be like an extra added-on attraction on many of the dances that I played for. They'd say, "Well, how much more would it cost to get Irma Thomas to play with you?" I'd say, "I don't know; I'll call Irma and see if she can come and sing with us."

I knew Esquerita when I was playing at the Dew Drop. So I got to play on the "Green Door," and all the stuff that Esquerita recorded with Allen Toussaint. I played all the early Lee Dorsey ones, then the new Lee Dorsey ones that came out after Allen got out of the service, like "Working in a Coal Mine" and "Ride Your Pony," all the stuff that was heavy on the guitars. Through the years I had cultivated a good friendship also with other producers like Wardell Quezergue, Harold Battiste, Eddie Bo, Dave Bartholomew. And once you play on a few hit records, everybody think you got the magic touch. They say, "Let's get him. He played on 'Mother-in-Law.' Let's get him. If we get the right cats, we can have another hit record."

This was mostly in Cosimo's studio. I go way back with Cos. When he had, not the first J&M studio, but the second one he had was on Governor Nicholls, in the French Quarter. No air conditioning. He started out with one track, but I came into the scene when he had two tracks. We had to kind of position everybody to get a good balance of the instruments all on one track. Then he'd save the other track for the vocals. And many a time we had to record the vocals and the instrumental at the same time. Cos, being so creative and all, he built a booth where the singers would be isolated from the musicians. He had it on wheels, just like a telephone booth. The singers would go inside of there and sing while the band was playing, to avoid the bleedover into the tracks.

I was on the ground floor when all this stuff was happening. So I saw how all this stuff developed, playing on various recording sessions. And I saw the advent of the new technology. But I started out when they only had like two tracks. In the early days, before me, like Dave Bartholomew and Fats—they only had one track. So they had to do everything at one time. Dave said he used to try out different positions in the studio—"Let's put the bass over here, in the corner, so it won't bleed into the saxophone mikes, and put the drum here, build a drum cage around it to keep it from bleeding into the mikes." So he could get fairly good sound; he had to experiment. Sometimes those recording sessions lasted all day, because you had to go back and do other takes until you found the right positions in the studio to get a good recording quality sound. Because the singers had to sing at the same time. You couldn't come back and overdub the vocals. So that was quite a challenge to the musicians and the studio itself, with Cosimo Matassa.

By coming in on the ground floor, I got to know a lot of people, like Cosimo Matassa. All the top producers—Dave Bartholomew, Wardell Quezergue. Harold Battiste. Harold started out as a session musician, too. Then he got his own company together and started producing; he said, "Well, if I'm doing all this work for these other companies, why can't I do it for myself." So he organized a group of studio musicians. They had their first big hit with Barbara George's "I Know." He also did Prince La La. I played on a lot of those historic sessions with Prince La La—was the guitar player for "You Put the Hurt on Me." I played on a lot of Wardell's stuff with Nola, like "Barefootin'," "It Ain't My Fault," "Teasin' You," all the various artists Wardell had.

And I played on so many records that weren't hit records. Allen had a big roster of artists, besides the successful hit recordings. I think his philosophy was to do as many as you can, and some of them are bound to be hits. And he was right on the money. I mean maybe like two, three times a week he'd be in the studio cutting on different artists. Just by the numbers game, one of them was bound to come through and be a hit. And sure enough, a lot of them did come through.

During those days four songs was a typical recording session. The musicians union had structured a formula—no more than four songs, and each song can't be any more than three minutes long. You had to do it within a three-hour time period, because anything over that was overtime and double sessions.

We never got rich. The singers didn't get rich, either. Everybody has a different story for why they didn't get rich. Some of them, it was the lifestyles of the rich and famous—sex, drugs, rock 'n' roll. Touring and wasting your money. Getting ripped off by unscrupulous agents and managers. And having to compromise your songwriting abilities with the producers and record companies—you had to give away your publishing rights or make some kind of deal for just a small percentage. During those days, they were only paying the artist 2 percent from the sale of the records. And that 2 percent was just your mechanical money you made from the sale of the records. Because if you didn't write the song, all you could hope for was the mechanical residuals. And for you to make any money from that, they had to subtract all the money that it took to produce, advertise, distribute, and promote the record. You had to sell a lot of records to make money back in those days.

The same thing is true now, but now the record business is even worse. All of a sudden we have the technological displacement where the machine has taken over. I don't see a very bright future, because the technology has gotten so good that you can now make perfect copies. Most of the big sales of records is not in the millions like it used to be. If you've got a hit, a million and a half is very good. Back in those days, a few million was nothing. We created a monster that's eating ourselves up. That's the way I see it.

To make it even worse, big conglomerates control broadcasting now. Then you've got only like a handful of record companies. And in order to get recorded, they want all your rights—your publishing, your writers. Give it up. Because they say "You don't have the wherewithal to do this and distribute this and produce this. So this is what you got to give up. Bend over." And that's become the norm now.

So nowadays a lot of the companies are saying, "Don't expect to make any money off records. It's only a promotional tool to expose your music." I don't particularly subscribe to that, because I come from the old school. The worst thing I see now is that with all of this downloading and people making perfect copies. The publishers don't get paid. The songwriters don't get paid. Nobody gets paid. All the people involved in the production, the promotion, distribution—they don't get paid anymore now. Nobody wants a CD anymore because they can get 5,000 songs in the palm of their hand on a little iPod. And most of them they can get for free or they can just buy them by the song rather than buy the LP. When I was coming up, that's during the '70s, you'd get a whole album of songs, but you couldn't buy just the one you wanted. So now the consumers are the producers—"I'll just get this one by Aaron, one by Deacon. And I'll make my own CDs, and I can make copies for all my friends and share them with them. I can just put them on my iPod, walk around with five, ten thousand songs." And all of this is done to the detriment of the artist and the musicians, the record company. Everybody's getting screwed.

I think it's going to stifle the industry. And it's filtering down into the movies. Videos, all that, can be easily downloaded, because it's all digital now. So all of this stuff is coming into play now, bigtime. The worst thing is coming to the theatrical districts in New York, Nashville, California—they want to replace the pit bands with recorded music. So you have boombox ballet. They say, "Well, they don't see the band, so we'll just play a recording. The people ain't going to know. Just play a recording, and we don't have to pay all these musicians to play in the pit."

## The Live Music Scene

I've never seen the live music scene in New Orleans get this worse. It's the same principle applied—there's a plethora of musicians and not enough places to play. The schools are turning out a surplus of really talented musicians, and they have hardly any places to perform live. So what happens, you create a dog-eat-dog mentality. And the club own-ers and the live music purchasers, they're all hip to this stuff. They say, "Well, we shouldn't have to pay musicians." That's what's going on now. Some of the major clubs in New Orleans say, "Why should we have to pay a band if they don't draw a big crowd?" And the musicians are so desperate for getting gigs and having exposure so they can hit the big time or get discovered, anything, a big record company, a deal. That's one of the worst things. That, combined with the illegal downloading; it has devalued music.

The worst-case scenario is coming up. People are going to expect music to be free. The poor musi-cians, they're backed in the corner. Now, instead of the club owners having to pay for music, they'll just tell the bands, "Well, you just have to pass the hat around and get whatever you can. Because we can't guarantee you any money. And if you don't want to take it, we've got two, three other bands down there who will do it." Or you can get a percentage of the drinks and the bar, and the bartender's skimming off the top. Or you've got to get two, three bands to take the door. It's like pay to play now. And we all got to share the door receipts from that particular night—and you got, what, three bands going to split up a few hundred dollars, if they were able to draw enough people.

I'll give you a perfect example. One of the local clubs, they'll have like three bands playing, and each band gets the door receipts for the sets that they do. So if you first up and you get so much for the people that come in to see you, that's your money. And the second band, the same thing. The third band, the same thing. Of course, it creates a lot of confusion, because somebody comes in for the first show, they want to see the second band and not have to pay any more. You can see the scenario for that. It's just a lot of chaos.

And the record business is so bad; you don't have these long-term contracts any more, where there's artist development. If you don't make it on the first run—boom; they're going to drop you and get somebody else. And then some of the people who are not selling enough records, like Roberta Flack or something, well, boom—they won't record them anymore. So you lose your contract. I've seen a lot of big-name people in jazz and R&B, they get dropped by the record company because they're not selling enough records.

It's so hard to compete in a business where tech-nology rules. And the people's taste in music has degenerated, too. You have the dumbing down of America, which in my opinion came through rap, where people could just curse and scream and yell, and sell whole bunches of records, because, you know, trash is cool. The envelope of free speech is constantly being tested. Because the stuff that you hear now, when I was coming up there was no way you could entertain with that or get it played on the radio. Or even get it sold in the marketplace.

✣ Deacon John in his studio

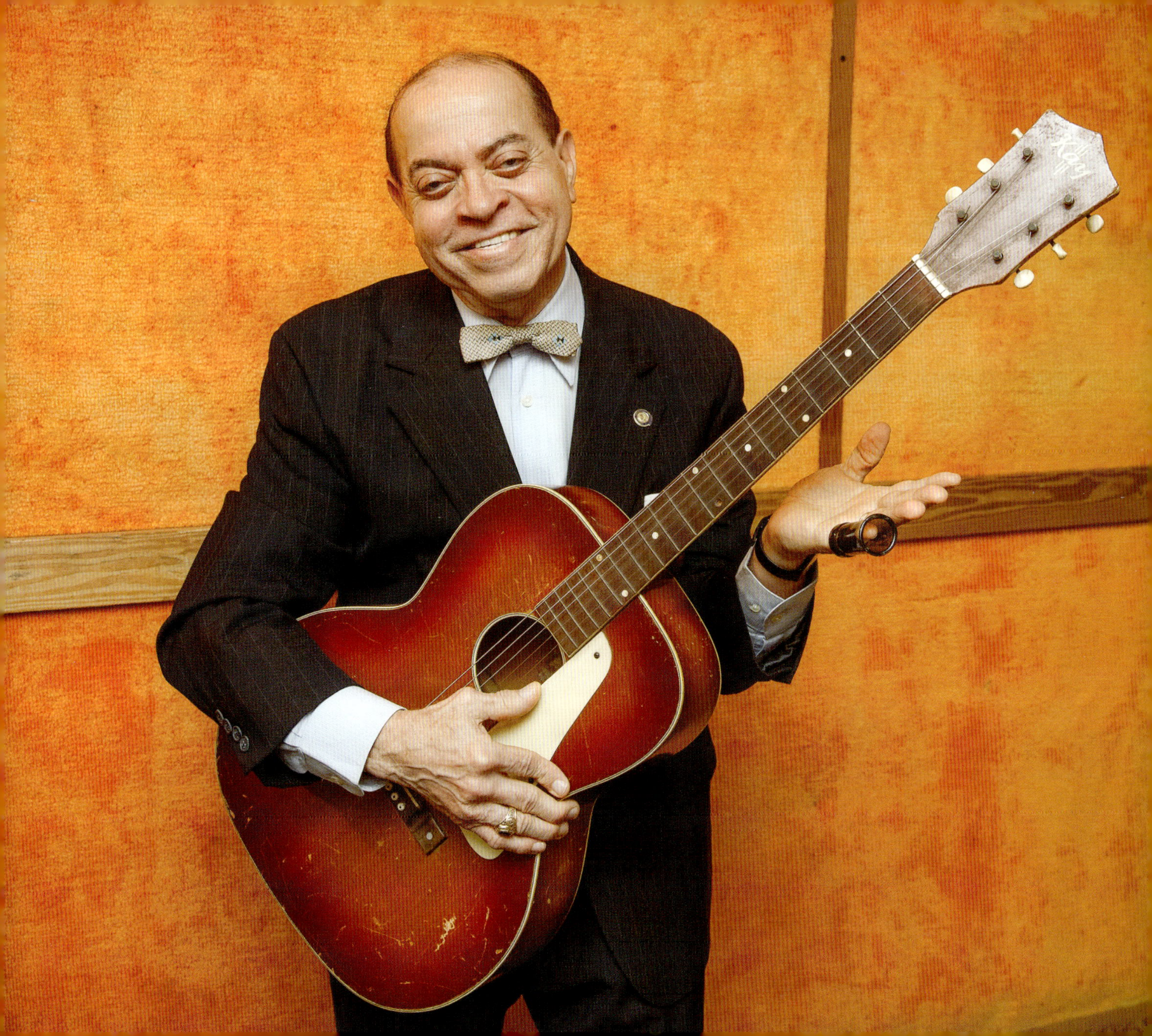

## Live Gigs

Live gigs are my mainstay. Over the years my success is attributed largely to being able to play in multiple markets. I attribute my success in live music as being able to play a huge variety of material. You look at that book on the music stand; I've got five hundred, some-odd, charts in there to cover all types of engagements. I can play a wedding reception, a carnival ball, a debutante ball, high school class reunions, festivals—all kinds of engagements. Over the years I've amassed a reputation about "That cat can play anything."

I've never been on tour in my life, and I haven't played in foreign countries or played all these festivals all over. I've been playing music fifty-five years; the little offers I've got to go in foreign countries, they're just laughable. Give you an example. A few years ago a guy called me from London, wants me to come play over in London—"I've got a few club dates, I'll get a little pickup band to back you up. But I can't pay you." He said, "I'll bring you over here and put you up in a hotel," he says. "You have to make it on selling your CDs." There are other people who go along with that. "Well, so-and-so came over here, and he sold his CDs. I didn't have to pay him. It's good promotion," and blah, blah, blah. I just laughed at him. Said, "Man, I make more money playing a wedding reception than to go all the way over there."

Back when I was coming up, you know, I was the prom king. I played for everybody's prom. People remember the band that played at their prom. So through the years, I played at your prom, I played at your college fraternity parties, and now these same people, they're calling me to play for their children's weddings, their grandchildren's weddings. I played a wedding last year, and the father of the bride said,

"You remember you played for my wedding?"

I said, "Oh, yeah."

He said, "It's my daughter's wedding tonight."

"Whoah. I played for your wedding, your daughter's wedding."

He said, "I got another daughter going to get married. I'm going to call you for that one."

So the business, just over the years, has accumulated into more and more things. I play casinos. I play all different types of engagements.

## Acting

I have another career, too, as an actor. I've been in television commercials. The big one I was in last year was, "What's in your wallet?" for Capital One. I did Snickers candy bars, Southern Comfort liquor, Miller beer. I also did bit parts in movies and television shows.

I was one of the actors in *Treme*. I was sorry when they killed my character in *Treme*, because they couldn't bring me back as myself. That was one of the regrets the producer said. "Yeah," he said, "One of the biggest regrets I had was that once Deacon John, the character that he played, died in the show, we couldn't bring him back as himself." But I really enjoyed, acting and playing the part of a trombone player. I didn't know how to play a trombone, but I knew how to make it look like I was playing it.

I like acting. I see that as maybe my future. I can still play the live gigs, but I would like to get more into acting, television commercials, movies. Opportunities might be a little limited because of my age, but there are parts for older people in everything that goes down, from the movies, the television shows, television commercials. I can be an actor/

musician, also—like in the Capital One commercial, I was a banjo player. I won the audition for the Capital One commercial because they liked the way I said, "What's in your wallet?" They said they liked me; they liked my smile.

If you've got a good smile, that's what they look for. I went through hundreds of auditions. You have to live with the fact that you have to be able to handle rejection if you want to be in that business, because you're going to get it all the time. I got the thing where, "I'm sorry. But this part is for a black man." I guess I'm not black enough. I'm not old enough. I'm not young enough. But anyway, sooner or later somebody's going to like you. I did a Miller beer national commercial; I just knew I wasn't going to get that because the part, the principal was a blues guitar mentor. I saw all these people, and they were all darker than me. And I said, "Oh man. I got Gatemouth Brown here—all these cats. I won't ever get this one." But they picked me. I asked the producer, "Why did you all pick me? You've got all these black guys out here, career bluesmen. Why did y'all pick me?"

He said, "We like your smile."

That just broke me up, and I started crying. All the years I've been trying to do things, I was always—wasn't black enough, wasn't old enough. I have a youthful persona that makes me look younger than what I actually am. That was working against me, too—you go and compete with people for an older guy part, and you see all the other older guys who look old. But you have to persevere. I'm just hoping that one day, a part will be written for somebody like me, and I will be the one that they select.

There's a whole lot of people you're competing with to try get into those movies. The first heartbreak I had was *Angel Heart*. I got an audition for the part, the old bluesman. I mean I could read the lines perfectly. I had everything. But I didn't look like the character that they wanted. So they got Brownie McGhee, who was perfect. But I still got a part in the scene, playing in the band, doing the movie soundtrack in the studio. I wasn't one of the main characters that I really wanted, but anyway I was satisfied with that.

I'm just waiting for the right part to come along, like maybe a Brad Pitt movie. He might need a character that looks like me. Or an elderly, Creole gentleman, you know.

Brad Pitt has a house down here. They love New Orleans. They say New Orleans is one of the few towns where they can walk down the street, nobody harasses them. Because we have so many quote unquote characters walking around, people just used to it. "Oh, there's Brad Pitt," you know—no big deal.

## New Orleans

New Orleans musicians have respect all over the world. You go anywhere and you tell them you're from New Orleans—"Whoa." Because historically New Orleans is the birthplace of jazz. This is where a lot of music started. It started in New Orleans because we have an amalgamation of various cultures, primarily the African slaves. And we have the European people, the different ethnicities came from Europe. So New Orleans became like a melting pot of cultures. This is why the music is so different from anyplace else.

And being from New Orleans, you're exposed to the culture. You come up in the culture, with the second-line parades, the Mardi Gras, all that. You're exposed to that ever since you were a little kid. Your parents bring you to Mardi Gras in your costume, and you see the Mardi Gras Indians, the brass bands, the jazz funerals, and it becomes a part of you.

And the way our musicians interpret the music is what makes it different from other parts of the country—our music is syncopated. It's highly improvisational. There's only three forms of pure American music. Blues, jazz, and gospel. Most of the rest of the stuff came from Europe. But those are the truly American forms of music. And I was just fortunate to be in the city where all of that evolved, from the slave ships to the auctions to the miscegenation that occurred, you know, with the Creoles of color.

**Identity and Music**

I straddle the line. My life has been the plight of the tragic mulatto. He's despised by one race and hated by another one. Through the years people think I've had it easy because of my skin color. They say that when white people see me, they see the sins of their father; they feel guilty. And so they'll make special accommodation, special treatment for people like me. Which is not true, because when I came up, I don't care what color you are, "You a nigger, you still a nigger. Ain't nothing you can do to change it."

Being African American doesn't always mean you come from Africa. It means you were raised in African American culture. I came up within the African American culture, even though I'm Creole—so I was a product of all that. And it came out in my music, also. I can play the syncopated music.

I'm a product of all that; you can look at my face and you can see the sins of my fathers. So I have mixed heritage, which is common in New Orleans. There are many people with mixed heritage, black and white.

And it's becoming increasingly common now, because young people are marrying in different races and cultures. I've seen things that I never thought I would see. A black woman marrying a white man—it was taboo. It was the black man that married a white woman, when I was coming up. But now you see the white men marrying Asians, Latinos. They're all intermarrying. It's real common, because our society has become more permissive, and the laws have been changed to accommodate different cultures and races and ethnicities being able to marry each other. I came up when it was against the law; when I came up you couldn't ride in the front seat of the car with a white woman, because the police would put your ass in jail.

But New Orleans is a melting pot of cultures; we have this history that's so important to music, because like Ernie K-Doe said, he said, "I believe all music started in New Orleans." New Orleans is the birthplace of jazz; jazz evolved from the blues. So the blues is the legitimate parent of all jazz. And the blues and gospel live right next door to each other.

The people who came in on the slave ships mixed with the Caribbean cultures, too. People don't know that some slaves came from the Caribbean. And their cultures were intermeshed, too, and that's why the polyrhythmic thing largely came from the Caribbean parts of the country. New Orleans music is characterized a lot with Caribbean music. You take Professor Longhair, "Go to the Mardi Gras." What is it? It's a mambo. The "Mardi Gras Mambo." Then you had the syncopated elements that came from ragtime jazz that grew into traditional jazz. I don't call it Dixieland jazz, because Dixieland jazz has all these connotations of racism. So most of the players now refer to it as traditional jazz. Dixieland jazz is the music that white people play.

**The Union**

I've been a union member since 1950. I joined when I was a teenager, and I've been in the union ever since. I saw what the union can do for musicians, and I still see the value of a union now, even though this is a right-to-work state. What disturbs me is all this anti-union sentiment among the younger musicians. "Man, fuck the unions; they don't get you no jobs. They just take your money." I look at the union as a valuable resource for guiding your career in music, because we have a system of by-laws and laws that will serve to help you with the ethical fair treatment of your fellow musicians. It's a good tool and a good guideline for how you should proceed in your profession. And we give you a lot of valuable information.

The musicians union is entirely unique because we deal in products of intellectual labor. We're the only labor organization where you see labor and management in the same umbrella—the bandleaders are in the same union as the sideplayers. Through the years we have been able to work it out. Sometimes there are conflicts, but we can resolve that.

More importantly, we have a structured system of getting paid—of what we think is a fair and ethical wage for our services. I'll give you an example: if you play a casual engagement like a wedding reception, there's a scale for casual engagements—so much, and nothing less. Our philosophy is that if we adhere to a minimum wage scale, we all can benefit because people who are purchasing our services will have to pay a certain minimum amount to engage us.

The big problem comes with the musicians themselves, who don't want to adhere to the minimum standards that we advocate. We get calls all the time, "Well, how much should I charge if I'm going to be in *Treme*? I'm just doing a scene in there, where we don't have to play, but we have to look like we're playing. And what about if we do a scene where we actually do play? What about if they use my music in the soundtrack? How much does it cost for me to do a recording session for a company or one of my own?" We have a structured pay system for soloists that perform at weddings in the church or for someone who plays a reception. Or we have structured pay scales for people who march in the second-line parades, people who play in nightclubs, people who play in hotels and lounge gigs, people who have season engagements that last for weeks and months. There's a pay scale for the jazz festival. It's higher than the pay scale for playing in a nightclub. It's different from playing in a movie soundtrack. And we encourage you—"Hey, you don't have to play for that. We like for you to play for even more."

We have a pension plan—some of the younger musicians, "I don't care about all that." But as you become older you become more concerned—"Hey, I played for all these recording sessions, and there's no money in my pension fund account for me to get when I'm old and eligible to retire." I found that to be true for a lot of people who played all these recording sessions, where the companies weren't signatory with the union.

The worst part about musicians is that they subscribe to the survival mentality. It's like they live their lives by two maxims: "A little something is better than nothing." And "If I don't do it, somebody else will." As long as you think in that mentality, it's hard for us to make progress as a group of musicians. This has been the number one stumbling block of many of our musicians. They say, "Gee, I ain't doing nothing tonight. I'm going go make these thirty, forty dollars." But they don't realize when they do that they're lowering the market value of their own music.

It's been the endless quest my whole life to try to get musicians to behave in an ethical manner and not play below the minimum standards that are proscribed by the union. The philosophy is if we all adhere to that, the marketplace would be a lot more prosperous for all of us as a group, because we're working against each other and we're lowering the market value of music.

You know, it's every-man-to-himself philosophy. The people who are purchasing music take advantage of that. On Bourbon Street now, most of the bands play by the set. Something new came up; you know, "We'll pay you $10 a set, $5 a set. You come down here to work, and we look around, and if there's nobody in the club, well, we can't pay you for that set. Just hang around, and maybe some people will come for the second set, and we'll pay you for that. Plus, you know, you can make some tips. But if you sell your CDs, we want a piece of the action, too, because you're using our club to sell your CDs."

It's crazy what's happening. Some club owners are signatory with the AF of M and pay the musicians' pension and stuff like that—like Preservation Hall or Palm Court. They'll actually pay the minimum scale wage and pay the pension for the musicians that work there. But for the majority of the clubs, it's that same thing—"If you don't work for this, I got three or four other bands that will." You find yourself in a predicament, and "Fuck the union; I need this little money. My rent is due." It's those same two things—a little something is better than nothing. And better than staying home and watching TV, I could be here making a little money.

Then there's all kind of schemes going on in these clubs, you know—where they find out what your habits are. So it turns out you working for the man.

If you got a alcohol habit, well, they supplying you with drinks all week at a discount rate, and at the end of the week you have a bar tab. And they say, "Well, your pay is so much, and we subtract a lot of money for drinks." Or if you're buying drugs, some of the clubs have schemes with drugs—the guy you buying the dope from, he working for the club owner, too. So as soon as he pay you off, you give him the money right back. Consequently, they'll pick out the musicians with the habits, so that when they pay you off, you give them the money right back. Sometimes, you owe them money. I mean the music business is the worst business in the world. Wherever you see fast money, there's always going to be a lot of crooks hanging around. The sharks. You know, "The shark bites with his teeth, dear."

**In Conclusion**

I'm a product of New Orleans. My success, I say, is largely attributed to being versatile, because I made a living playing music but I just didn't play gigs. I did a lot of other things that were music-related. And that's why I'm still around today—because I outlived the competition.

# SCOTT BILLINGTON

## Record producer, Vice President for A&R, Rounder Records

[ Interviewed December 29, 2011, in Newburyport, Massachusetts ]

In 2011 *Offbeat* Magazine conferred its Best of the Beat Lifetime Achievement in the Music Business Award to Rounder Records producer Scott Billington. "If good New Orleans or zydeco music was recorded in the past two and a half decades," *Offbeat*'s David Kunian and Roger Hahn wrote, "There's a good chance that Scott Billington made it happen." That wasn't Scott Billington's first award from the influential New Orleans music publication. In 1996 he shared the Best Producer award with Allen Toussaint. That puts him in rarefied company. I'll return to Allen Toussaint in a moment.

In the record business, a producer is positioned between an artist and his or her listening public. The producer organizes recording projects, often on behalf of a label. In many cases, it's the producer who brings repertoire to the artist and who, in conjunction with the artist, shapes the sound of the final product. You can liken record producers to film directors, bringing their artistic vision and practical expertise to a project. In that analogy, the audio engineer is akin to a cameraman, the person with the technical skills to best realize the artistic vision behind a project.

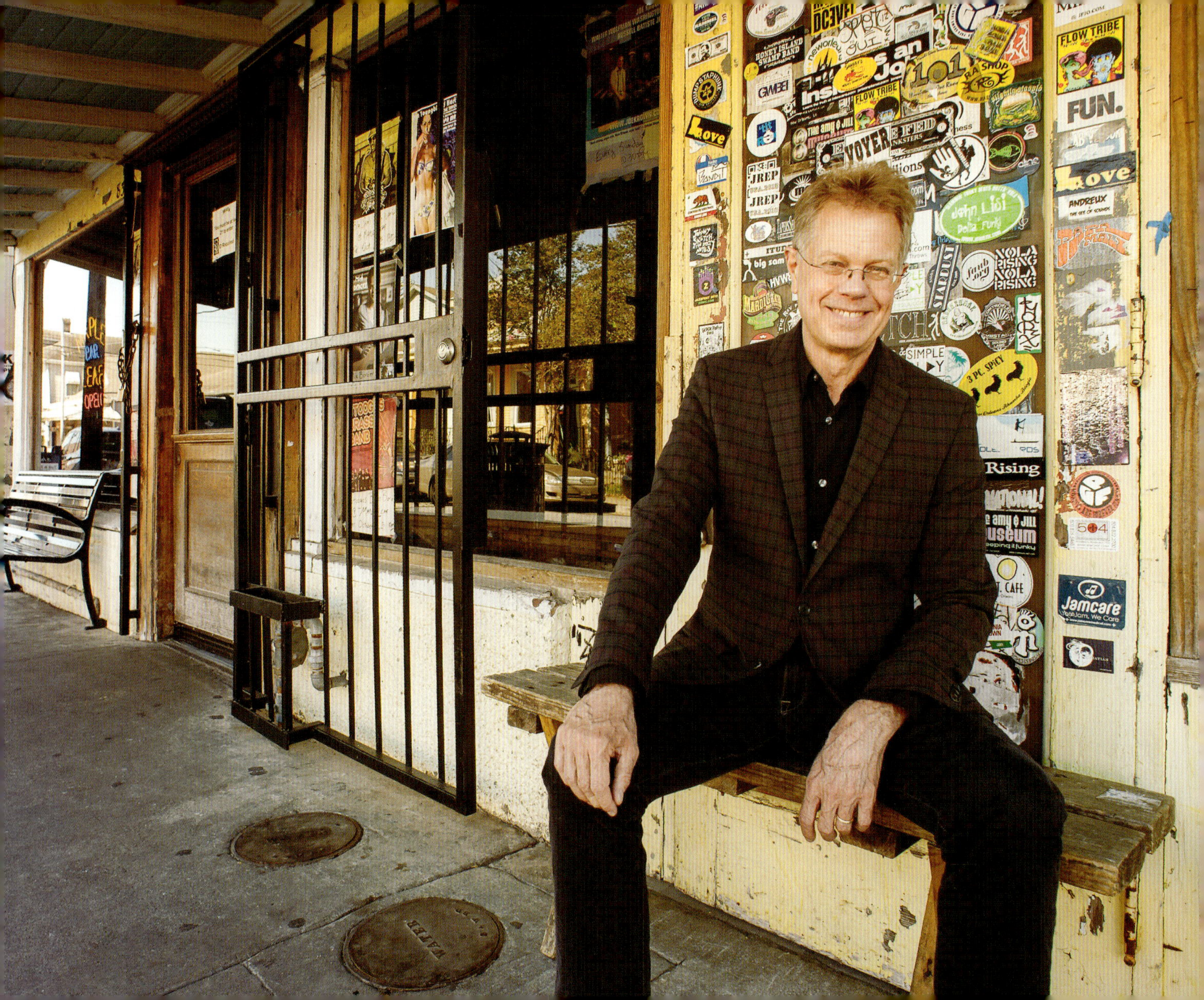

All in all, Scott Billington has produced in the vicinity of 150 albums, many of them presenting New Orleans musicians. He has been perhaps equally prolific in working with artists, especially zydeco musicians, from southwest Louisiana. His resume goes far beyond Louisiana. It includes work with musicians such as bluesmen Robert Jr. Lockwood and Johnny Shines, singer-songwriter Bill Morrissey, country musician Charlie Rich, Zairean vocalist and songwriter Tabu Ley Rochereau et L'Orchestre Afrisa International, Bahamian guitarist and singer Joseph Spence, and the Klezmer Conservatory Band.

His story begins in Massachusetts, where he was born. His family moved around a bit, but I interviewed him at his house in Newburyport which he'd owned for thirty-five years. In his late teens he was active in the Boston Blues Society, playing mouth harp with various groups and—at nineteen—managing a large record store in Boston. He also got to know the three founders of the Rounder record label, roots and funky music enthusiasts who eventually built one of the most influential independent labels in the world. He went to work for them, and his productions have had a great deal to do with the label's artistic success. His first project as a producer for Rounder, with Texas blues musician Clarence Gatemouth Brown, was released in 1982. It won a Grammy. Today he is vice president for artists and repertoire for the label.

His interest in New Orleans grew; he was going to Jazz Fest and getting the lay of the land, impressed by how many masterful musicians were on the local scene. Inspired by a set of releases on another label that had focused on Chicago blues players, he began a series, Modern New Orleans Masters, on Rounder. The first releases featured Johnny Adams, Irma Thomas, Red Tyler, Walter "Wolfman" Washington, and Tuts Washington. In her interview elsewhere in this book, Irma Thomas says that Rounder—in the person of Scott Billington—is the "label that really took care of the mature artist who had been in the business for a long time and had not

gotten any kind of national recognition the way they should have. I mean, I'd had some national coverage, but nothing of the magnitude of some others out there." The series was the start; over the years, his work has swept across the musical world that is New Orleans. He's worked with brass bands—from the Dirty Dozen to the Soul Rebels. He's produced projects by the most influential of the city's piano professors, from James Booker to Professor Longhair to Davell Crawford. His work with vocalists Johnny Adams and Irma Thomas brought national, and then international, attention to two of America's most distinctive voices. His work with Walter "Wolfman" Washington was what first made me want to go to New Orleans. It's no exaggeration to say that Scott Billington's work in New Orleans has helped shape contemporary understanding and appreciation of that city's extraordinary musicality.

For a time, Rounder kept an apartment in New Orleans to enable this work. They lost the apartment to Katrina. But these days, Scott Billington, married to New Orleans's children's musician and author Johnette Downing, divides his time between New Orleans, Nashville (where Rounder recently moved from its Massachusetts location), and his place in Newburyport.

Rounder continues its commitment to New Orleans. At the same time, as Scott says here, the record industry has changed dramatically since he first began producing albums. Many New Orleans artists fund and produce their own recordings these days. And, founded in 1997, a local label—Basin Street Records—is now the home of a number of leading New Orleans musicians, including Kermit Ruffins, Dr. Michael White, Henry Butler, Rebirth Brass Band, Jon Cleary, and Davell Crawford. Some of those artists appeared earlier on Rounder.

New Orleans's first great record producer was—is— Allen Toussaint. Toussaint's career as a New Orleans musician, songwriter, and hugely successful producer began in the 1950s. An extraordinary pianist and vocalist, he wrote

✤ Scott Billington in front of the Maple Leaf Bar, Uptown

many of the songs that established New Orleans rhythm and blues. Working with local studios—especially Cosimo Matassa's J&M, he produced some of the iconic music in that genre. About 250 singles produced in Matassa's studios charted nationally, and Allen Toussaint played a role in many of those (as did Dave Bartholomew, another name in the pantheon of New Orleans R&B and jazz history). Toussaint went on to collaborate with musicians such as Elvis Costello and Eric Clapton, but he has never lost his foundation in New Orleans.

A native New Orleanian—born in Gert Town—Toussaint found his métier in the single, the 45-rpm record. A native of Massachusetts, Scott Billington's medium has been the album, a sign of changes in the record industry. Allen Toussaint produced early work by a number or artists—notably Irma Thomas and Johnny Adams—whose careers were revitalized decades later by Scott Billington's work. And in an interesting twist in the lives of these two influential producers, in 2013 Rounder released a live set of Allen Toussaint playing and singing many of his most well-known songs. Scott Billington brought that project to the label.


### Coming to Music


I was born in Massachusetts. I grew up partly in Arizona and also in New Jersey, and then came back to Massachusetts. I've been in this house in Newburyport for thirty-five years.

We moved to Arizona during the Cuban missile crisis. My father worked for the American Sugar Company, and all of a sudden all of their sugar plantations had been nationalized by the Cuban government. He and a whole team of engineers got shipped out to Arizona to develop a beet sugar industry. So they were planting the beets as they were breaking ground on the refinery. We were there for a few years and then New Jersey.

My dad died when we were living in New Jersey. I was fourteen. So my mom moved us back to Massachusetts. I went back to school in Arizona for a year. But I've been here ever since, although sort of living in New Orleans about half the time for about twenty years, too. Rounder had an apartment down there—up until Katrina.

I got bit by music really early. When we were living in Arizona, my mother gave me a harmonica for Christmas. She got it with Green Stamps. So I was listening to Bob Dylan and some things like that, and learned to play that style. When we moved to New Jersey, my friends and I would go into Greenwich Village and hear the Grateful Dead at the Café Au Go Go, the Mothers of Invention at the Garrick Theater, and I started getting serious about it. Then I heard the Junior Wells *Hoodoo Man Blues* record; I heard Paul Butterfield.

So, by the time we moved back to Massachusetts, I was playing some. I had a little band called the Picket Fence Blues Band when I was a junior in high school. Then, in my senior year, I ended up playing with a really talented guitar player from Austin, Texas, named Mike Allen, who, sadly, no longer plays. His wife, Lana Pettey, played acoustic bass. We had a kind of a folk blues trio. We played coffee houses all around New England—Y Not coffee house in Worcester, and the Sword and the Stone, and the Turk's Head on Charles Street. Every Monday night Mike ran a hoot at the Catacombs, on Boylston Street, which was two flights down, right by Berklee, underneath a pool hall. Loudon Wainwright was a regular there. He would show up every other week. So I caught the very, very tail end of the '60s folk scene.

I'd known the three Rounder founders prior to when they started the company. I was working in a record store in Boston—New England Music City—which I ended up managing by the time I was nineteen. It was probably the biggest record store in Boston at the time—829 Boylston Street, not far from Berklee, right across from the Prudential Center. I think it's a hair salon today.

I became involved with an organization called the Boston Blues Society—Peter Guralnick, Jack Viertel, Dick Waterman, Erika Brady, Steve Frappier. I was the enthusiastic kid they invited to come and be part of that team. Durg Gessner was part of it, too, somebody who's still in the music business in Boston. We put on concerts at Harvard University—Houston Stackhouse, Son House, Doctor Ross, Mance Lipscomb, Joseph Spence, Roosevelt Sykes, Little Brother Montgomery—kind of the last of the first generation of bluesmen. They would come and play for these very polite audiences in Cambridge. The three Rounder founders would come there and sell records. They were distributing records on other labels, partly to earn money so that they could fund their own recordings. When the first Rounder record came out, I was working at New England Music City, and I already knew about the records. Ken Irwin was my salesman at the time—one of the founders. He'd come by and show me what they had new.

### Rounder, Producing, Gatemouth Brown

I was working in the record store. I'd been there five years, and I was playing in a swing band called Roseland. We played everything from Benny Goodman and Duke Ellington to Ella Mae Morse, some western swing—just a five-piece band. We started working all over the place, in New England, anyway. Often four or five nights a week. I really couldn't hold down the record store job and do that at the same time. Somebody I knew who did promotion for major labels approached me about being in business with him as an independent sales and promotion company. And he approached Rounder about both of us going to work for them. He would promote the records to radio stations and so forth, and I'd be the salesperson.

He didn't work out. But Rounder hired me directly. I'd had a lot of experience in dealing with salespeople from major labels and so forth who'd come in my store every week. I won't say I came from the sort of straight record business, but I was someone that had actual record business experience back then. I was their first employee to have that background, however modest it was. We definitely shared a lot of musical interests, too.

At first, I was selling records. The environment at Rounder, at that time—and it really didn't change for a long time—was that if you saw something that needed doing, you could do it. And if you did it successfully, then you could keep doing it. So, I started preparing the new release sheets that we'd send out in the mail and give to our accounts, and writing little blurbs for records that came in. We were distributing a lot of other labels at the time, too. It wasn't just Rounder. At one point we were up to about 400 labels.

One thing just led to another. Durg Gessner, from the Boston Blues Society, had recorded Johnny Shines at one of our concerts. Peter Guralnick and I knew about this tape; we got in touch with Johnny and asked Rounder if they'd like to put this out. So, Rounder released it—the Johnny Shines concert

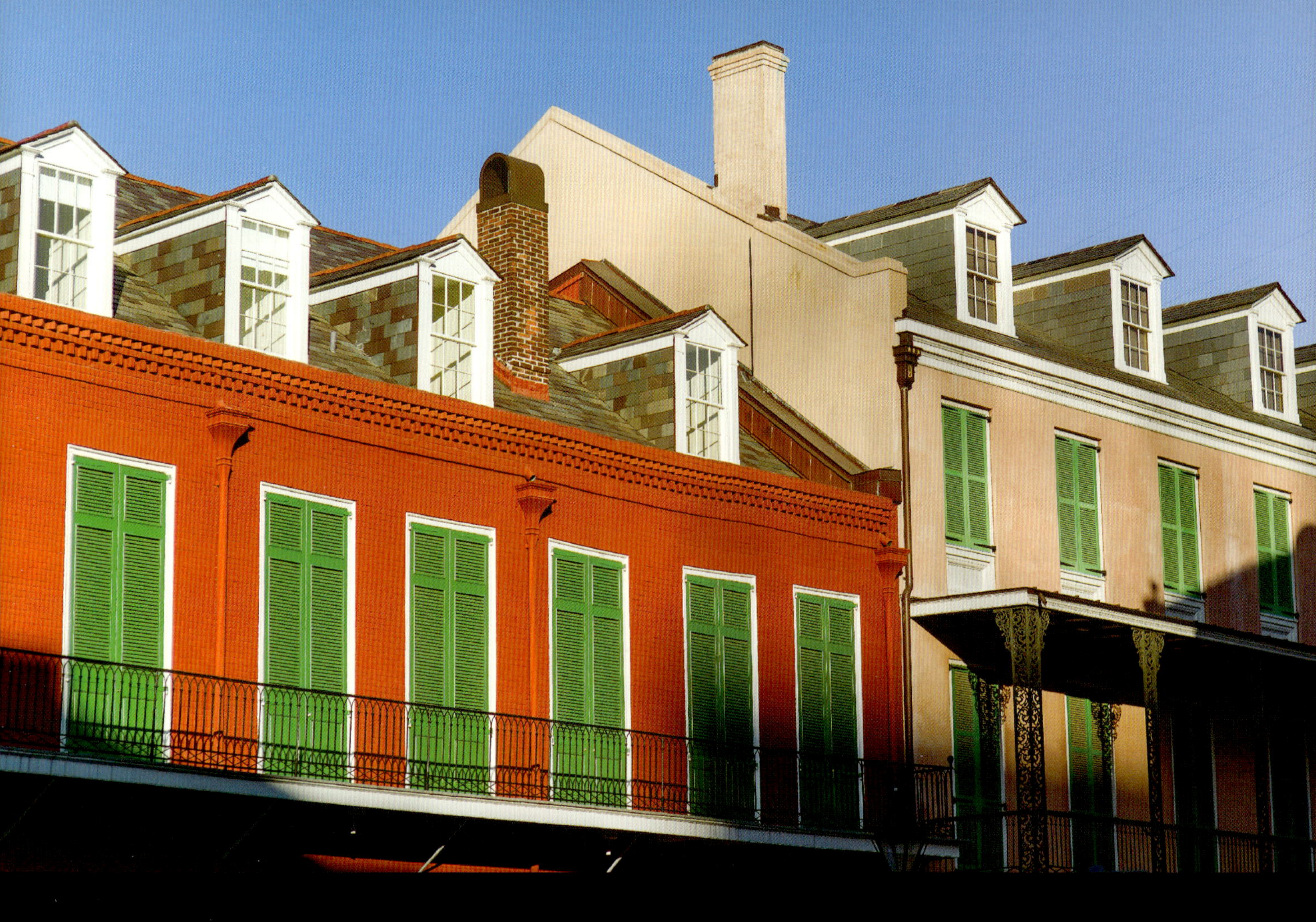

from the Boston Blues Society. I designed the cover, and Peter wrote the notes. I think that was the first one that I actually had hands-on, record-making experience—editing and everything that goes into making a record. And little by little I started doing more with Johnny Shines and Robert Junior Lockwood. Bill Nowlin and I went to the Bahamas and recorded Joseph Spence, whom I'd known because he stayed at my house for a few days when we was playing a concert here.

The big change came with George Thorogood and the Destroyers, because in 1977 they had a major hit record on Rounder. That convinced every blues player in the world that Rounder Records had the magic touch that was going to bring them success. Everybody wanted to record for Rounder all of a sudden. One of those was Clarence Gatemouth Brown. His manager, Jim Bateman, approached us about recording Gate, and the three founders said, "Hey—want to go do this record?" So Jim and I coproduced it. The idea was to bring him back to this big swinging big band sound that had been part of what he had done when he made his first recordings for Peacock Records in Houston. It was a style that I loved.

When I was in high school in Boston I used to go into Skippy White's record shop in Roxbury every Saturday afternoon. I had a job at the Automatic Radio Company that made auto air conditioners and auto radios. I'd get my paycheck and head right for Skippy. I learned a lot from him, too. One of the records he sold me—he would say "You need to get this; you need to buy this"—was Percy Mayfield's album called *My Jug and I*, which was on Tangerine Records. It was the Ray Charles Band, with Ray Charles on piano and Billy Preston on organ, and Percy Mayfield singing his great songs. So it had this jazz sensibility to it, but it was blues. Percy was

a poet. He was a wonderful storyteller and songwriter—all of those things coming together. We even recorded one of the songs from that record, "Give Me Time to Explain," with Gate.

I think that was the first time that I started thinking "Boy, I can bring songs to people, if they're right. And maybe that can be part of what I do in terms of production." So we'd be rehearsing the rhythm section in one part of the studio, while the horn players were scrambling to write these charts for a five-piece section. Gate had three horns in his band at the time, but we augmented that with Red Tyler, who was a great New Orleans sax player and kind of a legendary session player on so many hit records that came out of New Orleans in the '50s and '60s.

It all came together. We recorded it in Bogalusa. It was all kind of exotic to me, too. I remember riding into Bogalusa, and the first building you saw was the KKK headquarters back then. And going to a little restaurant there and seeing "wop salad" on the menu—a very different sensibility from kind of the politically correct concerts and environment in Cambridge.

We had eight days—and that included mixing—to make this fairly ambitious record. It came out in 1982, and it won a Grammy. That was really the first time I'd actually had a role as producer. It was a good way to come out of the gate.

It took twenty-five years to win another Grammy, of course.

### Modern New Orleans Masters

I started spending more time in New Orleans. I started going to Jazz Fest, and it seemed that there were so many great musicians there who were working. You could go out on any night of the week and hear Johnny Adams at Dorothy's Medallion Lounge, or James Booker at the Maple Leaf. But nobody was making records, at all.

My friend, Bruce Iglauer, at Alligator Records, had done the Living Chicago Blues series, where he looked at people who were on the scene who hadn't been recording, or recording a lot. That was sort of the idea behind this Modern New Orleans Masters series we did on Rounder, although Bruce's records were more samplers. They would have two or three bands on each record. Instead, we decided at Rounder that we would just make these individual records and sort of brand them as part of a series to try to bring a little more focus to what we were doing, from a marketing perspective. I guess the series is still going, although we stopped using the logo a while ago.

The first records were Johnny Adams, Irma Thomas, Red Tyler, Walter Washington, Tuts Washington. It did well. It put Rounder on the map of a different kind of roots music than the founders had explored before, which had been more oriented toward old-time music and bluegrass, and people from those traditions who were doing more contemporary things, too. We just kept going from there.

So many seeds were planted with that first Gatemouth record. David Farrell, the engineer at Studio in the Country in Bogalusa, and I went on to make probably fifty or sixty records together. There was a place called Studio Solo in Slidell that he moved to, then a studio called Southlake in Metairie, and Ultrasonic, which is where he stayed for the longest time—where he'd probably still be if it hadn't gone underwater in Katrina. It was right on a canal where one of the main breaches in the levee occurred. And Bill Samuel, who was one of Gate's horn players,

ended up arranging horns on a great many records that I've made. Red Tyler became an ally on many projects, and we ended up making a couple of his own records, contemporary jazz records, which I'm really glad we made, because that was a side of him that nobody had really heard. One connection led to another within the community of musicians. I think I eventually got to the point where I could imagine just about any sound that I might envision as being on a record, and I would know the person there who could make it.

**Johnny Adams**

I was introduced to Johnny Adams by Jeff Hannusch, who's a writer in New Orleans. He was a great resource, actually, Jeff—he introduced me to a number of people. I remember going to Johnny's house. He lived with his mother in the projects on Orleans and Claiborne, which were just torn down, actually. He had a regular gig at a club called Dorothy's Medallion Lounge on Orleans Avenue; he could practically walk there. I went to hear him at a couple of different places. There was a big African American nightclub called Steve's on the West Bank, and he was playing sort of what was left of what they called the chitlin' circuit in Louisiana and Mississippi at the time, really not doing a whole lot. He never stopped making records, and he'd been recording with a guy named Senator Jones. His pattern had always been to have some sort of record that was on the marketplace in the New Orleans area or regionally, and that enabled him to go out and work. The more I heard him, the more I realized this is one of the great voices of our time. I mean, there's no doubt about it. Johnny was one of the greatest singers of the last century.

Anyway, Johnny would arrive at Dorothy's Medallion Lounge, which may be the smokiest place I have ever been in my life. It really didn't get going until about midnight. It was decorated with Christmas lights. They had three-hundred-pound go-go dancers in cages in there. I saw my first shake dancer at Dorothy's Medallion Lounge—a woman with some very well-developed muscles in her derriere. And sometimes there would be somebody who would dance with a snake. I mean it was sort of this throwback to something—I don't know what. This old-time entertainment sensibility. But it was relatively small. Dorothy would always have on a great big wig and chains with medallions, of course, just to go along with the theme of the club, I guess. And Johnny would arrive at Dorothy's at ten or ten thirty in the evening, always immaculately dressed. Johnny loved clothes and wasn't afraid to spend money on clothes, either. So he has his little pocket handkerchief, and his silk tie, and everything just in place. Walter Washington would roll in at twelve thirty or one o'clock, sometimes looking like he'd just been working on his transmission or something. But the two of them—they just had an amazing musical bond. They were like brothers, really. I think Walter today gives a lot of credit to Johnny Adams for showing him the possibilities that existed in music and where you could go with them.

We made our first record with Johnny's working band at the time. It was Walter Washington and the Solar System. Walter went on to record for us and has had a really great career of his own. The record had a few songs that I had brought in, including a Percy Mayfield song, which seemed to be a recurring theme on some of the records I was making back then. It came out well. It was definitely a more aggressive modern sound than somebody might have associated with Rounder, although it still wasn't what you would call contemporary R&B. But it had those elements in it.

That began a relationship that went on for the next fifteen years. We made nine records together, and he sang on a couple of other projects along the way. It was just the greatest partnership, I think, that Johnny and I had. He benefitted from having someone around him that could help him with infrastructure and with thematic unity in the different records that we made, and in putting together the right musical situation. I don't like the second record we made together at all; I felt like I learned then, no, this isn't what Johnny needs to hear. One called *After Dark*. It's okay. I ended up using Walter Washington's rhythm section again, but Walter had left the band at that point, to pursue his own career. Without him there to glue it together, it wasn't quite the same.

The next record we made—I hope I had learned from my mistakes—basically used Dr. John and his rhythm section at the time. Walter came in and played guitar on that, and Duke Robillard played guitar. That was *Room with a View of the Blues*, and that was when I felt that we started to hit our stride.

The next couple of records were songwriters' records. We did a whole album of Percy Mayfield's songs. Then we made what I think is the record I'm most proud of in my career—the album called *The Real Me*, which is Johnny doing all Doc Pomus songs. Doc became a great friend and supporter. I would talk to him every week or two on the phone. He'd always say, "You know, you know what you're doing. Just stick with it, and everything's going to be okay." That kind of thing. The songs that are on that record are the last songs that he worked on before he passed away, most of which he wrote with Dr. John.

Mac and I actually coproduced that record—Mac Rebennack, Dr. John. That combination of really good, beautiful songs that told stories, Johnny's voice, but more important than that, I think, is the collective feeling, or soul, or whatever you want to call it that the musicians were able to put into it. If Johnny could hear that going on behind him, then he would soar. And Johnny Adams even at his very worst was always really, really good. But there was that space that we tried to attain where he kind of entered another realm as a singer. Not just a great technical vocal, but a real spiritual element to it as well. I think we hit that quite a few times when we went into the studio.

I've almost never made a record where I'm tracking individual musicians. I like to try to capture a moment, something that that really happened. That isn't to say that you don't go back later and work on keyboard parts or a solo, or that Johnny might want to sing the song again. Johnny loved to sing so much, he would ask to overdub his vocals even when he didn't need to, just so he could play with the melody some more or try some different things. That often became a dilemma in mixing him, because I'd have five or six really great vocal tracks. And it's like, "Gee, which pieces of which ones are we going to use here?" But, really, when he was at his best, he just nailed it with a track. That certainly happened most of the time on that Doc Pomus record. In particular, working with a singer, Ruth Brown or Solomon Burke, Charlie Rich, or Irma Thomas, they're always there, singing with the track. Otherwise, it's just never going to happen, in terms of attaining that other, more spiritual thing.

In some ways I think Johnny and Walter Washington were like fire and ice, and yet when they came together it was such a beautiful combination.

Walter understood absolutely intuitively what Johnny needed to hear. Just like Dr. John understood that. I think I came to understand with Johnny that having that pivotal person there, who understood the harmonies that Johnny wanted to hear—Johnny had a really sophisticated ear. But it still kind had to have a little bit of church in it if he was going to really feel it. So that person might be David Torkanowsky, the piano player. We made a record with Dr. Lonnie Smith, the Hammond organ player. I always try to have a key musician in there, too, who would sort of glue everything together.

## Irma Thomas

When I met Irma Thomas, she was living in the same house where she is now in New Orleans East. Irma's a real smart woman. We're all so accustomed to hearing stories of R&B singers from the '60s or something who are destitute, who lost their way. Irma may never have been a hit artist in the way Aretha Franklin was, but she was very careful managing her life. And when she met Emile Jackson, her husband, who she's still with today, they were a good team. She told me once, "We didn't want to be poor when we got old." So they've invested their money really carefully over the years. She had a very comfortable life when I first met her. She was forty-two or forty-three years old, and that's also been another relationship that just kept going.

With Irma, for a while I think we kind of mined this '70s-'80s R&B kind of sensibility with the records that we made. But five years ago, just after Katrina, we made a record called *After the Rain*. We'd actually picked out the material for this record before the hurricane. We had to postpone the recording, of course, when Katrina hit. We couldn't do it in New Orleans, because Ultrasonic had been completely destroyed. I mean the building got leveled after the storm.

I remember having a conversation with Irma about that record. I had some country blues material, some country stuff, with the idea that why not just find songs that Irma sings really good—that her voice is going to express in the best way. Let's ditch the horns; let's get rid of this whole R&B thing. I mean why should she have to do that for the rest of her life? So, it's a more acoustic record than anything she'd ever made before. And, eerily, the songs that we had picked out before Katrina all suddenly seemed to be about the storm.

We got together at Dockside Studio in Maurice, Louisiana, outside of Lafayette, about two months after Katrina. It was the first time that many of these musicians had seen one another since the storm— it was a very emotional time for everybody. That, I really think, is her crowning achievement as a record. And that one won a Grammy, too. When I first sent her these songs, I said, "Irma, I'm going to send you some stuff. And you may think I'm crazy, but hear me out on this." I think there's a Blind Willie Johnson, and Mississippi John Hurt doing "Make Me a Pallet on Your Floor." She got the CD, and she called me back a couple of days later, and said, "Scott, you're out of your mind. I mean, what am I going to do with this stuff?" And then she said, "But you know, we know one another well. You know what I can do. I'm going to roll with you on this. I'm going to approach this with an open mind and just see where it goes." And, really, from the first note in that studio, she connected with it, and all of a sudden she said, "Okay. I can see where you're going with this. I'm with you." I don't think we would have gotten that record without the long relationship that we had had before then. She sings so beautifully on that record.

Irma's just great. At seventy years old, she hasn't lost anything in her voice. She's astonished, I think, at how well her voice has held up.

If the records I made for her and for Johnny, both, accomplished anything, I hope it was to get them out of being oldies artists, or somebody who had made records in the past and, okay, we bring them out and they sing their hits. By working with different musical concepts and bringing in new material and so forth, I think they were able to find voices that were relevant to what was going on in the world today. Johnny ended up touring the world—going to Japan and Europe. He maybe never quite became a star. I think he liked to play golf as much as anything else. So he wasn't the most ambitious person when it came to his career.


**Walter "Wolfman" Washington**


Walter Washington's another really spiritual player. I think I learned with the James Booker record that the musicians, and this is probably true for other artists, who are most capable of transporting the listener to another place, of delivering something that touches a realm beyond music, or as far as you can go with music—they're the most difficult people to record. You can't just push a button and get that out of somebody. It takes time, and it takes the right environment. Walter's a lot like that. His sets at the Maple Leaf Bar at two o'clock in the morning are still sort of legendary. The band just hits this plane and stays there for a while, and it's a pretty exciting thing to be around. And, again, the first record with Walter—it's a little more song-oriented, a little more,

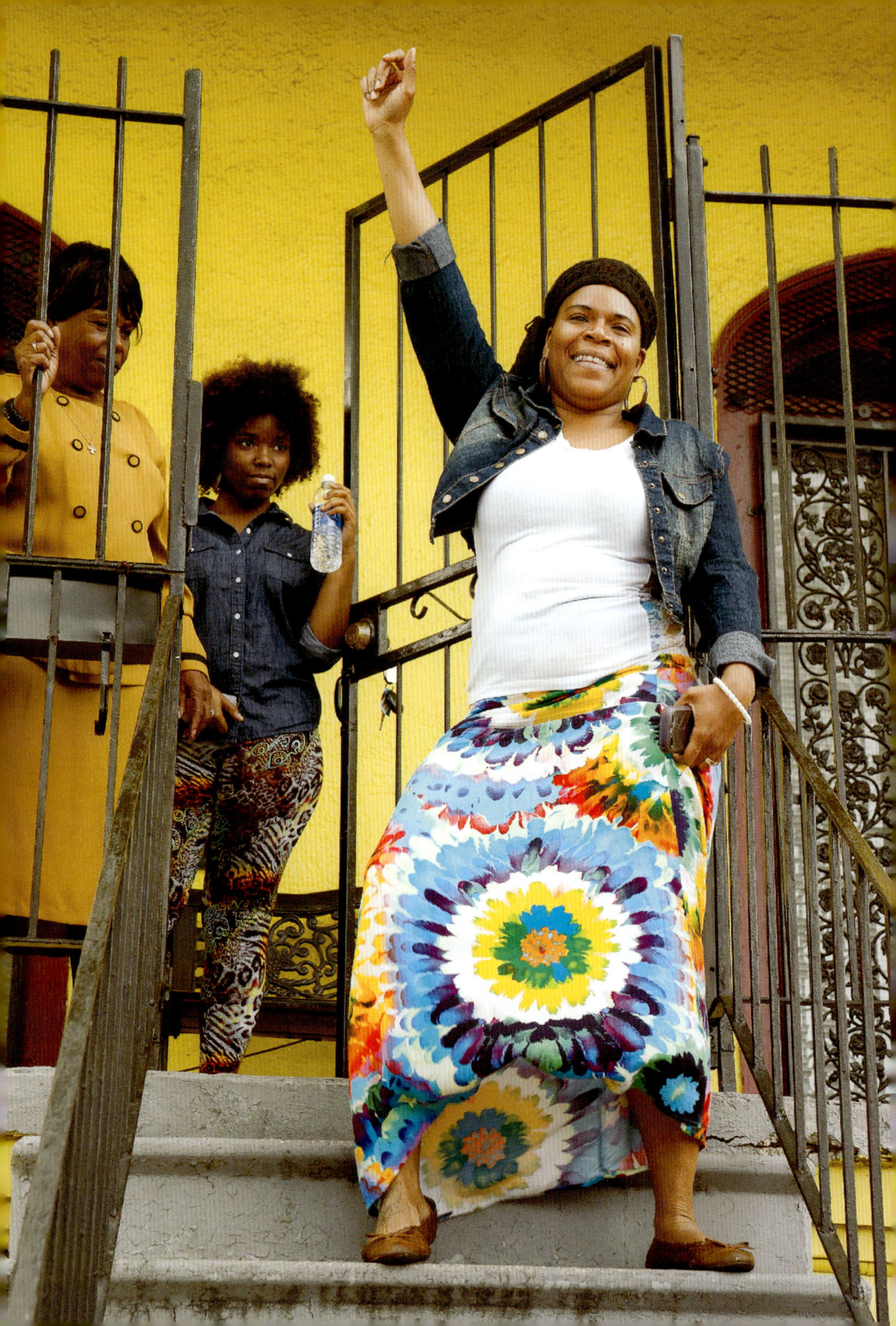

"Okay, let's put this together in the studio." I think you can hear some of where Walter could go, on that record *Wolf Tracks*. But the second record we made—*Out of the Dark*—I think we really got that spirituality out of it.

We made three records, and then he recorded for a while for Virgin. We made another one about ten years ago. I think we hit it pretty good on that one, too. He's just got such a distinctive sound with his guitar. You hear Walter play the guitar, and you know it's him immediately. Just like you know B.B. King or Elmore James or somebody like that—just such a distinctive thing. And he's a soulful singer, too.


**James Booker, Dirty Dozen Brass Band**


I did one record with James Booker. He died not long after that. He had his problems with substance abuse. And, yeah, I mean, he only made two studio records in his whole life, which was amazing. Joe Boyd had done one a few years earlier, at Sea-Saint, which I think probably is the great James Booker studio record. But, yeah, there are so many factors that can be involved in trying to get that great performance out of somebody.

I started with Johnny and Irma about almost the same time. Johnny was first. But when we decided we'd do this Modern New Orleans Masters series and make it something, Irma came in then. And Walter. And Red Tyler. Not long after that, Marian Levy, who's one of the Rounder founders, arranged for us to release the Dirty Dozen Brass Band's Montreux record, a live record that I mixed. We also acquired rights to a Professor Longhair record that he'd made for Bearsville, that they never released. I also mixed that with the engineer, Gregg Lunsford, up here in Boston. That one

won a Grammy. So it's interesting. Rounder's first two Grammys were not in the bluegrass field. It was Gatemouth Brown and Professor Longhair.

*Live at Montreux* was the Dirty Dozen Brass Band's second album. After that, we started a record for Rounder, called *Voodoo*. At that point, it wasn't quite George Thorogood, but it seemed like the thing might need a bigger label or that there might be a bigger opportunity for them out there. My friend, Steve Berkowitz, who's originally from Boston, was doing A&R at Columbia, and he became really interested in the band. So Rounder ultimately made a deal with Columbia to allow the band to move on. Actually, that was something that we'd had to do with George Thorogood, because even though his second record was a huge hit, we were being distributed, at the time, through a network of independent distributors who might pay you in 90 or 120 or 150 days, if you were lucky. In the meantime, the pressing plant needed to be paid in thirty. So we just didn't have the infrastructure at the time to do justice to the potential of an artist like that. As I say, it wasn't quite the same thing that was happening with the Dozen. But they had this opportunity to move on to Columbia. So the record that I had made for Rounder—it has Dr. John, Dizzy Gillespie, and Branford Marsalis on it—ended up coming out on Columbia. We went on to another three records after that for Columbia. And the band just asked me to continue with them as their producer after that point. And I'm just now in the middle of making another record with them, all these years later.


**Red Tyler**


Producing a record means different things for each project. With Red Tyler, for instance, he had written an album's worth of new material. I think he'd always had it in him to write these kinds of tunes, but he just never had the situation in which he could record them before. The band that he and I put together mostly were musicians that he'd been working with—Johnny Vidacovich on drums, James Singleton on bass, David Torkanowsky on piano, and Clyde Kerr on trumpet. There it was just a matter of getting the right sounds in the studio and being patient and supportive. We cut that record entirely live. So there was very little creative input from me on that record. We did bring in Germaine Bazzle to sing one song and Johnny Adams to sing one song, which I thought would be a good idea just in terms of making it a little more accessible, not being strictly an instrumental jazz record. With some of the singers that I've worked with I've become much more a part of the whole creative process in trying to create for them the absolute best situation for them, all around—the songs, the musicians, the arrangements.

## Rounder in New Orleans

I think most of the New Orleans musicians saw Rounder as a step up. There was also sometimes an expectation that they were going to have a hit again, which seldom came to pass. But I think it made a difference to most of them in that it gave them a platform to not just play the local stage, but to be able to travel around the world and around the country and have audiences there who'd heard the Rounder records, who knew who they were. I think generally people started coming to Rounder then, wanting to be recorded, when they saw what had happened with Walter, with Johnny, or whatever. They began to understand that, "No, we're not going to have a top-40 hit here, but this is a good career move, to make a record for Rounder." And we also always paid the musicians; the artist would get a modest advance. I think that was a positive thing, too. The musicians went home with a paycheck for the week of work that they did on these records.

## The Record Business Today

The record business has changed so much. Today with Tower gone, with Borders gone, and with people simply not buying records the way they used to, now we might only be able to sell a fraction of what we used to sell. Making roots music records for niche audiences is no longer a sustainable business model unto itself. As a result—and I don't think this is all bad—many of these musicians are now in a position of having to fund and distribute their own records. So perhaps they have less access to the best musicians, who you want to pay, and access to a team of professional craftspeople to help them make their record, especially engineers in studios. Everybody says you can make a record in your bedroom now, and, sure, there's going to be that one or two percent of kids who do this, that will make great records in their bedrooms. But most kinds of music, and most musicians, I think benefit from having a team around them that knows what they're doing when it comes to making records.

So the stakes are so much higher for us today in understanding the story that we need to tell to get people interested enough that they'll actually buy a record. We just signed the Soul Rebels this year; they've been around for about twenty years, but they've got four young guys in the band now and have just hit a stride. It's something more than a

✢ Girl with snowball, Uptown Super Sunday

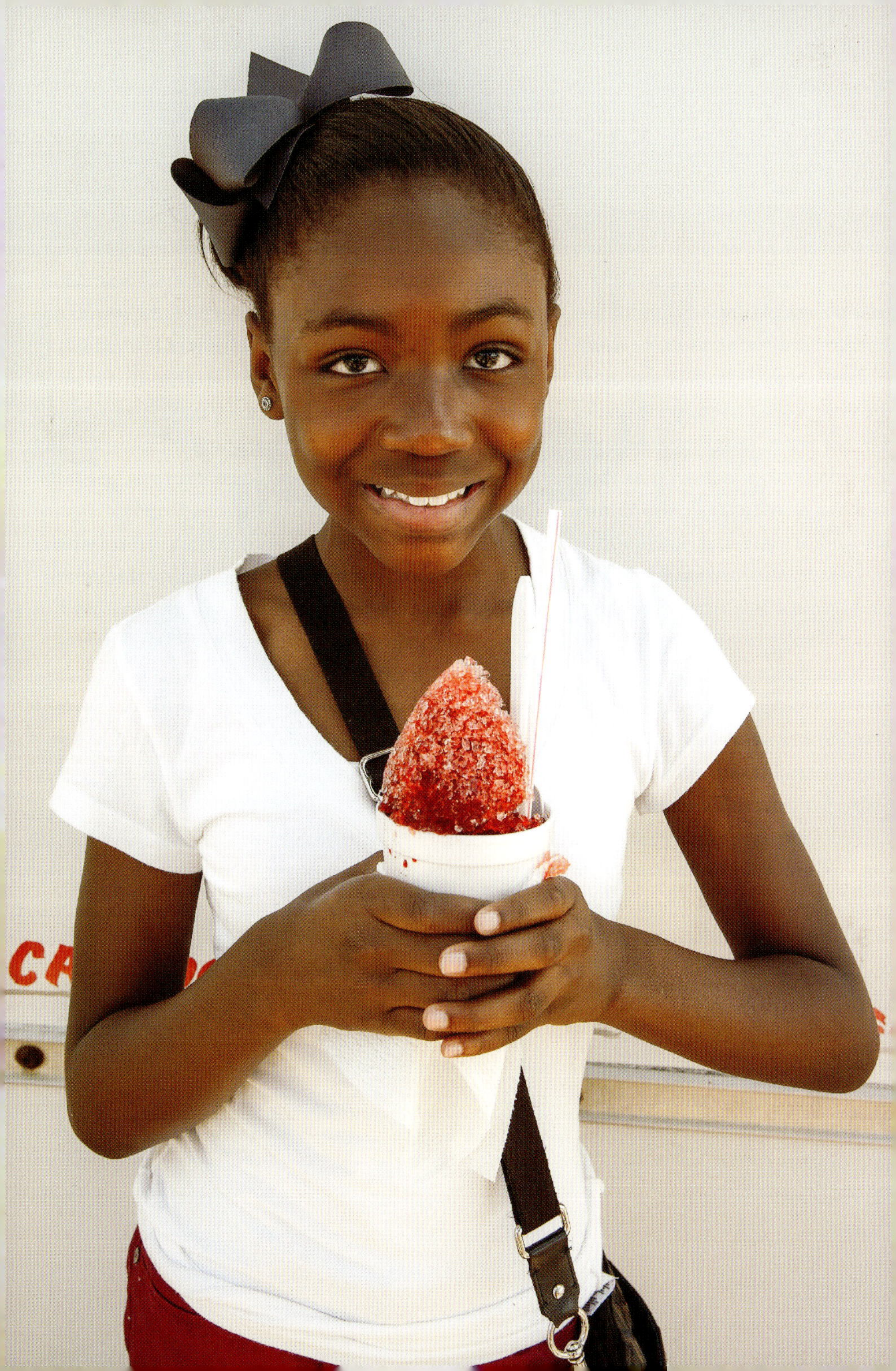

CA

brass band at this point. It's almost like a pop record played by a brass band. It was a band that I wish I had recorded ten or fifteen years ago. But we weren't able to go forward with that record until they had management and booking structure together. And we really have to go for it now—you know, Internet marketing, blogs. We did a re-mix contest on a website called Indaba for them, getting this whole community of remixers involved by giving them these stems, these bits and pieces of a Soul Rebels track, that they could then remix. Getting the band out there touring. You've just got to hit with all cylinders firing these days or you don't stand a chance. So, it can't be done in the kind of more low-key and self-sustaining way that it was done before. Which isn't to say we didn't promote things as vigorously as we could then. It's just the stakes are so much higher today.

One good thing that's changed at Rounder is that we do have the infrastructure now to deal with a hit record if one comes our way.

A&R work? Well, I guess I've been doing it anyway for a long time, but mostly the artists that I would sign I would end up producing as well. With A&R, well, it's sort of all the work and not as much fun. I mean it's more the business side of what goes into a successful record label, which is maintaining good relationships with your artists and with their management, and being the initial liaison with the Rounder team. And making sure all the bases are covered once a record comes out, or before the record comes out, because setup is so important these days.

Setup involves the promotion and generation of materials—that has to happen before the record comes out. The way the record business is set up today, the sales you get on your first week are pretty much accurately tracked now, through this company called Soundscan that picks up all of the barcodes that go across the scanners in stores and tracks also all the digital sales. If you haven't created enough of a story that you've made an impact in your first week, your record kind of disappears. That's something that we really have to take seriously. So press, TV, touring, marketing, getting advertising set up with the remaining retailers, with Best Buy or maybe with Walmart, if we get a record into Walmart. All these things are critical to those first week's sales, which are so important to the life of the whole project then.

But I also look for people to sign that would be good for Rounder. We'll see if this happens by the time this interview comes out, but I think we're going to sign the Preservation Hall Jazz Band and put out their fiftieth anniversary concert at Carnegie Hall. So those are the kinds of things that I'm involved with. Yeah, so A&R is more sitting behind a desk and talking on the phone and sending emails.

### How to Produce a Record

Producing requires a lot of involvement. In working with Ruth Brown, I spent a couple of months looking for songs, contacting songwriters that were going to work with her, contacting some people that I knew at publishing companies who I thought would have a sympathetic ear to what Ruth would sing best. I sent her probably twenty-five songs after going through that process. Then we got together in New York, where she was working, with a rehearsal pianist and started going through the songs. It was clear right away that some of these were great—they were going to work; she just lit up when she sang them. Others not so.

And in that process I was able to get an overall tempo for each song, kind of a groove, and her key. So I then took these rehearsal tapes to several different arrangers—Wardell Quezergue in New Orleans, who's a fantastic arranger, person, musician. He just passed away this year. And Victor Goines who works with Wynton Marsalis's band often, but who had actually played with Ruth a little while when he was younger. And they wrote arrangements for everything.

I would sit with Wardell at his kitchen table, and we would talk about the song—"Okay, we're going to go verse, verse, bridge, and then let's have a trombone solo here. And then why don't you write a horn ensemble section to come back in to the vocal." That sort of thing. We'd just go back and forth on ideas. I picked up Ruth Brown at a casino. She was playing at a casino in Mississippi. I drove back down to New Orleans with her and her two sons and her keyboard player. When she showed up in the studio that first day, here are twelve musicians with their arrangements all written out and somewhat rehearsed. That was a moment of some anxiety for me when Ruth stepped up to the microphone, and she hit off that first song—was this going to click or not? She just had the biggest smile on her face, says, "Oh baby, this is going to be fun." Again, so there we were, cutting her live with this twelve-piece band, kicking along behind her. Most of her great vocals on that record were cut that way, live with the band. We did one more with her, too.

At the exact opposite end of the spectrum is a record that one of my engineer partners—Steve Reynolds—and I made, calling ourselves Tangle Eye, working with Alan Lomax's field recordings. There we were starting with these fantastic vocal performances, the nature of which we couldn't reproduce anywhere today. Alan Lomax had recorded these in homes and prisons and churches in the South. They were part of a series called Southern Journey that came out on Rounder. So Steve and I programmed beats and rearranged the vocals sometimes, maybe putting them into a more formal verse and chorus structure, or something like that. We had to lock everything to a time grid so that things could be moved around. We played a few of the instruments ourselves. Steve played bass. I played harmonica on one thing; I played keyboard on one thing. But mostly we enlisted all the great musicians we knew. Once we had the bed for each track down, the basic rhythm thing, maybe an idea for how the harmony was going to go. So Henry Butler, Davell Crawford, David Torkanowsky on keyboards. Delfeayo Marsalis on trombone. Jeff Raines from Galactic on guitar. Ron Stewart from Nashville on fiddle. Tony Trischka on banjo. Everybody just kept adding their parts to this. So there was a record that was totally dreamed up and created from scratch using a production technique that has nothing to do with capturing something live.

**After the Storm**

New Orleans, post-Katrina, has certainly changed. You can see that it's becoming more gentrified. There are a lot more Hispanic people there now than there were before Katrina. And some of the neighborhoods that had the deepest cultural activity still aren't back. The lower Ninth Ward is still kind of a wreck. And it dispersed people all over the country. Some of them still haven't returned. Henry Butler and Davell Crawford are still living in New York

City. And yet it's not as bad as some people thought it might be. There are still second-line parades most every Sunday during the cool months of the year; the gospel community is still as active as it ever was.

I think that the great tragedy, though, is that so many working poor people were not able to return. And these were often the African American people that were the heart of everything that everybody loves about New Orleans—the jazz, the brass bands, the food, gospel music, the second lines. That's the tragedy to me, that people that owned modest homes went to Atlanta or Houston, wherever they had family. They got new jobs; they put their kids in school. They're paying rent on an apartment in their new place of residence. In the meantime, the bank wanted them to keep paying the mortgage on their wrecked home in New Orleans. And now there are these new regulations calling for the elevation of houses, particularly in the lower Ninth Ward. And there's just no way. The economic barriers are too imposing for people to be able to afford to come back. There's also the kind of ironic thing about New Orleans culture—that it was often those poorest people in which the culture ran most deeply.

Everything changes. But Katrina certainly did change things a lot more rapidly than they otherwise might have. Maybe one of the good things about the change that's happened is the schools have gotten better—mostly charter schools now. And it really made people take a hard look at the poverty that was there.

It's not quite as funky as it was before Katrina. Neighborhoods are getting more gentrified, maybe a little more generic. New Orleans was such a different place from the rest of the country, where a kind of mass-market, corporate kind of sensibility just never permeated that culture too much. Walmart came in, off of Tchoupitoulas Street, just before Katrina.

And that was quite controversial. New Orleans was a city of neighborhoods, where people really lived and interacted with one another. That fabric of neighborhood and community hasn't quite come back.

For the music, I think things have gotten really healthy lately. Katrina put a focus on people like Allen Toussaint and Irma Thomas. These are cultural treasures that we have, and I think they've gotten a little bit more of a spotlight shone on them since Katrina. I think there's a little more emphasis on music education now. I was just there a couple of weeks ago, at the national park where Delfeayo Marsalis was presenting this band of kids that were playing jazz. These were eleven-, twelve-year-old kids, and they were really good. The brass band thing also has exploded since Katrina. There are young players coming up. You go to the corner of Canal and Bourbon Street any night now, and there's this kind of ragtag bunch of maybe fifteen or sixteen teenagers out there playing Rebirth Brass Band songs. They may be a little ragged, but it sure does feel good. And that's maybe their entrée into music there.

New Orleans has also had its first new star since Katrina. Trombone Shorty—Troy Andrews—has just taken the jazz festival stages across the world by storm, playing something that's a little more contemporary, more of a fusion with jazz or a fusion with R&B sometimes. But you can hear the New Orleans in there. It's unmistakable. We're hoping that something like that can happen with the Soul Rebels, too. So there are still young people coming up. You mentioned earlier that many of the artists that we've worked with did have a previous history. But there are also many that didn't, like Davell Crawford, just a brilliant young keyboard player, singer. Well, even the Dirty Dozen when we started with them; they were kind of new on the scene.

One more thing I guess I would say about New Orleans. The funk has not gone away. There are a lot of young bands playing that music now. Galactic, who, of course, were popular before Katrina, too— they continue to grow and attract bigger audiences. In fact, that's the great bill for this spring—Galactic and the Soul Rebels are going to be touring all over the country.

I'm optimistic. New Orleans is not going away.

# A NOTE ON MARDI GRAS INDIANS AND THEIR MUSIC

Mardi Gras Indians are an African American carnival tradition in New Orleans, and their music is close to the heart of what makes the city's music so distinctive and important. Organized in tribes or gangs, black men, mostly working class—and, increasingly, women and children—mask and parade, singing and chanting in magnificent hand-sewn and beaded suits inspired by Native American garb. To sew a suit is an enormous commitment of time, creative energy, and money. The tradition dictates that every carnival requires a new suit. And the music, which began on the streets as part of the parade tradition, is anthemic in New Orleans. It's hard to image that anyone who lives in the city doesn't know "Hey Pocky Way" or "Iko Iko."

In putting this book together, I was fortunate enough to obtain an interview with a Mardi Gras Indian chief. But at the very last minute—in fact, as the book's copyeditor was finishing his work—the chief chose to withdraw his interview. We didn't want to go to press without acknowledging and celebrating the majestic black Indian tradition and its music. Hence this note.

♣ Chief Irving "Honey" Banister of the Creole Wild West, performing with Cha Wa, Harrah's Casino fifteenth anniversary

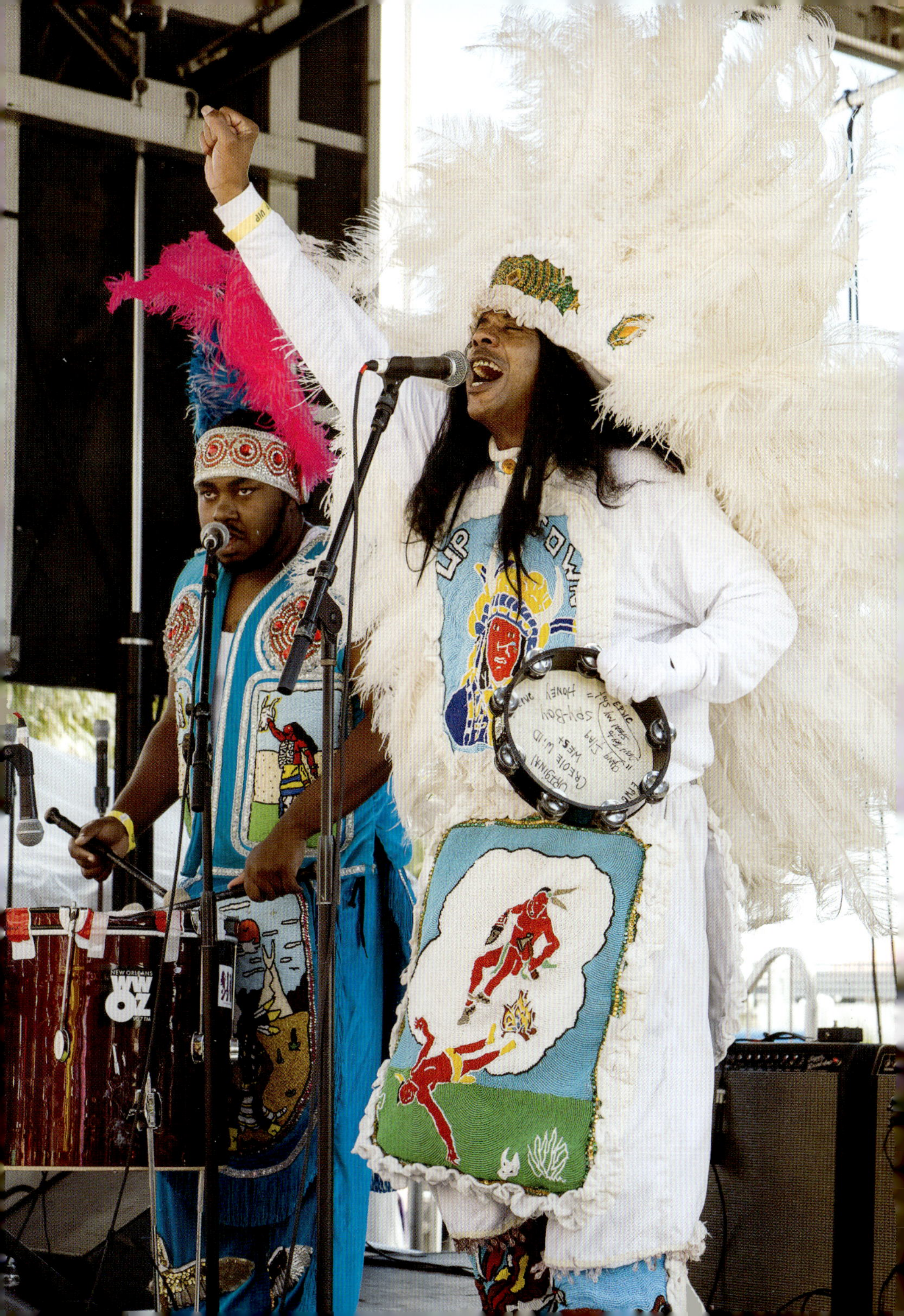

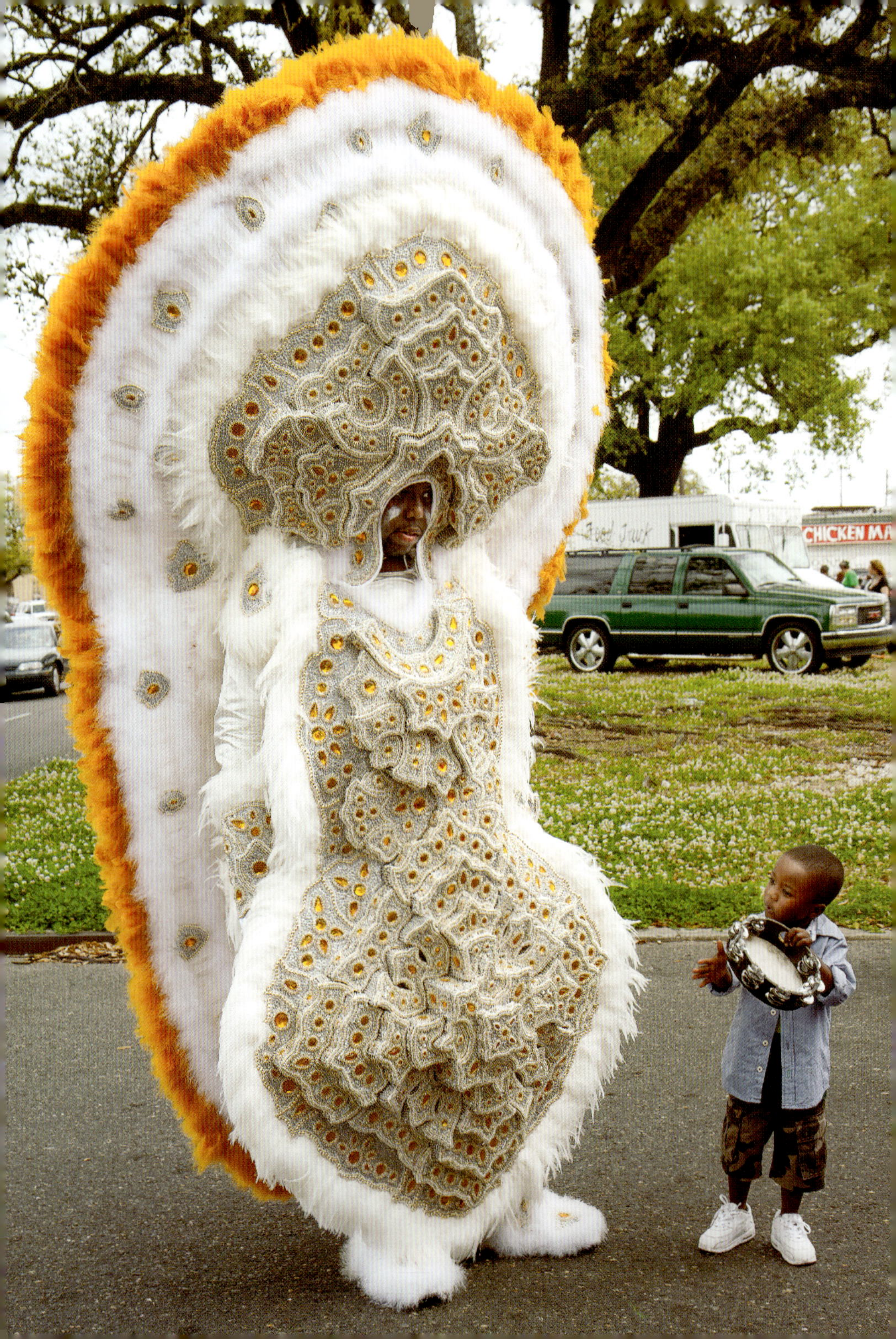

New Orleans has perhaps thirty or forty Indian gangs, organized into uptown and downtown tribes. They have names such as the White Cloud Hunters, the Wild Tchoupitoulas, and the Yellow Pocahontas. Each gang has a chief and a number of other traditional positions. Many now include a queen. Early on, encounters among parading tribes sometimes led to violent confrontations. But today, the competition is to see which chief has created the best suit—who, as the Indians say, is the *prettiest.* In his interview earlier in this book, Dr. Michael White speaks eloquently about the tradition and its importance.

Mardi Gras Indians have a distinctive body of music, which they often chant as they parade. In his extensive 1938 conversations with Alan Lomax, published as *Mister Jelly Roll,* jazz musician Jelly Roll Morton says:

> Now everybody in the world has heard about the New Orleans Mardi Gras, but maybe not about the Indians, one of the biggest feats that happened in Mardi Gras. Even at the parades with floats and costumes that cost millions, why, if the folks heard the sign of the Indians—
>
> *Ungai-ah!*
> *Ungai-ha!*
>
> —that big parade wouldn't have anybody there: the crowd would flock to see the Indians. When I was a child, I thought they really was Indians. They wore paint and blankets and, when they danced, one would get in the ring and throw his head back and downward, stooping over and bending his knees, making a rhythm with his heels and singing—*T'ouwais bas q'ouwais*—and the tribe would answer—*Ou tendais.* (14)

The song Jelly Roll cites, which Lomax seems to have decided to render in French, is, of course, "Two Way Pocky Way," another name for "Hey Pocky Way."

The tradition dates at least to the late nineteenth century. Many Mardi Gras Indians say that it is a tribute to Native Americans who helped enslaved African Americans and with whom there was a considerable amount of intermarriage. Some Indians and other scholars also cite the influence of Buffalo Bill Cody's Wild West shows, which wintered in New Orleans, 1884–85, and included Native Americans in regalia. The Creole Wild West was probably the first of the gangs. It's worth pondering, too, that descendants of African slaves practice a range of carnival traditions in the New World, many of them also involving parading in elaborate costumes.

Because African Americans were excluded from the krewes that march in Mardi Gras celebrations, black New Orleans neighborhoods developed their own celebrations, and it's here that Mardi Gras Indians began parading. They still parade on Mardi Gras, in the neighborhoods, away from the elaborate floats and processions that many associate with Fat Tuesday in New Orleans. Indians also parade in their neighborhoods on the evening of St. Joseph's Day, in March, and they hold public parades on Super Sunday, the Sunday closest to St. Joseph's Day. They are always a featured part of Jazz Fest.

Tribes are hierarchical and territorial. Big Chief is the leader, responsible for sewing the most spectacular suit, for leading the singing, and, in a general way, for the wellbeing of his tribe. Spyboy walks ahead of the gang, on the lookout for other gangs. Flagboy sends signals from Spy to the Chief. Wildman holds the crowd back. Queens and children, and Second and Third Chiefs, are also part of the entourage.

✤ Mardi Gras Indian and child, Uptown Super Sunday

Spectators and supporters second-line in the street alongside the Indian processions.

The music, often in a call-and-response pattern, is distinctive. Its origins are as a parade tradition, chanted on the street, sometimes accompanied by percussion instruments. The roots of some of its vocabulary are disputed, with claims ranging from Native American to West African origins. And the music shows up on commercial recordings, helping reinforce the repertoire and bringing it to wider audiences. As early as 1927, Louis Dumaine's Jazzola Eight 1927 disc "To-Wa-Bac-A-Wa" (there's "Pocky Way" again) refers to the music, even if the piece itself is pretty much a standard jazz dance side. Prominent New Orleans musician and arranger Dave Bartholomew's 1950 release on Imperial, "Carnival Day," includes a callout to a big chief and a number of Indian chants, including a bit of "Two Way Pocky Way." In 1958 music researcher and writer Sam Charters released field recordings of Mardi Gras Indians, including a track he called "To-wa-bac-a-way—The Indian Race," on the Folkways label, selections of which are now available on Smithsonian Folkways Recordings. Charters's tracks are the first publicly available documentary recordings of authentic black Indian music.

In the commercial realm, Danny Barker released a number of Mardi Gras Indian songs in jazz settings on the King Zulu label, dated by various sources as having come out between 1946 and 1954. James "Sugar Boy" Crawford released "Jock-a-Mo" on Checker in 1953. Twelve years later, the Dixie Cups released a version of Crawford's record, calling it "Iko Iko." That reached number 20 on *Billboard*'s R&B chart, and a New Orleans anthem, derived from Indian chant, was born. In 1968, early in his career using the Dr. John persona, Mac Rebennack, released "Mama Roux," which contains Mardi Gras Indian references, and he has continued to record and perform music from the Mardi Gras Indian repertoire.

The first commercial recording of Mardi Gras Indians performing their own music dates to November 1970, when the Wild Magnolias released "Handa Wanda, parts 1 & 2" on Crescent City Records. That recording adds a strong dose of funk backing to the traditional music. It became a local dance favorite and led, in the early 1970s, to a number of albums by Big Chief Bo Dollis and the Wild Magnolias. Thanks to the Wild Magnolias records, another distinctive New Orleans sound was born, this one blending Black Indian street music and funk. A 1976 release in that genre, *The Wild Tchoupitoulas*, featured Big Chief George Landry. Landry was Uncle Jolly to Art, Charles, Aaron, and Cyril Neville, who are featured on the album, accompanied by the Meters, who had developed a distinctive and influential New Orleans funk sound. That release, produced by Allen Toussaint, led to the formation of the Neville Brothers. It is on the Library of Congress's 2012 National Recording Registry, an annual listing of nationally significant sound recordings.

And the beat goes on. Big Chief Monk Boudreaux of the Golden Eagles, who performed early with the Wild Magnolias, is probably the best-known performer on the music scene these days. Performing in his Indian suit, he is typically backed by funk musicians. Chief Bo Dollis Jr. has been performing, sometime with Boudreaux, and recording lately. A group called Cha Wa features Mardi Gras Indians Irving "Honey" Banister and J'Wan Boudreaux on vocals. Dr. John routinely includes Indian songs in his stage shows.

Jazz historian Tom Morgan's website (http://tlmorgan.com/next/indian.html) has a very helpful overview of the recorded history of Mardi Gras Indian music. You can hear some of the music where it comes from—on the streets—in three fine films about Mardi Gras Indians. *Tootie's Last Suit*, produced and directed by Lisa Katzman and released in 2009, centers on the late Tootie Montana, a deeply respected member of the Mardi Gras Indian community (www.tootieslastsuit.com). *Bury the Hatchet* (www.burythehatchetfilm.com), produced and directed by Aaron Walker, features three Indian chiefs telling the story of the tradition through their lives. The 2014 *We Won't Bow Down* (www.wewont bowdown.com), directed by Christopher Levoy Bower and produced by Monica Cooper, uses a broader view to give a powerful portrait of the tradition in its neighborhoods and in the lives of many participants. And the Mardi Gras Indian Council, an organization of about twenty tribes, has a useful website (www.mardigrasindiancouncil.org).

# SOME NEW ORLEANS MUSIC RESOURCES

If you want to hear music in New Orleans, you have many options. You can go to Frenchmen Street, where you'll find a concentration of clubs and an exuberant street scene. I especially enjoy d.b.a., where it is often possible to hear Walter "Wolfman" Washington and the Roadmasters or John Boutté, among the musicians featured in this book. Snug Harbor, on Frenchmen, is the leading jazz club, and Charmaine Neville has weekly shows there. The Original Pinettes often appear at Vaso, and many other leading musicians play in other clubs up and down the street. Uptown, the Maple Leaf Bar is a major venue, often featuring Rebirth Brass Band. There's also the well-known Tipitina's, a club started originally as a communal venture by friends of Professor Longhair. Bruce Daigrepont and his band often do dances there on Sundays. And there are less well-known venues in various neighborhoods. For example, Bullet's Spots Bar in the Seventh Ward has for some years featured Tuesday night shows by the charismatic trumpeter Kermit Ruffins, and they have expanded to feature other acts, including the Original Pinettes,

✦ Vocalist Nayo Jones at Bullet's Sports Bar, Seventh Ward

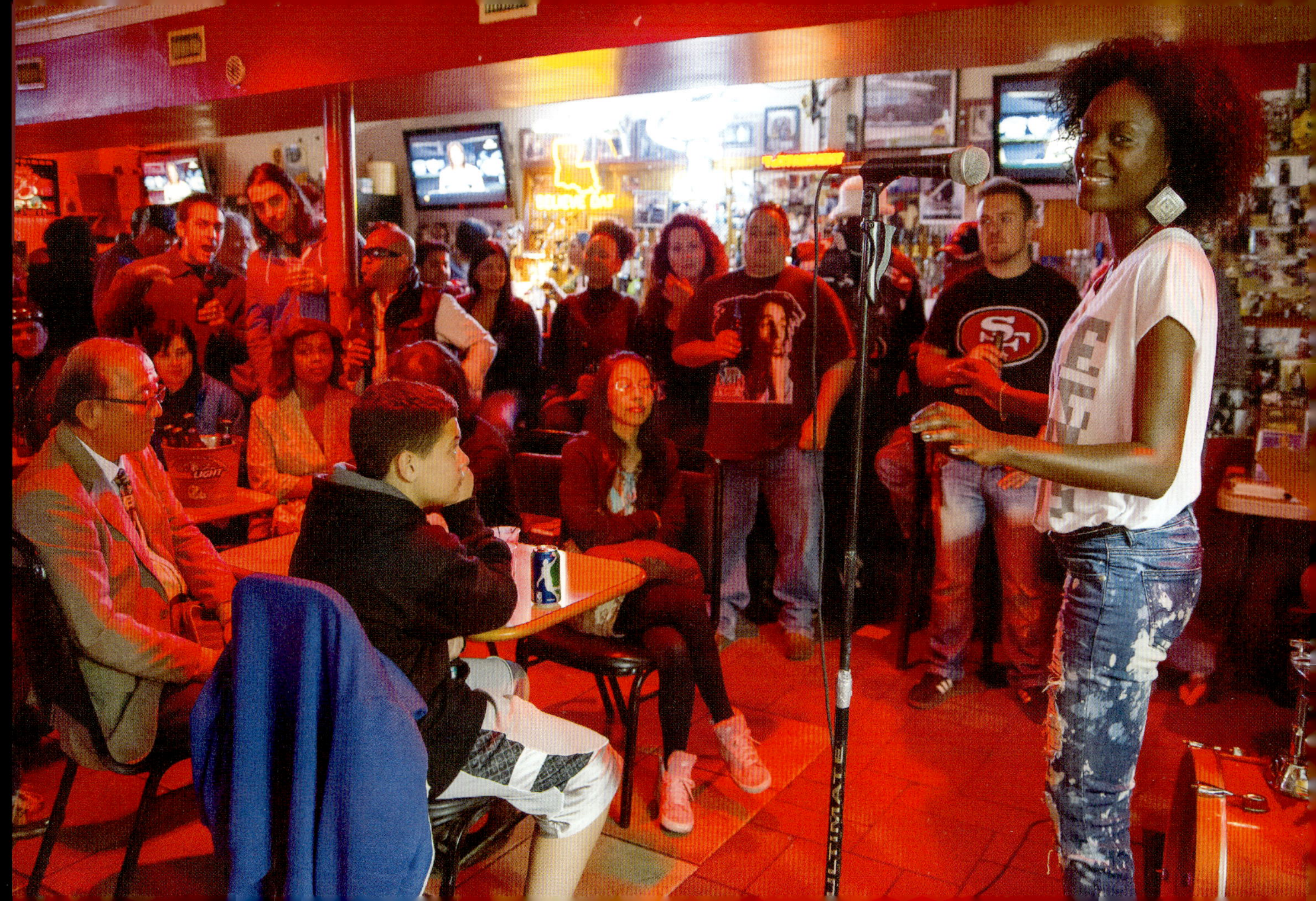

on occasional other nights. In the Treme, Kermit Ruffins has recently reopened the Mother-in-Law Lounge, which was originally associated with Ernie K-Doe and his wife, then widow, Antoinette, and you can sometimes find the exuberant Ruffins playing there. Also in the Treme, the Candlelight Lounge often has Wednesday night brass bands, typically the Treme Brass Band. In the Bywater, Vaughan's Lounge became a legendary venue because of Thursday-night shows by Kermit Ruffins and his band, the Barbecue Swingers. Ruffins no longer does those shows; as of this writing, Thursdays at Vaughan's features the excellent Corey Henry's Treme Funktet. Ironically, although there are a few venues in the French Quarter—the Palm Court Jazz Café on Decatur Street, Preservation Hall, and Irvin Mayfield's Jazz Playhouse in the Royal Sonesta Hotel—most of the local music is no longer to be found in the Quarter. And Bourbon Street is mostly for tourists, with cover bands in many of the bars.

The club scene, though, keeps changing, and what I've written here is the tip of the iceberg. The best way to track the clubs is to use the extensive online resources at WWOZ.org. 'OZ is a community radio station, and it has a laudable dedication to its home community. Stream it if you're not within range. Two free publications also include extensive music listings. There's *Gambit*, with its website, bestofneworleans.com. And there's *Offbeat*, a glossy with a fierce dedication to the music. You'll find that around town, distributed for free. It's online at offbeat.com; if you live outside the area, you can subscribe to it. You should, if you want to keep up.

But you should also look for music outside the club scene. To my mind, this is the best way to hear the music. The street is theater—public theater—in New Orleans, and it's the foundation for the music.

Strut along with second-line parades, dancing to the brass bands, getting a sense of the importance of the social aid and pleasure clubs and other organizations that sponsor the public events. Follow Mardi Gras Indians, marveling at the majestic tradition, dancing to the chanted music. One wonderful way to hear the Indians is to go to one of the Super Sunday events, generally in March and in May. It's in the streets where you'll really appreciate how deeply rooted these musics are. The best way to track the events is the "Takin' It to the Streets" section of the WWOZ website.

And there's Jazz Fest, officially the New Orleans Jazz and Heritage Festival. Held over two weekends, at the end of April and early May, this huge celebration of New Orleans began in 1970. It's centered on the Fair Grounds Race Course. For many, the gospel tent is a highlight of the festival. Clubs and other venues add their own unofficial programming. And the festival created both a foundation and an archive; they support and preserve the music with programs and projects throughout the year. There are many other festivals. Among them, the French Quarter Festival has a strong focus on local performers. Admission is free, and the event's not quite the mass scene that Jazz Fest is.

If you want to buy CDs and vinyl, ground zero is the Louisiana Music Factory, recently relocated to Frenchmen Street. What a place it is, with its huge selection of sound recordings from New Orleans and the rest of Louisiana, its large selection of DVDs, many of them music and culture documentaries, and its fine selection of books and magazines. The store often features performances by well-known local musicians. And, especially for collectors, Jim Russell's Rare Records in the Lower Garden District, on Magazine Street, is an important source for rare

✷ Dancing in Frenchmen Street club

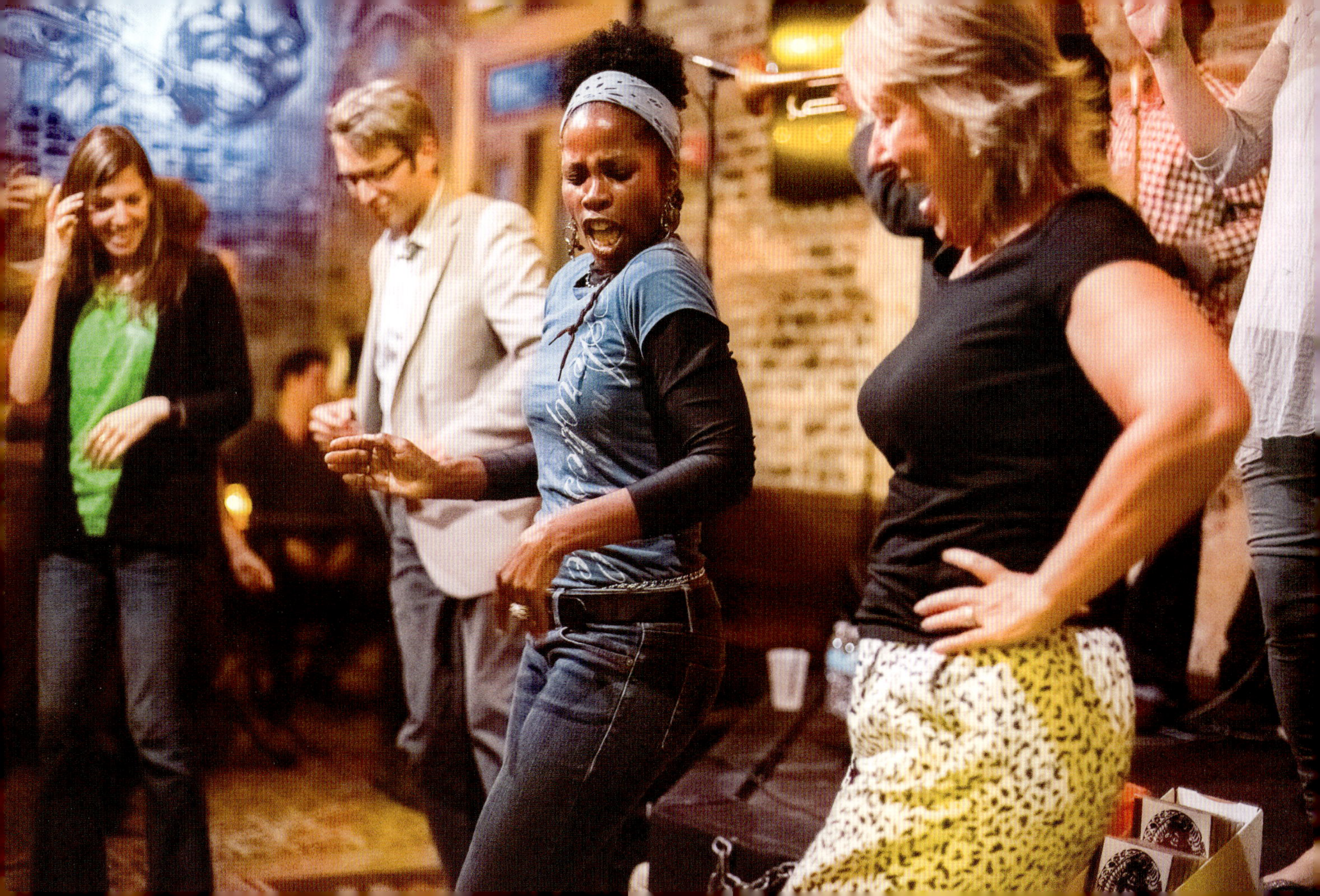

vinyl and CDs, with a very large collection. Jim Russell passed away in July 2014 at ninety-four; as of this writing, the store remains open.

Given that you're holding this one in your hands, for which Gary and I thank you, it seems likely that you're someone who likes books. If so, here's a short list of especially good and important ones.

Battiste, Harold, Jr. 2010. *Unfinished Blues: Memories of a New Orleans Music Man.* New Orleans: Historic New Orleans Collection.

Berry, Jason. 2009. *Up from the Cradle of Jazz: New Orleans Music Since World War II.* Lafayette: University of Louisiana at Lafayette.

Brothers, Thomas. 2007. *Louis Armstrong's New Orleans.* New York: W.W. Norton.

Broven, John. 1978. *Rhythm and Blues in New Orleans.* Gretna, LA: Pelican.

Burns, Mick. 2006. *Keeping the Beat on the Street: The New Orleans Brass Band Renaissance.* Baton Rouge: Louisiana State University Press.

Cohn, Nik. 2005. *Tricksta: Life and Death and New Orleans Rap.* New York: Knopf.

Friedlander, Lee. 2014. *Playing for the Benefit of the Band: New Orleans Music Culture.* New Haven: Yale University Art Gallery.

Hannusch, Jeff. 1985. *I Hear You Knockin': The Sound of New Orleans Rhythm and Blues.* Ville Platte, LA: Swallow.

Jacobsen, Thomas W. 2011. *Traditional New Orleans Jazz: Conversations with the Men Who Make the Music.* Baton Rouge: Louisiana State University Press.

Lichtenstein, Grace, and Laura Dankner. 1993. *Musical Gumbo: The Music of New Orleans.* New York: W. W. Norton.

Lomax, Alan. 2001. *Mister Jelly Roll: The Fortunes of Jelly Roll Morton, New Orleans Creole and "Inventor of Jazz."* Los Angeles: University of California Press.

Mazza, Jay. 2012. *Up Front and Center: New Orleans Music at the End of the 20th Century.* New Orleans: Threadhead Press.

Miller, Matt. 2012. *Bounce: Rap Music and Local Identity in New Orleans.* Amherst: University of Massachusetts Press.

Piazza, Tom. 2005. *Why New Orleans Matters.* New York: Regan Books.

Sakakeeny, Matt. 2013. *Roll with It: Brass Bands in the Streets of New Orleans.* Durham, NC: Duke University Press.

Sandmel, Ben. 2012. *Ernie K-Doe: The R&B Emperor of New Orleans.* New Orleans: Historic New Orleans Collection.

Smith, Michael. 1994. *Mardi Gras Indians.* Gretna, LA: Pelican.

Spera, Keith. 2011. *Groove Interrupted: Loss, Renewal, and the Music of New Orleans.* New York: St. Martin's Press.

Swenson, John. 2012. *New Atlantis: Musicians Battle for the Survival of New Orleans.* Oxford, UK: Oxford University Press.

Turner, Richard Brent. 2009. *Jazz Religion, the Second Line, and Black New Orleans.* Bloomington: Indiana University Press.

Vaz, Kim Marie. 2013. *The "Baby Dolls": Breaking the Race and Gender Barriers of the New Orleans Mardi Gras Tradition.* Baton Rouge: Louisiana State University Press.

Watts, Lewis, and Eric Porter. 2013. *New Orleans Suite: Music and Culture in Transition.* Los Angeles: University of California Press.

# ACKNOWLEDGMENTS

Gary Samson and I have worked together on various projects for quite a while now, and I can't imagine a better, more talented, and easy-to-travel-with collaborator. It's a treat to work with him. We're very appreciative that the New Hampshire Institute of Art recognizes the value of Gary's work on this sort of project. We should also acknowledge that many oysters gave their lives over the course of our work, and we should thank the friendly people at Markey's Bar and Vaughan's Lounge, among others, where we frequently debriefed.

It was a lunch with Tamarin Hennebury, an old and good friend of my sister, Betty Weinkle, that made me think this was a book I should, and could, do. A longtime New Orleans resident, Tamarin was enthusiastic about the idea, and she helped me overcome my uneasiness about whether, from my home in New England, I had any right to take this on. Steve Armbruster, Tamarin's husband, has for decades immersed himself in his city's music, food, and culture. Steve was remarkably generous and helpful with his thoughts and his Rolodex. Steve and

Tamarin opened their guest studio to Jeannie and me on a couple of visits. Likewise, my friends and folklorist colleagues in New Orleans, Frank deCaro and Rosan Jordan, were encouraging and very supportive. They also gave their guest room to Gary, who stayed with them on one of our visits.

Heartfelt thanks go to all the musicians who gave their time to us. Requests for interviews are nothing new to most of the people in this book. We'd like to think that this project stands out from many of those requests, in the way we tried to go deeper and longer than most journalistic interviews do. Although he's not featured in the book, I also want to add a note of thanks to Davell Crawford.

At the University of New Hampshire, Special Collections Librarian Bill Ross, who teaches a much-loved course on New Orleans, was a fine friend and resource. He and Dale Valena, curator of the University Museum, put on an exhibition, *The Beat on the Street: Second Lines, Mardi Gras Indians, and the Photography of Gary Samson*, that featured Gary's photography and gave me a chance to try out some thoughts on the interpretive side. The opening for that exhibition was the largest in the museum's history. Thanks to the New Hampshire Humanities Council for their support on that front. Also at UNH, Professor Mary Rhiel *rettete mir Arsch* by helping out with some German transcription. I'm lucky enough to work with Katie Umans and Jessica Fish in the UNH Center for the Humanities. Their remarkable competence made it possible to carve out time to work on this book. The UNH Department of English helped fund one of my research trips to New Orleans. Funds from the UNH College of Liberal Arts supported indexing this book. For that, I thank Dean Ken Fuld and Associate Dean Alasdair Drysdale. And Gary and I owe a huge note of gratitude to interim dean of the the university's Dimond Library, Annie Donahue, and Bill Ross for the generous subvention that helped this book look as good as it does.

Joe Compton made it possible for me to see his excellent documentary, *By and By: New Orleans Gospel at the Crossroads*, which was very useful when I wrote the section on gospel music. In addition, Joe helped us arrange a photo shoot at the Ebenezer Baptist Church, for which we also have to thank James Williams and Pastor Jermaine Landrum, as well as the congregants who were there that night in October 2014. Monica R. Cooper was very generous in providing access to *We Won't Bow Down*, her powerful film about Mardi Gras Indians. Thanks, too, to Jack Cruz, Walter "Wolfman" Washington's bass player, who arranged my interview with Walter. I'm sorry we never got to hear Jack rehearse with James Andrews. Thanks, too, to my old friend Dwight DeVane, with whom I always enjoy talking music and New Orleans.

At the University Press of Mississippi, Assistant Director and Editor-in-Chief Craig Gill believed in the project from the start, and it's been a pleasure to work with him. Managing Editor Anne Stascavage saw the book through production. Editorial Assistant Katie Keene was always responsive and helpful. Will Rigby was everything a copyeditor should be. Art director John Langston and designer Todd Lape transformed a manuscript and a set of tiff files into a beautiful book, making Gary and me very happy indeed. Then Shane Gong Stewart guided the manuscript through the production process. Steve Yates directs the marketing effort, which probably led to your reading this. Courtney McCreary was also involved in the marketing. We appreciate that others at the press, with whom we've not had direct contact, contributed mightily to making this book. And an evaluation provided by an anonymous outside reader was unusually encouraging and helpful on a number of matters of fact.

I'm lucky enough to have two daughters, Sophie and Hannah, who, when they're not marveling at the fact that I have the freedom to do this sort of project, are always interested in and supportive of the work itself. And I'm very fortunate, indeed, to have Jeannie Thomas, my significant other, colleague, muse and enabler, and companion. I've had wonderful times in New Orleans with her, and her knowledge and gently critical eye have made this book better than it would otherwise have been.

—BF

Durham, New Hampshire

November 2014

# INDEX